Song on Record   2

Edited by
Alan Blyth
Music critic, *The Daily Telegraph*

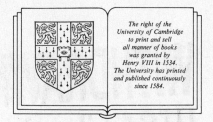

The right of the
University of Cambridge
to print and sell
all manner of books
was granted by
Henry VIII in 1534.
The University has printed
and published continuously
since 1584.

Cambridge University Press

Cambridge
New York   *New Rochelle*   *Melbourne*   *Sydney*

Published by the Press Syndicate of the University of Cambridge
The Pitt Building, Trumpington Street, Cambridge CB2 1RP
32 East 57th Street, New York, NY 10022, USA
10 Stamford Road, Oakleigh, Melbourne 3166, Australia

First published 1988

Printed in Great Britain at the University Press, Cambridge

British Library cataloguing in publication data
Song on record 2.
1. Songs – Discography 2. Sound
recordings – History and criticism
I. Blyth, Alan
789.9'1364   ML2500

Library of Congress cataloguing in publication data
Song on record.
Includes indexes of singers' names.
Contents: v. 1. Lieder – v. 2. [without special title]
1. Songs – Discography. 2. Sound recordings –
Reviews. I. Blyth, Alan.
ML156.4.V7S6   1986   016.7899'124   86–12926

ISBN 0 521 26844 3 (vol. 1)
ISBN 0 521 33155 2 (vol. 2)
ISBN 0 521 36173 7 (the set)

Contents

v

Introduction

For this second and final volume of *Song on Record*, I have endeavoured
to include the songs of as many countries as possible, the sole proviso
being that there should be enough recordings of each as to make a survey
of them worthwhile. Where *mélodies* are concerned, the major composers
in the genre are fully covered, and I have added a chapter on some of the
minor masters with the underrated Hahn given special prominence. Bizet
and Massenet have been excluded because their simple songs do not
present many interpretative problems. With Russian song, we have concentrated on the three main masters in this field, again because they have
been most often recorded. It seemed best, Britten apart, to deal with
English song in a single chapter. In the case of Spanish, Scandinavian and
American song, a collective chapter on each seemed the right solution as
no single composer has dominated either field. I considered it would be
entertaining to end the project with a chapter on those trifles, frequently
recorded, with which singers love to end their recitals; John Steane has
obliged.

Again I have thought it right to allow the subject of each chapter to
dictate its format. It seems foolish to impose a uniformity where there is
none. Where French song is concerned, a fairly consistent view has
emerged of a decline in interpretation in most recent times, at least since
the prime of Gérard Souzay, probably due to the fact that singers today
tend not to specialise in one genre but try to master too many.

Discographies of cycles and records exclusively devoted to single
composers are included where applicable but they do not claim to be comprehensive. Where individual songs and records are concerned, the
numbers are given within brackets in the body of the text according to the
following principles. Where applicable, the first number is that of the
original 78rpm record followed, after a semi-colon, by its most recent
LP reissue, or that considered most readily accessible today. EMI has continued to expand the refurbishing of its archive material under the
knowledgeable control of Keith Hardwick.

1

Introduction

The name HMV has not been repeated endlessly because its prefixes DB, DA, D, E, C and B are reasonably familiar. Col. stands for Columbia, Parlo. for Parlophone, Od., for Odéon, Poly. for Polydor. Discs originally issued in the US by Victor but later brought out in Britain by HMV are given their British numbers. Where titles were issued in the double-sided DB (twelve inch) and DA (ten inch) series, these numbers have been preferred to their single-sided equivalent. In the case of records issued only on LP, the most recent number is given. CD numbers of the latest discs are preferred to their LP equivalent; most have the suffix –2.

Once again thanks are due to my fellow-contributors for their many hours of fruitful labour, and to John Hughes, who has helped with editing and with the loan of many rare LP records. Peter Lack has done a similar service as regards French song 78s. Derek Lewis, BBC Record Librarian, has again given inestimable assistance. Penny Souster, as publisher's editor, has been a constant source of encouragement.

Berlioz

DAVID CAIRNS

Les nuits d'été

Ameling, Atlanta Symphony/Shaw	Telarc CD 80084
Armstrong, Veasey, Patterson, Shirley-Quirk, LSO/Davis	Philips 6500 009
Baker, New Philharmonia/Barbirolli	HMV ASD 2444
Baltsa, LSO/Tate	Philips 416 807–2
Behrens, Vienna Symphony/Travis	Decca 411 895–1
Crespin, Suisse Romande/Ansermet	Decca JB 15
Danco, Cincinnati/Johnson	Decca 411 961–1
de los Angeles, Boston Symphony/Munch	HMV ALP 1368
Greevy, New Irish Chamber/Prieur	NIRC NIR 013
Laplante, Durand	Calliope CAL 1883
Minton, Burrows, BBC Symphony/Boulez	CBS 76576
Norman, LSO/Davis	412 493–2
L. Price, Chicago Symphony/Reiner	RCA SB 6566
Te Kanawa, Orchestre de Paris/Barenboim	DG 410 966–2
Souzay, Baldwin	Decca 414 336–1
Steber, Columbia Symphony/Mitropoulos	Odyssey Y 32360
von Stade, Boston Symphony/Ozawa	CMS MK 39098

1. Villanelle
2. Le spectre de la rose
3. Sur les lagunes
4. Absence
5. Au cimetière
6. L'île inconnue

Considering how popular *Les nuits d'été* has become with sopranos and mezzo-sopranos and how often it is recorded (five new versions have come out in the last four years), it is remarkable how few singers succeed in penetrating below the surface of the music. For all the work's high

3

reputation (the *Penguin Stereo Record and Cassette Guide* calls it 'probably the most beautiful of all orchestral song-cycles'), a really satisfying performance is rare. Of the seventeen recordings which have appeared so far, only two or three come near to being so. Of the rest, some are let down by undistinguished orchestral playing or excessively slow (occasionally, fast) tempi. In some cases the singer succeeds with two or three of the six songs, only to fail with the others.

To listen to these seventeen versions is to be reminded that, for all its immediate appeal, the cycle is difficult to bring off, for conductor as well as soloist. Berlioz's chamber-music textures are so spare and finely calculated, so exposed, that every wrong note, careless note-value or unrhythmical phrase shows, and to combine accurately balanced ensemble with the sense of freedom and lyrical expansiveness which the character of the music required is far from easy. The fact that many singers succeed only with some of the songs, not with the work as a whole, is an indication of the severity of its technical and expressive demands. These six songs embrace, vocally and interpretatively, a very wide range. The singer is asked to sustain exceptionally long melodic spans of great intensity and precisely controlled dynamics, but must also be able to reduce the voice on occasion to a teasing playfulness. She (or he) must encompass both the skittish charm of 'Villanelle' and the large dreamy radiance of 'Le spectre de la rose', the dark, passionate outbursts of 'Sur les lagunes' and the salty gaiety of 'L'île inconnue', quite often at an exactingly high *tessitura* and without the comforting surge of a sonorous symphony orchestra to support the voice.

Not surprisingly there is a good deal of downward transposition in these seventeen versions. Only two singers, Suzanne Danco and Victoria de los Angeles, perform all six songs in the keys of Berlioz's orchestral score. Régine Crespin sings 'Villanelle', 'Absence' and 'Au cimetière' half a tone lower; Janet Baker and Frederica von Stade transpose 'Villanelle' a major third down, from A to F; Agnes Baltsa does the same, as well as singing the F sharp major 'Absence' in E and 'Au cimetière' in B instead of D. Von Stade's 'Au cimetière' is in B flat; so is Bernadette Greevy's. The cycle, in short, has often had to be adjusted to make it lie comfortably for a single voice.

In fact Berlioz himself made adjustments when he orchestrated the *Nuits d'été* songs. Whereas the original voice-and-piano score, published in 1841, was for 'mezzo-soprano or tenor', the orchestral score of 1856 specifies several different voices: (1) mezzo-soprano or tenor for 'Villanelle'; (2) contralto for 'Le spectre de la rose'; (3) baritone (with optional alternative of contralto or mezzo-soprano) for 'Sur les lagunes'; (4) mezzo-soprano or tenor for 'Absence'; (5) tenor (without optional alternative) for 'Au cimetière'; and (6) mezzo-soprano or tenor for 'L'ile

inconnue'. (At the same time the original key-scheme – A–D–G minor–
F sharp–D–F – was changed, no. 2 dropping from D to B and no. 3 from
G minor to F minor.)

This division of forces is, on the face of it, a practical acknowledgement
of the songs' wide diversity of style, weight and emotion. It seems to be
saying that more than one singer – a minimum of three, in fact – is needed
to do justice to the work. In the 1856 score the composer dedicated each
song to a different singer – all of them artists whom he got to know during
his tours of Germany and to whom he felt specially grateful (four of them
had taken part in Liszt's production of *Benvenuto Cellini* at Weimar).
From it we can deduce his ideal line-up: (1) mezzo (or tenor), (2) contralto, (3) baritone, (4) mezzo (or tenor), (5) tenor, (6) mezzo (or tenor) –
four separate singers.

What he would have done in practice we cannot say: the cycle did not
figure in any of the remaining concerts he gave between the publication of
the full score and his death; he conducted only two of the six songs,
'Absence' and 'Le spectre de la rose'. We should certainly not conclude
that he thought of the work simply as a collection of separate songs published together for convenience. He gave few concerts after 1856; and as
for specifying different voice-types, that has more significance today than
it would in the nineteenth century, when it was not uncommon for several
singers to be billed in the same concert programme. *Les nuits d'été* most
palpably is a cycle, held together not by a quasi-narrative thread, as in
Schubert's *Die schöne Müllerin* and *Winterreise*, but by a common theme,
romantic love, seen in various aspects – light-hearted and extrovert in the
first and last songs, more intense and passionate in nos. 2–5. The songs
are also linked by recurring musical figures, phrase-shapes and intervals;
and the progression from one to another and the shape of the whole are
consciously and carefully moulded. For example, 'Le spectre de la rose',
though altogether grander in manner than 'Villanelle', retains something
of that song's playfulness in the rich but sparkling textures which match
the subject, the poetic 'conceit' of a rose returning as a ghost to haunt the
dreams of the girl who wore it at her first ball; at the same time the music's
largeness of style leads naturally to the next song, the tragic 'Sur les
lagunes'. The final song, 'L'île inconnue', rounds off the cycle more
satisfyingly than by simply recalling the mood of the opening number
'Villanelle'. Though it sets out to mock the romantic assumptions of the
previous four songs (and breaks the claustrophobic atmosphere of 'Au
cimetière' like a douche of cold water), it cannot help responding to them.
There is a shift of emphasis, reflecting the depth of passion lived through
in between. In the end the music succumbs to the same irresistible illusion:
the enchanted shore where love lasts for ever is just over the horizon, if we
could only find it.

David Cairns

Being a cycle, *Les nuits d'été* is nearly always entrusted to a single voice, and almost invariably to a soprano or mezzo. But we have only to hear 'Sur les lagunes' and 'Au cimetière' sung by male singers to understand why Berlioz preferred a baritone for the one and specifically demanded a tenor for the other; the character of the two songs can be fully realised only in this way. A baritone voice fits 'Sur les lagunes' like a glove and brings out its dark, passionate colour. In 'Au cimetière' something of the essential trancelike, hermetic feeling of the music is lost if the vocal line is detached from the muted strings of the accompaniment by being raised an octave (a practice as inauthentic, one could say, as giving Handel's *castrato* roles to a baritone). The most veiled, mysterious *mezza voce* of a soprano or mezzo can't give the effect of a tenor moving with and among the orchestra like a sleepwalker; the pitch and timbre of a woman's voice are very much a second best.

And yet . . . Because it is a cycle, from instinct as well as habit we expect to hear it sung by one singer. Psychologically and even aesthetically, despite what has just been said, that seems on balance the best solution – if one singer can be found who combines all or most of the qualities required.

To my mind the singer who comes nearest to doing so on disc is **Eleanor Steber**. She has arguably the most beautiful voice of all, and indisputably the most complete control of her vocal resources. The timbre is even and ample throughout the compass, the breath control exemplary. Her *legato* and her feeling for Berlioz's long melodic spans are unsurpassed; only Janet Baker, among the others, approaches her. At the same time there is a brightness and directness about her singing that saves it from heaviness or undue solemnity. True, an ideal performance would be more playful in the final song and would sound a little less determined, more spontaneous, in 'Villanelle'. On the other hand 'Villanelle' benefits from her marvellous line and phrasing, as well as being the only performance of the seventeen which comes near the metronome mark, crotchet = 96. Most take it anything up to a third as fast again – *allegro*, not *allegretto*. The slowness of the marking reminds us that Berlioz was one of those conductors, like Beecham, who could give life to a tempo which in other hands would sound sluggish. Dimitri Mitropoulos, Steber's conductor, for all his qualities as a Berlioz interpreter (he is one of the most engaged of those under review), cannot do so here; the repeated woodwind quavers are nothing like the *leggiero* asked for. Even so, the purpose of the tempo of 'Villanelle' is made clear in this performance. At this moderate speed we can register the little shifts in the harmony and the gradual growth in the orchestration from verse to verse which give the extra quickening of tension and the touch of melancholy to the outwardly carefree melody, but which are lost in the rapid patter we usually hear. In the four middle songs Steber is splendid, not only singing gloriously, with phrase after soaring phrase perfectly weighted and shaped, but responding keenly to the poetic atmosphere. At many points she provides a touchstone against which to measure her rivals.

One whom we might expect to challenge Steber more closely than she does is **Régine Crespin**. She has the advantage of a large but not unsupple voice and good diction, and French is her native language, which it is not for most of the others. Her performance, indeed, is widely admired. But quite apart from the cavalier way she places 'Sur les lagunes' after 'Absence' instead of before, I must say I find much of it unconvincing – regal but mannered and lacking in vitality. She sounds detached from what is going on. Her 'O grands désirs inappaisés' in 'Absence' is an expression of civilised regret, not a cry of longing for the distant beloved. At 'J'arrive du paradis', the glittering climax of 'Le spectre de la rose', what she chiefly conveys is a sense of being fatigued by the journey. It is the same with her handling of the other changes in expressive intensity which vary and enrich the underlying strophic pattern of the 'Spectre': she glides imperturbably through them, and her often quite generous *rubato* seems to me contrived, not a spontaneous response to the music. Its main effect is to confuse the conductor, Ansermet; the ensemble is less than impeccable. In 'Sur les lagunes' the orchestral work is at times downright sloppy, and 'L'île inconnue' is marred by unrhythmical accompaniment. In these two songs, however, Crespin is at her best, especially in 'L'île inconnue', where her Parisian sophistication comes into its own and she gets the right mixture of the playful and the passionate. Here at last she achieves the note of surprise, of being caught out by sudden emotion, that is missing from the rest of the performance.

Suzanne Danco, the only other French-speaking singer to record the cycle with orchestra, does far more with smaller vocal resources. She is not helped by a slightly dim accompaniment (the recording places the orchestra very much in the background: the poignant horn phrases in the B flat major section of 'Sur les lagunes' are barely audible); and at times the unvaried colour of the clear, diamond-bright voice is a drawback that cannot be compensated for. But much more often Danco makes you forget such limitations in the sheer intelligence and vibrancy of her singing. Her 'Sur les lagunes', which she sings in the required key of F minor, evokes a keen sense of desolation; the shaping of the musical line and the inflecting of the text, for all their sophistication, seem to proceed spontaneously from the singer's identification with the song. How authentic the *frisson* of unappeased longing she conveys at 'Entre nos coeurs quelles distances, que d'espace entre nos baisers' in 'Absence'. At 'un air maladivement tendre' in 'Au cimetière', how vividly the sense of the words, the morbidly felt fascination of the churchyard at dusk, speaks in her singing – and this in spite of a tempo a little too quick to capture the full hypnotic mood of the music. 'L'île inconnue', by contrast, suffers from too slow a speed; it makes a disappointingly sluggish end to a version that has much to offer.

The disadvantages of a sumptuous voice and grand manner are apparent in **Jessye Norman**'s performance. The big moments like 'J'arrive du paradis' come off memorably; the tragic 'Sur les lagunes' is very fine (at least until the last 15 bars, where the tempo is all over the place). But the cycle also demands delicacy of nuance, a sense of spontaneity, a touch of mischief. Norman is often laboured where there should be no feeling of effort and the singing should seem perfectly natural. 'Le spectre de la rose', distinguished though much of the phrasing is, sounds too momentous; it lacks ease. Partly this is a question of the problems posed for a singer of her type by the vocal writing, the awkward octave leap within a long *cantabile* phrase in the melody of the 'Spectre' (varied in the final verse by a further rise of a third), the testingly high *tessitura* of the A sections of 'Au cimetière', the sustained E sharps and F sharps and the slow rise and fall of the long-drawn melodic line in the thrice-heard refrain of 'Absence'. In the latter song the problems are compounded by the slow tempo chosen by her and her conductor, Colin Davis, and there is some uncertain intonation. In general the orchestral work is good – and in 'Au cimetière' excellent – and Davis's care for dynamics and textural detail marks him out from many of the sixteen conductors. But the version as a whole is disappointing.

Heard immediately after it, the performance by **Kiri Te Kanawa** makes a refreshingly vivacious contrast. Though the exceedingly rapid speed of 'Villanelle' excludes any hint of melancholy, the warmth and brightness of the singing, the clarity of the words and the infectious air of cheerfulness are such that you hardly notice it. Her 'L'île inconnue' is also one of the liveliest on disc, taken by Daniel Barenboim at the proper brisk pace, and by turns eager, teasing and seductive. The tempo of 'Le spectre de la rose', again, has the right slow swing, and Te Kanawa responds with well-shaped singing, if without anything in the phrasing or inflection to make you sit up. It is the three most emotionally charged songs, 'Sur les lagunes', 'Absence' and 'Au cimetière' that find out her limitations. They are very well done up to a certain point – the point where interpretation begins. She simply lacks the tragic intensity for 'Sur les lagunes', the depth of feeling to match the heart-searching directness of utterance in 'Absence', the poetic sensitivity to capture the stifling stillness of 'Au cimetière'. Here, in addition, the atmosphere is undermined by fluctuating tempi (due to careless tape-editing?), though the character of the song presupposes an almost unwavering evenness of pulse.

Similar virtues and defects mark the performance by **Victoria de los**

Angeles. The notes are very well sung, with lovely clear tone and shapely phrasing; but like Te Kanawa, de los Angeles is much happier with the light-hearted songs – 'Villanelle', and even more 'L'île inconnue', which she sings with an irresistible playfulness – than with the intensity of the more dramatic pieces. She makes little of the rose's triumphant 'J'arrive du paradis', and floats on the surface of 'Sur les lagunes'. 'Absence', even though not really intense enough, has an attractive simplicity; and here, as elsewhere, Munch is a sensitive and exact accompanist.

A singer who combines beauty of tone and line with expressiveness is **Frederica von Stade**; but the expressiveness is strictly limited to the elegiac vein. 'Le spectre de la rose' soon becomes monotonously wistful, and this same dreamy melancholy falls far short of the dark despair of 'Sur les lagunes' (where Ozawa's conducting, too, is passionless). The big moments lack power, and the cycle's constantly changing moods are evened out and lose distinctness in the flood of creamy tone. Von Stade sometimes sings straight through the rests, ignoring their function of quickening tension, as if to suggest that smoothness of line, not vitality of expression, has become the chief preoccupation. As you would expect, the Boston Symphony's playing is excellent, and Ozawa's responsiveness to nuances of texture, especially in 'Au cimetière', is finely tuned. But nowhere does he strike deep.

In **Elly Ameling**'s seductive performance sensitivity to the poetry of the music goes some way – though only so far – to compensate for vocal shortcomings. Ameling, with slightly reticent but musicianly accompaniment by the Atlanta Symphony under Robert Shaw, offers some lively touches to make you forgive the white, fluttery tone in 'Villanelle' and the wobble on sustained notes at the top of the stage in 'Absence'. For two-thirds of the cycle that is, perhaps, possible; but the last two songs lose momentum, especially 'L'île inconnue', where the sea images become dulled in a tempo far below the composer's dotted crotchet = 96.

Hildegard Behrens makes a determined effort to adapt her voice and style, so compelling in Wagner and Strauss, to the demands of a radically different idiom. The effort shows. The music seems insufficiently familiar to her (and to the conductor, Francis Travis); so does the French language. You feel she is still grappling with problems that have to be overcome before a living performance, an interpretation, can begin. As a result, despite some expressive moments, as a whole it is lifeless; no essential experience is communicated.

Agnes Baltsa's version is certainly alive, though often raw and unpolished. Tone-production is sometimes uneven and gusty, there are ungainly scoops in 'Le spectre de la rose', and she tends to be careless of note-values, rhythms and words ('souvenir' instead of 'revenir' in 'Au cimetière'). On the other hand her singing can have an attractively salty vitality. She achieves some memorably rich, dark phrases in the lower register, especially in 'Sur les lagunes', which is sung with a passion missing in many other versions. 'Absence' (taken down a tone, into E major) has a moving submissiveness in the last, *ppp* refrain. In Jeffrey Tate, Baltsa has a conductor more alive than many to the light and shade of the score: the string *tremolando* in the final verse of 'Le spectre de la rose' is both truly *pianissimo* and tinglingly present. He is also one of the few who understand the need for a brisk tempo in 'L'île inconnue'. It is a pity that in two of the songs the tempo is unconvincingly slow: 'Au cimetière', where the crotchets' steady pulsation becomes clogged (especially when the music is transposed down a minor third, into B major), and 'Le spectre de la rose', where momentum is sacrificed to colour and incident.

Unlike Behrens', **Leontyne Price**'s performance suggests that a dramatic soprano can come to terms with the intimate character of Berlioz's song cycle. The splendid voice has a plangent quality, smoky but well focused, which sounds well in this music. Price is remarkably successful in scaling it down to 'Au cimetière' and at the same time sustaining the melodic line. In 'Villanelle' and 'L'île inconnue' she makes up for lack of subtlety by her exuberance. 'Le spectre de la rose', however, though suitably large and radiant, suffers from monotony of expression, and the Gluckian restraint and slowly unfolding phrases of 'Absence' overtax her. In this song, too, she conveys the voluptuousness of sexual longing, not the heartbreak of enforced separation. 'Sur les lagunes' is better done. The seventh bar from the end of the song is curtailed by two quaver beats (curiously, something similar happens in the Norman and Behrens versions); and in the refrain of 'Absence' the strings cut off with the voice on the third syllable of 'aimée' instead of holding their chord for a further beat – an error found in several recordings.

Some of Price's large-limbed physical vitality would not come amiss in the performance by **Bernadette Greevy**. Yet this is in many ways a likable reading, well thought out, musicianly, nicely phrased, securely placed in the pure, firm voice. Her account of 'Au cimetière', though sung a major third lower, in B flat, is one of the best on disc, and there is much to warm to in the other songs. The performance just lacks that special feeling, the sense of emotions touched to the quick. Its overall mood is a little too ladylike. The conductor, André Prieur, gets some quite expressive playing from the New Irish Chamber Orchestra, but allows the initial tempo to sag in both the 'Le spectre de la rose' and 'L'île inconnue'; and in transposing 'Au cimetière' the orchestral copyist has let some mistakes creep into the parts which have not been corrected.

Finally, to restore one's faith in the ability of a single voice to encompass the whole cycle, the version by **Janet Baker** – to my mind the best after Eleanor Steber's. It is also the only one by a non-French singer to deliver the text with something like a native feeling for the language: the words are invariably clear and well pointed, yet contained within the musical line. True, Baker can be self-conscious – a little too determinedly jaunty in 'L'île inconnue', a trifle arch in her response to the skittishness of 'Villanelle'. The abundance of expression for which her performance is notable sometimes sounds contrived. But far better too much intelligence than too little. Of all the singers she is the most sensitive to the touch and atmosphere of the verse and to the way Berlioz's music and Gautier's poetry interact, each intensifying the other. Time and again the quickening of mood, the deepening or lightening of colour are registered in her performance. Nearly always she finds her way to the heart of a song. Her singing is among the most technically secure and accomplished on record. Like Steber she takes the long wide-spanned phrase in the final verse of 'Le spectre de la rose' – 'Mon destin fut digne d'envie' – in a single breath, and beautiful it sounds. In all this she is tolerably well served by her conductor, Sir John Barbirolli, and by the New Philharmonia, who accompany admirably except for some untidy ensemble in 'Le spectre de la rose', where the tempo, as in the Baltsa version, is too slow. A wrong viola note in bar 84 of 'Sur les lagunes', and no oboe in the woodwind chord at letter D in 'Absence', are the kind of minor mistake which stands out in textures of such clarity and openness, and which should have been put right. None the less this is one of the most satisfying versions.

For the ideal version one would need an amalgam of Steber and Baker, with a seasoning of Danco, and a pinch of de los Angeles for the gaiety that might otherwise be lacking. Yet I continue to hope and believe such an interpretation may one day find its way onto disc, with the conductor to match it.

The alternative is the team performance suggested by Berlioz's orchestral score. Of the two recordings in this category, one merely divides the cycle between the two voices of the original vocal score, mezzo-soprano and tenor. The arrangement might work, given two spirited and sensitive singers and idiomatic conducting. But **Stuart Burrows** is disappointingly wooden (as well as singing a wrong note in each verse of 'Villanelle'), **Yvonne Minton** sounds laboured in the 'Le spectre de la rose' and only comes into her own in 'L'île inconnue' (taken at the right spanking pace), and Pierre Boulez conducts with characteristic clarity and meticulousness without conveying much sense of involvement. The whole thing makes a rather cold effect.

The other composite performance – part of the Philips Berlioz cycle – employs four singers and follows the orchestral score's preferences, where they are indicated, exactly. If the soprano, **Sheila Armstrong**, had been in fresher voice and if Colin Davis had not further drawn out an already slow tempo in the refrains of 'Absence', the experiment would have been more convincing still. As it is it casts striking new light on the work; the contrasts in vocal timbre throw into relief the changes in colour and mood from one song to the next, above all when it comes to the two songs in which Berlioz prefers or actually stipulates a male singer. To plunge straight from the contralto-ish tones of **Josephine Veasey** in 'Le spectre de la rose' into the dark sonority of **John Shirley-Quirk**'s baritone at the outset of 'Sur les lagunes' is to experience what the composer intended when he orchestrated the songs and made the colour of particular voice-types an integral part of the process. Equally **Frank Patterson**'s lyric tenor and rapt singing have a fitness that no female voice can match, in the account – perfectly paced by Colin Davis – of 'Au cimetière'.

I called the multi-voice performance of *Les nuits d'été* an alternative, and obviously it is no more than that. Clearly too it is not easy for a record company, still less a concert promoter, to set up; but it is something that would be worth attempting more often, perhaps in the context of a festival, especially now that the cycle is so popular.

A third alternative is to revert to the composer's original piano–voice version. There is a widely accepted notion among recitalists that Berlioz's songs are ineffective on the piano. Yet I have heard 'La mort d'Ophélie', with its utterly simple piano part, hold a large audience spellbound (sung by Sarah Walker, with Graham Johnson) and receive the loudest applause of the evening. Rudimentary though many of Berlioz's piano accompaniments may be, a sympathetic player can make them sound convincing.

In the case of *Les nuits d'été*, however, the task is complicated by the poor quality of the standard published accompaniment (not Berlioz's), a clumsy, inauthentic piece of work, full of octave displacements and unstylish thickenings, which at the same time leaves out essential subsidiary parts. A new accompaniment is badly needed, made by someone who has the sound of the orchestral score in his or her head and who knows what to put in and what to omit. If that were done, there is no reason why *Les nuits d'été* in this form should not work as well as a piano performance of Mahler's *Lieder eines fahrenden Gesellen*, another orchestral work which started life as a cycle for voice and piano. As it is, neither of the recorded versions is satisfactory. Of the two, the one by the French-Canadian baritone **Bruno Laplante** is the better. **Gérard Souzay** is both vocally and interpretatively far past his best, and his accompanist Dalton Baldwin plays without much understanding of the music. Though Laplante's rather backward voice-production and rapid vibrato are disadvantages, his intelligent intentions often shine through, and his pianist, Marc Durand, gives quite a lively account of himself. But in the process of transposing some of the songs he has let in several wrong notes, most notably in 'Au cimetière', a song whose subtly varied metric stresses also tend to make it accident-prone – Laplante loses his place at one point, and the pianist has to put in an extra beat. Cord Garben, the pianist on **Bernd Weikl**'s enterprising disc of French songs by Berlioz, Liszt and Wagner (Acanta 40 23511), plays with no little artistry, but even he changes a minor third into a major third in the coda of 'Sur les lagunes'.

Gabriel Bacquier's singing of 'Absence' (L'Art du Chant, vol. 2, Vega L 30 PO 357, with Jean Laforge accompanying) is fresh and expressive enough to make you wonder what his performance of the whole cycle would have been like. Yet it must be admitted that the lighter songs do not take kindly to being transposed down for the baritone voice. (The F major 'L'île inconnue' sounds positively sepulchral in Laplante's D major performance, as though the ship were a pirate vessel embarking on a mission of rapine and destruction.) They lie more naturally for a tenor, as **Cesare Valletti** shows on a recital disc (recorded live at the New York Town Hall in 1959, with Leo Taubman) which includes 'Villanelle' and 'L'île inconnue', as well as 'Sur les lagunes'. Valletti does not seem to have a great deal to say about the music, and he takes 'Villanelle' at breakneck speed, but his attractive voice, smooth line and phrasing and good breath-control give pleasure.

Of the recordings of separate *Nuits d'été* songs by female singers, four of the six I have heard are of 'Absence'. **Germaine Cernay**, an admired French mezzo with a well focused, soprano-ish quality who died relatively young in 1943, sings it with some character if a little carelessly as to note-values, accompanied by an unnamed orchestra (Odéon 123692; CL 99–111). **Jennie Tourel** recorded it twice, with piano, the first time as part of a French–Italian recital with Paul Ulanowski (Am. Decca DL 10013), the second time live as an encore at a recital in the Alice Tully Hall, New York, when the pianist was James Levine (Desto DC 7118–9). On the latter occasion she was seventy or nearly, yet her clarity and firmness of tone and her control of the sustained F sharp at the second 'reviens' are seemingly untouched by time. But the performance is marred by inaccuracies, and in both recordings she distorts the long, slowly unfolding phrase 'la fleur de ma vie', each time it comes, by making an *accelerando*. Much more interesting is the 'Absence' of **Maggie Teyte**, who recorded two of the *Nuits d'été* songs with orchestra in 1940, when she was 52 (HMV JG 177; COLH 139). 'Le spectre de la rose', taken at a hectic tempo (presumably in order to fit it onto one side of a 78 disc), is spirited but terribly rushed, and at times the orchestra under Leslie Heward sounds as if it is sight-reading; but the 'Absence' has charm and gives a glimpse of why Teyte was so admired as an interpreter of French song. There is an especially touching note of sadness in the final verse, and the slight pause and stress on the climactic 'loin' is a characteristically telling effect.

Ninon Vallin (Pathé PG 62; 2910023) sings 'Villanelle' with piano accompaniment. Vallin was 48 when the recording was made (in 1935), but her voice still sounds in its prime and the performance, sung at a restrained tempo with precise vocal control and clear diction, has a pleasing directness and simplicity.

In addition to *Les nuits d'été* there are fourteen solo songs in the retrospective collection, *32 Mélodies*, which Berlioz published towards the end of his life. Song – drawing-room ballads and *romances* – had been the main musical fare of his childhood and the medium of his own first attempts at composition, and he returned to it from time to time throughout his career, as a means of filling gaps in concert programmes but also because, with all his preoccupation with music on the grand scale, it remained a natural form of expression for him. In the process he played a significant part in the evolution of French song from the simple strophic *romance* to the flexible, poetically richer *mélodie*.

Five of the fourteen solo songs in *32 Mélodies* also exist in orchestral form. In style and structure they range from the strophic 'La belle voyageuse' and 'Le jeune pâtre breton' through the delightful 'Zaïde' and the rumbustious, rather facile 'Le chasseur danois' (three identical quick verses in 6/8 time giving way to a fourth, in a slow 4/4, followed by a shortened reprise of the 6/8), to the final version of 'La captive'. 'Zaïde' is a bolero with a racy refrain in F major (complete with castanets) and a plaintive D minor verse, the scoring and declamation different each time. 'La captive', originally composed as a strophic song with piano, evolved into one of Berlioz' most elaborate and poetically evocative vocal pieces.

All five songs appear on the reverse side of the multi-voice orchestral version of *Les nuits d'été*, adding to the unusual interest of that recording. Eleanor Steber's record of the cycle includes three of them, 'La captive' (transposed up into F), 'Le jeune pâtre breton' and 'Zaïde'. They are beautifully sung, especially 'La captive', and adequately conducted by Jean Morel though with less liveliness than by Colin Davis on the Philips record. 'Zaïde' also appears on *España*, a Songmakers' Almanac disc devoted to Spain (Hyperion A 66176), sung nicely if a little staidly by **Ann Murray** to the accompaniment of Graham Johnson.

Bruno Laplante, whose *Nuits d'été* has already been mentioned, includes four other Berlioz songs on the same record: 'Le jeune pâtre breton' (the alphorn *obbligato* played by Jean Gaudréault), 'Le chasseur danois', 'La belle voyageuse' and 'Les champs'. These less highly charged pieces go better than the *Nuits d'été* songs; and the same is true of Bernd Weikl, whose warm baritone is heard to advantage in 'Les champs', 'Petit oiseau', and 'Je crois en vous' which Berlioz later adapted for Harlequin's cor anglais melody in the Carnival scene of *Benvenuto Cellini*.

Berlioz's Thomas Moore settings of 1829 include five solo numbers. Three of them – 'Le coucher au soleil', 'L'origine de la harpe' and 'La belle voyageuse' – figure on a **Jill Gomez** disc of French song (Saga 5388, accompanied by John Constable). The best of them, 'La belle voyageuse', is sung with a charm and a distinction that promise well for Gomez's recording of *Les nuits d'été*, due for release this year. All five songs, together with the haunting 'La mort d'Ophélie', are on *Irlande*, a disc of Berlioz songs, duets and choruses, all with piano accompaniment (Oiseau-Lyre SOL 305, also featuring John Eliot Gardiner's Monteverdi Choir). The piano playing of the late Viola Tunnard is a model of its kind, and **April Cantelo** and **Robert Tear**, who divide the six songs equally between them, give sensitive, committed performances. The Moore songs contain characteristic Berliozian touches but, except for the turbulent 'Elégie', are quite comfortably contained within the polite conventions of the *romance*. 'La mort d'Ophélie', which dates from a year or two after *Les nuits d'été*, shapes strophic song with exquisite art into a single flowing continuum. It is better known in the later arrangement for two-part female choir and orchestra; but for once the voice-and-piano version enshrines the purer essence of the composer's invention.

Duparc

ALAN BLYTH

Complete sets:

Bouvier, Bonneau	Pathé DTX 278
Herbillon, Debuchy	Calliope CAL 1801
Kruysen, Lee	Telefunken 6.42113
Maurane, Bienvenu	Philips N00225L
Panzéra, Baillot-Panzéra	HMV DA 4880, DB 5000, 5075, 5084/5;
	Pathé Marconi FALP 50 024;
	HMV COLH 104
Rhodes, Ivaldi	Pathé-Marconi 2C 069–16387
Simoneau, Rogers	Westminster XWN 18788
Souzay, Bonneau	Decca LXT 2823
Souzay, Baldwin	Philips SAL 3434
Souzay, Baldwin	HMV HQS 1258

Panzéra's 78rpm records collected as above on LP were recorded between 1935 and 1938; he recorded several of the songs in earlier versions as mentioned in the text.

Henri Duparc's reputation rests, and rests securely, on the composition of just fourteen songs, one of which, 'Le galop', is not usually included in the canon, and has been too seldom recorded to be included here. This precious legacy has always presented a challenge of peculiar potency to recitalists: there are few who have not attempted at least four or five (Fischer-Dieskau appears, for once, to be an exception), but the secrets of interpreting these quite complex songs have been solved by few singers who are not Francophones; all too few of the latter have recorded complete sets. The saddest omissions are complete sets by Claire Croiza, Ninon Vallin and Pierre Bernac, the three singers best equipped to encompass them to judge by the examples of their art in Duparc that exist.

Important adjuncts to hearing Duparc's songs are two books: *The Songs of Duparc* by Sydney Northcote (Dennis Dobson, 1949), long out

16

of print unfortunately, and *The Interpretation of French Song* by Pierre Bernac (Cassell, 1970).

'Chanson triste'

Written in 1868, poem by Jean Lahor. Originally set for voice and piano in E flat.

This song is dedicated to Duparc's brother-in-law, and it has been assumed that it was designed for performance by him. On this evidence, as Northcote points out, he must have had an extraordinary compass, because the vocal line stretches quite boldly over an octave and a sixth. The alternative (lower) notes, given in the printed text, were probably later additions to bring the song within a more normal compass.

It calls for a perfect *sostenuto*, just what you might expect from one of its earliest exponents, Nellie Melba (DA 334; RLS 719), recording in 1913, to bring to it. In the event, her hurried, insensitive performance has little else to offer. She offers no softness on the 'doux' marking at 'mon', yelps the high A flat and seems to have no idea of what the song is really about.

A roughly contemporaneous performance by the Canadian soprano Eva Gauthier, a specialist in song, was included in vol. 2 of 'The Record of Singing' (Victor 69669; RLS 743). It is everything that Melba's is not: the voice itself is warm and expressive, the phrasing is thoughtful and long-breathed, the 'mon' is touched in delicately. The timing, 3′34″, more than a minute slower than Melba, is about right for the song, not too fast to skate over the surface of its feelings, not too slow to sentimentalise it.

But other sopranos, now in the era of electric 78rpm recording, delve deeper than Gauthier into its meaning, not least Maggie Teyte in 1941 (though she has to transpose down a tone). She sings primarily off the words, floats the 'mon' ideally, and gives that special Teyte accent to the repeated 'une ballade' (DA 1779; RLS 716). Her French contemporary, the legendary Claire Croiza (LF 59; ALP 2115), is even more personal, catching the elegiac intimacy of the song as well as anyone, not making it too extrovert in the modern manner, but intensely personal, though she needs more breaths (one before 'de tes bras') than are ideal. By timing it at 2′50″, she gives the impression of the poem and its setting as a single thought.

The slightly more dilatory Ninon Vallin (Odéon 123 562; EX 29 0946 3) is even more trance-like and soft-grained, floating the vocal line with the utmost expressiveness. This version with orchestra is, however, surpassed by the one with piano, much more difficult to come by (Pathé X 7230). Here words, tone and line come into a perfect alignment, and the expression, so mellow and intense, sets a standard simply not surpassed by anyone, certainly not by any of her fellow-countrywomen who followed her. Géori Boué (Urania URLP 7070) comes closest to Vallin in her peculiarly haunting and meticulous version, spoilt only by a too operatic treatment of the final stanza, a fault evident in several versions. Jane Rhodes travels through the song laboriously in seven-league boots. Régine Crespin (EL 29 0046 1), singing in the mezzo key, sounds sadly *passé* in her 1972 record. Hélène Bouvier, with the excellent Jacqueline Bonneau, is short-breathed and over-emphatic, creating a bumpy line.

In recent times a number of non-French sopranos (I count Teyte as adopted French) have essayed Duparc, but seldom with anything like the feeling for his idiom or for the language of even the least accomplished French soprano. Elly Ameling is quite likable. Her version with orchestra (Philips 410 043–2) is straightforward and unaffected but not particular enough in its accents. Jessye Norman (Philips 416 445–4), transposing down a tone, rushes the song and shows no special connection with the text. Margaret Price (Orfeo S 038831 A) takes a minute longer than Norman and thus conveys a stiff, wrongly grand impression far removed from Duparc's intent. Kiri Te Kanawa with the Brussels National Orchestra under John Pritchard (EL 27 0135 1) smooths away her consonants and delivers at a monotonous *mezza forte*. Nelly Miricioiu (ETC 1041) comes closer to catching the feeling of the song, but her words are indecipherable. Better than any of these is Bidu Sayão. Recorded in 1950 towards the end of her auspicious career (Odyssey Y 33130), the Brazilian soprano gives a sensuous, perfumed account of the song in well-articulated French, accompanied by orchestra.

Two mezzos are disappointing, Gladys Swarthout (ALP 1269) is plummy and chops her phrases, a souvenir of the singer, no more. Jennie Tourel (LX 1306) is unexpectedly laboured.

Tenors are perhaps better suited to this song than any other type of voice, so it is a pity so few have recorded it. Happily, all but one of the extant versions are worth seeking out. Among recent recordings, I enjoyed that by Ian Partridge (Pearl SHE 524). His tone may be a shade wanting in colour, his high A strained, but he has the measure of both the linguistic and musical idiom and conveys the poignancy of the piece. So does Cesare Valletti (RB 6622) who, towards the end of his career in 1965, is gentle and caressing. At a slower tempo, Léopold Simoneau sings with an observant eye on Duparc's markings and a subtle feeling for the right amount of *rubato*. The result is a shade affected and unspontaneous, but his soft-grained timbre is very much what Duparc's writing needs. But the palm for tenors, indeed for all male singers, goes to the unforgotten (among collectors) French tenor of the 1920s and 1930s, Charles Friant

(Disque P 450; GV 524). What poignant enunciation, what immediacy of feeling one exclaims as Friant provides the *tendresse* predicated by Duparc, Friant's quick vibrato here seeming peculiarly apt. His timing, 3′02″, feels exactly right too; so does the steadiness and flow of his tempo and line. Howard Haskin (Grapevine GV 002) could have listened to Friant with advantage before essaying the song; his version, recorded at a Wigmore Hall recital, is heavy-going, and he ignores most of the pauses marked by the composer.

Baritones by their nature and because of the downward transposition cannot provide quite Vallin's or Friant's qualities in this song, though several of them come close. Charles Panzéra seems to have recorded it at least five times, always with the 'speaking' tone, intimate refinement, and sense of a single arch of phrasing that made him such a renowned interpreter of *mélodies*. The 1932 version (DA 4808; 2C 151–73084/5), ideally sung, is the one to have and also the most easily obtainable on LP, but the earlier Disque version (P 497; GV 513) has a wonderful immediacy of emotion. The other readings are on Disque P 723, DA 4880 (listed at the head of this chapter) and DB 4971, with orchestra. No wonder Panzéra was such an influence on his successor, Gérard Souzay, whose three recordings, unlike Panzéra's, are variable in quality. The first, for Decca, is the most natural and impassioned. Made in 1952, the voice is in fine state. The vibrato is carefully controlled as are the dynamics with the repeated marking '*très doux*' scrupulously obeyed. Bonneau is a sensitive partner, but one wants to hear more of her than the recording allows. Dalton Baldwin is much more present in the 1962 remake for Philips. There may be more subtlety in this performance but less spontaneity. By the HMV version of 1972, the voice has hardened, the vibrato loosened, the *pianissimi* have become croons – all very sad.

Jacques Herbillon's over-emphatic version can be set aside. Michel Dens (2C 053–12507) has the style but the voice is worn. His near-contemporary, Camille Maurane, is gentle and lyrical but a little wanting in impetus. Willy Clément (Ducretet–Thompson 320 E 815) is unsteady, but his *baryton-martin*, Bernac-like in timbre, and manner, has the authentic touch. George London (American Columbia ML 4906) is firm and mellow of tone, but a little one-dimensional in accent, Jules Bruyère (RCA LM 2658) too strenuous. The Dutch–Swiss singer, Bernard Kruysen, in his soft, palpitating interpretation provides a modern *via media*, not as personal as the most noted of his predecessors but aware of tradition and of the complementary needs of notes and words. Above all, he shapes the songs in an unfailing *legato*.

Preferred versions are those of Vallin, Friant, Panzéra, Souzay I, and Kruysen.

Alan Blyth

'Soupir'

Written in 1868, poek by Sully Prudhomme. Originally set for voice and piano in D minor.

The emotional undertow in this eloquent song denies the apparent restraint of the setting, the extreme chromaticism of the piano part telling of lovelorn anguish in support of the adorned voice line. Bernac (op. cit.) declares 'it is a very touching and moving *mélodie* when it is performed with simplicity and sincerity'. Above all, it requires a sustained *legato* and a sensitive control of dynamics. Northcote (op. cit) points out that 'any trace of the sentimental will imperil the wistful intimacy which Duparc intended'. That predicates a basic tempo that is not too slow; indeed, Bernac's suggested crotchet = 56 is quite deliberate enough (he goes a touch faster in his own recording).

Rhodes is eliminated on grounds of tardiness, which makes the song sound merely lugubrious. Bouvier is much nearer the mark, indeed very good in a piece that doesn't require her to put pressure on her tone. Her words are clear and pointedly projected, her line well held, especially in the last verse. Margaret Price (Orfeo S 038831 A), singing in the original key, gives the best of her three Duparc performances, straight, unfussy, clean in text and music, but still wanting an essential identification with the song's sentiments. Miricioiu (ETC 1041) has only a vague idea of the idiom and language.

None of the baritones is disappointing though Herbillon, for all his sensitivity, starts too emphatically and comes into his own only in the last verse, softly breathed and tender. Beautifully supported by Noël Lee, Kruysen is at his appreciable best; dynamics, breathing, phrasing, and understanding of the text are held in almost ideal balance. Nobody, not even Bernac, sings the final stanza with a more palpitating inwardness on a thread of tone, the last 'toujours' exhaled longingly. That is an effect Souzay also manages well in the first two of his versions, but his slightly self-regarding approach, at a slow tempo, is less rewarding than the greater commitment shown by Kruysen. Souzay also makes too much of the song's two climaxes.

Maurane doesn't make that mistake. His finely modulated tones and natural singing cast the spell of this song and justify his slow tempo. In contrast, Panzéra is faster than Maurane by a minute. At first it seems he is slipping over its surface, but the quiet flow of the reading, particularly in the preferable first version of 1932 (DA 4808; 2C 151–73084/5), and the subtle enunciation of the text begin to convince you that 2'47" is all the *mélodie* needs to make its effect, an impression confirmed by Bernac and Poulenc (DA 4928; OVD 50036) at a similar tempo. What intense feelings and what terrible sorrow inform this reading, a greatly sensitive lover stretched on the rack, the final verse subsiding into resigned heart-ache, all so unobtrusively yet pertinently supported by Poulenc.

Howard Haskin (Grapevine GV 002) has the right voice for the song and sings it at the right pitch, but his voice sounds uncomfortable above the stave. You could never say that of Simoneau, whose plangent timbre is ideal here, but he takes an inordinately long time over his performance so that it tends to be maudlin, refined and fluent though the singing is throughout.

Preferred versions are those of Kruysen and Bernac, two baritones out of the same mould.

'Au pays où se fait la guerre'

Written in 1869, poem by Théophile Gautier. Originally set for voice and piano in F minor, later orchestrated by the composer.

This song, though not as immediately appealing as others, is peculiarly evocative, so that it is odd that so few singers have attempted it on record. Lotte Lehmann in *More than Singing* called it 'an intense dramatic scene'; Northcote rightly prefers 'drame lyrique' as description. Janet Baker, in both her 1970 recording with Gerald Moore (ASD 2590) and her 1978 version with André Previn and the LSO (ASD 3455), leans towards Lehmann's view of the piece, though the latter performance is in every way subtler and also, properly I think, a little more distanced, as if the girl was experiencing her longing in a trance-like state, rather like Marguerite in her 'Chanson gothique'. It is strange in the earlier record to find her taking the high A flat on 'n'ose' *forte*, when Duparc calls for it to be sung 'doux'. This has been corrected in the second version, where Dame Janet's French is also more idiomatic, her phrasing more fluent, yet there is some-thing immediate about the performance with piano that I miss with the LSO, who play in a markedly dozy fashion.

The song is intended for mezzo, yet the *tessitura* often lies quite high. It would have suited Vallin perfectly, Maggie Teyte too, so it is sad that neither saw fit to record it. On Kiri Te Kanawa's 1984 recording (CDC 7 47111–2) with the Brussels Opera Orchestra under Pritchard she sings with greater ease and warmer tone than Baker, but isn't quite so apprised of the song's histrionic import, though I like the way she darkens her voice and lets it take on a more vital tinge for the imagined appearance of the desired lover.

Both these singers adopt a slower tempo than the crotchet = 80 requested by the composer. Danièle Galland in her performance, which completes the Kruysen recording of the other songs, doesn't make that mistake and in consequence the march-like theme at the start sounds that much more urgent. Galland isn't a very personal interpreter, but her gallic timbre, light and on the breath, lets us imagine what Vallin might have made of it, and she rises finely to the despair of the close.

Of the two other French singers who have essayed the song, Rhodes sounds heavy and lugubrious partly because she transposes it down a tone. Not so Bouvier, who offers the most persuasive and idiomatic reading, in the original key. She successfully lightens her voice, catches the oddly uncomfortable melancholy of the song, and generally sings with subtlety and point at about the right tempo.

'L'invitation au voyage'

Written in 1870, poem by Charles Baudelaire. Originally set for voice and piano in C minor, later orchestrated by the composer.

One of the most widely sung of Duparc's output, it would figure in any pantheon of great *mélodies*. As Northcote comments: 'The exquisite nostalgia of the poem is translated into an unimpeded music, the vocal phrases rising like tall, swaying flowers out of a shimmering musical texture.'

As so often, modern accounts take a low priority of listening. Miricioiu (ETC 1041) is quavery and her diction is indistinct. Kiri Te Kanawa's 1984 performance with Pritchard (CDC 47111–2) is beautifully sung but indeterminate and hazy as an interpretation with the conductor in one of his lackadaisical moods. With the very slow timing, 4′41″, an ill-judged breath is needed before the climax at 'lumière'. Jessye Norman (Philips CD 416 445–2), transposing down a semitone, is at the opposite extreme from Dame Kiri. Northcote points out that the climaxes must be brought off by changes in tone colour not by dynamic emphases; Norman does just the opposite and consequently blows up the song out of all proportion to the sentiments being expressed. Much the most persuasive part of this performance is the piano playing of Dalton Baldwin, admirably clear and iridescent.

Ameling, in the original key, produces a poised line and captures something of the liquid dreaminess, not least the 'très doux' effect at 'larmes', but she misses something of the ecstasy in the counter-melody beginning at 'C'est pour assouvir'. In general, there is something a little tame about this version, though it is finely supported by the conductor, Edo de Waart (Philips 410 043–2).

Janet Baker, also with orchestra (the LSO under Previn), is certainly inside the song, but she falls into the modern fault of equating a slow tempo with meaning, thus losing the song's essential flow. Previn must take part of the responsibility for the pervading lethargy. More recommendable is Dorothy Maynor's controlled, finely etched, soft-grained but somewhat reserved record (RCA LM 3086).

22

Being French does not guarantee an ideal reading. Jane Rhodes wobbles uncomfortably in her clumsy version. Crespin (EL 29 0466) is as laboured as in 'Chanson triste' (q.v.) though nothing this artist did is without interest. Bouvier catches the intensity of the second verse, 'la vie entière' is especially vivid. By taking only a little over three and a half minutes over the song, she preserves its structure, but the quality of her voice is a shade thick for it. Herbillon's tone is also disturbing, too gritty in his case, but his fastish version has something to offer in its verbal acuity. Maurane again spoils an idiomatic reading by seeming uninvolved and so uninvolving.

We now move into an altogether higher bracket of inspiration. Souzay, it is true, favours an unduly slow tempo in his earliest version, but once more I find it the most worthwhile of his three recordings because he is able to shape the song with such urgency and freshness. The emphases in the second verse may be a little exaggerated but they come from a depth of passion missing in his later readings. The second has the advantage of Baldwin's accompanying, and the slightly faster pace gives the song a more natural flow, but Souzay's tone is no longer youthful, nor his approach so eager. By the time of the HMV disc (1972), the voice has become distressingly dry and unattractive. Kruysen is another to linger over the sensuous texture, but his reading, made in 1971, justifies the deliberate approach by virtue of its many subtle shadings and its affection for the text. George London's large but never unwieldy voice and caring approach (American Columbia ML 4906) is similar to Kruysen's. Even so, Panzéra proves conclusively that 3'30" is the most comfortable timing for this piece. Within the quicker tempo no point of interpretation is missed; the little *frisson* on 'pour mon esprit' is a typical example of Panzéra's innate understanding. The 'très doux' markings are scrupulously observed and the description in the second verse is alive with a realisation of the undercurrents of meaning implicit in the music. Madame Panzéra, as always, is a fitting partner for her husband's rewarding interpretation. His earlier, 1927 record with orchestra (Disque W 836; 2C 151–73084/5) is, if possible, even more rewarding in its conjuring up of atmosphere and revealing the emotional content of the song.

A few other singers are Panzéra's peer. Vallin, whose version (Pathé X 7230) plays a semitone below score pitch at 78rpm, gives a performance that is shaped with natural phrasing and softly voiced. The moments of heightened tension, as at 'la vie entière', are lovingly managed, yet the result is just a shade placid, which Teyte's reading (JG 178; RLS 716) in C minor is definitely not. Teyte catches the misty, mysterious mood of the words and music to perfection, places her high notes ideally, savours the trinity 'luxe, calme et volupté' on her tongue, and builds the second verse to an ecstatic climax. So does Victoria de los Angeles (SLS 5233), but her tone, though lovely, sometimes comes under stress. Croiza (Col. D 15081; ALP 2115), in the mezzo key, is possibly even more intimate than either Teyte or de los Angeles, probably because she is accompanied by a piano (Francis Poulenc, no less) rather than an orchestra, and she articulates the text as pointedly as Panzéra. Hers is a wholly absorbing account, imbued with the song's poetic essence and so not to be missed.

Bernac (DB 6312), reissued in EMI's 'Record of Singing, vol. 4' (EX 7.69369 1), also has the advantage of Poulenc at the piano. He is almost a baritone clone of Croiza, singing with as much immediacy and the same forward, immediate diction and confiding manner, and an extra shiver of feeling for the trinity of epithets. Above all he fulfils his own dictum (op. cit.) that one must sing this *mélodie* not with sadness but 'with an ecstatic sense of joy at the imagined realisation of a vision'. This is the version to present to a young singer who wants to verse himself or herself in the art of interpreting Duparc.

I have found three tenor versions, all worth hearing. That by David Devriès (Odéon 123553), a singer much lauded by 78 collectors, seemed a little four-square at first hearing, also too lacrymose, but the required feeling for the text is undoubtedly there and the voice itself has an appropriately elegiac flavour. Even if you find he makes the piece sound more like a Gounod aria than a Duparc *mélodie*, in the end it is hard to resist, so charming is the vocalisation.

Valletti (RB 6622) also tends to be too operatic, but his words are placed securely on his Italianate *legato*, and he seems to take fewer breaths than anyone else. His affecting version is, however, surpassed by Simoneau's. He shapes the whole first verse in a single arc, sings the 'très doux' high notes in a devastatingly beautiful *mezza voce*, and keeps the song on a level of sensuous, mesmeric intimacy that is unforgettable.

Teyte, Vallin, Croiza, Panzéra, Bernac, Souzay I, and Simoneau all have something individual and pertinent to tell us about this beautiful song.

'La vague et la cloche'

Written in 1871, poem by François Coppée from *Le reliquaire* (1866). Originally set for voice and orchestra in E minor.

Pierre Bernac (op. cit.) has written aptly of the 'tumultuous romanticism' of this *mélodie*, and the dramatic force of Duparc's setting of the somewhat overblown poem achieves an almost Wagnerian power. The poet tells of two successive nightmares, the meaning of which is enigmatic, but they provoke two anguished questions about the purpose, if any, of life. It is written for a powerful mezzo or baritone, and the piano version requires a player with a strong technique.

All the versions come from complete sets except two. Both women are rather impressive here. Jane Rhodes, sounding a bit like a French Gerhardt, sings with enormous conviction, and, as at 'l'inutile travail', an appropriate weight of tone, splendidly partnered by Christian Ivaldi. Bouvier isn't quite as effective, but finds a moving way with the questions. Both these mezzos take more than 5'30" over the song, giving it all they've got. Maurane adopts a somewhat more distanced approach. He has noted that the mark at the start is 'simplement et sans nuances' and that is how he sings the opening descriptive passage. He is not consumed by the song's feelings, but stands a little apart from them, but in a way that makes his intimate, almost hesitant voicing of the questions that much more eloquent.

Both Herbillon and Kruysen with their lighter voices take only five minutes, which gives their accounts an added urgency. Both employ a fierce, consonant-led declamation, but Kruysen's tone is the smoother and his identification with the terror of the nightmare is the more immediate, helped by Noël Lee's athletic playing.

Souzay's early version is again to be preferred to his later ones but not this time in all respects. I like the slightly untutored approach of I and the almost hollow reading of the questions, also the depth of meaning given to the arresting 'Puis tout changea', but Bonneau, backwardly recorded, is no match for the masterly Baldwin in the other two versions. By the third, the artists have quickened the pace and emphasised even more purposefully the melodrama. The hardness that has now entered the baritone's voice is here almost an advantage, and the questions have become weary rather than anxious.

Panzéra, on one side of a twelve-inch 78 record (DB 5085), has to squeeze the song into 4'12". Not surprisingly he sounds a shade flustered and distraught in the wrong kind of way. His later version, made in 1932 with orchestral accompaniment, on two sides of a ten-inch 78 (DA 4820; 2C 151–73084/5) is another matter. Though only a few seconds longer, this version evinces much more sense of excitement and atmosphere mainly because Panzéra is in stronger, more forthright voice. An apt comparison here would be with Schorr's famous account of Wolf's 'Prometheus'.

Michel Dens (2C 053–12507), coming from the world of opera, gives the song a weight of tone not found elsewhere, and shows a confidence and authority of phrase that etches the words forcibly on one's mind: 's'effondera' is just one superb example. He is well supported by Henriette Puig-Roget.

Simoneau, the only tenor I have found in this song, transposes the song up a third. While the voice is obviously a little light for the task in hand,

Alan Blyth

he brings a wealth of dramatic experience to bear on it, and finds a note of sad regret in the questions.

My preferred versions here are Kruysen, Souzay I, Panzéra II, and Dens.

'Elégie'

Written in 1874, poem by Thomas Moore ('Lament on the Death of Robert Emmet'), probably translated by Duparc. Originally set for voice and piano in F minor.

Duparc's admiration for Wagner is clearly felt in the expression and harmony: the beginning bears a striking resemblance to *Träume*. Yet, as Northcote points out, Duparc could 'absorb foreign influences without in any way sacrificing the native flavour of his music'. He adds, perceptively: 'Duparc's controlled romanticism is implicit in his expressive directions, which require a studied restraint and no disturbance of the smooth elegance of his melody'. If that is the criterion, Rhodes' clumsy version, at a funereal pace, is right out of the reckoning. So is Crespin's (EL 29 0446 1); she weighs down its already measured tread with ungainly phrasing and *portamento*. How sad she recorded her Duparc too late in her career. Bouvier's tone is also a little frayed, but her style is nearer what is wanted, catching the song's note of restrained melancholy.

These three versions all adopt the lower key as, of course, do the baritones. Herbillon, in one of the faster versions (2'37"), begins in a gentle, misty way, just right, but this promise is not fulfilled because his tone is apt to falter when he places pressure on it. Maurane is, as usual, too detached from its mood. None of Souzay's three versions is wholly satisfying. The first is beautifully voiced but too narcissistic at his slow pace (3'35"); the second is more purposeful, helped by Baldwin's eloquent piano, but still a little laboured. The third is acceptable, so far has the voice deteriorated.

Panzéra, though a little too quick, manages the sustained line and pointed enunciation that forms such an essential part of Duparc interpretation, and his emphasis on certain words, such as 'muettes, tristes, glacées', is admirable as is the corresponding *crescendo*. Kruysen is still better, managing to catch just those qualities predicated by Northcote and singing as though he absolutely shared the poet's and the composer's despair in the first verse, the hope suggested by the man's memory in the second. As always, Kruysen sings as if he had just thought up the sentiments of the song. Bernac (DB 6312; OVD 50036) is still better. He obeys his own injunction (op. cit.) for a slow tempo (dotted crotchet = 50), but never allows the song to drag: his timing of 3'17" seems ideal. Once more following his own advice, he sings the first two lines *pp*, making a small

26

crescendo on 'sans honneur'. With Poulenc's flowing accompanying, he takes the second verse marginally faster, makes no break for a breath in the second line beginning 'fera', and expresses faith in the unforgettable memory with due conviction by giving the word 'verte' an extra bite. Altogether this performance is an object-lesson in interpreting Duparc. It is a tragedy Bernac recorded so few of his songs.

Of versions in the original key, that by Michel Sénéchal (Philips N00681R) comes close to Bernac in catching the sad mood of the piece, but Sénéchal slightly spoils his version by becoming a little lacrymose. His pacing is excellent, but the white tone becomes tiresome before the end. Bonneau's fluent, thoughtful playing is an asset. Simoneau also tends to be pallid beside the template, Bernac, and noncomittal beside Sénéchal, but the style is always exemplary.

My preferred version is Bernac with Panzéra and Kruysen respectable runners-up.

'Extase'

Written in 1878, poem by Jean Lahor. Originally set for voice and piano in the key of D.

If anything, this song is more imbued with Wagnerian influence than *Elégie*, yet the result is once again peculiarly French in accent. Bernac – I wish that he had recorded it – says that it is a 'Wagnerian nocturne over which the vocal line floats in a dream-like manner'. The variations in speed among our interpreters here are truly amazing, ranging from Maggie Teyte, who extends it to 4′32″, to Herbillon's 2′26″. Teyte's is self-evidently too slow, but more important than tempo here is the impression created. Northcote quite rightly points out that 'concentrated intensity in tone quality' is what matters here, and the best of the singers have it. I also feel that the piece is heard at its very best in the original key; lowered a tone or more and the accompaniment can growl, the vocal line sound too heavy, but a few of the baritones manage to overcome their disadvantage. Not so the mezzos. Rhodes is truly awful, the insistent beat in her voice upsetting her line and the effect glutinous rather than dream-like at a dragging tempo. Bouvier is much better than this, with a real attempt at the mood-keeping so essential to the piece, but in the end her voice isn't quite reliable enough for comfort in the higher-lying phrases.

Herbillon, as ever, is tasteful, his gentle, hushed consonants a bonus in establishing the death-infected atmosphere of the song, but the pace is just too fast for sustaining the mood. Kruysen handles the climax to 'bien-aimée' with the expected sensitivity and once more gives the impression of spontaneity, helped by Noël Lee's soft-grained accompaniment.

Alan Blyth

Maurane, also well partnered, is still better. His withdrawn, contained style suits this *mélodie* excellently with the two occurrences of 'comme la mort' given just the right *frisson*, something Panzéra manages equally well. Indeed his slight hesitation before the final 'mort' is absolutely in character. At 2'28", this reading has a nice flow to it without ever seeming hurried, and the intensity of the tone is maintained throughout. The piano interlude between the two vocal utterances is beautifully played by the baritone's wife. Above all, the song's elegiac feeling is unerringly caught.

None of Souzay's three versions is quite on this level of achievement though the second comes close to it. The phrasing is immaculate, the rise to 'bien-aimée' finely negotiated, the restraint always evident. But neither here nor in the more lethargic first version can I find the refinement of accent, the special eloquence needed. George London, exhibiting warm tone and a sustained half-voice, is preferable, catching the piece's nocturnal beauty (ML 4906).

Teyte, the only soprano, transposes down a semitone (DB 5937; RLS 716). Hers is a classic of misinterpretation, quite extraordinary from one who had done two of the earlier songs so well. Gerald Moore makes all kinds of unwanted *ritardandi* in the prelude, which are then compounded by the singer. The result is desultory and self-indulgent, turning Duparc into a dripping sentimentalist.

It was a great relief to turn to Cesare Valletti (RB 6622), the first to sing the piece in D. But I had hardly been prepared for such a marvellous interpretation. His *legato*, Italian-based, is impeccable, his sad accents ideal, and he takes the phrase 'mon coeur . . . mort' in a single, unfaltering breath, something no one else attempts. The high A at 'bien-aimée' is sung in an exquisite head-voice, floating out into the air. What a shame his partner is such an insensitive pianist. The timing, 3'17", seems ideal.

After Valletti, Ian Partridge sounded a trifle too careful, even arty, his high A a shade precarious, yet there are refined things to like in his reading. Simoneau sings 'ou souffle . . . bien-aimée' in a single breath, and places the high A perfectly. His delicate, even winsome interpretation is among the best, and confirmed by preference for a tenor in this song, as in so many others.

Friant (Disque P 485; GV 524) is even more delicate and tender than Valletti, 'comme la mort' having a peculiarly French fragrance, the quick vibrato helping to suggest the hypnotic quality of the song. His high A, perfectly poised, is even more affecting than Valletti's or Simoneau's, and he makes a positive virtue of taking a breath before 'de' just before this climax by his slight emphasis on the word. This is the authentic voice of *mélodie* interpretation that is now gone.

The choices here, in ascending order of merit, are Maurane, Panzéra, Valletti and Friant.

'Le manoir de Rosemonde'

Written in 1879, poem by Robert de Bonnières (from *Contes de Fées*). Originally set for voice and piano in D minor, later orchestrated by Duparc.

This is, as Northcote says, 'a remarkable essay in dramatic vocal declamation', at least in its first half where the poet rails against his arduous life, this articulated by the insistent rhythm in the piano. The last two stanzas of the sonnet are set in slower tempo and express the emptiness of the poet's world: he has died without encountering the exotic manor of his beloved. Lotte Lehmann, in *More than Singing*, writes that 'something like madness rages through this song' and enjoins that its interpreter must 'imagine the terrible loneliness, the desperation, the crazy resolution of this man'.

And it should be a man who interprets it; none of the women makes a complete success of it. Certainly not Jane Rhodes, who is highly dramatic but too blowzy. Bouvier's declamation is much more precise than Rhodes', and she rightly makes the consonants in the first part explosive. She is to be admired for taking the final phrase in one breath, but as a whole the fiery rhetoric of the song is just beyond her. Crespin here is much happier than in the slower-moving songs on EL 29 0446 1. Her operatic attack in the first half is properly grand and she is rather touching in the slow section, especially at 'et blesse' and the repeated 'bien loin'. If only the voice was in better state . . . Janet Baker (ASD 3455), using the orchestral version, sings in the original key, unlike the other women, who transpose down; the high *tessitura* worries her, but she certainly enters into the desperate mood of the piece.

Most of the baritones are true to form. Herbillon, adopting a quickish tempo, is vivid and forward in the defiance of the first half, then brings a movingly sad quality of tone to the second, words very much on the breath in a Bernac-like way. Kruysen goes ever faster, breathing defiance at the start, finding an empty, weary voice for the last section, the expression almost lacrymose. By the side of these two subjective performances, Maurane is much plainer, more objective, as if retailing the inner drama from without and, as always, musical in his restraint. I like the way Jules Bruyère (RCA LM 2658) captures the crazed ranting of the first half and the anguish of the second; the torn nerve ends are all too keenly felt here.

Souzay is almost raw in his first version; 'chien' and 'mordu' are spat out. In the second-half lament, he brings a special eloquence to the last line. But I find more involvement and anguish in his Philips version with 'bien loin' almost dragged out of him. The tempo here is on the slow side. In his third recording it has become even more so, and for once the

Alan Blyth

deterioration in his tone is almost an advantage. This weary lover really sounds as though he has been through emotional hell.

George London (ML 4906), having been a noted Amfortas and Golaud, is well prepared for the mood of this song. His big tone and intense manner give text (excellent French) and music bite and immediacy. The second half is sung with world-weary, resigned tone, dying away to a defeated close, and he is to be thanked for encompassing the last line in a single breath. Mack Harrell (Remington 199–140), a noted Nick Shadow in *The Rake's Progress*, is a singer of a similar cast to London, and his splendidly intense reading sounds an even more haunted note than his colleague's.

Two pre-war baritones present very different aspects of the song. Panzéra, in much the fastest time of any (1' 55"), sings with open tone and fierce immediacy, but I find the second section passes by too quickly at his tempo, sounding almost perfunctory; it is one of his few failures. In stark contrast, Vanni-Marcoux's very free version (DA 1123) lasts 2' 51", and he makes marvellous use of the extra time. The declamation in the first half is melodramatic, bitter in the extreme, tone strong, words clear and full of meaning. Then, for the second half, there is a complete change; the voice becomes sad and weary. The two rising climaxes to 'monde' and 'mourir' are allowed huge *ritardandi*, entirely justified in the event, and the final line is intoned movingly. It is a memorable performance and – as luck would have it – very hard to come by.

Simoneau, the only tenor, is more histrionic than I would have thought possible with his voice, sounding almost heroic in his free declamation at the start. There is a perfect vocal accomplishment of the melancholy close, the 'bien loin' so plangent and the change in dynamics just right. So favourites here are Kruysen, London, Vanni-Marcoux and Simoneau.

'Sérénade florentine'

Written in 1880, poem by Jean Lahor. Originally set for voice and piano in F.

This is a miniature masterpiece that has been curiously neglected both at recitals and in the recording studio. Northcote avers that the 'vocal line is a charming melody, graciously phrased and possessed of a rare intensity of utterance, while a nervous chromaticism gives the musical texture an impassioned quality which is at once fervent and tender', and he goes on to comment that it calls for 'exquisite artistry' in performance. That is what it receives from the majority of the singers among our 'regulars', the only ones who appear to have committed it to disc. Of the two women, Rhodes is again out of court because of an insistent beat in her voice.

Bouvier captures the fragile stillness of the song and points the correct way in not making a break between 'ses yeux' and 'bénédiction', for surely the words 'and let fall upon her eyes the blessing of heaven' must be conceived as a single thought. Her pianist is also aware of the serenity called for by the gently rocking accompaniment.

Herbillon tends to be a shade jerky in his phrasing, but his light, airy tone and quickish speed catches the dream-like, floating nature of the piece. Kruysen is still better in capturing the intimate expression of the song, and his sense of spontaneity is as ever welcome: this, one feels, is how Bernac might have done it. But neither of these singers avoids that unwanted breath. Maurane doesn't need it and he, too, is tender and refined in his utterance, but – as usual – a bit detached, yet he is a fine exemplar of the French style at its best; that counts for much. So is Souzay in his first two recordings. As ever, he adopts a slightly slower speed than his colleagues, and employs more *rubato*. Nobody quite catches the wonder of 'Elle s'endort' as he does, and he is most sensuously accompanied by both Bonneau and Baldwin. But turn to one of his mentors, Panzéra, and you hear an even more wondrous, eloquent feeling though he, in contrast to Souzay, opts for another hurried tempo, just fast enough to disturb the trance-like sense of words and music. His earlier version (Disque P646; 2C 151–73084/5) is slower, the voice lighter, the reading less certain in 1926.

Turn to Simoneau, and the song sung in the intended key, and you find something else, a delicate ethereal tone that at once convinces you that the piece is intended for a tenor. Besides he, unlike Souzay and Panzéra, finds no need for a breath before 'bénédiction', nor one before 'rêves', indeed his version of 'alors rêves' up to a *pp* F is ravishing. Here song and singer are perfectly matched and the rest seem something less than ideal. Even so I would put the more accessible Kruysen alongside Simoneau as a recommendation.

'Phidylé'

Written in 1882, poem by Leconte de Lisle. Originally set for voice and piano in A flat; later orchestrated by the composer. Dedicated to Chausson.

Here Duparc is at his most voluptuous and expansive, though the passion is kept strictly in control. Northcote points out that it ought to be sung by a male voice, and that is what Duparc wanted, but even in his lifetime it was frequently being essayed by female ones, a situation that continues today, and still seems wrong.

It is of the essence here to convey the stillness of the afternoon, the

Alan Blyth

peacefulness of the summer landscape ineffably described in the poem, then the passion of the final verse where the man seeks the reward of a kiss for his patience while his beloved sleeps.

I have heard no fewer than twenty-seven versions of this long *mélodie*. The most striking difference in approach again concerns tempo. It seems to me that there is simply no means of reconciling Margaret Price's 6'05" with Panzéra's 4'12", one, or possibly both, has to be wrong. I am absolutely certain that Price and the others who take more than five-and-a-half minutes over the piece are mistaken, for at such a slow speed the song becomes static, almost boring. For instance, Rhodes (5'42") is simply ponderous and blowzy, tending towards sentimentality when she is trying to achieve sensuality. Crespin (EL 29 0446 1), singing in the mezzo key like Rhodes, is a little faster, but still too leaden. Although the smiling warmth of her approach is hard to deny, she cannot avoid the charge of clumsy vocalisation. Among other mezzo versions that of Bouvier at 5'25" is the most close-knit and appealing, but the climaxes of the final section strain her resources. At the same pace Janet Baker's 1970 version (ASD 2590), with Gerald Moore as perhaps the most telling of the pianists on record, is fluid and fluent in expression, with a sense of shaping towards the last verse, itself eloquently achieved. When she came to remake the song, this time in the orchestral version with Previn and the LSO (ASD 3455) in 1978, she opted for the original key, unwisely as it turns out because the strain of the high Gs and A flats is all too evident, and the bloom is sadly gone from the voice. She isn't helped by the leaden, unrhythmic support. Nan Merriman (EX 29 0654 3), in her 1954 record, paces the song carefully and interprets it stylishly without going to the heart of the matter.

Four other English-speaking sopranos have recorded the song with orchestra. Grace Moore's 1942 record (Victor 11–8258; VIC 1216) discloses a lovely voice but wretched French and little sense of the meaning of the words. Kiri Te Kanawa (EL 27 0135 1), with Pritchard and the Brussels Opera Orchestra, coasts through it as if ravishing tone were enough to encompass its meaning. Nothing happens here to make us awaken from our own slumber. Dorothy Maynor (LM 3086) sings with technical assurance and some eloquence, but remains a shade impersonal. Margaret Price (Orfeo S 038831 A) is lethargic and studied, listening to herself rather than concentrating on what the song should be telling us. Jessye Norman, in 1975, before her goddess image was born (Philips 416 445–2), has more sense of its meaning, aided by Baldwin's playing, but her voice and style remain too grand, the tone tending to be overblown. Teyte, recorded in 1940 with Leslie Heward as conductor (JG 178; RLS 716), is in another league. She proves conclusively that 4'33" is all you need to take care of all facets of this *mélodie*. Her unbroken *legato*, perfectly formed tone and poised 'Repose, o Phidylé', in all its repetitions, catch the sensuous ecstasy of the poem and its setting, not least because the words really mean something to her and, as in all the best versions, the tempi are related one to another. One point of interpretation is particularly subtle: the *diminuendo* on 'baiser'. A textual point: the end is changed with the singer finishing on a high E flat. Is this authorised?

Géori Boué (Urania URLP 7070) comes even closer than Teyte to the *vrai* French sound; in spite of her slightly acid tone, she gives the song a specially haunting accent, also at about four and a half minutes and that on an LP. Easily surpassing her is Vallin (Odéon 188595; Pathé–Marconi 291 0023), who – like Teyte – reconciles one almost to a woman singing this song by virtue of her ideal phrasing, based on a faultless *legato*, a smooth, firm tone and, as always with Vallin, an instinctive understanding of how to express the meaning of the text unobtrusively yet with no point missed. She is to be admired particularly for the repeats of 'Repose, o Phidylé', each different yet each imbued with the same languid, erotic feeling. Then the final verse is carried off with the touch of ecstasy that the words and music predicate. The recent reissue of this version is very welcome. By the way, Vallin takes 5'30" over the song, but that seems not a moment too long because the shape of the piece is always kept in mind. Victoria de los Angeles (ASD 530), though not quite in the Vallin class – her voice sounds awkwardly placed and her pitch occasionally doubtful, captures the mood well and the phrasing is admirable. Prêtre is a satisfactory partner as conductor.

Herbillon, among the baritones, suggests more than any other that a youth is singing and one amazed at the beauty of his Phidylé. The flow and immediacy of his performance is exemplary, but once more Herbillon's effort is vitiated by the restriction at the top of his range. Kruysen, with more voice, is hardly less vital at a slightly slower speed than Herbillon's, and he manages the phrase from 'Mais quand' to 'éclatante' in the final verse in a single breath.

Maurane achieves the same feat in his finely moulded account. His is the perfect *baryton-martin*, and it is here used exquisitely to convey the wonder of the protagonist. Souzay's first version shows a darker, more vibrant tone than Maurane's and a more leisurely, spontaneous way of approaching the piece, but Souzay rises as well as anyone to the expectant feeling of the final stanza. His second version is little different apart from the finely accomplished *diminuendo* on 'baiser'. The third is to be avoided.

Panzéra recorded it three times. The two earlier versions with orchestra (Disque W 591; GV 513 and DB 4820; 2C 151–73084/5) are to be preferred to the later one with piano listed at the head of the chapter. Indeed they are among the most rewarding of all. Panzéra's voice is in prime

Alan Blyth

condition. The *legato* is seamless, the inward feeling of the repeated 'Repose, ô Phidylé' most tender, and his tone opens out magnificently to the urgent desires of the final verse. DB 4820 is probably the record to have in its original or reissued form. It is the most expansive, at 4'32", of the three, and it is splendidly accompanied by Piero Coppola. The piano version is on a slightly lower level of inspiration.

Heavier baritones can make an altogether different impression in this *mélodie*. Michel Dens' voice, at 58 (2C 053–12507), is scarcely that of a youth, but his full-throated, unsophisticated account is an antidote to more inbred performances. George London, another generous-voiced singer, wraps it in his mellow, haunting tone, a most accomplished reading (ML 4906). Mack Harrell (Remington 199–140) is similar to London. Though not as technically assured, he makes an imposing sound. It is as if Hotter were tackling Duparc.

Georges Thill (French Columbia LFX 491) manages to inject virile, honest strength into his line without sacrificing sensitivity, with superb A flats in the concluding verse. If you find Thill too forthright and extrovert for this music, try Cesare Valletti (RB 6622). The sustained *legato*, immaculate diction and long breath (many phrases that others split in two taken in one), and the wonder of the scene-painting are pleasing throughout. Simoneau is even more mellifluous than Valletti, the soft grain of his tone well suited by this song, yet he still manages the fervour asked for by Duparc in the last verse. Simoneau takes 5'30", but it does not seem that long. On the other hand, Ian Partridge (SHE 524) sounds earthbound in his 1975 version lasting almost six minutes – another case of the unfortunate tendency today towards slow tempi.

A tenor is ideal in this song so Valletti or Simoneau would be my first choice, but I would not like to be without Teyte, Vallin, Maurane, Kruysen, or one of Panzéra's versions with orchestra.

'Lamento'

Written in 1883, poem by Théophile Gautier. Originally set for voice and piano in D minor. Dedicated to Gabriel Fauré.

As Northcote points out: 'The dedication of this song was no idle compliment for it is the most Fauré-like of all Duparc's songs'. While retaining its own identity, his style here resembles Fauré's in its 'supple elegance and graceful, sinuous, step-wise movement' in the vocal line. In every respect, Duparc here captures the elegiac mood of Gautier's sad poem. The singer must bring to it, to quote Northcote again, 'a tender melancholy and a studied restraint, smooth phrasing and an unhurried rhythm'. I would

34

add that he or she must, at all costs, avoid sounding lugubrious; gentleness must not slip over into the maudlin. On that count, Jane Rhodes must once more be set aside. Most of the other singers in the complete versions also run true to their by now familiar form. Among the baritones, I particularly admire the almost trembling quality in Herbillon's performance, the poised, hushed quality of Kruysen, the immaculate diction of Maurane, also his faultless phrasing – 'Où flotte . . . d'un if' taken in a single breath, a feat few others attempt, apart from Simoneau. As usual, Souzay is most natural and immediate in his earliest version. By the second the vibrato has already loosened, the responses are less immediate. Panzéra's contained, flowing performance, as if the song had been conceived in a single span, is attractive, but his wife's spreading of all the chords sounds woefully dated.

Simoneau phrases the song with as much distinction as Maurane and, like his baritone colleague's, his voice seems so right for Duparc in its French smoothness and the unaffectedly expressive way in which it is used. Hélène Bouvier, in the first two verses, is as good as anyone with Duparc's 'très doux' marking ideally observed, but in the song's one big outburst beginning 'Ah! jamais plus', the voice comes under strain. She takes the song down a tone as do the baritones. Croiza (LF 59; ALP 2115) sings it in key (though the LP transfer has her transposing it *up* a semitone, which can't be right), and in any case her interpretation easily surpasses all others, simply because of the way she scrupulously observes the composer's markings such as the *cresc.-dim.* on 'triste et seul au soleil' and the timeless quality of her *pianissimo* on the succeeding phrase 'chante son chant', repeated at 'Bien doucement'. Then the *forte* climax is quite piercing in its emotional strength. Altogether, she penetrates to the heart of this strangely neglected masterpiece, not least in her immaculate diction, and is more than adequately seconded by her pianist George Reeves. I cannot imagine that two tenors I have not heard, Jean Planel (Pathé PG 79) and Henri St. Cricq (Pathé X 3437), could be better. Among the other pianists, I would once more praise Baldwin, with Souzay II, for his singing tone and clear semiquavers in the last verse. Excellent, too, is Noël Lee for Kruysen.

First recommendation must be Croiza; if that cannot be found I would go for Kruysen or Simoneau.

'Testament'

Written in 1883, poem by Armand Silvestre. Originally set for voice and piano in C minor, later orchestrated by the composer.

With due respect to Northcote, who calls *Testament* 'one of Duparc's finest songs', I find it the least inspired of the set, wanting in musical and emotional focus, possibly because of the overblown nature of Silvestre's verse. Certainly it is not helped by the kind of heavyweight treatment it receives from Rhodes, though this is one occasion where she does not have to make downward transposition, as the song is composed for medium voice, going no higher than G flat. Hers, at 4′01″, is the slowest version I have come across, and gradually I came to the conclusion that the song must not last much more than three minutes or its sense of nervous desperation is quite lost. Nor does its meaning or style really suit a woman's voice, so it is hardly surprising to find Bouvier and Crespin (EL 29 0446 1), both of whom take almost four minutes over it, so unimpressive, and to put it politely both women might with advantage have recorded it earlier in their careers. Kiri Te Kanawa (EL 27 0135 1), the only record using the orchestral version, coasts her way through the song at far too low a voltage of emotional feeling.

Neither of my tenors seems well suited. Ian Partridge (SHE 524) is too anonymous and 'tasteful', although Jennifer Partridge plays the piano part better than perhaps anyone else except Noël Lee (see below). He sings the song in the original key; Simoneau transposes it up a minor third. He never quite gets inside the soul of the song.

No, the piece is most successfully interpreted by a baritone. The least fitted to it is Maurane, who, like Simoneau, sounds uninvolved though, as ever, immaculate in phrasing. Interestingly, both he and Simoneau take around three and a half minutes over the song, as does Souzay in his earliest rendering, all of which seems too slow in comparison with the best versions of this song. Among these is Souzay's second, bolder, more dramatic version, quicker than his first and expressing most of the remorse in the words and music. Still better are Herbillon and Kruysen, who traverse the song in less than three minutes, thereby imbuing it with a kind of fevered sense of remorse which, I am sure, Duparc intended. The storm of the heart is here expressed with immediate and unabated force. That Kruysen's version is the more impressive is again owing to his superior voice and accompanist. Indeed Noël Lee invests the raging semiquavers with more tensions and meaning than any of his colleagues, even Baldwin, excellent though he is for Souzay II. Which leaves Panzéra, fastest of all and giving the words a more pointed accent than anyone else, sometimes at the expense of *legato*. His tone also has a securer centre than those of his colleagues. For modern tastes, his version may seem almost too declamatory with the text but to hear him inveigh against the eyes of the loved one at 'sans merci' or inflect 'mort' with such bitterness is to discover the acme of Duparc interpretation. Versions to treasure are those by Souzay II, Kruysen and Panzéra.

'La vie antérieure'

Written in 1884, poem by Charles Baudelaire. Originally set for voice and piano in E flat. Later orchestrated by the composer. Dedicated to Guy Ropartz.

Appropriately enough, Duparc's final offering is among his best, as if the composer knew it might be his last. Here he adumbrates the most telling features of his style. Northcote, ever the perceptive observer, refers to its 'rare beauty', 'ethereal majesty', 'infinite sadness'. It is also one of the most difficult for a singer to encompass, particularly at two key points, following one another. After the solemn start, which Bernac enjoins should be sung in a rich quality of voice and broadly declaimed, the second quatrain calls for a big *crescendo* and *accelerando* over twelve bars; although the climax appears to be on the high A flat of 'riche', in fact the composer asks for the greatest *ff* emphasis at the end of the passage at 'yeux'. Nobody seems quite to achieve the desired effect. Then comes the tremendous affirmation 'C'est là!', repeated, succeeded by the section starting 'au milieu de l'azur' marked to be sung in 'almost a half-voice with no nuances, like a vision', something only the most perceptive interpreters manage. Then the pianist has to sustain the mood in the long postlude.

Neither Rhodes, once more much too slow, nor Bouvier manages to avoid a sense of fluster. Janet Baker, singing the orchestral version in the original key (ASD 3455), begins in too studied, almost affected manner, rises intensely to the climax of 'C'est là', but relapses into something a little mannered at 'au milieu'. Kiri Te Kanawa (EL 27 0135 1), also with orchestra (Pritchard), seems miles away from the meaning of the text, merely singing the notes, little more. Jessye Norman, with piano (Baldwin), is too generous with her voice throughout and expands the climax unduly, at the same time failing to imagine the words (Philips CD 416 445–2). Jennie Tourel (Am. Col. M 32231), with Bernstein at the piano in a 1969 Carnegie Hall recital, is well past her prime.

All the regular baritones do better than the women, even if the downward transposition robs the song of something of its recollection of a past ecstasy.

Herbillon relies on his innate understanding of Duparc's musical and textual diction to compensate for his somewhat parched tone; at last one discovers here what Duparc wanted in matters of dynamic level and word painting. As usual, Kruysen surpasses Herbillon because of the superiority of his vocal means and of his accompanist, the assured and comprehending Noël Lee. The sense of remembered joy at 'C'est là' is here as overwhelming as it should be, and Kruysen comes as close as anyone to that visionary touch at 'au milieu'; the blue skies and naked slaves are to this interpreter a most immediate memory. Souzay, in his earliest recording, uses too much voice at this point, but otherwise is in his element in spontaneous response to the piece, though the quicker tempo of both Herbillon and Kruysen gives their renditions that added *frisson* of an experience held so vividly in the mind's eye. Souzay II is more effortful, but the attack on 'C'est là' is more assured than before. Maurane is, as ever, too divorced from the song's feeling and shows himself too free with tempo in the concluding quatrain. Panzéra, on the other hand, here comes nearest to achieving the right rise to the central climax and then manages the vision with much imagination and a kind of palpitating accent that seems ideal. His is the fastest reading and once more he justifies his approach by reason of the interpretation's cohesion.

Michel Dens (2C 065–12507) has all of the reserve of tone to do justice to the climaxes and his enunciation is telling, but in the end he spoils his reading by a certain squareness in phrasing. Thill cannot be accused of that; here at last are all the resources the song needs, the volume, excitement, verveful attack at 'C'est là', and the plaintive timbre of the close, all recalling Thill's unsurpassed Werther, which is not inappropriate. Only in the vision, sung too loudly, does he disappoint us. That is just the place where our other tenor scores; Simoneau creates an almost hypnotic effect here, having already delighted us by building the climax seamlessly and finding reserves of strength for 'C'est là'. Of course, the expression is more contained than with Thill, and the results less elementally exciting, but both prove that the tenor voice is right for this wonderful *mélodie*.

Thill (Columbia LFX 491, not apparently on LP), Simoneau, Panzéra and Kruysen, in descending order of merit, are essential listening here.

The most essential complete versions are those by Kruysen and Simoneau; in their different ways, they are consistently stylish and involving performances, more so, I feel, than Souzay II, excellent though that is in an understanding of the songs. Also well worth seeking out are the various individual recordings made by Panzéra in the late 1920s and early 1930s; fortunately six of these are collected on the most recent reissue of this superb interpreter's art: Pathé-Marconi Références 2C 151–73084/5. The later performances, on COLH 104, are a little less compelling and were not transferred to LP in a manner that gave a true idea of the voice.

Gounod, Chabrier, Chausson, Hahn

This chapter is devoted to some of the most frequently recorded songs of some of the lesser composers of *mélodies*, all four of them underrated in my opinion. Before discussing the individual songs, I would like to list a few records that collect together rarely heard songs by these and other composers. They are mentioned in the text below but it may be of interest to know about their complete contents.

Jane Bathori (Columbia FCX 50030). This invaluable reissue finds this famous interpreter singing *mélodies* by Ravel, Debussy, Fauré, Hahn, Satie, Milhaud, and Paul Bernard, all to her own accompaniment with the exception of Milhaud's *Trois poèmes juifs*, which is accompanied by the composer.

Charles Panzéra (Références 2C 151–73084/5). A collection of records made by this great French baritone between 1924 and 1934, when he was in his prime. In addition to some arias and Lieder, the reissue includes songs by Sevérac, Milhaud, Ravel, Gounod, Duparc, Hahn, Fauré, Saint-Saëns, Chausson, Caplet and Debussy.

Ninon Vallin. The pair of two-record EMI reissues of Vallin are mentioned in the text of various chapters, but it should be added that EX 29 0946 3 includes Leroux's 'Le Nil' and Bemberg's 'Chant hindou', both worthy of revival.

Pierre Bernac and Francis Poulenc (Pathé Marconi OVD 50036, also issued under other numbers). Includes *mélodies* mentioned in the chapters on Duparc, Fauré, Chausson, Chabrier and Ravel, plus songs by Roussel, Milhaud and Auric, all originally issued on 78s in the DA and DB series. Essential listening for anyone interested in the genre.

Pierre Bernac and Francis Poulenc (PB 2, issued by the Friends of Pierre Bernac). Besides songs by Debussy and Fauré, includes Gounod's 'Au rossignol' and 'Ce que je suis sans toi', *Trois mélodies* by Satie and three

Alan Blyth

songs by Liszt. All rare and desirable records, originally published on DAs and DBs.

Gabriel Bacquier (Véga L30 PO 357). This excellent disc, made when Bacquier was at the outset of his career, then won the Grand Prix National du Disque: it includes songs by Berlioz, Gounod, Duparc, Debussy, Fauré, Hahn, Ravel, Poulenc, Sauguet and Yvain.

Michel Dens (EMI 2C 065–12507). Late in his career, this excellent French baritone turned to song. Here he tackles *mélodies* by Gounod, Saint-Saëns, Bizet, Chausson, Hahn, Massé, Pierné, Widor and Duparc.

Martyn Hill and John Constable (Saga 5419). An interesting disc of French Romantic Songs by Massenet, Hahn and Fauré.

Martyn Hill and Graham Johnson (Meridian E 77029). Entitled 'A French Collection', this record includes songs by Gounod, Franck, Bizet, Chabrier, Paladilhe, Delibes, Chausson, Dupont and Saint-Saëns.

Felicity Lott and Graham Johnson (Harmonia Mundi). 'Mélodies sur des poèmes de Victor Hugo' including songs by Gounod, Bizet, Lalo, Delibes, Franck, Fauré, Saint-Saëns and Hahn.

Elly Ameling has contributed several invaluable records to the French repertory. The numbers of her relevant CD recitals are Philips 410 043–2, 412 216–2 and 412 233–3.

Gounod

'Sérénade'

This mellifluous setting of Victor Hugo's delicate poem of love has always been a special favourite in recitals with performers and audiences. The three stanzas are set to the same music, and the art lies in varying dynamics and tonal colours. The song also calls for a sustained *legato* and, at the close of each verse, skill in rising coloratura.

Many of the older versions include only two verses, among them Emma Calvé's 1919 disc (Pathé 0275; GV 57), which is a little fruitily voiced but shows her famed command of *pianissimo* in the second verse, the last in her case. Selma Kurz (DB 677; GEM 122), recorded in 1924, is clear and pure but by the same token monotonous at least until the beautifully managed close of the last verse, the second in her case too. The contemporaneous Alice Verlet (2–033005; GV 18), with Harty at the piano, sings all three verses in her airy, free and *séduisant* account. She begins in just the right intimate, confiding manner, sings a teasingly erotic second verse, and *pp* third with a welcome *portamento* at 'harmonieux', but

40

spoils her card with a breath before the final 'toujours'. The last of these acoustic 78s is the delightful version by Geraldine Farrar (Victor 87257) with a harp accompaniment, poised and light with the peculiarly fresh timbre of her best records.

Among later sopranos, Eidé Noréna's extremely rare record (French HMV L 992) holds a special place in the song's discography for her secure, long-breathed singing and unique blend of the immediate and the other-worldly. Desmond Shawe-Taylor once said to me that her voice was oddly compelling but its quality was difficult to describe; I agree. By contrast Felicity Lott (Harmonia Mundi HMC 1138), though her piano (Graham Johnson) is to be preferred over Noréna's soupy orchestra, is strangely uncommunicative. The voice is lovely, the phrasing immaculate, the third verse exemplary in its *pianissimo*, but the sum total, perhaps because of studio nerves and the bathroom acoustic, is unsensuous. Valerie Masterson's rendering lacks variety of dynamic and tends to be one-dimensional (Pearl SHE 590). Suzanne Danco (Decca 414 635–1) is straight and stylish, with all the markings observed and the phrasing long-breathed, but here also the timbre is too cool.

Janet Baker earns bad marks for singing only two verses (ESD 1024391) and taking 3'33" over them (some sing the whole song in that time span). In consequence, after Moore's apt scene-setting, the performance is becalmed, too studied in spite of the singer's warm timbre.

Maybe it is really a man's song. Most of the male interpreters seem to prove that point. Joseph Rogatchewsky, my only tenor (Villabella has eluded me), makes a meal of his two verses but so caressingly does he spin out his attractively sensuous tone that we forgive him his self-indulgence, though he does overdo things in that final 'toujours' (LF 95). Roger Bourdin (Odéon 122663) sings one of the most unaffected and well-schooled of the baritone versions but regrettably offers only two verses even on a 12" 78. Michel Dens (C 053–12540) with orchestra adopts rather faster speeds than his confrères, and I like his forward-moving version even if his operatic baritone is a little heavy for the song. Gérard Souzay recorded the song twice, and for once I prefer the later, 1975 version (ASD 3083) to the earlier, 1963 one (SAL 3480), where both he and Baldwin seem a little bored with the piece and do not provide the essential contrast in dynamics until the end. In 1975 Souzay seems to have rediscovered the wonder of romantic expression in the *mélodie* and has brought a smile back into his tone. The slightly quicker speed helps him here, as does Baldwin's livelier playing. Fischer-Dieskau (Orfeo S 153861 A), recording in 1983, left it too late and adds a curious clarinet obbligato. Anyway I doubt if his style was ever really suited to this song.

The most rewarding version of this *mélodie* by a long way is that by Pierre Bernac (DB 6250; OVD 50036 and other reissues). Set on his way by Poulenc's joyous introduction, he follows his advice in his own book (op. cit.) to sing the first verse *mf*, the second *ff* and the third *pp*, and proves that his way is the right one. Then there is the ideal balance between the sweet, attractive tone and the keen diction, which evinces the admiration and adoration of the loved one's singing, smile and sleeping form. Just listen to the inflection each time at the words 'ma belle'. The final stanza is entrancing in every way, most of all in the handling of the last refrain. Throughout, the steady, temperate speed is justified by what is done within it. Just as desirable, by the way, is Bernac's lovely account of 'En prière' (DA 4915; OVD 50036), so plaintive and urgent.

After Bernac, I would recommend Verlet, Noréna and Rogatchewsky, all worth hearing if you can find them. I have not heard Vallin's rare Pathé.

Chabrier

Although Chabrier's song output was small, it is also choice. His *mélodies* are elegant, slightly whimsical in style, but can be acquitted of the charge of vulgarity once laid against them. As Ravel commented: 'How can one accuse a musician of vulgarity when it is impossible to hear two of his chords without attributing them at once to him, and to him alone?' The best known and most recorded of his songs is the delightfully airy 'L'île heureuse'.

'L'île heureuse'

Ephraim Mihael's poem is hardly distinguished poetry but it produced from Chabrier a lyrical outpouring of irresistible lightness and buoyancy. None of the performances I have heard is disappointing, yet each tends to be very different in character from the other. Martyn Hill and Graham Johnson (Meridian E77029) are delicate and also attentive to Chabrier's markings, but I have to say I found the reading a trifle studied and unspontaneous. So, surprisingly, is that by Hugues Cuénod (Nimbus 2112), made late in his career. Both tenors tend to slow down whenever Chabrier wants but too pointedly so. Elly Ameling (Philips CD 412 216–2) produces an aptly smiling, sensuous tone, and here the *rubato* is more naturally achieved. Rudolf Jansen attempts a grander style than Johnson; the music will take it. Both versions are overtaken by my third in the original key, that by Ninon Vallin (Odéon 188 667; EX 29 0946 3). Vallin as well as anyone conveys the sheer *joie de vivre* implied by Chabrier's music, its exuberant three-four rhythm and *con slancio* injunction at the head here exemplified to perfection. All the verbal nuances and subtleties, all Chabrier's wish for certain words such as 'rêves' to be given emphasis are here fulfilled exactly but without over-emphasis. The extra joyfulness Vallin discovers in the third verse is another pleasure in this generous reading.

My other singers have to make downward transpositions usually of a tone, but in each case the artists, being Frenchmen, have that *baryton-martin* timbre that makes you forget they are singing in a lower key. Jacques Jansen, a famous Pelléas, gives a slightly off-centre though not unappealing performance (LXT 2774). Both his tone and his range are somewhat 'short', but in compensation he uses the text in such an intimate way that one feels this telling of an idyllic love is directed just at the single listener. His Pelléas-like speech-song delivery cannot be the right one for the song, but it, and Jacqueline Bonneau's pellucid playing, make it a likeable and memorable reading. That is even more true of Reynaldo Hahn's semi-crooned version (Col. D 2020; Rococo R 5322) in that inimitable voice of his, dry as a Bath Oliver biscuit, which bounds along at a faster tempo than anyone else's. It is not particularly accurate as regards note-values, rhythm or obedience to Chabrier's markings, but who cares when it is so evocative of summertime caresses and an enchanted isle? Besides, his own piano playing, much more faithful to the score, makes his version literally single-minded in effect.

Pierre Bernac, in both his versions, seems to have everyone else's attributes – Vallin's gaiety, Jansen's gift for word-painting, Hahn's eager spontaneity – and coalesces them into an interpretation entirely his own, following all his advice in his book on interpretation (op. cit.). It is one of those occasions when it is preferable to listen and enjoy rather than to analyse, simply because Bernac tells us that if you follow what a composer has asked for, then add to his music a well-founded technique, the right timbre and an instinctive feeling for words, all will be right. And so it is here. It should be said that the earlier HMV pre-war version (DA 4892; OVD 50036) is to be preferred to the later Columbia of 1953 (Odyssey 3226 0009) on the grounds that Bernac is in marginally fresher voice and just that little bit more spontaneous. Poulenc is also more successful than any of his colleagues in projecting the broad sweep on the piano part. I should add that on DA 4892, Bernac also gives the definitive performance of Chabrier's 'Ballade des grands dindons', another delicious *mélodie*, while on LXT 2774 Jansen sings that song and also the appealing 'Les cigales' and 'Villanelle des petits canards' with the same vivid qualities shown in 'L'île heureuse'.

Chausson

Ernest Chausson wrote about forty *mélodies*, published in two collections. They tend to be romantic in style, often elegiac in mood, and call for a corresponding vein of expression in the interpretation. I have chosen to represent him by one of his happiest inspirations, 'Le colibri', a setting of Leconte de Lisle, and 'Le temps des lilas', the last part of *Poème de l'amour et de la mer*.

'Le colibri'

The humming-bird of the title dies having drunk the nectar of the golden flower on which it has alighted; so the poet wishes to expire of the first kiss from his beloved. The harmonies are lush and chromatic, almost Wagnerian in the second verse where the bird 'drinks so much love from the rosy cup that he dies'. Bernac, who sings it so superbly, is ecstatic about it in his book (op. cit.), writing of 'the beauty of the phrasing, the quality of the sonorities, the suppleness of the rhythm, the charm of the vocal curves'; just so.

The seven performances I chose to hear are all worthy of Chausson's inspiration. Jessye Norman (Erato NUM 75059), in a reading of five songs from this Opus 2, challenges earlier interpreters by virtue of her complete identification with the mood if not the diction of the piece; it forms part of a disc entirely devoted to the composer, including the complete *Poème*. But I do feel that 'Le colibri' needs to be defined by a more delicate brush. Maggie Teyte's perhaps (DA 1833; RLS 716)? Her performance is indeed remarkable for the clarity of her line and enunciation; that peculiarly plaintive timbre of hers is right for Chausson's intimate world here, but at times her phrasing is inclined to be casual, with breaths taken in the most untoward places. Her contemporary, Ninon Vallin (PG 100; EX 29 0946 3), makes no such mistakes of phraseology. Like Teyte, she takes a quicker tempo than their male colleagues, which allows her to build the tension of the second stanza and then produce a wonderfully floated climax at 'Vers la fleur dorée'. Mattiwilda Dobbs (33CX 1154) is delicate and plaintive, which is right, but tentative in accent, which is not.

Martyn Hill's version (Meridian E77029) with Graham Johnson is much the slowest at 3'32" and moulded with well-considered feeling, the moment of the creature's death 'Qu'il meurt' so affecting. He also manages the phrase in the last verse from 'Telle aussi' through to 'premier baiser' in a single breath. Hill's light, delicate tenor, like a good Chablis, is authentically French.

Gérard Souzay sings the piece on a rare Decca LP (LW 5201) wholly devoted to Chausson, a most treasurable disc with Jacqueline Bonneau his equal as pianist. This is one of Souzay's most natural, unaffected performances sung in a most mellifluous manner; he phrases the exhausted, detumescent chromaticisms of the third stanza with especial languor and beauty.

But all these versions are eclipsed by the most persuasive of all singers of *mélodies*, Bernac himself. The extra sensitivity of that tender, immediate voice of his is evident throughout, but nowhere more so than in the phrase D flat, E flat, F, then down to C at 'roi de collines' and again at 'ô ma bien-aimée', which he directs in his book to be sung up to a *piano* on the F, then a *portamento* down to the C. The second time this has to be just that much more tender, and so Bernac achieves it. Everything in this interpretation – tone, style, breathing, phrasing – seems so right and inevitable in capturing the essence of the song's mood and meaning that it is hard to imagine it being surpassed. One other point deserves particular mention: the precisely right amount of *rubato* at 'Du premier baiser'. Bernac recorded the song twice. The first version on a hard-to-find 78 (Ultraphon BP 1434) with J. Doyen as pianist shows a more reticent, lighter, more tremulous artist than the later (but still pre-war) HMV record (DA 4928; OVD 50036), which shows that much more confidence and personality with Poulenc in inimitable support. Both are sung in the original key.

'Le temps des lilas'

Chausson's Opus 19 is a setting of Maurice Bouchor's *Poème de l'amour et de la mer* for voice and orchestra of which 'Le temps des lilas' forms the closing section, its haunting melody having already been heard in the instrumental interlude between the two parts of *Poème*. It became well-known as a song in its own right, with piano accompaniment, its nostalgic, autumnal mood matched by the languorous, post-romantic mood of Chausson's setting. In this form, it has received several notable recordings.

Among the earliest is that by Melba, one of her rarest discs in its original form (2–033037; RLS 719). Her somewhat superficial reading is quite touching in its ingenuousness. In the climactic third verse she becomes wild and a shade inaccurate; elsewhere her *rubato* is generous but not very logically applied. It ends with empty tone at 'à jamais'.

Her version is quite eclipsed by Maggie Teyte's (HMB 15; RLS 716). Above all, Teyte conveys unerringly the sense of having been through the emotional experience delineated in the verse, the end-of-an-affair sensation sustained throughout. The opening is so sad and restrained, then in 'O joyeux', the start of the third stanza, where the singer recalls the springtime of love, Teyte allows a smile to enter her tone and rises splendidly to the climax at 'Las'. Then she almost empties her voice of feeling in the numbed expression starting at 'Et toi, que fais-tu?' when she wonders what her former lover might be doing. 'Point de gai soleil' has that peculiar Teyte poignancy, the words so touchingly inflected. Then 'ni

Alan Blyth

d'ombrages frais' calls forth a covered tone exactly apt to the text, and the final 'jamais' is drained, dark brooding. This is great singing supported with equal feeling by Gerald Moore.

Elly Ameling, in her 1984 performance, comes nowhere near Teyte's perceptions. Her rendering sounds altogether too comfortable, no sense of the heartbreak of the song, quite near its surface, being conveyed. The third verse is simply louder not more intense. Yet a case can, I suppose, be made for Ameling's good manners and musical accuracy. It is odd, however, that we have here a reversal of received thought on interpretation; it is the older singer who is interventionist, not the younger. So much for theories.

Nan Merriman (EX 29 0654 3), downwardly transposing, is more withdrawn and inward than Ameling. Her version has the merit of more seamless phrasing than any other: each of the first three lines is taken in a single breath; so are many others usually split in two. Yet for all its musicality and depth of thought I don't find Merriman quite communicative enough here; nor, surprisingly, Souzay (LW 5201), who sounds slightly outside the song's passionate expression, as though the studio were inhibiting him. But in terms of vocal beauty, this is the most telling version of all with a fine *pp* on 'des roses' near the end. Charles Panzéra, in his version with orchestra (DB 4971; 2C 151–73084/5), has that immediacy and commitment found wanting in Souzay. From the first, he gently strokes the line with that inimitably sensuous manner that informs almost all of his singing. Gradually the emotional temperature rises in verse two, then the third becomes the subjective outpouring of a soul in search of its past happiness that it should be, so that the last verse becomes almost unbearably moving. Panzéra adds an extra measure of vibrato to his tone at 'à jamais' to indicate moving resignation. With interpretations as satisfying as Teyte's and Panzéra's, the singer today has a hard time of it competing.

Hahn

The songs of Reynaldo Hahn have been underestimated and underperformed. Because of his unjustified reputation as a lightweight many have felt that his settings of some of the best French poems are too slight. But, as the old *Record Guide* (London, 1955) put it: 'His songs are unfailingly elegant, and sometimes (as in the case 'D'une prison') he achieves more by simplicity than others by subtlety and elaboration.' That has certainly been my experience listening to some of his most-recorded *mélodies*, and the performances suggest that these pieces bring out the best in singers. His own performances, fascinating as they are in themselves, must not be taken as law in their interpretation for his means were

46

too slight always to do justice to his own invention. More important is the series he made with Ninon Vallin, now reissued on the EMI and Références collections mentioned below; these can be regarded as authoritative but since most are of songs recorded by few others there are obviously no comparisons to be made. My selection is made from the songs that are most often heard in recital.

'Si mes vers avaient des ailes'

Victor Hugo's gentle, delicate expression of love has been more often recorded than any other Hahn song, not surprisingly considering its appeal to the singer and listener in terms of melodic ease. His contemporaries were obviously pleased with it, as the 1904 recording by Melba (DB 361; RLS 719) and the 1908 version by Marcella Sembrich (Victor 95202; RLS 7705) indicate. Melba's is typical in its somewhat cool, clinical vocalisation and curious French. She seems totally unaware of the deeper emotion lying just behind the deceptively simple line. Sembrich's version is delightfully airy; again the feeling is underplayed, but the carriage of the voice is so beguiling as to banish any regrets.

The song suits Maggie Teyte's particular gifts precisely. It was obviously a recital favourite of hers. Two versions are extant: her 1941 HMV (DA 1777; RLS 716) and an off-the-air version of 1937 issued by Decca in the 1960s (ECM 830). Both are considerably slower than the readings of her seniors and, with Gerald Moore on HMV, she captures to perfection the gradual slowing down of tempo enjoined by the composer although the final repetition of the first line is surely still too fast. Teyte has the ideal floating, plaintive timbre for this piece, also the command of *portamento*, such a lost art, that it requires. You feel without a doubt that this singer is aware of the ecstasy of love, not least in the breathing of 'amour' at the end, with the hint of a break in the line just before it. Good as the 1941 version may be, I prefer the earlier one, because the tone is just that much fresher and more sensuous, the feeling that bit more spontaneous. Both would be, and are, hard to beat.

I find nothing of equal merit in other versions by sopranos. Géori Boué (Odéon 188953) is free, carefree, an attractively airy performance which in the end wants poise and accuracy. Bidu Sayão (Odyssey Y33130) comes closest to it; her voice, like Teyte's, has that particular seductive quality so essential in Hahn, but the awful orchestra rather upends her effort. Joan Hammond's (1965) version in English (ASD 616) was made too late in her career when the high F sharp at 'jour' could no longer be taken *piano* – Teyte poises this ideally. Elisabeth Schwarzkopf's version (SAX 2265) is lovely as singing but too studied as an interpretation, as though she was determined to prove that she could achieve by artifice what others have achieved by natural means. She also omits the breath indicated for the obvious purpose of emphasis before 'nuit' but the F sharp at 'jour' is finely taken. A similar minus and plus apply to Felicity Lott's deliberate, sensitively shaped and timed version (on HMC 1138 – the one version to follow Hahn's marks precisely) with Graham Johnson as refined partner, but I find it less than spontaneous and a little cool. Grace Moore with a soupy Hollywood-like accompaniment (CAL 519) turns it into an item from some unwritten operetta.

Teyte's only rival in her register is her contemporary Ninon Vallin (Odéon 188579; EX 29 0946 3). She, above all others, notes the marking 'doux et expressif' at the start; she, more successfully even than Teyte, spins out the last two lines to the extent Hahn intended in conveying long-lasting love. Her line is faultless – as ever, her inflection of French unmatched, yet I do not capitulate to her as I do to Dame Maggie, simply because her one failing, a reluctance to sing quietly, is here bothersome; until the last line she refuses to obey Hahn's request for really *pianissimo* singing and indeed in that last line she doesn't quite achieve a *ppp*. Still, it is a lovely rendering.

Among the mezzos, Gladys Swarthout (ALP 1269) is soft and appealing but not individual, Jennie Tourel (ML 4158) is somewhat heavy in tone for this piece, but the style is right, and I like the catch in her voice at the final 'des ailes'. I wish I had been able to locate Nan Merriman's 78rpm Victor.

Of the five baritones I have heard, Jean-Christophe Benoit (Adès 14003) is no more than adequate, Michel Dens, late in his career (1973, 2C 065–12507), is unfussy, direct, warm, Francis Loring (Meridian E77005) too thin in tone. All three are easily surpassed by Gabriel Bacquier (Véga L 30 PO 357) in one of the most desirable versions of any *mélodie* I have heard. The timbre of the baritone, at an early stage in his career, is smooth, round, soft as velvet and the phrasing near perfection. It is one of those performances, replete with a wonderfully achieved high F sharp at 'jour', ideal, unforced diction, and spontaneous feeling, that doesn't deserve to be dissected. As is the way of the world it comes on a long unavailable record, though I note it justifiably won a Grand Prix National du Disque. Jacques Jansen on American Decca 143 574 is gentle and intimate with lovely *pp* high notes.

Martyn Hill's version (Saga 5419) is at once sensitive and a shade anonymous and non-committal. Tenors are better represented by Cesare Valletti (RB 6622), whose easeful flow of tone moves along both effortlessly and yet urgently. His F sharp is not as pleasing as Hill's, but the way he changes timbre, to something more erotically suggestive, in the final two phrases is right and persuasive. Preferred versions must be those by Teyte, Vallin, Bacquier, Jansen and Valletti.

'L'heure exquise'

Verlaine's marvellous evocation of a still, trance-like moment of peacefulness is perfectly reflected in Hahn's delicate setting. In her book *More than Singing* (London, 1945), Lotte Lehmann commented that it is a 'feast of the subtlest *piano* tones'. She goes on: 'There is not a *mezzo-forte* tone to be found, everything falls within the enchanting half light of feeling in the expression of which the French are such unsurpassed masters'.

Her dictum is certainly observed by Emma Calvé, the earliest interpreter I have come across (Pathé 3193; GV 57). Through the ancient, crackly recording made in 1919 can be heard just the poised, perfumed, pure rendering one would expect from a singer of the old school, with the final 'exquise' perfectly floated. Nobody else quite achieves this other-worldly quality; certainly not Alma Gluck in her 1917 record (DA 240), where the tinkly orchestra, carelessness over rhythm and excess of breaths suggest a matter-of-fact reading far removed from the intentions of the text and its setting. Maggie Teyte, in 1941 (DA 1821; RLS 716), offers some lovely phrases, intelligently shaped, and the expression is quite plaintive and touching with caressingly warm sound. The diction, too, is fine as at 'C'est l'heure' and 'L'astre irise'. So I find it hard to explain why I still find her unmoving, especially as Gerald Moore's accompaniment is so persuasive. It may be that Teyte's manner is just a shade too sophisti-cated for the simplicity of the piece. Or it may be that Ninon Vallin, in her roughly contemporaneous performance (R 20068; EX 29 0946), provides just the warm, unvarnished reading I miss in Teyte's version. Vallin's unfettered *legato*, finely judged *portamento* and dark-hued tone give her interpretation the sense of a single paragraph of thought. Her interpretation is flawed only by the absence of a true *pianissimo* at 'exquise' and by the taking of two breaths in the phrase starting 'Un vast' and ending 'irise'. Most singers make a single break before 'semble'. Janet Baker is unique in accomplishing it all in one breath. Altogether her 1973 version (ESD 1024391) is among the most worthwhile. With Moore again practising his peculiar magic on the piano part, Baker provides an inward, relaxed reading sung in a sustained *mezza voce* and an impressive float at 'exquise'. Another mezzo, Eliette Schenneberg (recorded in the 1930s – LF 257), provides more authentic French diction than Baker, and a more succulent tone, but shows none of her successor's sensitivity, sing-ing in a loudish, uncomprehending manner.

Of the men, Gérard Souzay is far and away superior to any rival. Indeed, more than anyone else, even Vallin and Baker, he captures the still rapture of the piece in his 1963 record (SAL 3480), when he was at the peak of his powers as both singer and interpreter. The first 'aimée', so gently intoned, is the clue to his whole, rapt interpretation, which is finely supported by Dalton Baldwin. By Souzay's side, Jean-Christophe Benoit (Adès 14003) sounds coarse, Martyn Hill (Saga 5419) anonymous, though Hill does manage to convey much of the song's reflective nature. Arthur Endrèze, the Chicago-born baritone who made his career in France and was closely associated professionally with Hahn, has the advantage of the composer at the piano (Pathé PG 89); indeed Hahn's liquid line is the best reason for hearing this rare version. Endrèze sounds dry and tremulous of voice and occasionally wayward in pitch, but he does catch the dreamy, timeless atmosphere of the song in his gentle, soft-grained singing. So does Jacques Jansen (Am. Decca 143574).

My favourite performances are those by Calvé, Vallin, Baker and Souzay.

'D'une prison'

It may be indicative of the simple perfection of this Verlaine setting that it has received nothing but excellent performances on record. The distant bell is the inspiration for Hahn's accompaniment – it rings persistently, evocatively through all but the middle section of the song, forming a background to the protagonist's description of the countryside he perceives from his cell, the key phrase being 'Cette paisible rumeur là'. As a contrast to this peace is the prisoner's heartache (and Verlaine's) at his misspent youth, a desperate cry from the heart, deeply expressed in Hahn's recitative-like passage.

Though it may be thought of as a man's song, several women have recorded it memorably, first of all Jane Bathori in 1929 (Col. D. 13099; FCX 50030). Though the voice itself is too mature, the expression of the text and its setting is deep, particularly the emotion of the middle section with 'ta jeunesse' rending the heart. However, Bathori was comprehensively surpassed a couple of years later by Ninon Vallin with the composer at the piano (Odéon 188738; EX 29 0946 3), a reading that remains a benchmark for all its successors, male or female. In line, diction, phrasing and accent, this is among the most telling of all Vallin's records. The *legato* of the opening, obeying Hahn's injunction for it to be sung 'avec la plus grande tranquillité', is ideal, while the start of the anguish at 'Mon Dieu' announces a real cry of pain before uneasy peace is restored.

Yvonne Gall's nearly contemporaneous version (DF 971) may not be so specific in its insights, but her cool, clear intoning of the main part of the song and the contained sadness of the outburst are beautifully read; it was this performance that first drew me to the song and I remain affected by it. Géori Boué (Odéon 188 959) is always an acquired taste; her shallow, slightly vinegary tone is not to everyone's liking, but here there is something in the immediate, untutored sound that gets under one's skin, most of all at 'de ta jeunesse', making one aware of the depth of melancholy here enshrined. Hers is much the slowest version on record but, with André Collard as perceptive accompanist, it seems not a second too long.

A year or so earlier than Géori Boué's record came that by her husband Roger Bourdin (Odéon 188635), who sounds a shade matter of fact beside his wife, yet on repeated hearing Bourdin's steady yet vibrant voice reveals a vulnerable quality that has yet something else to tell us about the piece.

Jean-Christophe Benoit's disc (Adès 14003) is not dissimilar, but here the vibrato, with the voice recorded so closely, can become obtrusive. Though a bit rough in phraseology and a little laboured in execution, once again the song seems to have profoundly touched its interpreter, who gives of his best. But there is no doubt that the most accomplished baritone version, indeed perhaps the best of all, is that by Charles Panzéra (Disque P 758, happily reissued in vol. 3 of 'The Record of Singing', EX 29 0169 3). Nobody, not even Vallin, captures the tranquillity of the beginning so movingly as Panzéra with his intimate, murmured rendering, the single word 'tinte' so gently uttered. No one finds more of the dolorous feeling in the middle section. These ingredients, seconded by Panzéra's marvellous diction, make this version well nigh unbeatable, except possibly by his own, even more gentle 1924 disc (P 489; 2C 151–73084/5) but this version is in the end less moving.

Charles Friant (Disque P 4520; GV 524), first of my tenors, comes close to matching his contemporary, Panzéra. Again there is the full comprehension of what Hahn was intending in this song, the view of a placid countryside, all exterior calm, shattered by the inner torture of the viewer, and Friant's extensive experience in opera, combined with that peculiarly plangent tone and incisive enunciation of his, creates yet another unforgettable interpretation. Tino Rossi (Col. DB 1864) is sweet, delicate. Jean Planel (Pathé X 93137), in his straightforward mellifluous performance, is accurate and pleasing but a shade superficial; so is Martyn Hill (Saga 5419), though his attempts at a facsimile of true French style are admirable. Cesare Valletti (RB 6622) achieves more than that. Though not especially effective at the start – he uses rather too much voice – his outburst suggests the anguish of Des Grieux at St. Sulpice, not wholly inappropriate, and the reprise and close are finely sung. I would not like to be without Vallin, Panzéra or Friant.

'Offrande'

Hahn's languorous, intimate setting of Verlaine's evocative, sensual poem is one of his most compelling achievements, indicating once again how simple means can sometimes surpass complex ones in getting to the soul of a text. As such I think it surpasses both the settings of Debussy and Fauré, under the title 'Green'. Gerald Moore understood the piece as well as anyone, as he showed when he commented in *Singer and Accompanist* (Methuen, 1953; revised edition, Hamish Hamilton, 1982) that 'its calm expression is deceptive so that we are almost unaware of the hunger which it masks of the longing surging through its veins.'

A select band of interpreters have turned their attention to one of the most moving songs in the *mélodie* repertoire, among them the composer himself (Disque 371; Rococo 5322). Hahn's dry, evocative baritone runs through the song rather more quickly than one would expect; I cannot make up my mind whether that is because he wants it to be heard as a single, trancelike supplication to the loved one with many phrases taken in a single breath, or whether his frail voice simply could not sustain it at a slower pace. I incline to the former view. Whatever the reason, it is a reading that is so haunting that repeat performances are imperative, like the need to drink yet another glass of a dry *eau de vie*. Particularly remarkable is the way he emphasises the words he has himself, as it were, underlined in the score, such as 'délasseront', 'derniers baisers' and 'que je dorme un peu' and the *rallentando* from 'Laissez-la s'appaiser' not marked in the music but obviously needed. Only Martyn Hill (Saga 5419) sings it as quickly as Hahn but, sensitive though he is, he can't manage the master's eloquence. Nor does the slower version by the baritone Francis Loring (E 77005), though Paul Hamburger at the piano is the composer's peer.

Jane Bathori, on her 1929 record (Col. D. 13099; FCX 50030) to her own accompaniment, sounds a little elderly (she was in her fifties) but gives a lesson in the meaningful declamation of French. The *rubato* is here laid on thickly perhaps, giving the song at 2'30", against Hahn's 2'07", slightly too much lassitude, but hear Bathori intone the final line and the whole era of great interpretation seems to be summarised.

Probably this isn't really a woman's song, but Maggie Teyte in her famous 1941 disc (DA 1821; RLS 716) almost makes you forget that. The *portamento*, the special accentuations and emphases are Teyte's alone and totally right for this song. She relishes words such as 'si beaux', and 'souffrons', and the whole is at once sensuous and sensual, as it should be.

Once one is used to Roger Bourdin's sombre, slightly querulous tone, his version (Odéon 188776) is peculiarly idiomatic, partly because, like the composer, he takes so many phrases in a single breath but does so at a slower, more accommodating tempo. That gives his version the sense of being a single statement of an emotional state. But Vanni-Marcoux (DA 1201), also long-breathed, surpasses Bourdin by virtue of his special quality of voice, plaintive, tender, seductive. Nobody manages to sing 'j'arrive' with such a sense of immediacy or change timbre for 'à vos pieds' or give such a palpitating sound to 'Toute sonore encore'. Possibly the reading, with its otiose string accompaniment, is a little too extroverted, even operatic, but it is nevertheless an interpretation carried off with such innate sincerity as to silence the criticism.

That leaves Jean Planel (Pathé X 93137), singing a tone up from the printed key of C. After the baritones, Planel can seem a little too sweet, even cloying, at least to begin with. Once accustomed to his timbre, one starts to think that perhaps this smiling, delicate reading by a kind of tenor no longer in existence offers a lighter approach not inappropriate to one view of the poem and its setting, for, like all great songs, this one can take many interpretations. I would recommend Hahn, Teyte and Vanni-Marcoux as essential listening.

Other songs by Hahn

A number of other, largely neglected songs by Hahn have inspired quite magical performances. I referred in the introduction to the long set, ten songs in all, recorded by Vallin, all but two made with Hahn at the piano. Besides those already mentioned in the text, Vallin sings the tender 'Tyndaris' from the neglected *Etudes Latines* and the subtle Gautier settings 'Lydé' and 'Infidélité' where the last line, after an effortless description of idyllic bliss with the beloved, tells all: 'Nothing has changed except you'. Géori Boué sings the latter with a deceptive nonchalance (Odéon 188953); on the same disc she offers the operetta-like 'Mai' delineating the pangs of parted lovers. It was written when Hahn was just 14. It was also recorded by Vallin (Pathé X 93082), which I have not heard.

In 1900, Hahn went on a visit to Italy resulting in the *Souvenirs de Venise*, dealing with gondolas, moonlight and the wiles of women. The complete set has been recorded by Graham Johnson's Songmakers' Almanac with Anthony Rolfe Johnson as main contributor (Hyperion A66112). 'La barchetta', the most famous of the set, has been recorded separately and memorably by Hahn himself, one of his winning efforts, and by Georges Thill (LF 103). Eliette Schenneberg made a charming 78 (LF 257) of the complete 1897 *Chansons grises*, from which 'L'heure exquise' comes.

Maggie Teyte was obviously fond of Hahn songs and not only the most popular ones. Unpublished when it was recorded with Gerald Moore in 1944, her rendering of the rarely encountered and highly original 'Belle lune d'argent' finally came out in the 1970s on a Historic Masters issue (HMB 15), and reissued in volume 4 of 'The Record of Singing (EX 7 69369 1). She also made a lovely record of 'En sourdine' (DA 1830; RLS

716), a setting of Verlaine's atmospheric poem that is quite the equal of Debussy's.

The Fauré-like 'Le rossignol des lilas' received a beautiful performance from Victoria de los Angeles (SLS 5233), less remarkable ones from Souzay (SB 6832), made too late in his career, and Martyn Hill (Saga 5419). Hahn marks it to be sung 'avec élan' and that is most definitely achieved by Géori Boué (Odéon 188953) but it does seem a little hurried for the 'modéré' marking. De los Angeles also offers the sad story of the pretty girl spied during grape-gathering who is next seen in her coffin. This is the Daudet setting, 'Trois jours de vendange' (ASD 2287), but it was much more idiomatically done on a matchless and rare record by Bernac made early in his career (Ultraphone BP 1566). On the reverse are two exquisitely fashioned songs, dating from 1893. 'L'incrédule', to a Verlaine poem, depicts the contrast between a superstitious girl and her sceptical lover; 'Nocturne', to a poem by Jean Lahor, with a gently synco-pated accompaniment, captures a moment of rapture very precisely, especially in Bernac's ideal performance. The even earlier 'Paysage' (1890) is a delightfully airy piece; it was recorded in the 1930s with a smiling, easy tone by Andrée Marilliet (Col. D 12042) and with a plain-tive voice by Villabella (Odéon 188588). I have not heard Vallin (Pathé X 93074) or Géori Boué in this song.

Finally Arthur Endrèze gave well-moulded accounts of the languorous, oddly neglected 'L'enamourée' (Pathé PG 89; GV 512), also recorded by Hahn and de los Angeles (ASD 651), and of the charming 'Phyllis' and 'Psyché' (Pathé PG 88; GV 512); and Vallin (Pathé PG 80) and Panzéra (Disque P 758) made fine records of the lugubrious 'Le cimetière de campagne'.

Fauré
Ten songs

RICHARD FAIRMAN

The *mélodies* of Fauré form a major part of the French song repertoire and have had their due share of attention on record. A complete discography, at least up until 1977 when the preparation for the book was completed, is available in the *Phonographie de Gabriel Fauré* by Jean-Michel Nectoux, published by the Bibliothèque Nationale de Paris (1979), an essential work of reference for any serious student of the subject. Its listings, song by song, show an impressive total of recordings and the only regrettable loss or omission is in the small number of singers who recorded the *mélodies* during Fauré's lifetime. Activity really begins in the late 1920s and early 1930s. From the LP era there are three complete recordings, or 'intégrales': the first on Pléiade (P 3060/4) shared by Renée Doria, Berthe Monmart, Paul Derenne, Jacques Dutey and Pierre Mollet; the second on HMV (2C 165–12831/5) with Elly Ameling and Gérard Souzay, accompanied by Dalton Baldwin; and the third on Calliope (CAL 1841/6) with Jacques Herbillon, Anne-Marie Rodde and Sonia Nigoghossian accompanied by Théodore Paraskivesco. Though each has some benefits – the playing of Baldwin on the HMV set is a constant source of pleasure – none can be recommended to a new listener without reservations and the best way to build a fine collection of these songs is certainly to search among the plethora of individual recordings elsewhere. In making this selection of ten *mélodies*, I have tried to select those songs which have been recorded most often and by the widest range of singers.

'Après un rêve' (Bussine)

One telling comment has been handed down as to Fauré's own opinion on how 'Après un rêve' should be sung. In the book *Un art de l'interprétation* Claire Croiza recalls how she heard a singer taking the piece so slowly that it almost ground to a halt. Sure that this could not be right, she questioned Fauré over dinner that evening about the correct way of interpreting the

55

song and the answer came straight back, 'Without slowing down, without slowing down'. The point was taken and Croiza's own recording (Fr. Col. LF 63; ALP 2115), made in 1930, keeps the pulse steady throughout. At just over 2'00", it is one of the fastest performances on record. The clean articulation of the words allows no feeling of sentimentality to creep into the music, but the singing is always sensitive and her hushed *piano* over the last phrase 'Reviens, ô nuit mystérieuse' captures as well as any the inner intensity of the song, its yearning for a blissful dream world. The record is living proof that in Fauré the *rallentando* is not necessary.

There are more recordings of 'Après un rêve' than of any of Fauré's other *mélodies*. Excluding the various arrangements for solo instruments (violin, viola, horn, piano, bass, trombone, saxophone and more than 40 versions of Casals' arrangement for cello) there are still more than 60 recordings with voice, either with piano or orchestral accompaniment. A wide range of nationalities is represented, and in no other song is the difference in style between the native French singers and the rest so easy to hear. When somebody like Ninon Vallin (Pathé 3222) or Charles Panzéra (Disque P 856) starts to sing the opening lines, the style instinctively sounds right. The rhythms of the French text fall naturally, the vocal line breathes, and the whole song has a straightforward appeal that is lost by non-French singers, who feel they have to add an extra layer of interpretation. Of the two, Panzéra is the more atmospheric and this early recording is certainly preferable to his 1937 re-make (DA 4911; COLH 103): the strong forward momentum there loses the previous sense of mystery. His call for the night to return with all its dreams and illusions sounds more a demand than an entreaty.

Vallin's record is less inward than either the early Panzéra or the Croiza – she makes little attempt to soften the dynamics – but the firm, clear, bright tone is typical of the French style at its best. Her later version (Pathé X 93081) is equally unforced. It is a tradition that has been well upheld in recent years by Suzanne Danco (Decca 414 635 1), the most obvious post-war equivalent; rather less well by Renée Doria (Pléiade P 3060), who has the same brightness in the voice, but also an intrusive vibrato that makes the singing insistently sharp and unaffectionate.

Among baritones the line follows through to Gérard Souzay, and his 1947 recording (Decca M 604) with Jean-Michel Damase is among the most cherishable of all the versions on disc. It is difficult to know where to breathe in this song – the phrases are long and some singers find themselves having to snatch breaths in the most awkward places – but Souzay lets the vocal line expand and contract so easily that the problem barely seems to exist. The dreamy tenderness of his singing in this period was exceptionally lovely and the only regret is that it did not last to his other two recordings: the second (LXT 2543), stronger and more ardent, is still an impressive achievement, but the third in the HMV set leaves a lot to be desired in all departments – the voice has become harsh, the manner of singing heavy and effortful. Heard immediately afterwards, Camille Maurane (Musidisc RC 693) sounds positively other-worldly, floating the voice on a light, plangent line that turns 'reviens, reviens' into a cry of yearning sweetness. Georges Thill (Fr. Col. LF 125; EMI 2C 153–11660/1) sings with an even, well-bound line and takes the triplets without lightening the voice. Jacques Herbillon (Calliope CAL 1841) aspirates them, which is a shame as they give the song its special feeling of languid grace. But then his speedy version has little time for niceties.

This leaves two French singers who view 'Après un rêve' in a more individual light. Pierre Bernac recorded the song twice, the first with Jean Doyen (Ultraphone BP 1483), the second with Poulenc (DA 4931; PB 2), and each time treats it as a single statement with no searching after secondary details. The opening two stanzas are cool reflection; then, as the poet wakes from his memories with the words 'Hélas! Hélas, triste réveil des songes', Bernac tellingly turns the song into sour disillusion. The feeling at the end is tauter, darker, less appealing than usual. By contrast, Régine Crespin (EL 2904461) goes to the other extreme. Indulgence is here in every bar (generous helpings of Fauré's dreaded *rallentando*) and her pianist, John Wustman, deserves to be shot for his compliance in providing a stop–go accompaniment. Yet here, more than with any other singer, we realise this is a love song: when Crespin sings 'pour m'enfuir avec *toi*' or 'les cieux pour *nous*' the voice speaks of a bond of devotion that is not heard elsewhere. It is, of course, the prerogative of an artist who is eloquent in her own language.

Most non-French singers have to manage without this advantage, as one soon becomes painfully aware. Kiri Te Kanawa's answer (CBS 76868) is to make beautiful noises and leave it at that, though her long *legato* phrases stretch further and more evenly than in most French performances. The loudly vocalised 'n' in the opening line 'Dans un sommeil' announces another foreign singer in Katia Ricciarelli (Bongiovanni GB 9), but she tries more positively to raise the level of intensity by creating a mood of breathless palpitation, an idea that is only partially successful.

Maggie Teyte made two recordings and in these the approach is still more creative. The 1932 version (Fr. Decca 40.300; LXT 6126) is alive to all the important moments of the song, such as the haunted, floating *pianissimo* at 'réveil des songes', though the *rubato* is already rather heavy. But by 1941 her performance (DA 1777; RLS 716) had become a parody of its earlier self. She races through 'reviens, reviens' only to put her foot firmly down on the brake for the next line 'ô nuit mystérieuse', and the growling chest register is highly doubtful. The obliging pianist is

Gerald Moore, who waits what seems to be an age at 'Je t'appelle, ô nuit' for his soprano to take a gulp for breath and carry on. After this Nan Merriman (EX 2906543) is a model of tact and her mellow timbre brings singing that is calmer and deeper in meaning than most.

Ian Partridge (Pearl SHE 524) is a touch fuzzy and nasal. With a voice that is just as typical of the English tenor, Martyn Hill (Saga 5419) sounds more youthful and lets the song float gracefully along in his head-voice. The elastic line that he stretches at 'triste réveil des songes', allowing John Constable to mark the suspension in the piano part, is sheer magic. By his side Nicolai Gedda (ASD 2574) is hard and unyielding with an unpleasant beat under strain. More convincing, among tenors usually associated with the opera house, is Cesare Valletti (RB 6622), who makes a surprisingly good case for himself in the proper style and only gives away his identity with some dramatically rolled 'r's' that would be more at home in Italian opera. The long vocal lines are probably a legacy from his Bellini.

Elly Ameling (ASD 2902) is all early morning sunshine and radiance – the dream and its disillusion seem long forgotten. Olga Haley (Vocalion X 9528), not listed in the French discography, goes at different speeds from bar to bar. Even this, though, is preferable to Frederica von Stade (ASD 4183), who keeps her *molto largo* religiously through to the end. Somebody has scribbled 2′30″ as a timing at the top of my score, but he or she has obviously not heard von Stade, who stretches the piece out to a funereal 3′45″, nearly twice as slow as Croiza. Her singing is not so much dreamy as plain soporific. Horrors of a different kind await the listener who is able to track down the 1935 live recording with Rosa Ponselle (EJS 191). These come not so much from Ponselle herself, who seems to have been in sovereign voice and attacks emotional moments such as 'je quittais la terre' with veristic intensity, but from her pianist, who is wisely left unnamed. At first he plays as though trying to remember the music after a long absence, fumbling along the bass line in a way that changes all the harmonies, but towards the end he gives up and just hammers double octaves with his left hand to keep up with the flood of sound emanating from his soprano.

Even a spurious orchestration could not be worse than that, one feels, and the first few of the recordings made with orchestra do indeed manage to keep decently within sight of Fauré's original intentions. The arrangement on Eidé Noréna's record (DA 4874; Rococo 5359) is more or less a straightforward transcription of the piano part, though the full body of strings does join in for the 'big tune' at 'Les cieux pour nous'. Noréna's singing is as clean and unmannered as anything on the records with piano – simple elegance with every note and consonant in its proper place.

Armand Crabbé's recording (Disco Nacional 82029; GV 78), another version that is not listed in the French discography, is also modest and unexceptional. A small group of strings, rather than a full orchestra, plays the repeated quavers of the accompaniment with a studied insistence that suggests they were still trying to learn the notes, while Crabbé himself sings with firm, strong tone and broad phrasing. Between them they make a dogged start, but towards the middle of the song suddenly start to put on speed as if they were worried they were not going to make the end of the 78 side. Best of all is Vishnevskaya (Artia ALP 157) with her outrageous orchestration of harp and swooning strings. Every bar of this record is stamped with the personality of a great singer: the shaping of the vocal line and the colours in the voice display a mastery that works on a grand scale, so much so that one minds less when the Russian consonants (she sings in her own language) come across like explosive cannonballs.

Lily Pons (Col. Odyssey 32 16 0270) is a mere peashooter by comparison – a thin, bright little voice with an unappealing tight vibrato. The only compensation of her record is the modest orchestration under Maurice Abravanel. Susan Lees (Pye TPLS 13061) has the novelty of a solo guitar for the accompaniment, but spoils its effect by over-interpreting. For erotic excess, though, nobody could do better than Barbra Streisand (CBS 73484), whose recording – replete with chromatic counter-melody on soulful strings – turns the music into an orgy of heavy breathing and husky crooning. Her suggestive mouthing of the word 'pure' deserves to be banned. Finally, there is Jane Gregory (D sharp DSS 1004), who recorded the song as a single with a synthesiser and a very active echo-chamber as companions. We have come so far from the 'Après un rêve' of Croiza and Panzéra that it is difficult to believe this is the same piece of music.

'Au bord de l'eau' (Sully Prud'homme)

As its starting point a song like 'Au bord de l'eau' needs tone just as firm and beautiful as any operatic aria. This does not, of course, imply that the voice needs to be a large one, though there is a special pleasure to be had in hearing a singer as sumptuous in vocal quality as the Wagnerian soprano Germaine Lubin (unissued on 78; 2C 061–96242), who recorded the song in 1944. The depth of tone and rich hue of the voice easily fill out the slow descending scales which are such a feature of the piece. It only seems a shame that she did not choose a slower tempo, which would have allowed those long phrases to expand in breadth, as they do with her French successor in the Wagnerian field, Régine Crespin (EL 2904461). Always one for slow speeds, Crespin evokes the song's river bank setting with all the languor of a summer haze. Her poetic handling of the word 'murmurer' is a typical feature, giving a delightful echo of the babbling brook, but this track of the record catches a tired, worn layer on the surface of the voice that ultimately precludes full enjoyment. Just how disturbing poor tone quality can be in Fauré becomes fully clear in the recording by Jacqueline Delman (Bluebell BELL 102). The voice curdles with vibrato and the unsteady line is disastrous.

On safer ground there is Ameling in the HMV set, who sings with her usual beauty of tone and brings a nice intimacy to the passage 'et seuls tous deux'; or Géori Boué (Urania URLP 7070) for evenness of motion as she glides over the phrases. Doria (Pléiade P 3060) also makes a better impression than usual, floating the rising fifths in the central section with a delicacy that eludes a surprising number of the others. Leontyne Price (RCA LM 2279) moves the song along quickly, but without much charm. Conversely Frederica von Stade (ASD 4183) has nothing but charm: the voice is shallow and the words are drained of interest. This is an especially pallid version. Perhaps the most attractive might be Victoria de los Angeles (ASD 2287), if only she did not worry the line so often and her pianist, Gonzalo Soriano, was not so self-effacing. One interesting point to note: de los Angeles is the only singer who breathes where Fauré directs, but the result – which is most unfair – sounds comparatively awkward when set against singers who ignore his instructions and breathe where they please.

Among the men Souzay (LXT 2543) holds the vocal line with such firm, well-focused tone that one is prepared to forgive him for passing over Fauré's *piano* markings – an unexpected fall from grace. The carefree contentment of the scene is affectingly captured by Martyn Hill (Saga 5419), who is light and fluent, truly 'sans nul souci', as the poem says. Jacques Herbillon (Calliope CAL 1841) is faster still, but leaves the music no room to breathe. Jacques Verhoeven (Charlin SLC 40), for quite different reasons, makes the breathing all too audible. Now we are back to breathy and poorly focused singing, where the discussion began.

I have unfortunately not located Vallin's rare 78 version (Pathé X 93081).

'Automne' (Silvestre)

The distant memories of 'Automne' can rouse marvellously ambivalent feelings. Is the song a sad reflection on time passing or an impassioned cry for the lost days of youth? In Bernard Kruysen's performance (Valois MB 765) nostalgia prevails. The movement is broad, the tone quietly expressive, as the singer looks out upon his 'autumn of the misty skies, the rapid sunsets, the pale dawns'. In moments of tender poetry Kruysen can be unbeatable and so he is here at the quiet return of the main theme, when the singer catches the scent of fallen roses so long forgotten: the voice sounds strong and healthy at *forte*, but almost fragile at *piano*, as though the slightest pressure might make it wobble, and the effect can be very moving. For Ameling in the HMV set, by contrast, this song lives very much in the pain of the present. From the opening bars of the accompaniment – Dalton Baldwin at his finest – the music pushes ahead with tension, as the rising sevenths of the bass line strain upwards to make their jarring clash with the chords in the right hand. (Baldwin makes the other pianists sound uniformly heavy and stolid.) When Ameling catches the scent of the roses, the sensation hits her with a jolt and on the final page she builds towards the climax with urgency and overt passion, though for a light-voiced singer it is surprising that she should experience such difficulty with the last G sharp. The note can hardly be too high for a soprano.

In the absence of so many masters of the *mélodie* – no Bernac, Croiza or Souzay – we have to look elsewhere for performances central to the French tradition. Panzéra recorded the song twice, both with his wife as accompanist: the first (Disque P 515; GV 513) moves grandly and has a gritty enunciation of the text; the second (DA 4911; COLH 103) is one of the fastest of all recorded performances and gains in fluency what it loses in its grip on the song's darker substance. As a general rule those who see the piece in a sentimental light are the least interesting. Irma Kolassi (Decca LX 3080) is sensitive, but pallid in expression. Arthur Endrèze (Pathé PA 1986) at a very slow tempo manages to keep the music moving forwards, which Camille Maurane (Musidisc RC 693) does not, but neither sounds positive in a song which has so much to be positive about. One might be tempted to say the same about Vallin, but her two performances have a quality of voice and *legato* singing that puts them on a higher level. The 1928 version (Odéon 188 578; EX 2909463) is natural and dignified, the less common 1935 (Pathé PG 60) more spontaneous with an extra urgency in the text giving it a tensile, live edge. Gregory Reinhart (HM 1117) follows a safe middle course. So does André Gaudin (Pol. 561017), a singer from the Opéra Comique, who is neither poetic nor really impassioned, but a strange slant is thrown on his performance by the accompaniment of the Quintette Ibos – piano in the middle, strings wandering aimlessly above and below. Huguette Vivers (BBC 30389) is rich in voice and more varied in dynamics. Uncertain which direction to take, Povla Frijsh (ED 517) tries to emulate both a different tempo in every line.

The bold last climax and weighty accompaniment make this an unusually strong song for Fauré and a relatively easy one to dramatise. Janet Baker with Gerald Moore (ASD 2590) is not always at her ease – she is too earnest in the reflective moments and lacks an intuitive feeling for French *mélancholie* – but she captures the hurt and resentment at the song's height most vividly. The way she lets fly with 'Ou jadis, sourit ma jeunesse' shows that a singer does not need perfect French pronunciation to make the words tell. Valletti (RB 6622) also tries to be dramatic and storms at the song, while his pianist Leo Taubman hammers ferociously at the triplets in the accompaniment. Heard in context, between two quieter items on their recital disc, the performance makes some sense, but as an interpretation on its own it is simply wrong-headed. Finally John McCormack (DA 1286; EX 2900563) chose this song for his only appearance in the Fauré discography: a fine ring in the tone, great personality in the use of the voice, but the cavalier attitude towards the score and the idiosyncratic pronunciation make this something of a collector's item in the wrong way. Why ever did Bernac or Souzay not show us how it ought to be done?

'Les berceaux' (Sully Prud'homme)

There is an extraordinary wealth of early recordings of 'Les berceaux': Félia Litvinne, Ernest Van Dyck, Jeanne Marié de l'Isle, Suzanne Brohly, Albert Vaguet and Maurice Sauvageot had all recorded the piece by 1920. If this was an operatic aria, the recordings would almost certainly be on LP by now, but instead they are rarities and the only one I have been able to hear is Van Dyck (Pathé 0976; IRCC 7028), whose 1902 cylinder vies with Litvinne's 78 for the distinction of being the earliest Fauré song on record. Unfortunately its historical value is not really matched by its artistry. What we hear is clean singing with little *rubato* and a firm, bright, well-focused voice that has plenty of strength to spare, as one might expect from a noted Wagnerian tenor. Of personal feeling for the song, there is less evidence. The long, swaying lines of 'Les berceaux' call out very obviously for careful *legato* shaping, but they meet with little response here – the crucial line 'Tentent les horizons qui leurrent' is even split in two places. No other singer finds the need to take more than one breath at this point and the most conscientious manage with none at all. Van Dyck's recording is a valuable souvenir of an important artist, but not much more.

As the recordings of this song cover such a long period, they offer a good opportunity to observe how the words have come to play a less vital role in interpretation over the years (a trend that is opposite to that shown in the performances of German Lieder). The 1930s recordings by Panzéra (DA 4909; COLH 103) – one of his best, very free and spontaneous – and Vallin (Fr. Col. LF 125; EX 2901693) get a grip on the text that is not found in many later singers, Vallin in particular declaiming key words like 'vaisseaux' and 'adieux' with great flamboyance. They remind us that a forward placing of the words is important not just for the sense of the song, but because the poetry, its choice of language and syntax, give a decisive impetus to the music. (Without words, as Schwarzkopf has pointed out, the voice is merely another instrument.) For this reason the performances of the inter-war years rarely seem dull, even when the tempo becomes slow and sticky – as it certainly does in Panzéra's earlier recording (Disque P 724) and with Alice Raveau (Pathé X 3490).

Even among singers who are not well known today there are some admirable things to be heard: Étienne Billot (Odéon 188 814) may pull the tempo back – he holds on to his top note as long as he dares – but the variety he brings to the vocal line keeps the song alive; and Roger Bourdin (Odéon 188 564) is still more attractive, always mellifluous and sensitive, but also disciplined with careful musical preparation. Endrèze (Pathé PA 1986) is fuzzy-sounding when he sings quietly, but the voice locks into gear in time for the climaxes. It is unfortunate that his accompanist Marie Endrèze-Kriéger (wife or sister?) puts the pedal down in the first bar and does not seem to take it up again before the end. Jean Vieuille (Parlo. 28518), a dark baritone, and Sophie Wyss (Decca M 529) are worthy but unremarkable. Martha Angelici (Lumen 33191) sings with an orchestral accompaniment – an unnamed ensemble conducted by Francis Cébron – and relies upon binding the notes of the vocal line into a firm *legato*. Verbal emphasis over a full orchestra is not so easy.

After the war, as the performing styles became more diverse (more nationalities, different backgrounds), so the recordings become less interesting in inverse proportion. Bernac and Souzay are the two exceptions, as usual, though neither is perhaps at his most inspired. Bernac (DA 1907; COLH 151), with that unique innate feeling that he always had for the right tempo, takes the song a notch faster than anybody else and places the climaxes with a powerful sense of inevitability. Souzay speeds up unconvincingly for the first climax in his earlier recording (ABL 3371) and, contrary to expectation, it is his performance in the HMV set that fares better, sustaining the thrust by keeping the dynamic levels high.

Most of the rest are disappointing. Jacques Verhoeven's version (Charlin SLC 40) is poorly sung. Maurane (Musidisc RC 693) bumps the dotted rhythms. Though Felicity Palmer (Argo ZRG 815) does not do that, the way she robs the voice of vibrato to get a feeling of immobility leaves the climaxes with no force or tension at all. Sarah Walker (Hyperion A 66165) has a limited impact; von Stade (ASD 4183) only a negative one, as she squeezes the voice with agonizing deliberation from the consonants to the vowels. The very act of singing seems to be in slow motion here, like a film playing at the wrong speed. Nor is the slow tempo managed well by Jennie Tourel (LX 1306), who lifts up into notes too often. Gregory Reinhart (HM 1117) is rhythmically unimaginative. For the most unlikely coincidence of people and places, nobody can do better than Leonard Warren (RCA LM 2266), who was caught live on a recital tour in Leningrad or Kiev – the venue is not quite certain – and gets rapturous applause for some honest, sturdy singing in tolerable French, a rather better experience than might have seemed likely in prospect. He takes the alternative line allowed by the composer at the bottom of the first page, but for some reason adds a second variant later entirely of his own invention. Finally, if you want to switch to another channel, there is Yves Montand (Philips 844 893) with the microphone between his teeth, turning 'Les berceaux' into a popular ballad. Come back Van Dyck, all is forgiven.

'Le secret' (Silvestre)

Some singers read the instructions, others pass them by with barely a notice. Listen to Bernac (unpublished 78; PB 2) and the purpose behind Fauré's detailed dynamic markings immediately becomes clear: while almost everybody else treats the three verses of this song the same, Bernac simply by observing what is written in the score gives each its own individual character – 'the dawn of love, the noon with its climax, the evening as it disappears with the setting sun'. The substance of the piece seems immeasurably greater. Although he does not sound in the best of vocal health (which may be why the original 78 of 1947 was never issued), he makes a lovely effect on the most important lines, not least 'Comme une larme il s'évapore' at the end of the first verse, which literally evaporates into nothingness.

That phrase – a long, slow scale that rises and falls *sempre piano* – is a test point of interpretation. Maurane (Musidisc RC 693) breaks it inelegantly half-way down. Maggie Teyte (DA 1876; RLS 716) leaves a gaping hole at the top and the *rubato* each time it occurs is too predictable, always fast going up and slow coming down. In other respects, though, this is one of her best Fauré recordings: much is handled with an attractive personality and she really gives the feeling she is letting the listener into a long-cherished secret. Perhaps the most musical is Ian Partridge (Pearl SHE 524) who floats the line at its apex and still has time to nurture it on the way down. Vallin (Pathé PD 45) manages it easily with a characteristic little *portamento*, whereas Vanni-Marcoux (DA 4814; EMI 2C 153–12845/6) is more studied. The line loses impetus at the top – the pause for breath is just too long – and the slow tempo allows the singing to stagnate despite his strong delivery of the text. He is also unlucky that the last note goes flat (a singer today would be able to have another try). A still slower tempo comes from Alice Raveau (Pathé X 93 077; Club 99 18), who has to work conscientiously to keep the line flowing, and her pianist Godfroy Andolfi turns Fauré's simple chords into rolled arpeggios, for which he would certainly be tried as a heretic today. Crespin (EL 2904461) is also too slow, though her singing gets the mood of hushed secrecy nicely. At the other extreme Maurice Sauvageot (P 378) and Povla Frijsh (Victor 2078) rush into the song as though they cannot wait to spill the beans. Both manage to squeeze another song on to the same 78 side.

The difficulty comes in trying to make the song interesting, while keeping within its intimate, small-scale boundary. Ameling's contrasts in the HMV set make little impression, while those of Valletti (RB 6622) immediately stretch out towards the opera house and his consonants are spat out too prominently. Even Gabriel Bacquier (Véga L30 PO 357) sounds too operatic in close-up, a risk Felicity Palmer (Argo ZRG 815) avoids by keeping well back from the microphone. As always, Souzay (Philips ABL 3371) can be relied upon to provide a sensitive, well-judged reading, but it is good to see an equally fine appearance from Susan Metcalfe-Casals (JG 22; EX 2901693). She places the last phrase with ravishing delicacy and in doing so, of course, only sings it exactly as the composer asks.

'Clair de lune' (Verlaine)

The standard in this song is set by Souzay (Decca M 606). The beauty of the single line 'Et leur chanson se mêle au clair de lune' is an object lesson in the singing of Fauré's *mélodies*: a perfect shape to the vocal line and a colouring of the words – the softness of 'mêle', the bright openness of 'clair' – that is absorbed effortlessly into the phrase as a whole. The music looks simple enough on the page, but it is typical that Souzay should make more of it than anybody else. His second recording (LXT 2543) recaptures much of the magic of the first; the third, on the HMV set, inevitably, does not, and the huffing and puffing at the opening are all too clear a signal that this is the Souzay of the later years, when the lovely *piano* singing had been lost. Any clumsiness of that kind sits poorly on the graceful manners of 'Clair de lune', an elegant picture from Verlaine of masked figures dancing in the moonlight among marble statues and fountains. Fauré set the poem as a minuet and ends it with a small 'jet d'eau' of his own, as the voice rises and falls on the last phrase, an effect beautifully carried out by Souzay in his early days.

Including versions with orchestra (an arrangement made by the composer in 1888), there are over 60 recordings of 'Clair de lune' and it is extraordinary how similar in their basic approach they are. Most move at about the same speed and even singers who can be way off-beam in other songs manage to put in a reasonably stylish performance in this one. A clean and lightly dancing accompaniment – it turns out to be Gerald Moore – alerts the ear to a fine recording by Mattiwilda Dobbs (Col.

33CX 1154), who spins the line on a silver thread of tone and touches deftly upon key words in the text. The refined elegance of singer and pianist here is all of a piece. Another pleasant surprise comes from Eileen Farrell (Am. Col. MS 6524), who strains a bit on the top notes (only Gs in this key – not much for a Brünnhilde), but shows a feeling for the poetry of the French language that one does not expect from a singer of her background. The same cannot quite be said of Leontyne Price (RCA LM 2279), though her singing is also more carefully schooled here than elsewhere. Even Nelson Eddy (Empire LP 806) makes an effort, despite the Hollywood backing which turns Fauré's liquid arpeggios into a sugary morass, and it is a shame that his Americanised vowels are as wide open as the prairies.

As a mark of special insight, the beginning of the third stanza is a good test point. A shimmering ray of moonlight, marked *espressivo e dolce*, has fallen over the music and the singer who finds a new tone colour for it – as Janet Baker (ASD 2590) so memorably does with a rapt, luminous glow in the voice – shows a sensibility to the mood of the piece that is missed by the average interpreter. Bacquier (Véga L 30 PO 357) seizes upon it, and after bumping through the first couple of pages finds a softness of tone that carries through to the end. Kruysen (Valois MB 765) typically brings the moment an unearthly stillness, moving the voice from note to note with a *legato* that is worthy of the very finest instrumentalist. The more one hears of this singer, the more underrated he seems. A similar effect to Kruysen, only transferred to the liquid head tones of a light tenor, can be heard on Martyn Hill's record (Saga 5419), which excels in Fauré's most limpid *mélodies*. His accompanist, John Constable, is one of the best and it is a pleasure to hear the long introduction played with such clean, well-articulated rhythms. Suzie Chereau on Jacques Verhoeven's recording and Théodore Paraskivesco on Jacques Herbillon's (Calliope CAL 1843) both over-pedal wildly, while Lily Bienvenu with Maurane (Erato EPR 15550) adds an infuriating amount of *rubato*. Even the tiny hesitations in Partridge's performance (Pearl SHE 524) are too much.

The easiest – and best – answer is to play it absolutely straight, which is what Moore does for de los Angeles (SXLP 30147). Not a hint of a *rallentando* in sight here, yet the performance loses nothing in depth and de los Angeles' unforced singing is supported by a firm sense of direction. When he recorded the song for Teyte (DA 1876; RLS 716), Moore was clearly asked for a slower tempo. Dreaminess is the essential quality now and, though that in itself does no harm, the slow pace tempts Teyte into a rash of mannerisms that make her sound like a French Schwarzkopf. Or, then again, perhaps not so French, since she pronounces 'quasi' as 'kwasi' – a fault also heard from Anne Thursfield (HMV E 452), recorded in 1926 with Ivor Newton. The one feature, though, that finally distinguishes an artist foreign to the style is a need to slow down for the moonlight episode discussed above. Unable to find the melting, moonlit colours of a Baker or Kruysen – his vowels are relentlessly open and bright in the Italianate style – Valletti (RB 6622) slows the pace by half, only to pick it up again a few lines further on. This is not a good idea (Bernac positively forbids it) and it says much for Valletti's lack of wisdom at this point that the only other singer on record to commit the same heinous sin is von Stade (ASD 4183), whose recital disc is a model, from beginning to end, of how not to sing Fauré.

This leaves the central group of French singers, who are usually to be trusted on matters of tempo. The exception in this case, sadly, is Crespin (EL 2904461), who deserves some sort of prize for taking 'Clair de lune' even more slowly than von Stade (the shame of it!) and fails to generate forward propulsion, despite her moving way with the text. Edmond Clément (Pathé 3165; Cantilena 6227) goes to the other extreme and races through the piece (the limits of the 78 side must take the blame). He barely has time to fit in all the words. Géori Boué (Urania URLP 7070) is bright and edgy in the Doria tradition; Vallin (Odéon 188 278; EX 2909463), the first of her three recordings, shining bright too, but with far more body to the tone and a strong presence. Her male counterpart of the period was Georges Thill (Fr. Col. LF 154), the Werther to her Charlotte, who sings with fine, clean, broad strokes, but cannot resist making the climaxes a public statement in full voice. The world of the Massenet opera seems too close to hand. Perhaps the most reliable of the group is Panzéra, who recorded the song three times, always with a sensitive appreciation of its nocturnal mood. Beware the LP transfer of the first (Disque P 489; 2C 151–73084), which plays at the wrong speed on LP and makes him sound like Larry the Lamb. The second (DA 4887; COLH 103) is just as good, and his orchestral recording (Disque P 739) is arguably the finest of the three, long-breathed and delicate, really confidential. With singing like this even the trills in the orchestra, when he mentions 'les oiseaux', hardly seem to matter.

'Mandoline' (Verlaine)

The delicate strumming of strings and light breezes give 'Mandoline' a special atmosphere. Nobody catches its mood better than Dalton Baldwin, whose *pizzicato* accompaniment is light and rhythmical, judging the (marked!) *ritenuto* at the end with a timing that catches the twist of harmony to perfection. With his wit and precision to hand,

67

Richard Fairman

Ameling in the HMV set can hardly go wrong. Showing a quick eye for detail, she introduces each of the elegant serenaders in Verlaine's picture – Tircis, Aminte and boring old Clitandre – as though they are individual personalities: little touches, like the bounce in the rhythm to describe their silk doublets or the long, rolling *legato* for their trailing dresses, give the whole piece a pictorial appeal, and her balance between *legato* and *non-legato* is ideal.

Imagination is crucial to a descriptive song of this kind. Felicity Palmer (Argo ZRG 815) clearly has no patience with 'l'éternel Clitandre' either and, despite a larger and harder voice than most of the singers on record, she keeps the music lightly on its toes. Indeed, the wafting runs of semiquavers go so easily in her hands it seems all the more puzzling that lighter singers should struggle over them with such effort. Herbillon (Calliope CAL 1843) aspirates all the runs heavily, as he rattles through the song at an astonishing speed. Gales are blowing here rather than evening breezes. Leontyne Price (RCA LM 2279) also makes hard work of them, though that is perhaps less surprising, and in the central section she starts biting into the consonants and bouncing the dotted rhythms, until she is enjoying herself so much that she dots the rhythms even when it is not written. A similar cheeky spring in the gait comes from Kathleen Battle (DG 415 361 1), but now it sounds as though Despina has strayed into the picture from *Così fan tutte*. Von Stade (ASD 4183) goes to the other extreme and dampens any life in the song by taking it at a deathly tempo. This is worse: 'Mandoline' without a sense of humour is no fun at all. Irma Kolassi (Decca LX 3080) makes her slow tempo work by bringing a dreamy sensitivity to the text, and a still greater feeling for the words comes across with Maurane (Erato EPR 15550), who makes 'leur joie' sound really joyful and hisses the 's' of 'les frissons de brise' with a little shudder of excitement. There are also good, central performances – like Ameling, but without her sharpness of wit – from Kruysen (Valois MB 765) and Hugues Cuénod (Vanguard VRS 414), both of whom balance words and line with a fine equilibrium. Their lithe singing is a good reminder that this should feel a youthful song, something one certainly does not sense in the wobbly, unsteady efforts of Berthe Monmart (Pléiade P 3062), who sounds well past serenading anybody.

This leaves one singer who falls outside the parameters set by the rest. Souzay recorded 'Mandoline' twice and his 1955 recording (Decca LX 3149), the earlier of the two, quickly captures the imagination: fleet and weightless, the first high note on 'écouteuses' floated gently, the whole thing gossamer-light, as though the distant sound of the serenaders is being wafted to the listener on the slightest breeze. It is a recording quite unlike any of the others and wholly delightful.

68

'En sourdine' (Verlaine)

Over rippling arpeggios 'En sourdine' spins a vocal line of infinite calm and beauty. It is a song which calls for pure singing of the highest quality and for that there is no need to look any further than the earliest recording by Souzay (Decca M 604), made in 1947. If a high point is sought in the recordings of Fauré's *mélodies*, this – together with a select handful of Souzay's other 78s – is surely it. Perfect vocal control, sensitivity, an unforgettable tenderness in the voice, the eloquence of the poetry: everything is there, and it is typical of Souzay's singing that he manages to impart so many nuances to the text while not losing for one moment the rapt stillness of Verlaine's 'silence profond'. If his two later recordings are not its equal, the decline is at least less evident than elsewhere. The 1950 performance (LXT 2543) has the voice still in its prime, though firmer and less intimate; and even in his last recording (Philips SAL 3505) the old magician manages to bring off the lovely ending of 'le rossignol chantera'. It is very rare for Fauré to write a vocal 'effect' in his songs and this *pianissimo* entry on a top note is one no singer can afford to bungle.

Bernac comments rightly on the song's 'impression of calm and amorous languor', and it is important that the singer should establish this feeling from the beginning. The attack by Doria (Pléiade P 3062) on the opening phrase is immediately too hard and edgy, and Verhoeven (Charlin SLC 40) sounds positively infirm. Nor does Palmer (Argo ZRG 815) or Baker (ASD 2590) create an easy impression, because they manage their voices in too self-conscious a manner, squeezing out the natural vibrato to try and keep a steady line, when naturalness of vocal emission is needed above all. If only he sounded more romantic, Cuénod (Vanguard VRS 414) might be in Souzay's class, for he clearly feels the music as keenly. The *dolcissimo* of 'Ferme tes yeux' is held as quietly as possible, but the effect is spoiled by the tight vibrato that comes into the voice at the same time. A little cough seems to be audible as he clears his throat before the phrase begins. Herbillon (Calliope CAL 1843) has a more appealing basic sound, but his pianist uses too much pedal and creates muddy textures. Ameling (HMV set) has both the beautiful tone and the best accompanist: Baldwin keeps the arpeggios clear and makes the top line in the right hand sing with the voice. The fluency that she always has in Fauré is usually the prerogative of French singers, and it is typical that the performances most like hers come from Maurane (Erato EPR 15550) and Ginette Guillamat (Fr. Col. DF 2485), who show how little conscious interpretation this music needs, so long as it is kept flowing forward and the words are clear. After them von Stade (ASD 4183) is all contrivance; and even Teyte (Glendale GL 8002) who sings 'En sourdine' with orchestra – a recording preserved from a radio broadcast of the Bell Telephone Hour in 1948, forces on the music flamboyant ideas that are unnecessary. At least with her, though, they sound strongly and personally felt. Only Vallin (Pathé PD 46) pushes the song harder, singing off the words with an urgency that puts a different interpretation on Verlaine's poem. Time is running out, she seems to be saying, the nightingale will soon sing and the lovers' brief night of ecstasy will be over.

While the text can support this approach, the languorous sound of Fauré's setting surely asks for singing with a deep inner contentment at its heart. Souzay has that in abundance, of course, but there are also worthwhile alternatives from Kruysen (Valois MB 765) and Panzéra (DB 4903; COLH 103), who are both at their finest. Indeed, Kruysen finds as much in this song as anybody. His treatment of the lines starting at 'Ferme tes yeux à demi' is so withdrawn and intimate that the listener hardly dares to breathe and in the last stan'a the dark colours in the voice subtly herald a change of mood. This is Vallin's presentiment of parting in a different guise. Panzéra, by contrast, is always soft, mellow and easy-going. He sings on this record as though he has all the time in the world, lavishing upon the music a dreamy affection that would be a path to ruin in a singer with half his spontaneity. It is recordings like these that make the job of comparisons a pleasure: so much beautiful singing, so much – of course – that is beautiful to be sung.

'Prison' (Verlaine)

The simple way to perform 'Prison' is in an unvaried mood of resignation. The slow, repeated crotchets in the accompaniment can be deceptive of the music's range and it is all too easy to pass through the song, as Pierre Mollet (Pléiade P 3063) does, with nothing but mellifluous tone and a sympathetic reading of the text. Maurane (Musidisc RC 693) and Herbillon (Calliope CAL 1844) take the song even more lightly, though Herbillon engineers an excitable climax in the second verse; and while Stuart Burrows (L'Oiseau Lyre SOL 323) works up a more convincing outburst at this point, the singing still goes only skin-deep. There is no grip on the words and the semiquavers in the vocal line have too light a spring. It is difficult to read Verlaine's poem, recalling his own days in prison after the attempted murder of his friend Rimbaud, and come away feeling that Fauré's setting of it should mean so little.

The description that Bernac gives of 'Prison' in his book on French song – 'a dramatic sense quite exceptional in [Fauré's] works' – makes it clear that he felt the same. It is unusual for Fauré to set feelings of personal bitterness so directly and the singer does him no favour by smoothing them over. Bernac's recording (DA 4889; 2C 153–12485/6 and PB 2) immediately opens the window on the full range of emotions: the opening stanza, in which the poet talks of the birds, trees and blue skies that he can see from his cell, is drained of warmth and feelings, but then the inner coil of frustration quickly becomes tightened to the point where Bernac lets fly at the climax 'Qu'as tu fait, o toi', biting into the words with unrestrained savagery. As always with this singer, the text is the driving force behind the performance as much as the music. Nobody else explores the same depths of hopelessness. There are, however, recordings that are effective on a more modest level: Kruysen (Valois MB 765) is at his best in the tone of sweet longing that haunts the opening phrases, and Gregory Reinhart (HM 1117) brings a fine cutting power to the climaxes. The nasal vowels of Baker's French singing (ASD 2590) are at their most jarring here – perhaps the intention was to catch the pain of nerves on edge in the voice itself – but the high point of the song is unerringly hit with desperation at its most intense. The indulgent style of Susan Lees (Pye TPLS 13061) and her guitar accompaniment do not sound right at all. Von Stade (ASD 4183) is half as slow again as anybody else and eases the voice on to the top notes in a most uncomfortable way. Most tempting of all, the Fauré discography lists a recording by Claire Croiza with Poulenc as the accompanist (D 13033), which I have unfortunately not been able to hear. It seems this is a rare record and may, indeed, never have been issued.

Apart from Bernac the most essential performances come from Souzay, who recorded 'Prison' three times. The first of these (Decca LX 3149) is so heartrending in its tenderness, every phrase so beautifully shaped and full of humanity, that it is difficult to imagine the song ever being better sung. By the time of the second (Philips SAL 3480) the interpretation has grown one size bigger – the drama is more incisive, the bitterness more keenly felt and, like Bernac, Souzay hits out at 'Qu'as tu fait' with an explosive force that singers who are not French by birth do not quite dare. (Baker is perhaps the only exception there.) His third performance in the HMV set is a disappointment. Between them, however, Souzay and Bernac at their best have the measure of this song from end to end. (See also the chapter on Hahn for comparisons of his settings of Verlaine's poem. *Editor*.)

'Soir' (Samain)

For Croiza the music of 'Soir' aroused very specific emotions. When she was asked how she understood the song, she replied that it gave her the impression of being in the country and going for a walk after the rain, when the atmosphere is so captivating that one hardly dares to speak. Her pupils were told not to make the song too bright. She felt the mood of the piece should rather feel 'nocturne, enveloppé, chaud' – a description that suits her own recording of it (Fr. Col. LF 63; EMI 2C 153–12845/6), made in 1930. As we know that Croiza was close to Fauré himself, it is possible that this interpretation came from him and in that case the very steady tempo that she adopts may also be authentic. At nearly 3'00", she gives almost the slowest performance on record: the singing is not fault-less (some phrases are broken and the voice sounds shaky at the top) but the sense of oppressive surroundings is well sustained, especially on the last page where she does not take the climax *forte*, as marked, but floats it and keeps the dynamics hushed to the end. Fauré's magical 'jardins de la nuit' are convincingly evoked.

Although the score is only marked *andante molto moderato* (no metro-nome mark is given), it is noticeable that the major interpreters of Fauré follow her example and take a slow tempo. Kolassi (Decca LX 3080) is withdrawn in much the same way, though with additional *ritardandi* that Croiza would have abhorred. Souzay (Philips ABL 3371) also aims for the same mood, but this is a late recording (1960) and he finds it difficult to sustain the quiet singing. The *rubato* is too heavy in Crespin's perform-ance (EL 2904461), but with this voice there is a resonance of Wagnerian depth that turns 'Soir' into a night of luxuriant, Tristanesque romance, closer in feeling to Croiza's description than anybody else. She, too, goes against instructions and floats part of the last climax to delicious effect. Like Crespin, Teyte (DA 1819; RLS 716) wants individual moments to tell. The gardens of the night, their lines and colours, are vividly described and she addresses 'ma soeur' anxiously, as if another person is really present. The mixed feelings of the poem, at once sad and erotic, are beautifully pointed by the catch in her voice at the end. Of Bernac's two recordings, the earlier (Ultraphone BP 1493; Rococo 5276) is relaxed and lyrical, its exquisite shaping of some phrases matched only by Souzay, while the later version with Poulenc as accompanist (DA 1907; PB 2) is taut and swifter. The clipped phrases and emphatically rolled 'r' at 'si tristes' bring more intense emotions into play. Panzéra also recorded the song twice: both straightforward in outlook, though the later version (DA 4905; COLH 103) is half as fast again as the first (Disque P 852), an extraordinary difference from one interpreter.

The rest of the singers understand *andante* as meaning a more flowing tempo and treat the song accordingly. There are fewer opportunities for making points at this speed and the simple, fluent performances by Herbillon (Calliope CAL 1844) and Kruysen (Valois MB 765) are fairly typical of an approach that sets most store by the overall shape of the piece. In the HMV set Ameling allows the voice to pour out radiantly in the last couple of lines (the dynamic markings are a clear invitation) and the two recordings by Vallin, made in 1938 (Pathé PG 101; EX 2909463) and 1946 (Pathé PD 45) do the same. The soothing calm of Vallin's timbre would be welcome in Doria (Pléiade P 3063); and her sensuality in Baker (ASD 2590), who could afford to soften her sturdy mezzo tone at times. Maurane (Musidisc RC 693) is too uneven. The only eccentricities in 'Soir' come from Metcalfe-Casals (JG 22), who tails each phrase away in an affected *pianissimo* and makes her way lightly through the central section of the song on tiptoe. It would be interesting to know what Croiza thought about that.

Fauré
Song cycles

RICHARD FAIRMAN

A survey of Fauré's song cycles on record is not the undiluted pleasure it ought to be. While popular individual songs, such as 'Après un rêve' or 'Clair de lune', have been treated to continual reappraisal by leading singers from all possible artistic backgrounds, the song cycles have been comparatively neglected. It is easy to see the reasons why (less easy, perhaps, to sympathise with them): with the exception of *Poème d'un jour*, a small triptych written during his early years, these works represent Fauré at an advanced stage of his musical development, a true 'third period' in the manner of Beethoven or Mahler, in which the composer has begun fully to explore his most inward, personal style. The last four cycles, in particular, the summation of his career as a composer of *mélodies*, follow this path to its ultimate and most rewarding destination. Where the early songs had easy-to-hum tunes, these modestly keep close to the inflections of speech; where before one might have found senti- mental harmonies, the late cycles feel their way towards a new purity of harmonic language, where a single key change is such an event that the power of the modulation can be felt several lines in advance. The music is, in short, bad box office and the record companies have reacted accord- ingly. From the 78 era there is just a handful of recordings. After the war the number increases, but the quality remains doubtful. Foreign singers generally stay well clear, because the style demands an even more intimate contact with the rhythms and sounds of the French language than the early songs of Fauré did before. But perhaps the saddest feature is the lack of complete recorded performances from the major figures of the French tradition: no Croiza, despite the fact that *Le jardin clos* was first per- formed by her; no Noréna; no Endrèze; no Clément; no Vallin or Thill, except for *Poème d'un jour*; no Bernac that has been officially issued; no Crespin; no Bacquier; not even much Souzay, and that mostly from his later years, though one is always glad to have his thoughts on this com- poser. The roll-call of absentees is far more impressive than that of those taking part. For the rest – with a couple of glorious exceptions – mediocrity rules. The way remains open for future generations to make good the shortfall.

As the number of recordings is relatively small, I have tried to be comprehensive wherever possible. Some issues always remain elusive but their existence, at least, is noted here. For the purposes of this chapter the *Cinq mélodies de Venise* Op. 58 have been regarded as a group of individual songs, rather than a cycle, and therefore do not appear. Although they share some thematic material and for that reason might be seen to constitute a single work, recordings have tended to deal with them individually and it seemed best that a study of them on record should do the same. Two of them, 'Mandoline' and 'En sourdine', can be found in the preceding chapter.

Poème d'un jour

(with piano)

Friedmann, Zubal	Da Camera SM 90 004
Gedda, Ciccolini	EMI 063–10000
Herbillon, Paraskivesco	Calliope CAL 1842
Maurane (I), Bienvenu	Pathé ED 23
Maurane (II), Maillard-Verger	Musidisc RC 693
Mollet, Gouat	Pléiade P 3061
Panzéra, [Panzéra-Baillot]	Disques P 765
I. Partridge, J. Partridge	Pearl SHE 524
Sciutti, Bonneau	Philips A 76705
Singher, Gilchrist	1750 Arch S 1754
Souzay, Baldwin (I)	Philips ABL 3371
Souzay, Baldwin (II)	EMI 165–12831/5
Thill, Fauré	Fr. Col. LF 157; EMI 153–11660/1
Tourel, Reeves	Am. Col. ML 4158; Odyssey Y2 32880
Turp	CBC Expo 26
Vallin, Darck	Pathé PG 61
Verhoeven, Chereau	Charlin SLC 40

(with orchestra)

Noréna, Orchestre du Gramophone, Coppola	Disques K 7202

The early cycle *Poème d'un jour* happily begins on a positive note. In 1924 Charles Panzéra recorded the first song, 'Rencontre' (Disque P 497); in 1925 he recorded the third, 'Adieu' (Disque P 515); and in 1926, a strange trio of engagements, he returned to the studios to record the whole cycle

(Disque P 765), which in any case consists of only three songs. The repetitions are hard to explain, as there is no great change in his view of the pieces, but among them Panzéra's short series of records has as much to tell us about the cycle as anything that came later. The point of the songs is that they follow the three stages of a romance. 'Rencontre' portrays amorous attraction before the first meeting; 'Toujours' is the prospect of parting; and 'Adieu' marks the end of the affair with a casual wave of farewell. As the poem says, 'Hélas! les plus longs amours sont courts . . . Adieu!', an unfortunately trite ending that leaves one longing for the superior poetry of Verlaine that Fauré was to set so eloquently later. Nevertheless the music brings to Grandmougin's tawdry prosody an expressiveness that is not found in the words themselves and this little cycle, with its openly personal feelings and strongly dramatised progression of emotions, offers songs that are easy to characterise in a way that Fauré's *mélodies* – and the song cycles, in particular – usually are not.

Panzéra realises this and the success of his performances lies in the very different colours that he finds for each song. To anyone familiar with the cycle it may seem that he takes 'Rencontre' slowly, but in fact it is he who follows Fauré's metronome marking almost to the letter, while other singers generally take the song too fast. The tone is marvellously affectionate throughout and at the words 'Une mystérieuse et douce sympathie' he achieves just the new mood of hushed, inner intensity that the words demand. (This effect, or something like it, is specifically requested by the score, in which the phrase is marked *dolce*, and it is disappointing to find how many singers fail to make such an obvious point tell.) The forceful attack of 'Toujours' is easily grasped, though Panzéra commendably keeps the *legato* line intact; and then, in 'Adieu', he stretches the long phrases out in the softest of colours, all pastel shades of tenderness and devotion. He was in fine voice at the time and this small clutch of recordings is as fine a representation of his art as anything he did.

The recordings by Ninon Vallin and Georges Thill are more straightforward. Both are ideally clear with the text, incisive and purposefully projected, but there is a lack of the intimacy that makes Panzéra so engaging. In Thill's case one senses that the climaxes are the *raison d'être* of the singing: the adrenalin begins to rise as he approaches the top notes and a chance to let his voice ring out with its full power. Perhaps an orchestral backing, such as he would have had in the opera house, might have offset the monochrome of the voice to better effect. Jennie Tourel sounds more at home with the smaller scale of the *mélodie* and, although she cannot match Vallin for sheer splendour of voice, keeps the music bubbling with nervous excitability. Her tempo for 'Adieu' is unusually fast – no sentimentality here.

Tourel's recording dates from 1949 and it may be that other post-war singers knew it, as the tendency on more recent discs is to take the music quickly. Camille Maurane's second recording – I have not been able to hear his first – is typical in this respect, light and eager, continually pushing the momentum on, but all too often the singing seems facile in the way it dispatches the most telling moments of the score. Maurane's matter-of-fact handling of the rhyming couplets ('aimées/fumées', 'aveu/Adieu' – a cloying idea) in the last song is especially deadening. Pierre Mollet is not dissimilar, though he digs more deeply into its feelings. After these one inevitably turns to the two recordings by Gérard Souzay with higher expectations, which are only partially rewarded: Souzay's earlier performance comes from one of his least successful recital discs dating from 1960 when deterioration of the voice had already set in, and the interpretation is depressingly short on spontaneity. In 'Toujours' he even takes the extraordinary step of changing the vowels ('cher-*at*' for 'cher-*it*') to enable himself to get the top notes more easily. In the complete HMV set the voice has some ugly moments on nasal vowels but at least there is some honesty about the performance. The words are cleanly sung as written, whatever the passing vocal difficulties, and the singing as a whole shows welcome signs of life. Dalton Baldwin is the expert pianist on both. The accompaniment of 'Toujours', which is essentially nothing more than slowly rolled chords, is cleverly arranged so as to allow inner parts to throw up brief snatches of counter-melody and Baldwin sifts the textures to perfection, keeping them clear enough for the inner patterns to be heard but allowing the pedal to absorb all the notes of the underlying harmonies.

The recordings by Graziella Sciutti and Nicolai Gedda have been impossible to find, which is a shame, as that leaves very little else worthy of mention. Gérard Friedmann is perhaps the most interesting – a fluid and light reading, which is still able to find serious, darker colours for the central song, 'Toujours'. One point, though, cannot be right: his accompanist, Franz Zubal, plays the repeated chords in 'Adieu' sharp and detached, a most unlikely interpretation of Fauré's *staccato* dots covered by a *legato* line which is not copied by any of the other pianists on record. Jacques Verhoeven is prosaic and vocally pushed to his limits. And over Martial Singher's recording it is best to draw a veil – preferably a thick one. The gramophone caught him about 40 years too late in this cycle. The major drawback of Jacques Herbillon's performance is the insensitive playing of his accompanist, who brings confusion to the harmonies of 'Rencontre' (a far cry from Baldwin's beautiful clarity) and launches into the drama of 'Toujours' with heavy-handed emphasis. Ian Partridge's record, by contrast, is sensitive to a fault. For once all the *dolce* markings are observed and the vocal line is moulded with infinite care, but how quickly this music can come to sound soft-centred and over-

Richard Fairman

sweet. Even 'Toujours' lacks bite. The words, crucially, need to be more forward in the French manner. What *Poème d'un jour* needs is a combination of these delicate shades and the healthy, straightforward singing of Thill and Vallin – but, as yet, the only artist who has successfully found that middle road is Panzéra.

There are few recordings of individual songs from the cycle. The tenor Miguel Villabella (Odéon 123 517; ORX 143) sings 'Rencontre' with large *rallentandi* at the end of each verse. I have not heard the versions of this song by Madeleine Mellot-Joubert, Madeleine Sibille or Janice Harsanyi. Stuart Burrows (L'Oiseau Lyre SOL 323) makes 'Toujours' still more wan and mellifluous than Partridge; Victoria de los Angeles (ASD 2287) gives it more life, but lifts up into all the top notes. I was not able to hear the version of 'Adieu' with orchestra by Edmond Clément or that with quintet by André Gaudin.

La bonne chanson

(with piano)

Ameling, Baldwin	CBS 74027
Bernac, Poulenc	HMV DB 8931–3 (unissued)
Bogard, Moriarty	Cambridge CRS 2775
Brainerd, Paull	Concert Hall CHC 49
Cuénod, Holetschek	Westminster XWN 18707
Danco, Agosti	Decca 414 635 1
Derenne, Houdy	Charlin CL 2
de San, Robin	Duchesne DD 6090
Fischer-Dieskau, Moore	HMV BLP 1106
Herbillon, Paraskivesco	Calliope 1844
Kruysen, Lee	Telefunken SAT 22526
Maurane, Maillard-Verger	Erato STE 60 0062
Mollet, Gouat	Pléiade P 3062
Palmer, Constable	Argo ZRG 815
Panzéra, Panzéra-Baillot	HMV DB 5020–2; Jap Angel GR 2162
Pears, Britten	BBC Transcription 97180–1 (not commercially available)
Souzay, Baldwin (I)	Philips ABL 3371
Souzay, Baldwin (II)	EMI 2C 165–12831–5
Sussman, Maillard-Verger	Club National du Disque CND 10
Wyss, Long	Decca AF 9414–8

(with piano quintet)

Fischer-Dieskau, Sawallisch and members of the Berlin Philharmonic Orchestra	BASF EA 22765
Singher, Goode, Tree, Naegele, Molieri, Grebanier	Am. Col. MS 6244
Walker, Nash Ensemble	CRD 1089

(with orchestra)

Stappen, Orchestre dir. Coppola	HMV K 7327, K 7368, K 7458–60

1. Une sainte en son auréole
2. Puisque l'aube grandit
3. La lune blanche
4. J'allais par des chemins perfides
5. J'ai presque peur
6. Avant que tu ne t'en ailles
7. Donc, ce sera par un clair jour d'été
8. N'est-ce pas?
9. L'hiver a cessé

La bonne chanson (1894), the most frequently heard of the cycles today, is a setting of nine poems by Verlaine, which describe the joy of a new and perfect love. The piece was not much liked when it was first performed. Fauré's contemporaries found it 'needlessly complex' and complained of its 'lack of order and logic'. The music is densely packed, an extreme point in Fauré's creative style both for its rapid modulations and use of tiny melodic cells, and it is no surprise to find that the score contains more instructions on tone and dynamics for the performer than any other. It would be interesting to know how rigorously singers in Fauré's day would have been expected to follow such detailed markings. The earliest recording, a highly regarded set of 78s made by Panzéra in 1936, does not find him in the mood to make much of them. In 'Une sainte et son auréole' he ignores the dynamic markings on the words 'de grâce et d'amour', turning the *forte* on 'amour' into a *piano*, and though he does provide some moments of *dolce* tone, they are rarely the ones that Fauré demands. Against that he knows how to shape a song in the most natural way and the performance is always alive with spontaneity, such as his sensual way with the memorable line 'C'est l'heure exquise'. Panzéra's virtues on this record are strong, sure technique and an idiomatic approach to the music.

His singing throws up an important feature of style. Like many artists of his generation, Panzéra observes a clear distinction between *legato* and *non-legato* phrasing, giving a variety of shape to the vocal line which has been lost by the majority of later singers. In 'J'ai presque peur', for example, he makes little attempt to mould the phrases into beautiful lines until the final words 'Que je vous aime, que je t'aime', where the notes are suddenly joined with a thread of infinite tenderness, a perfect example of the very even *legato* singing that he chooses not to employ elsewhere. No other singer delivers this first declaration of love in such a heartfelt manner. Some support for this approach comes from Jane Bathori, a singer and accompanist who studied *La bonne chanson* with Fauré. In her recollections we read that this cycle was conceived in 'the most pure and measured French style, with no *portamenti* and no excessive *rallentandi*' at all. In the light of that description perhaps even Panzéra goes too far.

From here to Souzay is a small step in terms of style. There are obvious similarities in the quality of voice, especially its weight and the natural shaping of the words, but this time it is Souzay's artistry that is the more complete of the two. His 1960 recording of *La bonne chanson* comes from the same session as *Poème d'un jour* but with far more positive results. Indeed, the performance ranks as one of the most indispensable interpretations of any Fauré song cycle on record, and it makes one think what the singer might have made of it, if he had recorded the cycle when he was in the prime of his youth. From the opening song, where Verlaine describes the girl he loves, Souzay builds up a vivid picture: a lively humour for the 'rougeurs de femme enfant', a tenderness in the 'aspects nacrés blancs et roses', an evenness of tone and slight broadening of the notes for the 'doux accord patricien'. Like the poet, we feel that we can 'see and hear all these things'. Where Panzéra found little to interest him, Souzay goes quickly to work, shaping phrases, varying their length and colour to pin down in each its full significance. The cycle has more depth, more variety, more meaning. It is also well sung, showing off an ease and fullness of tone from the softest *piano* to a fine, strong *forte*. The swift speeds keep close to Fauré's metronome markings and there is excellent support from Dalton Baldwin, who again keeps the textures of the piano accompaniment clear and light. Unfortunately Souzay's later recording in the complete HMV set is not on the same level. A comparison of 'Rêvons, c'est l'heure', the central moment of the third song, shows what has been lost: in the earlier recording the singer was able to sustain a perfectly focused, hushed tone over the arch of the whole phrase, but by 1970 the focus has gone and he has to resort to a gasp in mid-phrase to try and inject the same sort of effect. The technical details are not academic; the magic of the moment has been lost and the climax of the song has gone with it.

The same phrase is a good introduction to the recording by Hugues

Cuénod. Here the markings in the score are even more acutely observed, the hairpin *crescendo* over the words 'c'est l'heure' executed with pinpoint precision. That is typical of a performance over which much care has been taken. The words are clearly enunciated and phrases are spun out over an unusually broad span; only when *rubato* is applied with a heavy hand are liberties unexpectedly taken. What the performance lacks is romance and spontaneity. Even in the enchanting moonlight of 'La lune blanche' a feeling of intellectual rigour persists, accentuated by a tenor voice which is tense, bright and tight with vibrato, sufficiently restricted in its production to hinder the easy flow of softer colours that the music needs. Although *La bonne chanson* concentrates on one central emotion – total happiness at a new love – it does so within a complex mesh of secondary feelings, from relief at escaping an uncertain past to determination for the future. If the singer is to match the complete human picture of Verlaine's poetry, he must be able to draw on a wide palette of tone colours or inflexions in the voice.

None of the other performers on record has the range to do so. The best is the baritone Bernard Kruysen, whose swift tempi and lithe, youthful timbre work together in a fresh and unaffected reading of the score. Even here, though, variety is wanting. Perhaps if Fauré had written a cycle with obvious dramatic shape, settings and characters (like, say, Schubert's *Winterreise*) there would be less of a tendency for singers to allow all his songs to turn out the same. As it is, the music invariably comes across as pleasant and innocuous, but little else. It is no coincidence that most singers choose speeds slower than indicated. Both Pierre Mollet and Jacques Herbillon are fairly typical of this approach, making the cycle sound generally soft, relaxed and dreamy. Camille Maurane sings off the words more consistently but is rhythmically stolid and still fails to use the text to convey specific statements about the songs. Not much in Paul Derenne's version even qualifies as pleasant and innocuous, least of all the ungainly phrasing or the off-centre intonation. That leaves the 1958 recording by Dietrich Fischer-Dieskau. (The Electrola record listed by Nectoux in his discography is merely a reissue of this original.) Here we encounter a different phenomenon of interpretation: a singer of outstanding technical mastery and insight, but one who works essentially outside the French idiom. His singing of 'Une sainte et son auréole' is the slowest on record, every phrase studiously moulded and enveloped in a hazy romantic aura. The song is smothered with affection. As the cycle unfolds, countless details register but any natural, spontaneous feeling for its shape (so well grasped by Panzéra and Souzay) has been jettisoned. Even the timbre of the voice – a smooth, rounded Germanic baritone – sounds wrong by the side of so many sharp, bright Frenchmen.

The French women, what is more, sound brighter still. Although

Richard Fairman

Verlaine's poetry speaks from a male point of view, *La bonne chanson* was originally written for Emma Bardac, and Fauré accompanied female singers in it himself. The best of the women's recordings to date is the one by Suzanne Danco, a performance which was not greatly liked when it first appeared. Certainly the criticism that she does not have enough variety of tone colour is justified and one longs for the sharp edge to be taken off the voice in the more intimate moments, but the singing is fresh and straightforward with a lively response to the words. The bubbling energy she brings to 'L'hiver a cessé' shows just how much sheer joy there is in this cycle. The recording by Sophie Wyss is on the same lines, though she lacks individuality.

Elly Ameling also fails to imprint ideas on the memory, but the radiance of the voice and sensitivity of phrasing afford a degree of purely musical pleasure that is not often available elsewhere. Some of her incandescence would not come amiss on the record made by Felicity Palmer, whose strong soprano can sound hard and unlovely by comparison. Here, for a change, is a bold and direct singer, but one with little feeling for musical grace: Palmer and her accompanist really go at some of the later songs with a will, leaving the climax of 'Avant que tu ne t'en ailles' ringing in the ears. At least they are not dull.

Two of the most important recordings have not achieved full circulation. Pierre Bernac recorded *La bonne chanson* in 1945, but two of the songs – 'J'ai presque peur' and 'Avant que tu ne t'en ailles' – are believed lost and the remaining discs have never been issued. Although he may not have the vocal quality of a Souzay, Bernac is a formidably perceptive and intelligent interpreter. His book *The Interpretation of French Song* (Cassell, 1970) instructs performers on how to tackle this cycle in some detail, setting standards of discipline which these records show the author had fully mastered himself. Demands that the singer should be faithful to the score are unswervingly met. Bernac is, for example, the only singer who takes the beautiful 'La lune blanche' up to tempo and keeps it there. In addition, he gives due weight to Verlaine's poetry. A sampling of all these recordings in chronological order shows that later singers put increasing emphasis on drawing a shapely, moulded vocal line at the expense of the text; whereas Bernac, recorded at the end of the war, tips the balance decisively towards the words, using the natural colour of vowel sounds and the rhythm of the sentence to give each phrase its shape. It follows that his singing is strong in variety, capturing the moments of darkness and uncertainty in these poems with more point than anybody else. A subtle extra weight in the accompaniment and feeling for harmonic movement denote a pianist of unusual distinction in his regular partner, Francis Poulenc.

By coincidence the pianist on the other limited circulation record is also a major composer. Peter Pears and Benjamin Britten gave a performance of *La bonne chanson* at the Aldeburgh Festival in 1958 and a live recording of that has been preserved by the BBC on a transcription disc (not for public sale). Like Poulenc, Britten is not content to play a merely secondary role. Solo lines in the accompaniment are projected with sufficient weight to make them tell, the strands of melody in 'Donc, ce sera un clair jour d'été' duetting as virtual equals with the voice. At times, indeed, one senses that it is Britten's hand on the helm. 'La lune blanche' starts at an exceptionally slow tempo, so still and quiet that the audience could hardly have dared to breathe, and only moves forward at the words 'O bien aimée', where a passionate climax is built up. This goes way beyond what any other pair attempts and might well sound contrived if voice and accompaniment did not mirror each other so exactly. Given Britten's importance, it is a shame that the piano was not balanced more closely. Pears was in fresh voice at the time, but the microphone is unflattering towards his slow vibrato and neither the idiosyncratic tone nor the pronunciation sounds idiomatically French. Nobody else, however, has matched his extreme sensitivity in floating a long, slow *legato* line.

A couple of excerpts were recorded by Maggie Teyte with Gerald Moore. In the first (DA 1893), made in 1942, she offers a rather wilful account of 'L'hiver a cessé', energetically sung, but with some questionable *rubato* and the last note taken up an octave. The other (GSC 22) dates from five years later and shows a sad decline in the voice, with frayed tone and a lack of vocal control. Neither the *legato* of 'La lune blanche' nor the more varied demands of 'J'ai presque peur' is any longer within her power. It is a pity the gramophone did not catch her in this work earlier.

In 1898 Fauré was persuaded to make an arrangement of *La bonne chanson* for piano and string quartet accompaniment, a move he soon came to regret. His own preference was always for the simple piano accompaniment. Even though this version has never been published, there are three recordings of it, which repay close study. Perhaps because it is well known that Fauré himself was dissatisfied with the arrangement, other people have subsequently decided to help him out and no two of these recordings are the same. A copyist's score has been made by Fauré's publishers (Hamell) and is available for inspection. The discrepancies arise, for example, in the last section of 'Donc, ce sera': here Sarah Walker's recording follows the Hamell score; Martial Singher's record adds off-beat quavers, present in the original piano version, to the viola part; and the third recording with Fischer-Dieskau gives the off-beat quavers back to the pianist and puts the violin parts up an octave. This last version has the most differences of the three. It not only includes the optional double-bass part (despite a sleeve-note which consistently talks

Richard Fairman

about 'the quartet'), but also decides that the player looks underemployed and gives him a lot more to do. None of this is in Hamell's score.

So, to hear what Fauré wrote, the best bet is almost certainly the record with Sarah Walker. This is also a very worthwhile performance, sung in creditable French and with phrasing that is sensitive but firm, while the relatively close balance of the instruments shows off their parts to good effect. The other two recordings are less successful. Singher, much respected as the first singer of Ravel's *Don Quichotte* songs, is a disappointment, constantly under strain at the top of the voice and unreliable in intonation. Fischer-Dieskau is much improved since his earlier piano-accompanied version, especially in his French pronunciation and choice of tempi. Indeed, in the last section of 'Donc ce sera', where the poet imagines the peaceful, star-lit night after his wedding, he comes near to perfection, tracing a soft and inflected vocal line of almost unbearable tenderness. But still the interpretative ideas often sound hardworked and the wide contrasts between, or even within, songs are exaggerated. As a postscript, there is a full orchestral recording of the piece with Suzanne Stappen. This arrangement, made by Maurice Le Boucher in 1933, is so horrendous in its overcolouring of the score that the conductor Piero Coppola might well have asked himself why he was associated with it. Trilling violins and tinkling bells take over – enough to make Fauré rise from his grave and sue for damages.

La chanson d'Ève

Ameling, Baldwin	EMI 2C 165–12831–5
Curtin, Edwards	Cambridge CRS 1706
Doria, Gouat	Pléiade P 3063
Kolassi, Collard	Decca LXT 2897
Rodde, Paraskivesco	Calliope 1846
Shelton, Orkis	Nonesuch H 79106

1. Paradis
2. Prima verba
3. Roses ardentes
4. Comme Dieu rayonne
5. L'aube blanche
6. Eau vivante
7. Veilles-tu ma senteur de soleil
8. Dans un parfum de roses blanches
9. Crépuscule
10. O mort, poussière d'étoiles

La chanson d'Ève (1906–10) was planned as a pendant to the previous cycle, though the styles of the two works are poles apart. Fauré's score evokes van Lerberghe's picture of the Garden of Eden with spare textures and a rapt stillness. All but two of the songs are marked *andante* or *adagio*. From this point on Fauré slowly pares away the instructions in his scores and the pages tend to look increasingly empty of ideas, a dangerous temptation for any singer to assume that there is indeed nothing there. Recordings of *La chanson d'Ève* do not, in general, dispel this fear. Most are deficient in either personality or atmosphere to some degree. The performance by Anne-Marie Rodde is sung with affection, but its manner does not begin to enter this cycle's special world, the 'paradis bleu' of God's kingdom. Renée Doria keeps admirably close to Fauré's metronome marks, but the bright, edgy sound characteristic of so many French sopranos is heard here at its most acerbic. The Garden of Eden, of all places, deserves more beautiful singing than this. It is worth noting that Doria's pianist, Simone Gouat, plays in the old style with the left hand out of synchronisation with the right, an effect that can also be heard on Fauré's own piano rolls.

For a more sensitive appreciation of the calm and timeless mood of this cycle one might turn to Irma Kolassi, but her intonation is not exact and the slow speeds are held back still further by *rubato*. The highest level of purely musical accomplishment comes from the partnership of Elly Ameling and Dalton Baldwin, who have a genuine feeling for the beauty of the music combined with lovely tone and first-rate technique. Yet still one feels no specific contact with the substance of this poetry. The American Phyllis Curtin does try to probe further. The verses of 'Roses ardentes' are painted in different colours (darkness for the deep sea, brilliance for the sun, and so on) and in 'Veilles-tu ma senteur de soleil' she is the only one who asks the many questions in the poem as if she wants to know the answers. But too much is exaggerated and in her desire to make the words tell she invests the French text with sounds and rhythms that are not idiomatic. For a cycle that engages the senses so temptingly with the sights, smells and sounds of the Garden of Eden, *La chanson d'Ève* has not enticed many singers to bring its delights graphically to life. Souzay has recorded a couple of excerpts. On a 1964 disc (SAL 3505) he offers a refreshing 'Eau vivante' and 'O mort, poussière d'étoiles'. A later recital record (Decca 414 336 1) has 'Eau vivante' again, but with a distressing lack of vocal control. For *La chanson d'Ève* it seems that Paradise is still a long way off.

Le jardin clos

Ameling, Baldwin	EMI 2C 165–12831–5
Herbillon, Rodde, Paraskivesco	Calliope 1845

Richard Fairman

Maurane, Bienvenu	Erato EPR 15550
Monmart, Gouat	Pléiade P 3064
Pérugia, Benvenuti	French HMV DB 5157–8

1. Exaucement
2. Quand tu plonges tes yeux
3. La messagère
4. Je me poserai sur ton coeur
5. Dans la nymphée
6. Dans la pénombre
7. Il m'est cher, Amour, le bandeau
8. Inscription sur le sable

If anything, *Le jardin clos* (1914) has fared even worse. The only performance which provides a striking insight into this elusive cycle is the earliest recording, made in 1941 by Noémie Pérugia. This soprano starts with the disadvantage of an unremarkable voice with an inherent fast vibrato, but she really understands what the poems mean and her urgent delivery of the text penetrates to the secret of van Lerberghe's mysterious, walled garden. Sensuality is the emotion locked in here, its potent force quite unmistakable in the poet's erotic language. In 'La messagère', which tells of a girl meeting her sisters in the garden's dark shadows, Pérugia builds up pace and intensity in a flush of ecstatic joy. Her thrill at the words 'Tes lèvres touchent leurs lèvres' sends shivers down the back. None of the other singers matches this.

Ameling once again sings very beautifully and uses her slow speeds to explore the strange harmonies of the piece in greater depth. Maurane finds a fairy-tale atmosphere for the opening of the cycle but cannot sustain an even *legato* without letting odd words or consonants protrude. In Calliope's complete set the songs are shared by Herbillon and Rodde, but their combined intelligence does not come up with much to say about the songs. Their performance is brisk, sweetly sung and superficial. Berthe Monmart's recording is almost painful in its lack of vocal control, the low point in a disappointing series. There are a couple of excerpts. On a disc devoted to music in the time of Proust (Arion ARN 37169) Michel Carey sings 'Inscription sur le sable' in a pleasing, light baritone. Souzay and Baldwin (SAL 3505) offer 'Exaucement' and 'Je me poserai sur ton coeur' with their usual understanding. Surprisingly there is no complete recording of Souzay in this cycle. It is also a shame that the gramophone did not capture anything from *Le jardin clos* with Claire Croiza, who gave the first performance of the work with Fauré at the piano in 1915. In her book of reminiscences she recalls that Fauré was 'a walking metronome', accompanying her with an unrelenting drive that bore no relation to any expression or shading in his music. The generous *rubato* heard in some of these later recordings would clearly not have appealed to him.

Mirages

Daniels, Benvenuti	L'Oiseau Lyre OL 27–8
Derenne, Cox	Pléiade P 3064
Gehrman, Walker	Nimbus 45001–4
Herbillon, Paraskivesco	Calliope 1845
Kolassi, Bonneau	Lumen LD 2406
Kruysen, Lee	Telefunken SAT 22546
Maurane, Bienvenu	Erato EPR 15550
Pérugia, Bon	Voxigrave V 6929–31
Reinhart, Baldwin	Harmonia Mundi HM 1117
Souzay, Baldwin (I)	Philips SAL 3505
Souzay, Baldwin (II)	EMI 2C 165–12831–5

1. Cygne sur l'eau
2. Reflets dans l'eau
3. Jardin nocturne
4. Danseuse

L'horizon chimérique

Allen, Vignoles	Hyperion A 66165
Anspach, Visell	Pavane ADW 7046
Bastin, Van Den Driersche	Pavane ADW 7038
Carey, Curé	Solstice MNO 5
Herbillon, Paraskivesco	Calliope 1845
Kruysen, Lee	Valois MB 765
Maurane, Bienvenu	Erato EPR 15550
Mollet, Gouat	Pléiade P 3064
Martin, Brilli	Colosseum SM 636
Panzéra, Panzéra-Baillot (I)	HMV DB 4972
Panzéra, Panzéra-Baillot (II)	HMV DB 5009; EMI 2C 153–12 845–6
Panzéra, Panzéra-Baillot (III)	Mercury MG 10097
Reinhart, Baldwin	Harmonia Mundi HM 1117
Singher, Gilchrist	1750 Arch S 1754
Souzay, Damase	Decca K 1693
Souzay, Bonneau	Decca LXT 2543
Souzay, Baldwin (I)	Philips SAL 3505
Souzay, Baldwin (II)	EMI 2C 165–12831–5

Richard Fairman

1. La mer est infinie
2. Je me suis embarqué
3. Diane, Séléné
4. Vaisseaux, nous vous aurons aimés

In the last two cycles – *Mirages* (1919) and *L'horizon chimérique* (1921) – the musical style has been refined to the furthest point of simplicity. The questing harmonies have gone and the vocal lines seem to do little more than follow the intonation of speech, yet Fauré has used this very ordinary basic material to explore inward-looking emotions with ever greater depth and subtlety. Over this music lies the shroud of a deep 'ennui', personified in *Mirages* by a black swan which longs to glide off in search of strange lands, perfumed gulfs and immortal isles. Of all Fauré's song cycles, this is the most visionary and illusive. Two recordings, by Kruysen and Souzay, demand attention, though the character of their performances is quite different, as a direct comparison of 'Jardin nocturne' shows. Here, as always, Kruysen's singing is exquisitely poised. The single phrase 'en des voiles d'or fluides et légers' is a model of vocal control, its liquid consonants cleverly bound into the vocal line, the tone as fluid and light as the golden veils it describes. Souzay cannot equal this, for by 1964 his voice was apt to lose its focus in quiet singing and become breathy. Yet, as the song progresses, he stirs its emotional depths: an increase in sensual warmth at the 'caresses sensibles', a quiet affection for 'votre paix délectable' and a powerful release of intensity as he reaches the words 'vos charmes troublés de désirs et d'ennui', the central emotion of the cycle. With singing like this it is made quite clear that the pictures we are shown are not to be taken literally, but as visual representations of the poet's innermost feelings. None of that is evident in Kruysen's performance. For him the song is just a simple watercolour to be tinted and shaded with delicacy and there is inevitably little of the cumulative power that makes Souzay's recording, as a whole, so compelling. How marvellous Souzay is in the last song too, rhythmic and light, magical and evocative. The last words 'Vaine danseuse' hold a world of understatement. As before, his later recording, made in 1974 as part of HMV's complete set, does not have the technical control to equal his earlier achievement.

The other recordings of *Mirages* rarely make the listener think what the songs mean. Herbillon's performance is cleanly sung and sensitive, the surface calm of the music attractively presented. Kolassi and Maurane dig a little deeper into the words but still fail to pin down specific emotions. Despite obvious signs of diligence in preparation Gregory Reinhart's singing is a touch too prosaic for songs so far-sighted in their visions. Lise Daniels is ordinary. Derenne, for all his fine reputation in this field, sounds unpleasantly hard and bright, while his fast tempo for 'Jardin nocturne' is insensitive in the extreme. Shura Gehrman rolls the French nasal sounds round his mouth and generally lets his imagination run riot. None of them fully gets to grips with the special sentiments of lost opportunity and desire for the unknown which make this cycle so compelling. Unfortunately I have not been able to track down a copy of the live recording made by Pérugia, who did just that in *Le jardin clos*. There are a couple of recordings of excerpts. The earliest is a 1936 record of 'Jardin nocturne' (DA 4889) with Bernac and Poulenc, distinguished by the clean enunciation of the text and complete fidelity to the score that one would expect. 'Cygne sur l'eau' is sung in an outgoing manner by Yvon le Marc' Hadour with Maroussia le Marc' Hadour as his accompanist (Boite à Musique 31).

L'horizon chimérique is the only cycle in which we have the chance of hearing the singer for whom the piece was written on record. This work was dedicated to the French baritone Charles Panzéra in 1921. Over the next 45 years he made four recordings of the cycle, three complete and one incomplete, and also included advice on how to perform it in his book *Mélodies françaises*, a teaching manual on the French song repertoire. The earliest of the records is the single disc featuring 'Je me suis embarqué' and 'Diane, Séléne', made in 1925 (P 519), only three years after the work was published. In this the young Panzéra gives his best account of the songs on record. The chapter in his book recommends that 'Je me suis embarqué' be sung with 'a certain harshness' in the striking of the syllables and 'a kind of severity' in the voice, both of which are magnificently heard here with a bite to the consonants and strong, masculine cut to the vocal timbre. Perhaps the most striking thing about Panzéra, as always, is that he has no time for the wan, pretty style affected by so many singers in this repertoire. The complete recording of 1936 is much the same. Panzéra's way with the music is fresh and spontaneous, going straight to the high point of the song without fussing over passing detail. *Portamento* is sparingly used and then only when he wants a special effect. Later singers, by comparison, sound smooth and over-indulgent. The singer defends the way he slows up in the great last phrase of the cycle by saying that Fauré advised a *rallentando* privately, even though he was frightened to print one in case the effect became exaggerated. The last of Panzéra's recordings, made in 1952, is disappointing. The voice no longer goes what he wants and the sharp edge to the singing has become blunted.

Many of this artist's strengths can also be heard in the singing of Souzay – the same clarity of text, the same vocal strength, the same sure focus. Souzay recorded *L'horizon chimérique* four times, and in these records, made over a span of 25 years, we can chart the progress of his career from its extraordinary early successes to the slow vocal decline of the later years. The first two performances, dating from 1948 and 1950, count among the finest records of French *mélodies*. Brilliant and biting in its attack, the voice sounds ideally suited to this bracing, sea-borne cycle. The tone speaks immediately with no wasted breath in between the consonant and the vowel. If the first recording can sometimes seem a trifle stiff or formal, its inhibitions are soon cast off in the second, where Souzay finds a multitude of inflexions to colour the text: in the second song he varies the mood with an unexpected sadness to the line 'A vivre parmi vous, hélas!' and, at the end, allows a broad *legato* to cast a heartfelt shadow of regret over the words 'ou vous ai-je laissée'. (This goes against the advice of Panzéra, who recommends that the line be kept at *forte* until the last syllable.) By the time of the 1964 recording much of this power and spontaneity has been lost. The poor balance between the voice and piano, as with *Mirages* on the same disc, does not help. In that respect the 1974 HMV set is to be preferred, as it keeps the singer to the fore. The singing here is also more than a shadow of its former self, a remarkable tribute to three decades of outstanding performances in this field.

Both Panzéra and Souzay seize these songs by the throat. The 'air and salt' and the 'foam of the sea', which give this cycle its special character, come across with a vigorous, outdoor energy in their singing, quite enough to make all the other performances sound tame by comparison. Pierre Mollet is gentle and affecting, as before, but does not generate enough power for the long phrases of these songs. In 'La mer est infinie' Maurane even takes the early climaxes *piano* instead of *forte* as marked, though it is interesting to note that he is the only singer to span the whole of the great final phrase of the cycle in one breath. Kruysen sounds taxed by 'Je me suis embarqué', where his vibrato loosens under pressure, but he makes a typically fine job of the hushed 'Diane, Séléné'. He also rises to the challenge of the last song with some powerful, committed singing. Singher, 70 by the time of his recording, is too unsteady to do himself justice. For no apparent reason he changes the rhythm of 'Diane, Séléné'. Lightness of voice, swift speeds and a welcome eagerness to communicate the words keep up the interest in Herbillon's performance. Thomas Allen is too cautious and soft-grained. More grit and salt sea air are needed here. Reinhart is fortunate to have Baldwin as his perceptive, idiomatic accompanist, but for all the singer's sterling work there is a lack of vocal colour and spontaneity. Jules Bastin sings with a cultured, light bass timbre and shapes the music in long, elegant paragraphs. I have not been able to hear the recordings by Martin or Anspach. Fauré is reputed to have said that it was amateurs who sang his songs best. So far only a handful of professionals on record have proven him wrong.

Debussy

'Complete' recording

Ameling, Command, Mesplé, von Stade, Souzay/Baldwin	EMI 2C 165 16371/4

Records solely devoted to Debussy

Cuénod, Isepp	Nimbus 2127
Danco, Agosti (*Fêtes I*, Villon)	Decca LW 5145
Danco, Agosti (the other songs)	Decca LX 3052
Kolassi, Collard	Decca 417 559
Kruysen, Richard	Valois MB 729
Kruysen, Lee	Telefunken SAT 22540; Astrée AS 58
Laurent, Arbaretaz	Harmonia Mundi HMC 5150
Pons, Laforge	Victor 1905; Am. Col. ML 2135
Souzay, Orchestre de la Société des Concerts du Conservatoire/Lindenburg	Decca LXT 2566
Souzay, Baldwin (1962)	DG SLPM 138 758
Souzay, Baldwin (1972)	EMI 2C 065 12049
Teyte, Cortot and Moore	HMV 2904 021
Wend, Lee	Valois MB 407

Debussy wrote at least 85 songs for solo voice with piano – undoubtedly more (and at least one duet). All but 22 were composed by 1892, when he turned thirty: before even the String Quartet and *L'après-midi d'un faune*, long before the *Nocturnes* and *Pelléas* and the mature piano music, almost a quarter of a century before the *Études* and the chamber sonatas. Until quite recently only fifty-five songs had been published, including all the 'mature' ones, but more and more of the songs of Debussy's twenties – and even of his 'teens – are becoming available. So far as the songs are concerned, 'mature' needs its inverted commas because so many of the

David Murray

pre-1890 ones are as assured and polished as they are fresh: unlike his tamely derivative piano music of the same period, they are 'immature' only by the reckoning of hindsight – they offer only meagre clues to the composer that Debussy was to become.

Quite rightly, singers have not been historically snobbish about them. Many of them make severe technical demands (young Debussy favoured high sopranos with *coloratura* skills), but they promise dividends of immediate effect and charm. Some have been much recorded: a baker's dozen by Mady Mesplé in the EMI album (of which more below), expertly bright, more by Anne-Marie Rodde – tidy, interpretatively cautious performances with some strain in high places – and four by Edita Gruberova, whose practised glitter shows how well these early songs can do without the nuances of 'mature' Debussy style. There are many more recordings of individual songs which I set aside with regret.

For lovers of Debussy the 'complete' EMI album of the songs must be indispensable, uneven though it is. Its guiding spirit was Gérard Souzay; I take his performances of *Fêtes galantes II*, *Le promenoir des deux amants* and the Villon *Ballades* to be identical with his much earlier EMI versions, though with enhanced sound. I shall discuss only the song-sets (hardly 'cycles': Debussy came to favour triptychs), but that does not incur very grave omissions – after his burst of song-publishing around 1890, which involved some much earlier songs as well as the new *Poèmes* after Baudelaire, I skip over only a Verlaine trio, three odd songs, the two *Chansons de France* after Charles d'Orléans and the 1915 'Noël des enfants qui n'ont plus de maison', patriotically mawkish to the composer's own words.

There is a general impression of what Debussy songs are like (Anna Russell is partly responsible), but in fact from the *Proses lyriques* forward none of Debussy's sets has much in common with any other. Ravel's songs divide neatly into the sets, which mark decisive points in his development, and the marginal one-offs; *all* Debussy's 'mature' songs are marginal to the progressive steps registered in his music for piano and for orchestra, and in the opera *Pelléas et Mélisande*. He set only poetry that seized his imagination, and never used it to his latest revolutionary ends. From 1892, seventeen productive years added only the *Proses lyriques*, the *Bilitis* songs, *Fêtes galantes II* and the *Chansons de France* to his song output; from 1910 onward there are only *Le promenoir des deux amants* (which filched one of the *Chansons de France*), the Villon and Mallarmé sets and the unhappy last 'Noël'.

Of all the early songs, only the Verlaine 'Mandoline' demands inclusion. Debussy composed it at twenty, while revisiting the family of Nadezhda von Meck – Tchaikovsky's great patroness – in Vienna. It is an unimprovable setting, and a pre-emptive strike against Fauré (always perceived by Debussy as an Establishment stifler), whose elegant, wryly detached version appeared almost a decade later (q.v.). Fauré's is a pure words-and-music serenade; Debussy's loses none of Verlaine's irony, but it invites the singer to be swept along with the mannered parade, to surrender to the thrill that it mocks.

The earliest recordings of it are by Lillian Nordica – whose version (Am. Col. 30657–1; SYO 6) sounds quite crazy now, casually rewritten and subjected to bizarre switches of tempo – and by Nellie Melba (DB 709), small and tight and very slow. The young Lily Pons (DA 1726) sounds hasty and rushed, though very free with pauses; her later recording (Am. Col. ML 2135) is tamer but clumsier. Irène Joachim, a distinguished Mélisande, is thin and innocent (BAM 54/5), though much more expert; Géori Boué (Urania URLP 7070), neatly articulate, is flat on quick top notes; Roger Bourdin (Odéon 123 670), using the Beydts orchestration, is elegantly languid to the point of seeming to doze off at the end. Gladys Swarthout's late attempt (RCA LM 1793) was a frightful mistake.

The more recent versions are generally happier. Nan Merriman (EX 29 0654 3) is suavely excellent at a moderate tempo; Phyllis Curtin's *faux-naïf* manner is pretty and suggestive (Cambridge CRM 706). Caballé is brisk to the point of heartiness (Vergara L 110005), and Gedda's lively intelligence is a touch over-emphatic (ASD 2574). Ceasar Valletti's crisp flexibility (RB 6622) wants more wit (and a less cack-handed pianist); Sarah Walker (Unicorn DKP 9035) and Hugues Cuénod (Nimbus 2137), stylish though they are, fall short of the essential brilliance. Anna Moffo (RCA LSC 3225) is pointedly clever, even arch, but not so elegant as Souzay; neither is Fischer-Dieskau (SLPM 138 115), though he is daringly quick, and captures precisely the feeling of *emportement*. Schwarzkopf (SAX 5268), wielding a lot of self-conscious vocal colour, fails to sparkle. Elly Ameling (Philips 412 628–1) offers a breathless on-the-spot report by a featherhead, not a bad act.

That leaves us with Souzay and Bernard Kruysen, who between them can claim many of the best recorded Debussy performances since the last World War. In 'Mandoline' Kruysen is more enigmatic than Souzay, a little less dashing – but it is a lovely performance. Souzay has offered at least three versions: most recently with Dalton Baldwin in the EMI album, delightful despite some loss of voice and of panache, earlier and even better on DG, and best of all with Edouard Lindenberg and the Paris Conservatoire orchestra (LXT 2568) – a performance of unequalled vitality, poise and wit. It sets a standard.

Now to the song-sets, among which the first book of the *Fêtes galantes* and the six *Ariettes oubliées* include songs written long before the publications of the two collections. In both, all the texts are by Verlaine.

93

There are at least ten recordings of *Fêtes I*. Maggie Teyte's (DA 1471–3; 2904021), with Cortot in 1936, is authoritative and direct, if hardly spontaneous. Merriman, with Gerald Moore (EX 29 0654 3), is sombrely intense in 'En sourdine', refined and romantic in 'Clair de lune' (both poems also set by Fauré), a trifle slow and effortful in the middle 'Fantoches'. In the latter song Moffo (RCA LSC 3225), with her accompanist Jean Casadesus at his (rare) best, is cleverly light and playful, though her manner in the outer songs – creamily romantic – is so different as to imply play-acting in all three. Charlotte Lehmann (1C 065 46356) is sensuous in 'En sourdine', loudly exuberant in 'Fantoches', fervent and slightly flat in 'Clair de lune'. With Noël Lee, Flore Wend (Valois MB 407) flanks her bright, airborne 'Fantoches' with a less remarkable 'En sourdine' (too simple) and 'Clair de lune' (thoughtful but frail). Ameling's 'En sourdine', in the EMI album, is sincere but lightweight, 'Fantoches' calculatedly charming; 'Clair de lune' runs along pleasantly, but the words get vaguer and vaguer. Noël Lee – as recorded – offers a thunderous accompaniment to Anne-Marie Rodde's 'Fantoches', and her carefully plain 'En sourdine' matches her innocently pretty 'Clair de lune' all too well (Etcetera ETC 1026). Much like Barbara Hendricks, she is too self-effacingly respectful to leave her own stamp upon any song, though everything she does is attractive and in unimpeachable good taste. Hendricks (EL 27 0294 1) allows herself more open involvement in 'Clair de lune', just where her stylish pianist Michel Béroff becomes prosaic. Her sedulous French lapses on high notes and at speed.

All three of the remaining *Fêtes I* recordings leave deeper impressions, at least as wholes. Though the set is clearly designed for a high voice, Souzay's suppressed intensity in 'En sourdine' is gripping, and the marvellous lyrical swing that he finds in 'Fantoches' is answered by his wistful serenading in 'Clair de lune' (which makes any un-serenadish version sound square). Victoria de los Angeles (ASD 2287) is liquid but also pungent in the first song, deliciously fined-down in the second, and in the third she offers a beautiful view downward from a great height. Suzanne Danco (Decca LW 5145) – with the priceless musical assistance of Guido Agosti, a superlative Debussy pianist – follows a superbly poised, restrained 'En sourdine' with a good, lively 'Fantoches' and a most elevated 'Clair de lune'.

The individual songs of *Fêtes I* have not been neglected. Jacques Jansen's lightly mocking, urbane 'Fantoches' (LXT 2774) is let down by Mlle Bonneau's rather ordinary piano; Madeleine Dubuis' (DA 6012–3) is neat and pretty, Michel Sénéchal's (Philips N 00681 R) very exactly pointed. Irma Kolassi's resembles Merriman's, with the addition of slick period swoops (and a heavier piano), but her 'En sourdine' is impressively opulent. There Melba – at 50 – sounds limply passive, not really at home

(IRCC 35). Neither Pons version is convincing, and her 'Clair de lune' is appealing without the aid of anything like interpretation. Valletti's carefully attractive account (RB 6622) ignores atmosphere. Like Souzay, Curtin (Cambridge CRS 1706) makes it a serenade, but rapt and visionary; her dark, coolly impassioned 'En sourdine' is probably designed to contrast with her lightly romantic Fauré setting, since it shares her record with that and the other five Verlaine songs set by both composers.

There are many accounts of individual *Ariettes oubliées*, but only nine of the whole set. In the EMI album of the (provisionally) 'complete' Debussy songs, Frederica von Stade's *Ariettes* stand out as wilfully personal. Her 'C'est l'extase langoureuse' is indeed that (and very Artistic), her 'Il pleure dans mon coeur' – very swift – displays some odd French, and 'Green' and 'Spleen' are comparably idiosyncratic; 'Chevaux de bois' gets a heavily accented accompaniment from Dalton Baldwin. There is even less verve in Halina Lukomska's 'Chevaux', and she manifestly fails to understand what 'Spleen' is about, though her 'C'est l'extase' is warmly seductive and her 'Green' shyly, attractively hesitant; her 'L'ombre' is gluey, her 'Il pleure . . . ' slow and verbally indeterminate (Muza SXL 1050). Hendricks, as before, is graceful, shy about adding colour, reluctant to seize any phrase too firmly – rather than *making* the music, she follows it at a loyal distance. An anxious question, 'Was that all right?' is continually implied; generally it was, but one would like not to have been asked.

Charlotte Lehmann (1C 065 46356) is consistently mild, but more solid: a smooth 'Extase', a poised 'Ombre des arbres', 'Green' warm and simple. Some spark is missed. Her 'Il pleure . . . ' is *very* slow, unlike Ameling's; in other respects their *Ariettes* are rather similar. Ameling's 'Spleen' is prettily morose (both singers betray some strain at the climax), her 'Green' charmingly effusive, her 'Chevaux de bois' lively and confiding. Flore Wend (Valois MB 407), with Noël Lee, is better still with an extra touch of horse-power in that song, and she offers a *soigné* 'Extase' and a flowing, subtle 'Ombre'.

I value most highly two performances. With Poulenc as accompanist, Lucienne Tragin (Col. LFX 650–1; 2C 047 12538) lends a beautiful timbre to her knowing 'Extase', flirts delightfully in 'Green' and puts a haunted shadow over the fading 'Chevaux'. In 'Il pleure . . . ' she is expressive over Poulenc's quick, unyielding accompaniment (much like Debussy's: see below), and though she too is taxed by 'Spleen' she makes something tensely personal of it. Suzanne Danco (Decca LX 3052) manages 'Spleen' more easily and no less vididly, again with Agosti's exquisite playing, and each other *Ariette* is graced with her intelligence, her elegant simplicity and her transparent style.

Of the *Ariettes* recorded separately, Mary Garden's 1904 perform-

ances with Debussy (33448–52; CHS 7 61038 2) have to be revered.
In 'Il pleure . . . ' Debussy confirms Poulenc's impersonal briskness (the
piano is only the rain, not the grieving heart); there Garden is svelte, with
a quaver, and they make 'L'Ombre' as fascinating and persuasive as their
'Green' is excitably eager. (The recording is noisy, but the voice at least is
quite clear.) The redoubtable Jane Bathori accompanied herself as well as
other singers – she was a favoured interpreter of many composers: her
own duet-performance of 'Extase' is a beautiful dry sketch (Col. LF 50;
FCX 50030), and with her accompaniment in 'Green' Joachim (BAM 55)
sounds delighted, fresh and full-voiced. 'Green' suited Lily Pons particularly well (her second recording is more winsome), and even in 1941
Maggie Teyte sounded bright in it, if also stretched. Phyllis Curtin's is
sophisticated and mercurial, and Eileen Farrell's astonishingly light and
vernal – irresistible, I think (Am. Col. MS 6524). By contrast Boué
(Urania URLP 7070) is sober and clever, almost abrasive. The only male
recording is by Souzay (DG 138758), marvellously balanced with the
piano and winningly eager.

Souzay has also recorded 'Chevaux de bois' (DG SLPM 138758), with
more vitality than mischief, hyper-delicate toward the end. Poulenc also
recorded 'L'Ombre', 'Extase' and 'Il pleure . . . ' with Geneviève Touraine
(BAM LD 012): keenly expressive in the first, hushed and intense in the
second, gently sensitive – with Poulenc unbending a little – in the third.
Hugues Cuénod sustains 'L'Ombre' gently and perfectly, and manages a
forceful climax. Jennie Tourel (Col. LB 125) recorded a refined, ravishing
'Extase', notably attentive to the words, and a goodish 'Il pleure . . . ' – less
subjectively felt, and less effective, than Curtin's (with beautiful playing
by Ryan Edwards), less sharp-edged and assured than Boué's, far less vital
than Claire Croiza's (with Poulenc again) (Col. D 13084; ALP 2115) –
where Pons merely pipes away. There remain three versions of 'Extase' to
mention: slow ones by Caballé (Vergara L 110005) (cultivated and very
definite) and Valletti (RCA RB 6622) (sensitive in a generalised sort of
way), and Curtin's languorous account – a bit shrill in places – with much
vibrato and many *frissons*.

With the *Cinq poèmes de Charles Baudelaire*, published at about the
same time as the *Ariettes* and *Fêtes I* but composed closer together as a
cycle, we reach the newly developing Debussy, a precociously proficient
composer suddenly inspired by Wagner – and by a poet of grand rhetori-
cal power. The poems are long, and of intricate structure; Debussy rose to
the new formal challenge as none of his interpreters on record – or rather
his *pairs* of interpreters, for the piano parts are musically demanding – has
so far done. Cuénod, with the excellent Martin Isepp, is perceptive but
frail: he has to be cautious at climaxes, and the late-Romantic surge isn't
felt. Michèle Command (in the EMI 'complete' album) and Lukomska

(Muza SXL 1050) both improve from the third song onward, but Command makes an impression more of steadiness than of depth and Lukomska's phrasing is short-breathed. Command gains from Dalton Baldwin's confidently stylish accompaniments, and Lukomska from Godziszewski's moment-to-moment energy. Hendricks is yet again fluently sinceire, without muscle, bite, irony or any large, decisive shaping: Béroff's piano supplies helpful authority, but Baudelaire's poems absolutely require more knowing declamation than this.

Colette Herzog has recorded the Baudelaire set twice. With Jean Laforge (Inédits 995 020) she is purposeful and light, but also lightweight (the resonance of the texts is diminished); with the veteran Jacques Février (DG SLPM 138822) she seems to acquire an appealing, definite *persona*, disarmingly simple, by way of a defence against Février's aggressively rich, forward, unpredictable playing. Their uncomfortable partnership strikes sparks, but nothing much like a consistently pointed reading. The only other complete recording of the Baudelaire *Poèmes* is by Anna Moffo (RCA LSC 3225), speedier than the others and sharper in a *prima donna* sort of way – her accompanist is Jean Casadesus, whose cultivated discretion fixes him as a lesser partner. In this cycle there *is* no lesser partner; we still await equal partners who will do justice to the scale of Debussy's conceptions and to the (erotic) depth of Baudelaire's poems.

Only the astutely shaped 'Jet d'eau' has been separately recorded, always quite happily. Souzay is subtle, acutely attentive to the grand shape of the song; Maggie Teyte – admittedly elderly-sounding and 'dated' – is less dignified and more pressing, but still insightful. Croiza (this time with Ivana Meedintiano (Col. LFX 109; ALP 2115) is flexibly strong and affecting, with a wonderful timbre, and Merriman (with Gerald Moore (EX 29 0654 3) delivers the song with magisterial dignity and polish.

After the Baudelaire cycle came the four *Proses lyriques*, to Debussy's own texts. Two of those prose-poems were sufficiently attuned to avant-garde literary tastes to earn publication on their own, but none of the four – derivative, quirky and feline by turns – has a strong form. You might expect Debussy-the-composer to make explicit what Debussy-the-poet leaves evasively half-realised. It isn't so: the composer's freewheeling new style, with only intuitive connections between successive passages, precisely needed precise texts as foundations, not effusions like his own 'Proses'. Interpreters find themselves without clear guidance, though many an imaginative passage calls up an imaginative response.

That must explain why singers have been so shy of recording them. Of the five complete accounts, Maggie Teyte's is a composite – 'De grève' recorded in 1936 with Cortot, the other songs with Moore in 1940. Moore is palpably a less sophisticated partner, in what was the most advanced piano-writing Debussy dared to publish by 1893. Teyte's model diction, composed manner and directness have the effect of simplifying the songs. Dalton Baldwin makes an aggressively forward partner for Ameling (again in the EMI album), who is whitish in 'De rêve', suave in 'De grève', elegiac and then violent, even harsh, in 'De fleurs' and oddly, deliberately child-like – while Baldwin continues hyper-energetic – in 'De soir'.

Francine Laurent, a Joachim pupil, is consistently interesting, with her creamy, languid tone contrasted against an accompaniment (by Marie-Claude Arbaretaz) of a crisp Ravellian cast (Harmonia Mundi HMC 5150). With another insistent pianist, Ulf Björlin, Dorothy Dorow (SCLP 1019) manages very telling changes of mood – excellent for defining the forms of the songs – despite strained climaxes in 'De rêve' and 'De fleurs'. Jill Gomez, with John Constable, is *hors concours*: vividly personal in everything (with some exceedingly peculiar vowels), fascinating throughout. So bold a re-creation must be controversial, but it is just what the *Proses lyriques* deserve (Saga 5389).

There is no single recording of 'De rêve'. Sarah Walker (Hyperion A 66165) gives a sensible account of 'De grève', but Roger Vignoles' accompaniment is bumpy. In 'De soir' Souzay begins alert and vital, calms gracefully but lavishes too much voice on phrases in the epilogue. Bidu Sayão (Odyssey Y 33130) recorded a striking 'De fleurs', fretful and irresistibly keen.

Four years later came the *Chansons de Bilitis*, on texts by Debussy's exotically-inclined friend Pierre Louÿs. They presage *Pelléas* unmistakably, but their glassy eroticism is quite special. Since they sit comfortably on most female voices, there are twice as many complete *Bilitis* recordings as of any other Debussy song set. As the Sapphic name suggests, the songs are mock-classical confessions: 'La flûte de Pan' reports a tremulous erotic spark at a clandestine meeting, 'La chevelure' (like Mélisande's) inspires a piercing transport, and in 'Le tombeau de Naïades' Bilitis hunts a satyr in winter but finds (probably) only a knowing man. This ambiguous last song is the most difficult to shape; the narration in the last two songs includes some direct male address; all three, like the *Proses*, are free-form, with flexible, magical accompaniments that blaze up briefly.

With the admirable Cortot, Teyte is a poised narrator in the outer songs, taut and ravished – with lots of *portamento* – in 'La chevelure'. Singing to her own piano, Bathori (Col. D 13086; FCX 50030) is no less stylish, and her naturalness is disarming; she also accompanies Joachim's quick, alert, excited Bilitis (BAM 54–55). There are two other Bilitises in the Mélisande mould: Madeleine Dubuis (DA 6012–3) vulnerably naïve, her simplicity shadowed by things unspoken, and Flore Wend (Valois MB 407) – in a superb performance with Noël Lee – transparently girlish, clear and bright, ecstatic in 'Chevelure'. Danco's luminous modesty and grace are enhanced by Agosti's rapturous piano: another treasurable recording.

Régine Crespin (SXL 6333) brings candid maturity to her performance – a beautifully steady 'Flûte' with a sudden intimation of worry at the end, a 'Chevelure' of great, contained passion and dignity, an unerringly purposeful 'Naïades'. In a similar vein, Irma Kolassi's vibrant warmth somehow misses the poignant surrender in 'La chevelure'. There, Marilyn Horne (Decca SXL 6577) is less a Bilitis than a Dalila; in all the songs her cultivated dramatic effects get heavy-handed accompaniment. Like her, Janet Baker (ASD 2590) is over-expansive in 'Naïades' – but it has its own conviction, despite a mannered air, like her gently plangent 'Flûte' and strong, clever 'Chevelure'.

Of the darker voices, Merriman (EX 29 0654 3) also benefits from Gerald Moore's partnership, and her controlled sensuousness is potent. Her *Bilitis* is crowned by an inspired 'Chevelure', where the lover's speech assumes her voice completely and eerily – 'Que je devenais toi-même' indeed! Sarah Walker (Unicorn DKP 9035) is more sensible than sensuous, though her shapely 'Chevelure' has a fine post-coital coda, and a conversational note is missed in her urgent 'Naïades'. In the EMI album Command is honest and decorous, but makes nothing much of 'Naïades'; neither does Julia Hamari (Hungaroton SLPX 12406), whose generally lush sound (with a tame piano) discloses no specific point in *any* of the songs, nor does von Stade – but her delicately troubled 'Flûte' is good, and her total-surrender 'Chevelure' is a memorably haunting experience.

Of two Jennie Tourel recordings, the one reissued on Odyssey Y 32882 (with swimmy piano-sound) doesn't flatter her ageing voice, though as pedagogy it is admirable; she casts a more effective spell with James Levine – free and insightful – as her pianist (Desto DC 7118). Nadine Credi (Pye GSGC 14031) is pedagogical too, and unappetisingly dry. Anna Moffo's hushed, subtle 'Flûte' and sexy 'Chevelure' lead to a languidly non-committal 'Naïades' (RCA LSC 3225). Elly Ameling's *Bilitis* is among her best performances, with an eager 'Flûte' and 'Chevelure' – rapt and persuasive – and a 'Naïades' in which the dialogue is neatly rendered, with musical intimations of an antique rite. Victoria de los Angeles is bright, even febrile in that song, almost too overtly dramatic in 'La chevelure', irresistibly fetching in 'La flûte' (ASD 2287).

There are single recordings only of 'La chevelure'. Rosa Ponselle's 1957 version (RCA LM 2047) is formidable, almost carnivorous; Eileen Farrell's (Am. Col. MS 6524) is beautifully curved and suspended, acutely felt, with a daringly stretched-out conclusion.

I pass over the 1904 *Trois chansons de France*, from which Debussy later subtracted the Tristan Lhermite 'La grotte' for inclusion in *Le promenoir des deux amants*. But in the same year came the second set of Verlaine *Fêtes galantes*, much less like the earlier *Fêtes* than like the *Bilitis* songs – although sadder, wryer, more detached, tonally ambiguous. Again the earliest recording is by Bathori (Col. D 15196; FCX 50030), dry-eyed and very straight. Teyte, with Cortot, offers magisterial diction and fine, dark colour in all three songs, and some special damping device (Kleenex between the strings?) lends an uncanny quality to the throbbing bass of 'Le faune'. Teyte and Cortet are now on CD (CHS 7 61038 2).

That quality is missed in Charlotte Lehmann's 'Faune', but her bright, passionate 'Les ingénus' and sensitive 'Colloque sentimental' are excellent (1C 065 46356). For Sarah Walker (Unicorn DKP 9035), Roger Vignoles is more aptly dry in 'Le faune'; she dramatises 'Les ingénus' better still, and is both livelier and more sentimental in the 'Colloque'. Souzay and Kruysen have both recorded *Fêtes II* twice. On DG Souzay's 'Ingénus' is brilliant and teasing, less mature than his ripely definitive EMI account (borrowed for the later album), his earlier 'Faune' faster and more secretive, the disembodied *repliques* of the 'Colloque' gently remote rather than (as later) infinitely weary. Though Kruysen's 'Colloques' – the first with Jean-Charles Richard, the second with Lee – are similarly contrasted, he makes more of the dialogue; his fine earlier 'Ingénus' acquires speed and a sharper mocking edge later, as well as more of a dying fall, and 'Le faune' becomes more whimsical, brisker, much less distanced.

Among the versions of single songs, Pierre Bernac's 'Colloque' (DB 6386) begins touchingly frail; the central dialogue gets an eager First Voice, all yearning, against a dull, bemused Second Voice – these ghostly past lovers are very plain and very moving. In the same song as orchestrated, the great Charles Panzéra (DA 5015) lets the orchestra (under Jean Fournet) suggest the former raptures while he reports the dialogue evenly, with bitten lip. A Farrell version of 'Faune' (Am. Col. MS 6524) is lovely to hear, but detached from any evocative sense.

The next six years, up to the publication of *Le promenoir des deux amants*, saw the definitive fixing of Debussy's mature orchestral and piano style: from then, his songs were suggestive but reticent exercises, unlike the Mallarmé songs or the *Chansons madécasses* of Ravel, and they have to be taken on their own modest, introspective terms. Teyte recorded *Le promenoir* with Cortot – a solemn, full-voiced 'Grotte', 'Crois mon conseil, chère Climène' warm and mild (Cortot goes deeper), 'Je tremble en voyant ton visage' as closely felt but equally cautious at climaxes. The other female versions are Kolassi's – 'La grotte' deliberate and deep, 'Climène' attractively tender, a candid, dignified 'Je tremble . . . ', all with refined support from André Collard; Baker's (ASD 2590) – a sincere, dullish 'Grotte', a merely superficial 'Climène', an exacerbated 'Je tremble . . . '; and Danco's with a marvellous account of the last song to cap her quietly intense 'Grotte' and intimate 'Climène' (where Agosti shines). Walker's 'La grotte', by itself, is cool and tasteful.

Among the male interpreters Bernac (with Poulenc) (Am. Col. ML 4484) is uncharacteristically stagey and effusive, though his 'Climène' is keenly pointed. With orchestra, Roger Bourdin (Odéon 123 670) is comfortably bland: the claim of 'Je tremble . . . ' is egregiously false. Jacques Jansen's 'La grotte' is stylish but a bit limp, his 'Climène' very light; with 'Je tremble . . . ' his vitally engaged Pelléas is recalled most happily (Decca LXT 2774). Fischer-Dieskau's slow, awe-struck 'La grotte' is full of suppressed excitement (DG SLPM 138115). Again the strongest complete performances come from Souzay and from Kruysen. The latter is smooth and sincere with Richard, exaggeratedly soft (though subtle) with Lee; Souzay's earlier DG performance is erotically entranced and fresh, his later EMI one (again with Dalton Baldwin) more settled but still rapt and heartfelt, and splendidly searching. Earlier than either, he recorded an orchestral version of 'La grotte' (with the Paris Conservatoire Orchestra) that is swifter, delicately exalted and imperishably beautiful.

That leaves the *Trois Ballades de François Villon*, from 1910 like *Le promenoir*, and the *Trois Poèmes de Stéphane Mallarmé* of 1913. The Villon set proves astonishingly rich, with a lover's close-to-the-bone plaint ('Ballade de Villon à s'amye'), a devout old woman's simple profession ('Ballade que Villon feit à la requeste de sa mère pour prier Nostre-Dame') and a racily *risqué* number ('Ballade des femmes de Paris'). Though there are harmonic pre-echoes of Debussy's music for d'Annunzio's mystical-decadent *Martyre de Saint Sébastien*, the virile Villon *persona* seems so sympathetically captured – even when the agnostic poet speaks for his credulous old mother – as to rule out female interpreters.

Records prove otherwise. *Maman* Villon's prayer of course provides a feminine *entrée*: Danco's clean-lined sincerity there matches her sadder-but-wiser plaint and her brightly pointed last Ballade, as Flore Wend's disarmingly naïve plea to Our Lady matches her personal (but stylish) involvement in the plaint and her *staccato* teasing in the ditty. Though Teyte recorded 'Femmes de Paris' (not a feminist song by a long shot!) with much more energy than conviction, there is a Merriman version – with canny injections of chest-tone – that is genuinely exciting.

Jansen (Decca LXT 2774) is simple and heartbroken in the plaint, light and unforced in the prayer, crisply confident in the ditty. With Poulenc, Bernac (DB 6385–6) delivers reproaches from the heart in the first song, plain piety in the second – with a lovely last verse – and light mischief in the third. With Karl Engel at the piano in 1960, Fischer-Dieskau (DG SLPM 138115) was despairing and lyrical in the first (if never convincingly French), softly intense in the second (impersonation only in the delivery, not in the timbre) and vocally sophisticated – without real high spirits – in the last; later with Barenboim and the Orchestre de Paris (DG 2531 263), his plaint is bitter to the point of violence, the prayer almost romantically suave (with some self-conscious frail moments) and the ditty at once elaborately bright and bland. Martial Singher (Am. Col. 17579–81 D; ML 4152), also with orchestra, pleads aristocratically in the first song, treats the second urgently and anxiously, and in the third is dashing without any particular wit.

With Baldwin, Souzay is soberly frank 'à s'amye' (his tone occasionally unctuous), determinedly insouciant but not much fun with the 'Femmes de Paris'. In the prayer, much lighter, he presents a wide-eyed, modest old lady; it is moving to compare this with his much earlier version (with Lindenberg and the Conservatoire orchestra) – fine, fresh and fervent, disconcertingly youthful. Panzéra recorded the second and third songs with Piero Coppola (DA 4810), the one eloquently humble and the other brimming with panache and passion. Franz Mertens's version (HLP 26) of the prayer is slow, gentle and pious, with distinguished diction.

Among all the excellent Villon sets two are especially remarkable. There is a magnificent orchestral version (with Inghelbrecht) by Bernard Plantey (Ducretet Thomson 320 C 154): the plaint broken, almost drained, the prayer fluent and pointed with discreet impersonation, a terrific 'Femmes de Paris' with hints of raucous market-place delivery and infectious wit. The orchestra matches him. Kruysen, with Lee again, offers the most searching account on an intimate scale. Full of refined dramatic detail, his first *Ballade* is anxiously intense, almost bitter, the second swift, fragile and confiding, the third brittly elegant and excited.

Where the *Ballades* are organised firmly around their refrains, the *Trois Poèmes de Stéphane Mallarmé* are as fleetingly elusive as their texts. By a famously strange coincidence, Debussy chose two of the same poems as Ravel for his exactly contemporary triptych. 'Soupir' and 'Placet futile'; but Ravel preferred to close with a hermetically perfect sonnet, Debussy with the fluttery 'Éventail'. The etched silhouettes of Ravel's settings, with their iridescent accompaniment for nonet, ask less for interpretation than for *soigné* musicianship, whereas Debussy's – whimsically dainty – require keen (if baffled) appreciation of the words. Non-native speakers are disadvantaged, though Margaret Price (Orfeo S 038831) manages a smooth, opulent 'Soupir' (with dark, covered vowels) and a *prima donna* playfulness for 'Éventail' (clever assistance from James Lockhart); her 'Placet futile' is dull.

In the EMI album, Ameling is more flexible with that song (though Baldwin is brisk and unambiguous), sustains 'Soupir' delicately – one line goes flat – and is prettily feathery in 'Éventail'. Cuénod's *Poèmes* are jewelled miniatures: a flawlessly poised first song, a properly precious second and an airily puckish third (with a witty gleam in Martin Isepp's piano). But it is Kruysen, in both his recorded versions, who responds most imaginatively to the words and gives the fullest sophisticated life to the songs: each record (they were made more than a decade apart) has its own insights. His 'Placet futile' is masterly both times, flirtatious and seductive. The soft intensity of his 'Soupir' with Richard (much lighter than Baldwin) is further hushed in the version with Lee, at the expense of any climax; his earlier 'Éventail' is as volatile as Ameling's but much more coherently narrated, his later one less firmly led forward but even subtler in detail, brilliantly 'characterised' where any character would seem an impossible figment. He illuminates the music through the words: just what Debussy wanted.

Ravel

JEREMY SAMS

Histoires naturelles

Bacquier, Baldwin	HMV EX 27 0139 3
Bathori (self-accompanied)	Col. D 15179; FCX 50030
Benoit, Ringeissen	Adès 10.002
Benoit, Ciccolini	HMV CUB 2175
Bernac, Poulenc	Col. 33CX 1119
Crespin, Entremont	CBS 76967
Fischer-Dieskau, Höll	Orfeo S 061831
Jackson, G. Johnson	Hyperion A66149
Kruysen, Richard	Valois MB 469
Mruysen, Lee	Telefunken 641873
Palmer, Constable	Argo ZRG 834
Souzay, Bonneau	LX 3077, LX 3149
Souzay, Baldwin	Philips 6527 154

1. Le paon
2. Le grillon
3. Le cygne
4. Le martin-pêcheur
5. La pintade

Shéhérazade

Ameling, San Francisco Symphony/ De Waart	Philips 410 043–3
Baker, New Philharmonia/Barbirolli	HMV ASD 2444
Berganza, Capitole Orchestra of Toulouse/ Plasson	HMV EX 27 0139 1
Crespin, Suisse Romande/Ansermet	Decca JB 15
Danco, Suisse Romande/Ansermet	Decca GOS 602/3
De los Angeles, Paris Conservatoire/Prêtre	HMV ASD 2260
Harper, BBC Symphony/Boulez	CBS MK 39023

Norman, LSO/Davis	Philips 412 493–2
Te Kanawa, Brussels Opera/Pritchard	HMV CDC7 47111–2
Teyte, Covent Garden Opera/Rignold	DB 6843/4; RLS 716
Tourel, Columbia Symphony/Bernstein	Col. 33CX 1029
Tourel, New York Philharmonic/Bernstein	Am. Col. MS 6438
Von Stade, Boston Symphony/Ozawa	BS 36665

1. Asie
2. La flûte enchantée
3. L'indifférent

Cinq mélodies populaires grecques

De los Angeles, Paris Conservatoire/Prêtre	HMV ASD 2260
Fischer-Dieskau, Engel	DG 138115
Fischer-Dieskau, Höll	Orfeo S 016831
Kolassi, Bonneau	Decca 417 559–1
Kruysen, Richard	Valois MB 969
Kruysen, Lee	Telefunken 6.41873
Mesplé, Baldwin	HMV EX 27 0139 3
Palmer, Constable	Argo ZRG 834
Souzay, Paris Conservatoire/Vandernoot	HMV FALP 30330
Souzay, Baldwin	Philips 6527 154
Van Dam, BBC Symphony/Boulez	CBS MK 39023
Von Stade, Boston Symphony/Ozawa	CBS 36665

1. Chanson de la mariée
2. Là-bas vers l'église
3. Quel galant
4. Chanson des cueilleuses de lentisques
5. Tout gai!

Deux mélodies hébraïques

Benoit, Ringeissen	Adès 10.002
Bernac, Poulenc	Col. 33CX 1119
Danco, Suisse Romande/Ansermet	Decca GOS 602/3
De los Angeles, Paris Conservatoire/Prêtre	HMV ASD 530
Grey, Ravel	Polydor 561075, 627063; World Records SH 196
Kruysen, Lee	Telefunken 641873
Souzay, Paris Conservatoire/Vandernoot	HMV FALP 30330
Souzay, Baldwin	Philips 6527 154

Jeremy Sams

Van Dam, Baldwin	HMV EX 27 0139 3
Von Stade, Boston Symphony, Ozawa	CBS 36665

1. Kaddish
2. L'énigme éternelle

Trois Poèmes de Stéphane Mallarmé

Baker, Melos Ensemble/Keeffe	Decca SDD 368
Benoit, Paris Orchestra/Jacquillat	HMV CVB 2175
Danco, Suisse Romande/Ansermet	Decca GOS 602/3
Gomez, BBC SO/Boulez	CBS MK 39023
Lott, Orchestre de Paris soloists/Plasson	HMV EX 27 0139 3
Palmer, Nash Ensemble/Rattle	Argo ZRG 834

1. Soupir
2. Placet futile
3. Surgi de la croupe et du bond

Chansons Madécasses

Baker	Decca SDD 368
Benoit	Adès 10.002
Fischer-Dieskau	DG 138115
Fischer-Dieskau	BASF EA 22765
DeGaetani	Nonesuch H 71355
Graf	Claves P 604
Grey	Polydor 56106/7; World Records SH 196
Jansen	Decca LXT 2774
Kolassi	Decca 417 559–1
Kruysen	Valois MB 469
Ludwig	Col. SAX 5274
Norman	HMV EX 27 0139 3
Norman	CBS MK 39023
Palmer	Argo ZRG 834
Souzay	HMV FALP 30330
Souzay	Philips 6527 154
Von Stade	CBS 36665

1. Nahandove, ô belle Nahandove!
2. Aoua! Aoua! Mefiez-vous des blancs
3. Il est doux de se coucher

Don Quichotte à Dulcinée

Benoit, Ringeissen	Adès 10.002
Bernac, Poulenc	HMV DA 1869; PB3
Fischer-Dieskau, Engel	DG 138115
Fischer-Dieskau, Höll	Orfeo S 061831
Huttenlocher, Lausanne Chamber/Jordan	Erato STU 71126
Kruysen, Richard	Valois MB 469
Kruysen, Lee	Telefunken 6.41873
Singher, orch.?/Coppola	HMV DA 4865/6
Souzay, Paris Conservatoire/Vandernoot	HMV FALP 30330
Souzay, Baldwin	Philips 6527 154
Van Dam, BBC SO/Boulez	CBS MK 39023
Van Dam, Baldwin	HMV EX 27 0139 3

1. Chanson romanesque
2. Chanson épique
3. Chanson à boire

Maurice Ravel does not belong in the mainstream of the French *mélodie*. It was only in his earliest songs that he explored the world of Debussy, Chausson and Fauré – but he soon found that poetic introspection in symbolic landscapes was not for him. His first successful song, *Sainte*, showed that the statue of an angel strumming frozen music from her harp was more moving to him than all the hot houses, classical gardens at night – all the poetic 'states of mind' which the contemporary poets could muster. And so it proved throughout his career. The greater his detachment and distance from naked emotion the more possible his music becomes. This is true of almost all his songs – the settings are frequently foreign places which he never visited, and in some cases (the Orient, Madagascar) which his poets never visited; he is fascinated by children, animals, machines, the past, prose rather than verse, declamation rather than long *legato* lines. He will frequently prefer a female voice in a male song – disguise, paradox and personation are everything.

His first full-scale voice-and-piano cycle, *Histoires naturelles*, is a case in point. Its text, by Jules Renard, is a series of prose sketches about animals. Quaint, witty but wordy, they are hardly the stuff of song – Ravel admitted that he wished to add nothing, merely to interpret the texts. To that end every rise and fall of declamation is precisely notated in the vocal part, which seeks to reproduce the cadences of real, as opposed to 'poetic' speech.

Jeremy Sams

The first performance was given in 1906 by Ravel and Jane Bathori, who recorded 1, 2 and 4 23 years later. Both the voice and piano parts in this historic recording contain inaccuracies – but this is hardly surprising when one realises that she is accompanying herself. The most fascinating aspect of these performances is their total lack of sentimentality: 2 rattles along at an astonishing rate and 4, potentially poetic, is merely matter-of-fact. One can assume that Ravel would have detested too much sentiment, but there must be room in this cycle for colour and character. These are amply supplied in a classic reading by Pierre Bernac with Francis Poulenc. Bernac is extremely faithful to the printed music but manages through virtuosic vocal timbre to depict the animals in question – he becomes pompous for the peacock, fastidious for the cricket, whilst still maintaining a sympathetic detachment from them. The general mood is one of gently ironic melancholy – and it is matched by a Poulenc on his best behaviour – never slushy or slovenly but pert and precise.

Without sympathy and colour this cycle is potentially dry as dust. This is exemplified in more recent recordings. Jean-Christophe Benoit makes the mistake of interspersing his performances with readings of the text by an actor, Henri Virlojeux, who provides all the characterisation which Benoit lacks. He redeems himself on a record with the pianist Aldo Ciccolini, who inspires him to marvellous moments, such as a lovely yawn on 'lasses de l'admirer'. The pianist's depiction of the peacock's tail opening is breathtaking, as is their rendition of 4, in which time seems to stand still as they recreate a magical memory. Bernard Kruysen is another singer frightened to comment on or to colour the words. His recording with Richard is the less dull, though his other partner, Noël Lee, proves the better accompanist. John Constable, who accompanies Felicity Palmer, has an aridity and accuracy in his playing which, though normally unsuitable for French song, fits this cycle very well. Palmer herself adopts a very sophisticated manner here, rather scornful, but misses many chances for humour and colour – mainly because of the lack of precision in her French diction. A similar stance is adopted by Régine Crespin, who sounds full of pity and, in 5, scorn for these poor animals – each song is slow and sad and her voice often sounds uncontrolled and strained.

Of course coloration can be overdone, as two prominent Lieder-singers show. Fischer-Dieskau's recording, very well played by Hartmut Höll, contains such a range of vocal devices that it distracts us from the music. In 1 he is often almost speaking, which totally misses the point of Ravel's 'musical declamation'. Gérard Souzay's recording with Baldwin contains some marvellous things. 2, for example, is a miniature miracle of precision and discretion. 3 is splendidly smooth but spoiled by a horrid chuckle at the end. 4 is lacking in any atmosphere, real or remembered, and Souzay is often too loud. 1 and 5 are frustrating – excellent performances undermined by eccentric vocal mannerisms. The playing is exemplary.

The two recordings that strike the most happy medium are the two most recent – and they could not be more different. The young baritone Richard Jackson occasionally uses rhythmic over-emphasis as a compensation for a lack of vocal beauty, but there is a sympathy and above all an intelligence in this recording which is extremely touching. In 1 the roles are very clear. The pianist (Graham Johnson, excellent) is the peacock – strutting along, head held high, whilst the voice is the commentator, dry and precise but always with an underbubbling of irony. In 2 we are drawn into the fascinating tiny world of a fastidious creature whom the singer never patronises. Similarly the bathetic last line of 3, referring to the swan's greed and obesity, is not mocking but, rather, full of self-reproach at having got so carried away. 5 could be more grotesque, but 4 could not be more spellbinding.

Lastly there is Gabriel Bacquier, a veteran performer who seems to combine the best of Bernac and Souzay. His colouring of words and his prosody are a delight; such care adds to the atmosphere of sympathy and concern for the creatures he describes. His is a large honest voice best suited for 1 and 5, so 4 becomes a larger-than-life angler's tale and 2 makes no concessions to the insect's size. Only in 3 do we miss a simple lyrical impulse from both singer and pianist.

Ravel's prosodic experiments in this cycle are the logical extension of those he began three years earlier in the songs for voice and orchestra entitled *Shéhérazade*. The texts are from a large collection by Ravel's friend Tristan Klingsor (a pseudonym to conjure with) of semi-pornographic poems about a totally imagined and geographically impossible Orient. In composing his songs Ravel, it seems, transcribed the poet's precise inflections as he read his work aloud. Passionate extravagance may be the immediate effect of these songs, but painstaking precision is at their heart.

Very few of the sopranos who have recorded this cycle achieve both. There is an early recording by Maggie Teyte that achieves neither. Her French is surprisingly idiosyncratic and the orchestral tuning is execrable. Her rather ugly repetitions of 'je voudrais voir' in 1 sound unfortunately like the petulant protestations of a spoilt child. A happier reading is given by Jennie Tourel in her two recordings with Leonard Bernstein. The Columbia Symphony Orchestra produce a very stormy and percussive version of 1 with a brassy climax redolent, and by no means inappropriately so, of Cecil B. de Mille. Tourel's singing is not beautiful but thoughtful and arresting. In 2, however, she insists on explaining everything in a tiresome and pedantic fashion. 3 is too slow. In her second version, with the New York Philharmonic, the orchestral sound is more integrated and impressionistic. Unfortunately she comes to grief on her climactic top note in 1. She falls off it and gives a little unhappy scream. 3 is still too slow.

The finest orchestral playing of this cycle comes, without a doubt, from Barbirolli and the New Philharmonia Orchestra. His tempi, the sense of urgency which binds the disparate elements of 1, the lazy languor of 2 and 3, the oboe and flute solos at the beginning of 1 and 2 as well as the shattering climax of 1 are all beautifully judged. Although Janet Baker can, in purely technical terms, match these thrilling sounds, she is let down by her unimaginative interpretation and her unidiomatic French. She is the mistress of mis-stress. Final syllables and feminine endings are triply underlined, consonants are doubled, her vowel-sounds are as unpredictable as her 'r's', which are variously rolled and guttural, and her *portamenti* suddenly swoop in either direction. Heather Harper is another sufferer from an excess of Englishness. She is further hampered by Pierre Boulez, who, though holding a tight rein and coaxing fine playing, seems out of his element. He misses the sweep of 1 as much as the ease and sensuality of 2 and 3. John Pritchard's Brussels Opera Orchestra capture most of these qualities in spite of some peculiar sounds from his wind soloists, but there is no disguising the fact that he and Kiri Te Kanawa are just not together a lot of the time. Her line and tone are beautiful, but this problem of ensemble, coupled with her unreliable pronunciation and intonation, spoils one's enjoyment. Frederica von Stade's French also becomes extremely strange under pressure. Her strength is the laid-back lassitude of 3, but in 1 she seems unwilling to join in with the excitement, exoticism and manifold changes of mood provided by Ozawa and the Boston Symphony.

This relaxed mood is taken one step further in the beautiful version by Jessye Norman, Colin Davis and the LSO. 1 is an epic conception which unfolds slowly and vastly. The soprano's style suggests not so much a longing for the Orient as an opium dream, a vision being enjoyed, here and now. The last two songs are equally seductive, particularly the yearning orchestral sighs of 3. Elly Ameling, by comparison, sounds like a schoolgirl looking longingly at a map of the Far East: lyrical and excited but tentative. The San Francisco Symphony under Edo de Waart produce an antithetically brash accompaniment. Both she and Jessye Norman have a fine command of French.

The three most successful singers of this cycle have voices as large, as lustrous and, on occasion, as lubricious as the songs themselves. Two of them are Spanish – perhaps not surprisingly considering Ravel's ancestry and the very Mediterranean languor that informs this music. Victoria de los Angeles is least idiomatic. Her French stresses and pronunciation are unreliable, but her technicolor palette of vocal and verbal effects seems to cover this adequately. 2 and 3 are very precisely characterised – one recognizes and sympathises with the women here portrayed – and 1 is full of surprises, sudden *diminuendi* and exotic swoops and slides. The intonation is occasionally uncertain, both in the voice and almost parodistically French-sounding orchestral playing. Teresa Berganza is less rapturous but more precise. She puts into the words what de los Angeles puts into the line. She is the only performer who seems to understand and sympathise with all the subtle changes of mood in 2 and have the courage not to get over-excited in 3, which receives a very mature reading – a precise portrayal of a woman of the world neither too mad about the boy nor too regretful at his passing. The Capitole Orchestra of Toulouse, under Plasson, seem to supply all the sensuality which she is suppressing – a fascinating balance. The conducting and playing are exemplary.

Would that the same were true of Ansermet and the Suisse Romande. They give uneven and heavy-handed accompaniment to two sopranos: Suzanne Danco and Régine Crespin. This matters more for the latter than for the former, for Danco's reading is prosaic and unenticing. Crespin's is the opposite. From her first cries of 'Asie' we find ourselves under the thrall of a spell-binding storyteller – a real Shéhérazade. With broad brushstrokes she conjures up a huge canvas in 1; and the shorter songs, 2 and 3, are no less generously lavished with longing and languor. All this, alas, is in spite of Ansermet, whose contribution is unlovely (note the acidic oboe playing in 1) and uneven.

Having, as it were, visited the mysterious East, Ravel continued his armchair travels over the next few years with special folk song arrangements. The most popular of his *Chants populaires* are the Greek and Hebrew songs. These have been much recorded and pose few problems for the performers – for the simple reason that only the piano part in the Greek songs is by Ravel; in the case of the orchestral version only 1 and 5 are Ravel's, the other orchestral accompaniments are spurious. Souzay seems to feel this in his orchestral recording – his readings are overstated and unconvincing. But with Baldwin at the piano he is sedate and unaffected particularly in 2 and 4. 5 still doesn't sound as gay as its title implies. The same is true of Irma Kolassi; 5 is a bit sluggish but the slow simplicity of 2 and 4 shine through. Kolassi has two trump cards, however: firstly the peerless playing of Souzay's erstwhile accompanist, Jacqueline Bonneau, and secondly the fact that she sings the songs in their original Greek – rendering them totally incomprehensible but extremely authentic! Not so Frederica von Stade and Fischer-Dieskau. Von Stade's French, no less eccentric here than usual, lessens the impact of pleasant singing and felicitous tempi. Fischer-Dieskau's French improves between his first recording (with Karl Engel), where he can't sing 'matin' or 'brulée' in 1, and his second (with Höll), where he has learnt how to. In both cases 1 is too breathy, 3 is stodgy and transposed down, and 2, surprisingly, is excellent. Kruysen has also produced two recordings – in the first with Richard, the voice sounds a little pinched, the songs a little careful and the pitch a little flat. Everything is happier, more easy-going and more convincing in his second recording with the excellent accompaniment of Noël Lee. My preferred recordings all come from sopranos. Palmer and Constable seem to slot into absolutely correct tempi in these songs: bouncy and uncomplicated in the faster ones and suitably pliant but matter-of-fact in 2 and 4. Only the odd vocal scoop in 3 spoils the enjoyment. Mady Mesplé also finds the right speeds as well as the brightness of voice and lack of musical sophistication needed to make these 'concert' folk songs credible. Lastly there is de los Angeles, who has the knack of making anything connected with folk or national music sound thoroughly authentic, unpatronising and, above all, simple. She sings these songs beautifully.

And the *Mélodies Hébraïques* no less so. These songs pose fewer problems than the Greek harmonizations. 'Kaddish' is merely an extended cantorial *melisma*; 'L'énigme éternelle' is a world-weary folk song written in Yiddish. The definitive performance is given by Madeleine Grey with the composer at the piano. Her voice is extraordinarily modern, without any of the pseudo-operatic excesses associated with the period. Her singing in 1 is free, yet controlled in timbre. 2, interestingly, is extremely fast. Bernac matches this tempo but cannot match Grey's beauty of tone in 1. For once Bernac the master interpreter has nothing to interpret, and his voice sounds rather high and dry. Souzay's colourings of 1 are also rather wasted on such a simple song, but the beauty of his natural voice, a fine orchestra, and flattering synagogue echo see him through. 2, however, is very downbeat and depressing – as it is in his version with piano. Kruysen (with Lee) also adopts this approach in 2, assuming the persona of an old man; rather weary, but not without wry humour. Occasionally bad intonation intrudes. In 1, however, he is on fine vocal form, credible as a cantor, singing with simple and unforced fervour. Benoit lacks Kruysen's straightforwardness and beauty of voice; and a good tempo in 2 does not compensate for a rather prosaic reading of 1. Danco (with orchestra and Ansermet) does not even provide this compensation; 1 is dull and 2 is duller.

The two finest versions of these songs both adopt the slower speed in 2 but manage by dint of sheer vocal beauty to make it credible. Von Stade sees this song as a lament and she sings it with such conviction that it makes a perfect counterpart to the soaring passions of 1. José van Dam also accentuates the threnodic nature of the music – and his melancholy *melismata*, especially in 1, are most moving. As in all folk-singing it is beauty of voice and honesty of intention that finally win the day.

The contrast with Ravel's Mallarmé settings could not be greater – sophistication, artifice and detachment are everything. It has been said of Mallarmé's poetry that it is untranslatable, even into French. These highly precious poems have an extraordinary effect on Ravel's music. He produces a sort of frozen lyricism, rapturous but static, carefully descriptive but distant and haunting. The successful singer of this cycle requires not only a cast-iron technique but also the selflessness to remove indulgent vocal effects, replacing them with precision of colour and diction. Only a handful of singers has taken up this challenge on disc – and only a few of them have done the music justice.

The wrong approach is exemplified by Janet Baker. The *tessitura* lies high for her. Despite a very fast tempo she is unable to maintain the forced 'soprano' tone and soon resorts to a more worldly, darker timbre. The brittle ice of this song thus soon turns to slush as intervals are sentimentally scooped, consonants are doubled, and guttural 'r's' add a bizarre music-hall flavour to the mix. Sentimentality is to be avoided in these songs – particularly in 2, which always threatens to turn into a soppily conventional love song. Baker falls straight into this trap with impossible *portamenti* on the repeated word 'Princesse', which give unwelcome warmth and immediacy to a song of courtly love. The fault is further compounded by throaty 'r's' on the words 'coiffeurs divins', reminding one not so much of *The Rape of the Lock* as of Vidal Sassoon. Further mispronunciations ('framboise', 'nommez') do not help. The third song is superbly played – by then it is too late.

Danco (with Ansermet in attendance) reminds us that there are certain subtle internal *rubati*, certain precise prosodic stresses which, especially in difficult poetry, only a native French speaker can attain. This is neither the most beautiful voice nor the most beautiful recording in the world, but the intentions are pure and often touching. The old-fashioned playing adds a pleasingly quaint touch to 2, as if the aged Abbé had commandeered an orchestra of his own vintage to assist his hopeless suit. Ravel preferred a woman's voice for these cycles – one can hear why in Benoit's recording. The amorous elements in the verse somehow seem too literal, too immediately credible. A baritone's falsetto is less suitable than the cold, high, floating head-voice of a soprano, and the octaves sound misplaced. Nevertheless Benoit produces a marvellous 'white' sound in 1 as well as several delightful character points in 2 (the stress on 'délire', the little sulk in the voice on the last line), although 3 is oversung and growly in the lower register. The playing, particularly from Aldo Ciccolini at the piano, is exemplary throughout.

Jeremy Sams

The three finest recordings come from British singers – and it is hard to voice a preference. Palmer produces lovely long lines in 1, as flowing as the fountain she describes. Perhaps there is a *portamento* too many, perhaps the vibrato is occasionally over-wide, but the whole effect is mesmeric. 2 is particularly well played, Palmer's only fault being a rather worldly scoop on the second 'Princesse'. 3 is suitably cold and haughty. Jill Gomez has the advantage of the clinical intelligence of Boulez's conducting. This music is as natural to his musical temperament as *Shéhérazade* is unnatural. The high soprano is also well suited to this music, particularly to the purity of 1 and to the ineffectual pleading of 2. Only the occasional English vowel sound breaks the spell. Felicity Lott shares first prize. Michel Plasson is not the spellbinder that Boulez is, but Lott's beauty of tone, absolute refusal to slide between notes, and above all her intelligent understanding and interpretation of difficult verse make this a remarkable reading.

Thirteen years elapsed between the Mallarmé songs and Ravel's next cycle, the *Chansons Madécasses*. The musical difference is immediately audible – any remaining harmonic excesses or lushness of texture in the earlier style have now been expunged in favour of a pared-down style, a fascinating interplay of freely moving, often dissonantly clashing melodic lines. These settings are the apogee of Ravelian detachment – songs set in an imaginary foreign country to eighteenth-century prose texts by a poet who had never visited Madagascar. As in the case of the Mallarmé songs, indeed more so, the singer must subjugate emotional or poetic excess and perform a more restrained, instrumental, role. This can be backed up with the authority of Ravel's own definitive recording with Madeleine Grey, his preferred interpreter for these songs. The first surprise (after the shock of the appalling sound quality) in these performances is the sheer pace. There is no sentimentality, no dwelling on exotic detail; 'le plaisir passe comme un éclair', she sings, and indeed the first song goes past like lightning. This approach is a revelation in 2. Grey's voice sounds numb and drained of emotion – the perfect depiction of a race bruised and abused. As the song proceeds, the already fast tempo quickens as the catalogue of atrocity becomes more hysterical and accusatory before slowing down to its panting conclusion; very compelling. 3 is still fast, again prosaic to a degree which makes its final paragraph of lyrical description doubly moving, and the final line ('Allez, et préparez le repas') a mere return to a previous mood rather than the bathos it often becomes.

Restraint is everything in these songs, and the moments where anger and passion can no longer be contained are made the more moving because of it. Not every singer, however, has the courage or temperament to achieve this. Christa Ludwig (excellently accompanied, particularly by Amaryllis Fleming on the cello) starts with soupy scoops and exotic

114

colouring and very soon has nowhere to go. The effect of 1 is rather nauseous, 2 is over-accented and 3 over-enthusiastic; its last line is sung with unexpected urgency, as if depicting a sudden hunger pang. Baker is a similar offender. Her ensemble underlines every musical moment in 1 and 3 with the result that they die on their feet. Mispronunciation and misreadings (some of them quite grotesque) and wilful sentimentalisation go to make her singing unattractive and unacceptable. Palmer, whose voice is not dissimilar, is infinitely more attentive to detail; her tempi and approach are relaxed and easy-going. This seems to suit 3, but elsewhere more colour and urgency are required. The same is true of Jan DeGaetani, whose attempts at a 'laid-back' approach manifest themselves as rather limp and wheedling love-making in 1, as a feeble acceptance of oppression in 2 and a self-indulgence which makes 3 sound like an adver-tisement for sunbathing. Kathrin Graf, on the other hand, takes an entirely neutral stance which makes the performance sound like an emotionless, well-executed instrumental quartet. The same is true of von Stade, who seems to have no precise line on the songs – merely a generalised urgency in 1 and violence in 2. Her pronunciation is impre-cise, but her musicians are excellent.

Souzay and Fischer-Dieskau have both recorded this cycle twice. Souzay's first recording (with Jean-Pierre Rampal) has much to recom-mend it. The tempo in 1 is fast, supple and expressive and 2 has a frighten-ingly obsessive and measured pulse. Only 3 is self-indulgent and rhap-sodic. His later recording has more individual vocal mannerisms which distract the attention from the forward motion of this music. Although Souzay bawls a bit in 1 he has found the right restraint for 3 and a more exciting and uncontrolled tempo for 2. Fischer-Dieskau is also frequently guilty of excessive and surprising vocal tricks. This is particularly notice-able when he is not the master of the idiom. His French is imprecise and often (particularly in 2) swallowed and gabbled. The sheer beauty of his voice and the honesty of his intentions are, however, great compensations in his early recording. In his recent rendition his vocal confidence is less and his reliance on special effects therefore much greater.

Successful singing of this cycle stems from surprising sources. Kruysen's discs are always workmanlike but seldom startling. This recording, one feels, can only get better after the cello fluffs its first bar: and so it does. His reading is calm, factual and cumulatively very touch-ing. The same is true of Kolassi. She does not dwell on details but presses on in a very compelling, down-to-earth fashion. 2 is unfortunately beyond her vocal powers and her slow tempo only serves to highlight the fact. 3 is a showcase for her cellist and flautist, William Pleeth and Geoffrey Gilbert, both excellent. Benoit and his musicians produce a wonderfully dry and dusty sound, urgent and often ugly in 2 and compellingly rhythmic in 1. In 3 someone suddenly switches the echo on and the recording sounds unsuitably swamped and smoochy.

My two favourite interpreters, in a very strong field, could not be more different. Jacques Jansen with a first-class ensemble (Rampal, Bonneau and Maurice Gendron) seems to strike a wonderful balance between fact and fantasy. His old-fashioned vocal style seems to combine pace with lyricism, and the erotic with the commonplace. The tempi are always unambiguously urgent except in 3, which seems to have all the time in the world. This recording is a real collector's item. His present-day counterpart is Jessye Norman, who has, in recent years, made these songs her own. Her two recordings have little to choose between them. Her very personal approach and integrity shine through, particularly in her heartbreaking catalogue of suffering in 2. In the excitement of 1 and in the calm of 3 she succeeds in creating a very stylised, almost abstract sensuality which seems to capture the very essence of Ravel's musical intentions. A remarkable reading.

Ravel's song-writing career had its final flowering at a time when it was thought there was no more music in him. But the subject-matter of these last songs, *Don Quichotte à Dulcinée*, was enough to set Ravel's pulse racing and his music flowing. They concern a distinct country, Spain, a historical, fictional character, Don Quixote, and an unattainable mother–madonna figure, Dulcinea. These are themes so central to his psyche that it is no surprise that Ravel came out of his illness-induced retirement to respond to them.

These songs hold few perils for performers. The rhythms are dance-inspired and therefore immutable, the characterisation straightforward and consistent. All they must do is get the words and the notes right. I say this because Fischer-Dieskau and Karl Engel do neither. Those who know these songs will be astonished to hear what should be semitonal clusters, or the wrong rhythms on the line 'Est plus à moi qu'à vous ma Dame' in 1, and the pronunciation of 'foin' and 'vin' in 3. These misreadings are cleared up in his recording with Höll but replaced with new ones, such as his mispronunciation of the important word 'but' in 3. Without wishing to damn further with faint praise, one must add that Fischer-Dieskau's tempo in 3 is, in both cases, absolutely correct.

There is a historic recording, very fine, by Martial Singher, which was made in the presence of the composer. On it we can hear very clearly the *tackiness* of Ravel's made-for-the-cinema orchestration, which subsequent producers have tried to prettify by the hiding of the prominent woodwind and vibraphone writing. This is true of Huttenlocher's orchestral recording; the sound is ravishing but homogenised. The singing is strong and sympathetic but the songs start slow and get slower. Souzay presents a much more heroic and self-deluding persona undercut

116

in his orchestral version by vain falsetto work in 1 and irritating chuckles in 3. 2 is perfect, courageously slow and equally fine in the piano transcription. In this reading 1 is more clipped and self-deprecating – and the more moving for it, but 3 retains those chuckles and the strange conviction that being drunk means being amusing. Benoit is a much more serious drinker but a much less interesting singer than Souzay. 3 is good and rough but 1 and 2 are dull by comparison. Ditto Kruysen. Both of his recordings are mature and full of energy. But neither contains any musical or interpretative surprises.

These are to be found in two fascinating readings of this cycle, one recent, one vintage. José van Dam's voice suits these songs perfectly. He adopts the persona of an old man but a garrulous one – by turns hammy and self-deprecating, full of fervour in 2 and of Dutch courage in 3. Of his two recordings the one with Baldwin at the piano is preferable. Boulez attempts strange *rubati* in 1, which is, after all, a dance movement. Lastly there is Bernac with Poulenc. His Don Quixote is a very colourful creation; doddery, self-pitying but whether in love, in church or in his cups never less than seriously and sympathetically portrayed.

Poulenc

JEREMY SAMS

Complete set

Ameling, Gedda, Parker, Sénéchal, Souzay, Baldwin	HMV 2C 165 16231

Single records

Bernac, Poulenc	Rococo 5276
	PB 3
	EMI 2C 061 12818
	Columbia 33CX 1119
	CBS 54031/2
	Adès 7048/50

The story of Poulenc the song-writer and pianist is the story of his collaboration with Pierre Bernac. 'It is in accompanying him in Schubert, Schumann, Fauré, Debussy and Ravel', wrote Poulenc, 'that I have learned the craft of songwriting.' Bernac's extraordinary gifts, his musical intelligence and adaptability, not to mention sheer beauty of vocal timbre, made possible the music that Poulenc needed to write. And their many recordings, as well as their pioneering concert tours, opened up the mysterious world of French song to the musical public, put the *mélodie* on the map, and began a performance tradition which is still valid today.

The Poulenc–Bernac partnership looks and sounds like that of Pears and Britten. But despite initial similarities there are significant differences. There is, firstly, no question of emotional interdependence. Their partnership was based on professionalism and respect – summed up in their lifelong use of the polite 'vous' – and a shared love of music and poetry. What Poulenc discovered in Bernac is what we can hear in his recordings: seriousness, simplicity and above all sympathy with both poet and composer. And most importantly for Poulenc the ability to be lyrical, sensual, deeply religious and garishly vulgar without any sense of contradiction; and above all to be able to express all these musically.

Of course one cannot find without seeking. In 1934, when their partnership began, Poulenc's songwriting had lost its way, indeed stopped altogether. He was, in every sense, looking for a new voice. Songwriting is not a young man's art, and Poulenc is one of its few infant prodigies. *Le bestiaire*, to words by Guillaume Apollinaire, was written when Poulenc had just turned twenty. Its six tiny songs are perfect – and it is hard to say whether this was a stroke of genius or a stroke of beginner's luck. In 1918 small was beautiful and Apollinaire's little verses were all the rage. The two-and-four-bar phrases which added up to *Les Six* and their short-lived vogue was all that self-taught Poulenc was compositionally capable of. But his simplicity, real or feigned, struck a chord with Apollinaire's lyrical strain to make marvellous music. His next songs, *Cocardes*, turn away from this budding lyricism towards a more brittle self-conscious style which culminates in the five *Poèmes de Ronsard*, in which all the poetry is choked by a tangle of sub-Stravinskian complications. Indeed a lack of interest in poetry marks Poulenc's next works. The *Chansons gaillardes* are good, dirty fun but entirely superficial, and in *Airs chantés* the composer sets out to mangle a text with which he has no sympathy: surely rock bottom for a born song-writer.

In 1931, after a few years of silence, Poulenc returned to song-writing, to Apollinaire and his low-life counterpart Max Jacob. There is some lyricism in Poulenc's Jacob settings but it is almost parodistic, the bright pink in a brash palette. The only true glimpse of the music to come is in the warmth and nostangia of 'Hier', to words by Marie Laurencin (masquerading as Louise Lalanne). The next years were marked by personal crisis, recurrent melancholia and the realisation that you can't be an *enfant terrible* all your life. Most importantly he rediscovered his religious faith and with it a new sincerity in his music which enabled him to set the lyrical humanist poetry of Paul Eluard, and thus to revitalise his songwriting. A new sound needs a new instrument – and that was the voice and personality of Bernac, for whom Poulenc wrote the five *Poèmes de Paul Eluard* in 1935. As Poulenc put it, 'You could hear the key turning in the lock.' And the door which Bernac helped to open revealed not only a life-time of great songs but also the religious music which extends logically from Poulenc's Eluard songs (the two are full of cross-references) and his three operas, which only a song-writer could have written.

Poulenc was no stranger to the recording studio. As accompanist in his own music he had already recorded *Le bestiaire* in a very sweet and serious reading by his friend Claire Croiza (D 15041; ALP 2115) and the regrettable *Airs chantés* superbly sung by Suzanne Peignot (LF 5; COLC 317). Already we can hear the character of Poulenc the accompanist. In the latter songs he is *insouciant* to the point of recklessness but manages to give the impression of great dexterity within a great wash of notes. *Le bestiaire* is more carefully played and interestingly at variance with the printed score. He slows down where he shouldn't and plays the grace notes in 'La carpe' before the beat. His playing is, as always, highly coloured, with very clear dynamic areas garnished with precise but generous helpings of pedal. Poulenc referred to this variously as the 'butter' or the 'sauce' which his music required. And what good Frenchman could stint on either?

Bernac and Poulenc started their recording career in 1935 (Ultraphon BP 1531; Rococo 5276) with two of the *Chansons gaillardes*, of which Poulenc had given the first performance back in 1926, and three of the *Quatre Poèmes de Guillaume Apollinaire*. But in the next ten years they recorded no songs by Poulenc, for the simple reason that Poulenc was busy writing them, some forty songs inspired by and written for Bernac's voice. Before their retirement he was to write about thirty more, and their recordings of them are, by definition, definitive.

This next batch of recordings, dating from 1945–6, displays two musicians at the height of their powers. The range is extraordinary. In *Tel jour, telle nuit* (DA 6383/4; C 061–12818) Bernac veers from electrifying and melodramatic horror in 'Une roulotte' and 'A toutes brides' to the epitome of calm and wonderment in the mixed head-voice of 'Une herbe pauvre' and 'Une ruine coquille vide'. In 'Le front comme un drapeau perdu' and 'Je n'ai envie que de t'aimer' the infinitely supple and subtle use of *rubato* is as revealing an index of the artist's sympathy as is the courage to use none at all in the opening and closing songs. Here Bernac's sense of wonder and humility before the beautiful objects and people described by Eluard's verse is underpinned by an inexorable and therefore totally unsentimental accompaniment.

Compare this with 'C'est ainsi que tu es' from *Métamorphoses* (DB 6267; PB 3), where Bernac's voice is much more amorous and personal and Poulenc's *rubato* much more sensual and Chopinesque. Bernac caresses every feature of this very physical portrait, and when it is complete the words 'Voilà, c'est ton portrait' could not be sung with more love and simplicity. The ending of the song is beautifully controlled, down to the rather demotic aspirate in the word 'bien', the breath before 'connu' and Poulenc's pleasing postlude.

From the same year comes a delightful recording of *Le bestiaire* (DB 6299; C 061–12818), in which Bernac announces the title of each song with quite as much tenderness as he sings them (a performance tradition that seems not to have caught on), and the first recording of *Deux Poèmes de Louis Aragon* (DB 6267; PB 3), where the heavy grief of Bernac's voice in 'C' forms a remarkable contrast to the garish street argot of 'Fêtes galantes'.

The next recordings were made for American Columbia in the early 1950s (Am. Col. MM 951; Odyssey 32 26 0009) and include some of their finest work, notably their best recording of *Banalités*, which includes that masterpiece of laziness, 'Hôtel', and a matchless rendition of 'Tu vois le feu du soir', an extraordinary four minute *cantilena* of extreme beauty and difficulty.

It was near the end of their career that the bulk of Bernac's recording of Poulenc's songs was done. The Véga–Adès recordings date from 1958–60 (Adès 7048–50), by which time, it must be remembered, both artists were in their early sixties. Bernac's voice is, if possible, more elastic and highly coloured than ever, as if in compensation for his now restricted range. This is most sensible in the re-recordings of the Apollinaire songs 'Dans le jardin d'Anna', 'Allons plus vite' and 'Montparnasse', all of which are a cadenza of colour, ranging from ferocity and ironic humour to nostalgia and melancholy, which no singer has ever matched. We can also hear the song cycles *Calligrammes*, *La fraîcheur et le feu*, and *Le travail du peintre*, which Poulenc composed specifically for Bernac's voice as it grew deeper, and more expressive. It is only in the latest recording of the earliest cycles that the strain of age is sensible. Poulenc's line on transposition was simple and unimpeachable. Unless stipulated in his scores it was not allowed. Each phrase in a song occurred to him in a specific key; the balance of tonality was essential to a song cycle and indeed, to extend the metaphor, to a life cycle. Thus 'Bonne journée' and 'Pablo Picasso', though written 20 years apart, both belong together and must both be in C major; 'Sanglots' and 'Voyage' must both be in F sharp minor, Poulenc's key of love and longing, and 'La grenouillère' and 'Hôtel' both belong in D major, which, for Poulenc, meant sunshine. Rather than sacrifice this integrity Poulenc records his early songs in their original keys though palpably now too high for Bernac. *Tel jour, telle nuit* is a particular casualty here, for the lower alternatives in the vocal line occur at the moments of highest potential emotion. These Véga recordings comprise almost 70 songs, an extraordinary tribute to a great career.

Like the voices of many great singers, such as Pears, Fischer-Dieskau, Souzay and Schwarzkopf, Bernac's was individual to the point of eccentricity, not always technically perfect nor always, in the abstract, 'beautiful'. Certainly his use of falsetto, his extraordinary colouring of open vowel sounds and his rather 'old-fashioned' approach to *portamento* and *rubato* are very personal and do not appeal to everyone. But I do not believe that anyone who likes Poulenc's music could dislike Bernac's voice, any more than an admirer of Britten could hate that of

121

Pears, whereas a lover of, say, Schubert might. But as in the case of Pears, Bernac's supremacy in his own field and the longevity of his recording career had the unfortunate effect of depriving a generation of singers of the chance of exploring a composer's output.

Bernac had, or rather should have had, only one natural successor: the baritone Gérard Souzay. But Souzay was understandably reluctant to record any of Poulenc's music whilst his teacher and mentor was still singing it; and it was not until Poulenc's death in 1963 that he started his series of very individual readings of the songs. We are given a tantalising glimpse of what might have been by a recording Souzay made with Jacqueline Bonneau in 1949. He gives ravishing performances of 'Reine des mouettes' from *Métamorphoses* and 'La grenouillère', both soft and affectionate (BAM 63), using Bernac's precise approach to prosody but in a very unmannered and personal way. There is also a very tender reading of *Le bestiaire* (BAM 63) (Souzay announces the poems, as Bernac used to), pleasantly combining a young singer with the work of a young composer, full of humour and compassion.

By the time Souzay recorded his next Poulenc songs, it was 1963, and his voice and approach to singing had changed. No longer with the range of his youth and early maturity, various mannerisms creep into his singing, and they become more pronounced as his career develops, and as the natural beauty of his voice diminishes. This sounds harsh. Souzay is a singer of natural power and range, but when a 'Souzayism' appears, a sudden breathy *messa di voce*, slack consonants to achieve a a false *legato*, a bawled *subito forte*, a vulgar *crescendo* and *decrescendo* on an innocent held note – all this can decrease one's enjoyment of the song and call the sincerity of the singer's approach into question.

The 1963 record (Philips SAL 3480) mostly finds Souzay in good form. 'Air vif' from the *Airs chantés* is fast and furious, 'Priez pour paix' suitably slow and serious. 'Reine des mouettes' is less enjoyable; he now transposes it down and replaces the candour of his 1949 recording with breathlessness and ugly *crescendi* at the end. His next record of four song cycles (Philips SAL 3635) is extremely fine. *Le travail du peintre*, *La fraîcheur et le feu*, and *Calligrammes* are late cycles written for a lower voice with extremely dramatic piano parts, all of which suit Souzay and his virtuoso accompanist Dalton Baldwin extremely well, and the singer's stamina and sheer volume are well displayed in the mad mixture of Mussorgsky and Maurice Chevalier which make up the *Chansons villageoises*.

In Souzay's third Poulenc record of 1968 (RCA SB 6780) he unwisely turns to some more intimate songs. Little gems like ' . . . mais mourir', 'Rosemonde', 'Paul et Virginie', which merely need to be sung and felt, get crushed under a weight of effects. His *Tel jour, telle nuit* is in A major, which is so low that it muddies up Poulenc's precise piano writing and confuses Baldwin into playing, with great confidence, an extraordinary wrong note at the end of 'A toutes brides'. Nevertheless the more dramatic songs in the cycle work very well, as does 'Le portrait', a whirl-wind song of hate and accusation; and, surprisingly, 'Nuage', a late song whose lyrical *tessitura* suits Souzay superbly. The wittier songs on this album suffer from exaggeration – one does not need to laugh during a per-formance to show that it is funny as Souzay does in 'Avant le cinéma' and in the *Chansons gaillardes*. His performance of the latter songs is altogether too knowing, the rather obvious jokes are given away too early, the 'Chanson à boire' is much too drunkenly done. The main delight here is Baldwin's playing – you hear all the notes which you miss on the Bernac–Poulenc recordings.

The next record (2C 165–12158) again shows Souzay at his best and worst. There are cracking performances of *Parisiana*, where Souzay catches the grotesquerie of Max Jacob to perfection, and the *Cinq Poèmes de Paul Eluard* have a power and virility, especially in 'Amoureuses', which rivals the 1958 Bernac–Poulenc recording. But transposition is again a problem here; if the cycle must be transposed it should be done consistently. Here the opening song is transposed but the third is not. The same is true of an otherwise excellent *Chansons de Federico Garcia Lorca*. 'L'enfant muet' is sung in a beautifully controlled half-falsetto and 'Adeline à la promenade' is suitably Spanish and stormy. Only the 'Chanson de l'oranger sec' is a disappointment. It is transposed down and the dynamics, particularly the *subito piani*, seem overdone. This highly coloured and dramatic work suits Souzay particularly well, even in 1972, and one can see why Poulenc particularly admired his singing of it. Again it is the subtler songs that suffer on this record. In *Le Bestiaire* and *Métamorphoses* (the latter transposed down) Souzay's voice comes and goes unpredictably and is particularly uneven in the *legato* passages of 'La carpe' and 'C'est ainsi que tu es'.

This leads to a bit of a tragedy. The years 1974–7 saw the recording of a complete set of Poulenc's songs (2C 165 16231/5). Its only virtue was its completeness, for it came, frustratingly, at precisely the wrong time. As we shall see there were suitable artists both in the 1960s and the 1980s who could have performed this task. Instead we have Souzay at the end of his recording career with a very uneven back-up team. All of Souzay's recordings for this set are inferior versions of the performances discussed above. Many of them are transposed down, several are merely reissues from his last record (although the sleeve-notes do not admit it), and none of the songs previously unrecorded by Souzay ('Mazurka', 'Epitaphe', 'Le disparu') does singer or composer any particular credit.

Of the remaining singers in this set there are two operatic tenors:

Michel Sénéchal and Nicolai Gedda. Sénéchal is a high character tenor: Monostatos or Basilio rather than Tamino or Don Ottavio. Thus he is an excellent interpreter of *Cocardes*, where he spouts nonsense very seriously and good-naturedly like a white-faced clown. Similarly he is very fine in the *Poèmes de Ronsard*: he steers a cool and clear course through the neo-classical curlicues of Baldwin's brilliantly played piano part. But when it comes to Poulenc's Apollinaire songs 'Dans le jardin d'Anna', 'Le pont' and 'Allons plus vite', accuracy and a sense of fun are not enough. There is a whole world of tenderness, nostalgia and sensuality totally unexplored here. And to give Sénéchal 'C' is to miscast him totally. His rather edgy voice lends an unwanted cynicism which is as inappropriate here as it is appropriate in the second Aragon song, 'Fêtes galantes', which he rattles off in high style. Sénéchal's main contribution to this set is his po-faced rendition of Poulenc's children's songs.

As for Gedda, his versatility is admirable, but as a singer of *Tel jour, telle nuit* he is out of his element. The subtleties of phrasing and ensemble are totally lacking here, as is the emotional pull of a baritone at the top of his range – the strong high notes of an operatic tenor sound too easy and too obvious. 'Montparnasse' suffers similarly as well from a total lack of wonderment and yearning implicit in the song. Bizarrely it is in Poulenc's only mature song written for a tenor, 'Bleuet', that Gedda's sense of style totally deserts him. He slides hammily, is consistently out of tune and even incites the normally impeccable Baldwin to force his sound. The eight Polish songs, however, sung in the original language, are so well executed that almost all is forgiven. Miscasting is at its most ludicrous in the last male singer on this set, the American baritone William Parker. He has a fine lyrical voice and sings good French, but that is all. There is a total lack of colour, personality or the poetic imagination required to sing *Banalités*, *Calligrammes*, *La fraîcheur et le feu* or *Miroirs brûlants*, the most difficult cycles in the whole French song repertoire. It was perhaps not his fault. He is thrown in at the deep end and even the life-saving efforts of Baldwin's flamboyant piano playing are of no avail.

Elly Ameling is another extremely fine singer not quite at home in this very rarified repertoire. She is at her best in the *Airs chantés*, where the prime qualifications are a ravishing top to the voice and a cast-iron technique. Both of these she has and she even succeeds in making 'Air grave' sound like a decent song. The *Trois Poèmes de Louise Lalanne* are also well sung – with a good Ophelia-like mixture of breakneck lunacy coupled with lyrical introversion. This quality is well maintained in the Jacob songs, but here we find a missing ingredient. There is an ugliness and a grotesque quality in these songs (they do after all mention pimples, goitres and diarrhoea) which Ameling does not quite come to terms with; the resultant sweetness is therefore rather cloying. Similarly the *Trois*

Poèmes de Louise de Vilmorin and *Fiançailles pour rire* have much more to them than the beautifully lyrical performances given here. There is a febrile, rather aristocratic sensuality without which some of the songs, particularly 'Violon', 'Il vole' and 'Officiers de la Garde Blanche' seem musically dull and mechanical. Those, however, that deal merely with melancholy and nostalgia, for instance 'Fleurs', 'Dans l'herbe', as well as the Eluard song 'Ce doux petit visage' suit Ameling very well.

A more colourful reading of these songs can be found on a long-deleted compilation album called 'Poulenc et ses poètes' (CCA 1898). The singer and pianist are Liliane Berton and Poulenc's friend and collaborator Jacques Février. They give just the right mixture of blood-curdling passion and visionary poetry to the Jacob songs (of which they perform only three, alas) as well as the perfect mixture of breathlessness and sensuality in 'Reine des mouettes' and the first two *Poèmes de Louise de Vilmorin*. The third is equally successful: hypnotically played and very sexily sung – note particularly her vocal pout on the words 'consciences pures'. But the prize in this department must go to Denise Duval, who, in an otherwise unsuccessful live performance (with Poulenc gamely trying to follow at the piano), manages to endow the words 'certaines pensées' with totally indecent overtones (INA CLIO–001).

Duval, Poulenc's favourite artist in his later years, made only this one recording with him. It is full of delights, such as their duet rendering of a scene from *Les mamelles de Tirésias* and her definitive rendition of his mad music-hall song 'Toréador', complete with a very authentic-sounding spoken third verse. Poulenc never recorded with favourite female interpreters Suzanne Balguerie and Madeleine grey. But he did once make a record with an unfavourite artist, a singer called Rose Dercourt. This recording (Turnabout TV 4489) must be avoided – for it is only the strong-hearted who can listen to Poulenc playing away patiently while some of his finest songs are massacred a few feet away. It is a mystery why this ghastly record was ever contemplated, let aloane recorded and released.

He had better fortune in his association with Geneviève Touraine (BAM LD 5866), who gave the first performance of the *Fiançailles pour rire* and whose recording of it with Poulenc at the piano must be regarded as definitive. Hers is a rather middle-aged sound but capable of conveying great affection and sweetness in the opening songs, breathless excitement in 'Il vole' and a resigned melancholy in 'Fleurs'. After Poulenc's death Colette Herzog (DG SLPM 138882) recorded a beautifully poised version of this cycle let down only by Février, who is uncharacteristically cautious in his playing. It is coupled with a very tender reading of Poulenc's last songs, *La courte paille*. Both these cycles appear on a Poulenc collection from Felicity Palmer and John Constable (Argo ZRG 804). Palmer's particular strength is a wonderful way with Poulenc's patter songs; the faster numbers in *La courte paille* are excellent, as are 'Il vole' and 'Adelina' from the Lorca set. In the more lyrical songs she has a slight tendency to scoop the voice in a sentimental and inauthentic manner. This works well in cabaret-influenced numbers such as 'Violon' and 'Berceuse' (Max Jacob) but not in, for example, 'C'est ainsi que tu es'. Her biggest drawback is her pianist, who is very accurate but dry, prosaic and uninspiring.

Two more great sopranos who have flirted with Poulenc's *mélodies* are Régine Crespin (Decca SXL 6333) and Jessye Norman. Crespin has given definitive performances in Poulenc's *Stabat mater* and *Dialogues des Carmélites*, but a voice of such size and sensuality is hard to scale down to the more intimate world of the solo song. There is still a touch of the diva about her recording of Poulenc's songs. If she requires time she merely takes it, even in songs as implacable as 'Chanson d'Orkenise' and 'Les gars qui vont à la fête'. The highlights of this group are her outrageously self-indulgent reading of 'Hôtel', which is at once unforgivable and unforgettable, and a suitably vulgar rendition of Aragon's 'Fêtes galantes'. Norman, a pupil of Bernac's, is if anything too respectful and careful. In her two records of Poulenc her search for the perfect *legato* is conducted at the expense of the words. Her early, over-ambitious recordings (1C 053–28901) of *La fraîcheur et le feu* (superbly played by Irwin Gage) and 'Tu vois le feu du soir' are particularly muddy and unclear. She shines only in 'Les chemins de l'amour', where her characteristic combination of technical excellence, good fun and good taste are happily combined (Philips 9500 356).

Among male singers Bernac has no peers and few successors. Two of his contemporaries recorded selections of Poulenc's songs – but both waited until the composer's death to do so. Remarkably, they were both 70 when these recordings were made. Martial Singher gave the first performance of Ravel's Don Quixote songs and his reading of 'Sérénade' from the *Chansons gaillardes* (1750 Arch Records S1754) is in a similar style – fervent and mature. The words of 'L'anguille' feel good and slangy; whereas those of 'Fêtes galantes' come to grief at speed. 'Priez pour paix', however, is very touching. As indeed it is on Hugues Cuénod's recording with the surprisingly inaccurate Geoffrey Parsons at the piano (Nimbus 2118). Perhaps it is an old man's song. 'Bleuet' is about a young man going peacefully to his wartime death. Cuénod's white, quavery tenor adds a touching perspective to that moment, as if an old man were recollecting it.

The two singers who assumed Bernac's mantle as specialists in the *mélodie* were Jean-Christophe Benoit and Bernard Kruysen. They seemed to have shared out his gifts equally. Benoit's recordings of Poulenc's songs (CCA 1898) are marked by an extreme beauty of tone but very little to offer in the way of poetic insights. Kruysen has none of the beauty of sound but has learnt an enormous amount from Bernac in the area of colour and expression. His 1964 collection (Erato ERG 4009) with Jean-Charles Richard is confident but uneven. A recent record of four song-cycles, however, displays much intelligence and imagination (particularly in the *Chansons gaillardes* and *Tel jour, telle nuit* in B major) which transcend the audible vocal strain (Arion ARN 38744). Gabriel Bacquier, one of the finest singers of his generation, has recorded only a handful of Poulenc songs (CCA 1898) – but they are enough to make one long for more. There is an earthy quality to his voice which makes the two songs of the tragedy of the war, 'Le disparu' and 'Dernier poème', both to texts by Robert Desnos, particularly poignant – and the sheer power of his voice lends a suitably heroic stamp to 'Pablo Picasso' and 'Jacques Villon', both of which he sings to the hilt, with poetry and passion.

But the most exciting addition to the Poulenc discography is the most recent: the recordings by the Songmakers' Almanac accompanied by Poulenc's greatest advocate over the last ten years, the pianist Graham Johnson (Hyperion A 66147). The quality here is extraordinary and immediate. Anthony Rolfe Johnson weighs straight in with the finest version of 'Bleuet' ever recorded. The baritone Richard Jackson comes up with an extremely accomplished (if slightly arch) *Bestiaire* and even better 'Toréador'. Best of all is Felicity Lott, whose meltingly lovely voice is backed up by an intelligent sense of poetry and, most essentially, by a use-ful streak of vulgarity. Her Aragon poems, *Métamorphoses*, her wonder-fully calm *Tel jour, telle nuit* and dangerously seductive *Louise Lalanne* poems are the equal of any on record. She falls down only at the highest hurdles: 'Tu vois le feu du soir', 'Montparnasse', both of which are too slow, and in the latter case too self-indulgent. Johnson's playing is an abiding joy.

Le bal masqué, for voice and instruments, is one of his best works in any idiom. Poulenc long considered it too garlicky for Bernac, but eventually they recorded it, in 1956 (Véga C 35 A35). He does well, but one still feels he is slumming it. The earliest recording, by Warren Galjour CPT 518) feels authentic, the roughness gives it an appropriate sense of the circus. In Souzay's 1973 version (2C 065–12 158), the playing is excellent, each movement garish, lurid and sentimental as intended. Souzay's mannerisms here seem the valid stagecraft of the street theatre. Fischer-Dieskau (Acanta 40. 22765) mispronounces his French and sings a whole passage (from 'Quand un paysan de Chine') on the wrong note. Thomas Allen with the Nash Ensemble (CRDC 4137) is near-ideal. A sense of humour to match a voice at once mellifluous and melodramatic. Unfortunately, Lionel Friend lingers too often to admire the music's charms. As Poulenc wrote of this piece: 'The rhythm, whether slow or lively, should be implacable'. Conductors take note.

Spanish song

MICHAEL OLIVER

The recorded repertoire of Spanish concert songs, songs with piano accompaniment, is voluminous but at the same time severely restricted. In the first place, the art song was virtually non-existent in Spain until the twentieth century. There was a great age of Spanish vocal music, both solo and concerted, in the sixteenth and early seventeenth centuries, but throughout the next 200 years native professional composers looked primarily to the theatre for employment. Opera was cultivated (Italianate when not actually in Italian), but the truly national art forms were the hugely popular *zarzuela*, or light opera with spoken dialogue (from which a more serious style, the *zarzuela grande*, in due course developed), the shorter *sainete*, the intermezzo-like *villancico*, a form of religious drama with music performed as part of a church festival. Individual numbers from such theatre pieces could readily circulate independently as songs, but of a genuine Spanish equivalent of the Lied or the *mélodie* there was little sign (symphonies and chamber music by native Spanish composers of this period are almost as scarce). Various explanations have been put forward for this dearth: the long economic decline of the country and its further impoverishment by a sequence of brutal and disastrous wars; the taste of its rulers for music in the Italian manner, preferably both written and performed by Italians (the two most important 'Spanish' composers between the death of Victoria and the birth of Falla were Domenico Scarlatti and Luigi Boccherini); and the very late development in Spain of a concert-going, music teacher-employing, sheet-music-purchasing middle class.

The result was that when Spanish musical life did show signs of a renaissance (a convenient pair of dates for this would be 1866 and 1867, the years, respectively, of the first performance in Spain of a Beethoven symphony and of the first of Felip Pedrell's[1] (1841–1922) exhortations to

---

[1] The forenames of Catalan artists are often quoted in their Spanish (Castilian) form (Pablo for Pau, Felipe for Felip, etc.), thus obscuring their origin in a region with its

128

build a national music) it found few traditions of concert music either to build upon or to react against. It is significant that the two greatest monuments of Pedrell's legacy, aside from his polemical writings, his teaching and his scholarly edition of the works of Victoria, were the eight-volume *Hispaniae schola musica sacra* of 1898, a collection of Renaissance and classical choral and organ music, and the famous *Cancionero musical popular español* (1922), four volumes primarily of folk-songs and dances from all the provinces of Spain, but including also much composed material. Pedrell's objective was to demonstrate not only the great richness and antiquity of both repertoires but also (a cardinal point of his doctrine) their inter-relatedness. Indeed, the folk music of Spain, Pedrell argued, with its profusion of regional styles, its often sophisticated complexity and its deep roots (entwined as they often are with the roots of Spanish liturgical music as well as with the music of Islam) was the only foundation upon which a modern school of Spanish music could be built.

The Spanish heritage was indeed a great one (as well as an impressive corpus of sacred polyphony and an ethnic musical culture of formidable variety and vitality it included also a lively demotic music of the theatres and city streets), but it provided few models for those musical forms that had become the primary vehicles for serious composers elsewhere in Europe. Of the generation of composers following Pedrell (Granados, Albéniz, Falla, Turina) only Turina, the most rigorously and least Hispanically educated of them, found it possible to write a symphony, a quartet or a sonata.

As far as song was concerned, Pedrell himself provided the models: not his weak and surprisingly Gallic settings of Gautier and Hugo, but his arrangements, with piano accompaniment (still more surprisingly published under a pseudonym), of folk-songs from Andalusia. From that point on, until well into the second half of the present century, the characteristic Spanish song would be either a folk song arrangement or a song so carefully composed in folk style as to be virtually indistinguishable from an arrangement. The Spanish for 'folk song' is *canción popular*, and the folk style did indeed prove overwhelmingly popular, both in Spain and without.

Manuel de Falla

The *Siete canciones populares españolas* of Manuel de Falla (1876–1946) are his only 'nationalist' compositions in this narrow sense: none of his

own language and cultural traditions. With the exception of Victoria de los Angeles (whom it would be pedantic to call Victòria dels Àngels) such names appear here in Catalan.

other mature works uses genuine folk material at all extensively. But even in the *Siete canciones*, where not only several of the melodies but in some cases the accompaniments as well are derived from published collections, Falla has used his materials so freely and imaginatively, so fully in the spirit of Pedrell, that he must be regarded as their composer, not merely their arranger. We are fortunate in having a 'creator's recording' of them, with Falla himself accompanying the soprano Maria Barrientos (Columbia D11701 and PFX1/2; Pathé Marconi). Barrientos' performance is regarded as a touchstone by many collectors, but to my ears her voice (she was known as a lyric coloratura) is very white and innocent-sounding for such plangently vehement music, and by the time of the recording (1927) its precision and steadiness were far from perfect (although only in her mid-40s she had been singing major roles since she was fifteen). Falla's accompaniments, however, while not as virtuoso as some, can still serve as models: the sound is crisp, dry and never heavy even in the most forceful passages. The true classic among early recordings, though, is that of Conchita Supervia (Parlophone–Odéon PO 153/5; HMV HQM 1220), with the aristocratic accompaniment of Frank Marshall: his playing is as idiomatic as Falla's own and technically more secure. Supervia is incomparable: the almost snarling vibrancy of her voice has an extraordinary emotional directness that can range from aching pathos to black fury within a few bars of the concluding 'Polo' and searches out the bitter melancholy at the heart of most of these songs: in her interpretation 'El paño moruno' is not a shrewd peasant apothegm about the market value of virginity but a dark cry of lament at its loss; in the 'Jota' her voice hardens at just the point where most singers relax into tenderness, and we realise at once that it is not a charming epigram about the private language of lovers ('they say we are not in love because they do not see us talking') but a story of meetings so rare and so fleeting that their joy is almost eclipsed by the long partings between them. Her singing has the quality to which Federico García Lorca devoted an essay without ever clearly defining: *duende*, an intense and exalted expressiveness rooted in blood and earth.

Victoria de los Angeles has recorded the *Siete canciones* three times (I have not been able to locate a presumably early recording with the Spanish pianist José Tordesillas – HMV 7ERL 1030). Her 1951 version appeared while those of Barrientos and Supervia were still current, and it was adversely compared with theirs as too refined, too ladylike, even too beautiful (HMV SLS 5012). It now seems one of the very finest performances, the sorrows of the cycle seen as those of a touchingly vulnerable young woman rather than the ageless, tragic Lorca heroine portrayed by Supervia. The voice is in immaculate condition (duskiness shadowing the silvery sheen), and if her 'Polo' is lacking in throaty vehemence (and is, besides, a touch cautious in tempo) and if her 'Canción' seems slightly demure (only Supervia really searches out the pain of this song), the remainder have inimitable delicacy and poignant directness, and her pianist, Gerald Moore, is quite admirable. Even he is eclipsed, however, by the accompanist in de los Angeles' later, 'live' recording, Alicia de Larrocha (Angel S36896). The voice has by now taken on an edge, a slightly reedy quality, and this combines with tempi much faster than in the earlier performance to produce a greater urgency and intensity. The voice is no longer quite as steady as it once was, and the singer finds some of Larrocha's speeds uncomfortable, but the performance as a whole has considerable eloquence.

Anyone preferring the darkness of a mezzo voice but wanting a more recent recording than Supervia's will find Nan Merriman's account of the cycle, with Gerald Moore (EX 29 0654 3), very effective: the quality of tone is rather unvaried, and it hardens to shrewishness once or twice, but elsewhere her voice is splendidly smoky and vibrant, with an almost Supervia-like throb in the lower register. Teresa Berganza recorded these songs rather early in her career (Decca SDD 324), and her emotional projection of the 'Seguidilla murciana' and the 'Canción' is a little tentative, but in quieter numbers the lovely edged purity of her tone is most attractive, and she is one of the few mezzos since Supervia who are capable, without seeming exaggeratedly histrionic, to give a fervent, rasping throatiness to the 'Polo'. Marilyn Horne has the right vocal quality for these songs (SXL 6577): the sound itself is exciting even when not much is made of the words, but her performance is let down by melodramatic overacting in the 'Canción' (a baritonal cry of 'Madre!') and the 'Polo' (much of which is bayed rather than sung, with a wild shriek at the end). Shirley Verrett (SB 6625), despite an attractive grainy quality in quieter passages, is often loud to the point of vulgarity and her pianist is very harshly recorded. Sandra Browne (Enigma K53563) is another singer with the right vocal metal for the cycle, but her use of words is quite impassive and she takes the 'Polo' at a showily swift tempo that makes it seem merely petulant. Zara Dolukhanova (Electrecord ECE 0128) is efficient but excessively strenuous and makes little of her words, while Susan Daniel (Denon C37–7539) often pushes her voice beyond its limits into shrillness and insecurity. Recordings also exist (though I have not been able to hear them) by the mezzo-sopranos Ana Maria Iriarte (Pathé DT 1007), Cora Canne-Meijer (Musical Masterpiece Society MMS 76) and Alicia Nafé (Bellaphon 690 01010).

Fewer sopranos than mezzos have recorded the cycle. Montserrat Caballé brings to it much more throatiness and edge than one might expect, and her phrasing is wonderfully smooth. The earlier of her two recordings (Vergara L 110005) is somewhat bland, with inexpressive

Michael Oliver

words, but in the later one (SXLR 6888) even the 'Polo' has an exciting vehemence. Her fondness for scooping *portamenti* has also increased, however, and it marginally robs her of a place alongside de los Angeles among soprano interpreters of these songs. Nor does Lois Marshall (Hallmark RS1) earn that position, despite the expressiveness of her line and the incisive purity of her voice; she is another singer let down by insufficient pointing of words (and in this case by a quite dreadful recording). Jill Gomez (Saga 5409), however, uses her light and flexible voice with resourcefulness and great intelligence (aided by an exceptionally fine pianist, John Constable), roughening the tone effectively in the 'Polo' but elsewhere achieving more with understatement and simplicity of manner than the demonstrative vocal acting of many other singers.

The slightly cool elegance of that refined artist Ninon Vallin (Pathé X3460/PG 71; EX 29 0946 3) is better suited to the restrained sorrow of 'Asturiana' and the quietness of 'Nana' than to the rest of the cycle; the ache of the music is lacking, despite a surprisingly fiery 'Polo' and a thoroughly idiomatic command of the language.

Not many male singers have attempted the *Siete canciones*, though Charles Panzéra (P 749; 2C 151–73084/5) recorded three of them – 'Asturiana', 'Jota' and 'Nana' – with characteristic seriousness and elegance; oddly but effectively he dramatises the farewell of the closing lines of the 'Jota' by singing them from the far end of the studio. Gérard Souzay (Decca LX 3077) produces a studied performance, with lovely shadings and caressings of the words (an exquisitely tender 'Nana'), but for all the beauty of his sound the result is rather self-conscious: his Maurice Chevalier-like growl in the 'Seguidilla murciana' and his histrionic yelp at the end of the 'Polo' are absurd rather than expressive. José Carreras, for all the Italianate splendour of his tenor voice (Philips 411 478–1), gives a rather uninvolved reading, seldom quiet (save in the attractively gentle 'Nana') and with little sense of character or drama (though there is plenty of both in the hands of his excellent pianist, Martin Katz).

Mention should also be made of Falla's other songs, all of them cast in the shade somewhat by the popularity of the *Siete canciones*. The *Trois mélodies*, written to texts by Gautier during Falla's years in Paris, are intimate and Gallic in style (though the final 'Séguidille' tilts amusingly at French ideas of Spanishness); their only recent recording, and a charming one, is by Jill Gomez (Saga 5409). More characteristic, but until recently unpublished, are the 'Oración de las madres que tienen a sus hijos en brazos', Falla's touching response to the German invasion of Belgium in 1914, the 'Canción andaluza; el pan de ronda', very dark and sultry in the *Siete canciones* manner, and 'Dios mío, qué solos se quedan los muertos', a student work, already prefiguring Falla's 'Andalusian' style: all three have been recorded, adequately but not very strikingly, by the soprano Montserrat Alavedra (RCA SRL1 2466). Falla's only late song, the nobly declamatory 'Soneto a Córdoba', is scored for high voice and harp. Falla himself recorded it on the piano (accompanying Barrientos in a fill-up to their account of the *Siete canciones* referred to above). De los Angeles gives a far finer performance (one strained high note apart) and uses the correct accompanying instrument (ASD 2649). Barrientos is very splashy in a vaulting vocal line that is quite unsuited to her, and Falla sounds thoroughly ill at ease.

Enric Granados

Falla's later works show a retreat from the more obvious and colourful aspects of nationalism towards neo-classicism and an exploration of other aspects of the Spanish heritage. Enric Granados (1867–1916), his senior by nine years, was at least as influenced by eighteenth century Spain as by its folk music (and as much by Schumann and Chopin as by either). It is a pity that his two song collections, the *Tonadillas* and the *Canciones amatorias*, have been so seldom recorded in their entirety: both were conceived as Schumannesque *Liederkreise* rather than as narrative cycles, but it would be good for once to hear the *Tonadillas*, in particular, as Granados intended: with his evocative spoken text over the prelude to 'La maja de Goya', with the cor anglais *obbligato* in 'La maja dolorosa 1', with 'Las currutacas modestas' sung as a duet and with the solitary low-voice song of the set, 'El majo olvidado', given to a baritone (as it is, the texts of all the others being quite inappropriate for a male singer, this moving song with its strikingly imaginative accompaniment is practically never heard). The *Tonadillas* are a homage to Goya, to Scarlatti (Granados edited and performed numerous Scarlatti sonatas; the title-page describes the songs as *'escritas en estilo antiguo'*) and to the brief but pungent music-theatre pieces from which the collection takes its name: sung as a cycle, as a sequence of related dramatic *Goyescas* (or, to adopt the title of another of Granados' piano cycles, of *escenas románticas*), the vividness and economy of his invention are all the more apparent. The claim of many Spanish critics that the best of the *Tonadillas* are of a quality comparable with true Lieder seems extravagant only when a recital selection concentrates exclusively (as is often the case) on the lighter ones.

The only complete recording of *Tonadillas* that approximates to the composer's ideal plan is that by Lola Rodríguez de Aragón, accompanied by Félix Lavilla (London EL 93016). The spoken text is omitted (though Lavilla plays the long prelude to 'La maja de Goya' with such delicate expressiveness that it is almost possible to imagine it being read) and the baritone song (with its text fussily feminised as 'La maja olvidada') is transposed up an octave, but 'Las currutacas modestas' sounds delightfully and demurely witty as a duet. The cor anglais in 'La maja dolorosa 1', though dreadfully out of tune, gives at least a faint impression of Granados' poignant intention: the *obbligato* instrument represents the remembered voice of the dead lover whom the *maja* is so bitterly lamenting. Rodríguez was a pupil of Elisabeth Schumann (and the teacher of Teresa Berganza), and although her voice is a peasant-like and very nasal mezzo, penetratingly shrill at times and thus not ideal for the more gracious numbers in the set, it is capable both of charming humour (a deliciously self-possessed 'El majo discreto') and a poignant sincerity.

The other complete sets (both omitting cor anglais, baritone and duet partner) are by Conchita Badía (Vergara L 110010) and Pilar Lorengar (Spanish Columbia CCL 32037). Badía's voice was very worn and insecure by the date of her recording, and only in the quietest phrases can one hear traces of her famous subtlety of expression; elsewhere the sound is harsh and ungainly, most of the character of the music being sketched by her pianist, Larrocha. Lorengar was at the beginning of her career, and the voice is very fresh and bright, with its fast vibrato: rather unremittingly bright, indeed, and with an operatic amplitude that is best suited to the big songs of the *Maja dolorosa* sequence. There is not much humour to the lighter numbers, but she too has a fine pianist (Félix Lavilla) to make up some of the deficiency (a selection from the *Tonadillas* recorded on another occasion with Larrocha – SXL 6866 – unfortunately concentrates on very straight-faced performances of the lighter songs). A recording by Caballé, using an anonymous orchestration of the keyboard part (SB 6686), is of interest in that it provides the only decently played performance in existence of Granados' cor anglais line in 'La maja dolorosa 1'; alas, it is not confined to this one song, and others are embellished with a very prominent solo guitar. The voice is very beautiful, but there is little wit or incisiveness to her performances, and the songs emerge both over-scaled and over-sweetened; it is presumably not out of authenticist scruple that Caballé omits both the 'duet' and the 'baritone' numbers.

Selections from the *Tonadillas* have been recorded by a number of artists from whom complete performances would have been welcome. First and foremost, of course, by Supervia, who more than any other singer was able to portray both the anxiously tender woman and the scold in 'Callejeo', the ruefulness as well as the humour of 'El majo timido', the hint of malice in 'El tra la la y el punteado', and the respectable flightiness of 'Las currutacas modestas' (she also recorded 'El majo discreto', 'Amor y odio' and 'La maja dolorosa 3': RO 20324/5; HQM 1220). At one time or another de los Angeles has recorded all the *Tonadillas* save the first two of the *Maja dolorosa* sequence: a significant omission, perhaps, since she seems more at home with the charm of these songs than with their at times jarring depth of expression. However, her account of 'El majo olvidado', with Larrocha, is the best available, with its touching expression and exquisitely controlled *pianissimo* (the song also suits Badía rather well, calling as it does for much restrained quiet singing, quite low in the voice) and the same 'live' recording also includes a fine 'Amor y odio', a charmingly sprightly 'Las currutacas modestas' and a sharply characterised 'La maja de Goya' (Angel S 36896). An earlier group of *Tonadillas*, with Gonzalo Soriano, is beautifully sung but slightly underacted (CFP 40336); for sheer untarnished vocal colour and simple charm of manner a still earlier selection with Moore (HMV BLP 1037) is still outstanding. Berganza, by contrast, has tended to concentrate on the more serious songs of the set: the darkness of her voice is used to poignant, almost operatic effect in a selection including all three of the *Maja dolorosa* settings (DG 2530 598) – they gain greatly from being presented in sequence. An earlier recording of 'La maja dolorosa 1' and a couple of the lighter pieces (SDD 206) is marred by a touch of hardness and a lack of humour. Another excellent and still more amply operatic account of the *Maja dolorosa* triptych is that by Margaret Price (Orfeo S 038831); her gravity of manner and opulence of voice easily make up for a slight lack of point in her enunciation of the text. What can be accomplished by a much lighter voice is finely demonstrated by Jill Gomez's selection of *Tonadillas* (Saga 5409), which includes a highly imaginative account of 'La maja dolorosa 2', the drawn pallor of the sorrowful *maja* suggested by the quality of voice, the accompanist (the outstanding John Constable again) portraying her distractedly faltering steps in the postlude. Neither Sandra Browne (Enigma K53563), who is dull, loud and not always secure of pitch, nor Susan Daniel (Denon C37–7539) – also over-loud and often rather fast and inexpressive – measures up to the quality and the subtlety of these songs.

The high mezzo Ann Murray, however (Hyperion A66176), has both the intelligence and the variety of vocal colour that they demand; her accounts of the three *Maja dolorosa* songs (she and her pianist Graham Johnson both acutely aware of the unity of the sequence) are particularly expressive. Once or twice she makes less of the words than one might have hoped, but her 'Las currutacas modestas' (over-dubbing allows her to sing it as a duet with herself) is enchantingly done, with the phrasing of the repeat (as in her 'Callejeo') subtly and charmingly varied.

It is lamentable that the only complete recording of Granados' later collection, the *Canciones amatorias*, should be in an (albeit restrained) orchestrated version (SB 6686). Caballé is in free, warm and beautiful voice, but the presence of an orchestra, and her own tendency to the grand manner, lead her into a style of expression which robs these songs of some of their subtle intimacy. Her *cantabile* line in 'Mañanica era' is exquisite, but the innocence and delicacy of the song is understated; she rises splendidly to the big phrases of 'No lloréis ojuelos', but makes disappointingly inexpressive use of words (and how one misses the stormy turbulence of the piano accompaniment). Hers is an indispensable recording for lovers of these elusive, underrated songs, but a frustrating one. The recordings by Lorengar and by de los Angeles, however, are both with piano and both are *almost* complete (both understandably omit 'Descúbrase el pensamiento', which lies horribly low for a soprano). De los Angeles, in a 'live' performance with Larrocha (Angel S 36896), sounds slightly under pressure at times, but the momentary loss of control in a very fast 'Iban al pinar' is a small price to pay for her lightly touched blitheness. Her quiet, almost childlike manner in 'Mañanica era' is delicate and affecting, there is real charm to her 'Gracia mia' (the most *Tonadilla*-like song in this otherwise more veiled and ambiguous song-world) and her 'Llorad, corazón' is tenderly lovely. Lorengar (SXL 6866), also with Larrocha, is often too forceful for this music: the voice takes on a harsh edge under pressure, and only her restrained account of 'Mañanica era' bears comparison with de los Angeles. Conchita Badía, with a voice far more worn than Lorengar's, at least realizes that using a mere thread of tone in music such as this is vastly preferable to over-singing, but her selection (unlike de los Angeles and Lorengar she also omits 'No lloréis ojuelos') gives only very qualified pleasure (Vergara L 110010).

The few remaining songs of Granados are still more neglected, but worth investigating. Caballé has recorded three of them (all to Catalan texts) twice. Her earlier versions, from a public concert (Edigsa O1L 0481), are to be preferred to the later studio recordings (SXLR 6888), in which her tendency to indulge in drooping *portamenti* has become more marked: 'L'ocell profeta' is an ardent Lied, 'Cançó d'amor' a slow and intense love song, while 'Elegía eterna' is a passionate and declamatory scena. Of this latter there is also an earnestly expressive account by Margaret Price (Orfeo S 038831).

Joaquín Turina

Of the remaining composers of the Falla/Granados generation, Isaac Albéniz (1860–1909) wrote only a few, slight songs early in his career, while those of Joaquín Turina (1882–1949) are more problematical, at least for the non-Spanish listener. The weakness of the folk-derived, nationalist style is that it restricts the range of mood that a composer can adopt and the range of texts that he can set: one cannot imagine even Falla setting a Spanish equivalent of Goethe's 'Prometheus', or 'Ganymed' in the manner of the *Siete canciones*. Turina sought to broaden the compass of the nationalist style. His accompaniments, which betray a strong debt to his long years of study in France, are ambitious but at times thick and ungrateful, and his vocal lines (much more characteristically Spanish, even specifically Andalusian in colour) often seem to imply a voice of considerable range and strength: they call for big performances. Realizing this, most Spanish singers have been very selective in recording them (thus his rather carefully constructed short cycles of songs have been seldom recorded complete) while the dramatic, Italianate voices that he surely had in mind have as a rule ignored them. The *Canto a Sevilla*, to make matters worse, requires the services of a virtuoso pianist (the four songs of the cycle are framed by showily brilliant solos), and as a consequence only the picturesque evocation of the famous bell-tower of Seville, 'La Giralda', is at all often heard: there is a charming, rather lightweight recording of the song (in its orchestral version) by de los Angeles (SLS 5012) and a much more vehement one (with piano), much more expressive of pride in 'the arm of Seville lifted up to God' by Nan Merriman (EX 29 0654 3). In her complete recording (EMI 16380), Caballé has all the reserves of power for the big declamatory phrases of 'Semana santa' (she has the veiled delicacy, too, for the evocation of the ancient Holy Week *saeta*, though she does not always use it) but her pile-drivingly over-assertive pianist, Alexis Weissenberg, forces her almost to scream to make herself heard in 'La Giralda', and she is disappointingly melodramatic in 'El fantasma', that evocation of a spectre walking the city streets (it takes Berganza, in a grippingly acted performance – DG 2530 598 – to demonstrate that there is more in this song than immediately meets the ear).

It is again only the most obviously and picturesquely Spanish song of Turina's *Triptico*, the 'Farruca', that has proved at all popular in the recording studio. Here Caballé, with a more sympathetic accompanist (Miguel Zanetti), can give the song the large-scale performance it needs, despite the fact that her florid runs and low notes are not quite effortless (SXLR 6888). So can Merriman (EX 29 0654 3), with her biting edge and chesty vehemence. Verrett (SB 6625), with her mock-flamenco snarls (and a clangorously heavy pianist) cannot; nor can de los Angeles (SLS 5012), who tries heroically but does not have the weight for it (though her disc also includes one of Turina's best single songs, 'Tu pupila es azul', light, lyrical and with a transparent piano part for once; an elegant and charming performance). The single complete *Triptico*, which leaves one wondering why we have not heard more of its singer, is by Marilyn Richardson (World Records R 02423), a soprano with real urgent vehemence of manner, ample technique and an attractively dusky lower register: hers is the best account of the 'Farruca' on record. The incon-

Michael Oliver

siderate demands of the other two songs (they lie terrifyingly high) are also ably met, with just a touch of strain here and there.

Except for the popular, flamboyantly florid central 'Cantares', the four songs of the *Poema en forma de canciones* (plus a solo piano *Dedicatória* on a theme close to one in Falla's *Noches en los jardines de España*) are rather easier on the singer, and the cycle has received several recordings, most of them by tenors. Carreras (Philips 411 478–1) is rather beefy, and lets out an ear-splitting yell in *Cantares*; Aldo Baldin (RBM 3062) uses his slightly hard, Italianate voice with more restraint and a nice *mezza voce*; Nicolai Gedda (SAX 5278) is also rather hard, and cannot manage the difficult runs in 'Cantares'; none is half so effective as the apparently mis-cast Jill Gomez (Saga 5409), who is obliged to save her full voice and the sharp edge that it can take on for the most crucial moments (the bitter closing lines of 'Nunca olvida', the vehement outbursts of 'Cantares') but elsewhere finds far more delicacy and precision in these songs than any of her tenor colleagues. Of the isolated recordings of 'Cantares', Supervía's (Odéon 184212; Rubini GV 583) is electrifyingly urgent, Berganza's (DG 2530 598) scarcely less so, Caballé's (SXLP 6888) distinctly less so, but with stunningly flexible coloratura runs, Lorengar's (Spanish Columbia CCL 32037) shrill and slightly reserved.

It is a pity that Caballé has not recorded all three songs of the *Homenaje a Lope de Vega* sequence; her account of the central song, 'Si con mis deseos', shows her to be well-suited to its wide-spanned, slightly heavy-featured lyrical phrases (SXLP 6888). No doubt she looked at the opaquely heavy piano parts of the outer songs and decided that discretion was the better part of valour: Regina Resnik, who has recorded all three (Epic BC 1384), does not have the necessary steadiness of voice, and her dark mezzo congeals with the clogged accompaniment to glum effect. Nor does Lorengar (Spanish Columbia CCL 32037), in her account of the first two songs of the triptych, suggest that much is to be made of them. Berganza, though, in a song that is not dissimilar in manner, the 'Saeta en forma de salve a la Virgen de la Esperanza', shows what fearless vocalism and grave intensity can do for Turina: in both her recordings (SDD 206, DG 2530 598) a dark and profoundly Spanish earnestness emerges that is very impressive. A further indication of what large-scaled performances can reveal of Turina is provided by the curious but effective *Corazón de mujer*, in effect a ten-minute scena or linked cycle of brief songs. In its portrayal of the moods of a latter-day *maja* (specifically a *maja* of the fox-trotting 1920s), from worldly urbanity to bitter frustration, it makes great demands of both singer and accompanist, demands that are met with eloquent distinction by Ann Murray and Graham Johnson (Hyperion A 66176).

'Nationalists' and others

The folk-derived or folk-copying style satisfied a hunger for national pride and identity after the long, slow decline of the nineteenth century, as well as catering to foreign audiences' taste for the picturesque; it was natural that the first post-Pedrell generation of Spanish composers should seek to compose *música española* (though, as Falla, Albéniz and Turina agreed in Paris before the First World War, it should be, as Pedrell had envisaged, *música española con vistas a Europa*). But after the country had been torn asunder by the nightmare savagery of civil war, nationalism also provided comforting reassurance and the illusion that Spain had not really changed: it was prolonged and fossilised by the war and by the long dictatorship that succeeded it.

Most of the better-known songs of Salvador Bacarisse (b. 1898), Julian Bautista (1901–61), Jesús Guridi (1886–1961), Joaquín Nin (1879–1949) and his son Joaquín Nin Culmell (b. 1908), Fernando Obradors (1897–1945) and Joaquín Rodrigo (b. 1902) are so dependent upon folk material or other prior sources that they can hardly be classified as composed music. Of this group the most skilful and imaginative are Guridi (for his knack of supporting his attractive traditional melodies with simple but cunningly-wrought accompaniments), Nin (whose keyboard parts are sometimes close to Falla's in their boldness of gesture) and Rodrigo, who submits not only folk melodies but troubadour songs and melodies from sixteenth century song-books to charming and resourceful embellishment. By far the most interesting of the folklorists, however, is no composer but a poet: Federico García Lorca (1898–1936). An accomplished musician who accompanied Falla on his excursions to hear gipsy music, Lorca made striking arrangements of numerous folk-songs, mostly from Andalusia, in which the creative freedom of the musical editor is allied to the sensibility of a poet (quite a number of the texts have evidently been adapted rather than transcribed). A representative selection of his arrangements has been recorded, very stylishly and with meticulous care paid to regional dialects, by de los Angeles (ASD 2649).

The quality, the still current vitality and the rich regional variety of Spanish folk-song ensured that much pleasant music was written in this nationalist style (it is ironic, but not wholly irrelevant, that the very adjective associates the genre with Franco's regime), but it was difficult wholly to avoid a sense of escapism, of standing aside from time and history. And those composers of the Franco period (and even before) who chose not to write in this idiom have been, at least until recently, little performed and rarely recorded. Spanish critics write with an enthusiasm that whets the curiosity of the songs of Gerardo Gombau (1906–71; a convert, late in his composing career, to serialism), of Andrés Isasi (1890–1940), some of whose songs are Lieder in the strict sense, being settings, in the original, of Heine) and of Manuel Palau (1893–1966), a pupil of Ravel and Koechlin, whose style is said to be close to Respighi, but as yet there are no recordings to confirm or deny their talent. In the case of Conrado del Campo (1878–1953), however, a refined and striking musical language, somewhat diffuse but close at times to Strauss or even Pfitzner, is revealed by his five *Canciones castellanas*, only just tolerably performed by the soprano Pura María Martinez (RCA RL 35197). He confirms the existence of an 'internationalist' wing of Spanish composition, and even if only a few of his prolific output of works in all media confirm the expectation tentatively aroused by these songs, they should prove worth the search.

Neither Oscar Esplá (1886–1976) nor Xavier Montsalvatge (b. 1911) is a major composer, but both have written pleasing songs in a style largely independent of nationalism. Esplá's slight but pretty *Cinco canciones playeras españolas* have a touch of Gallic economy to them, and an appealing brightness of colour. De los Angeles' recording (ASD 505) has just the right winning charm, though she uses the composer's own bright-as-a-button orchestration; the original piano version (Berganza has recorded a single song from it (Spanish Columbia CCL 32031)) is no less dapper.

Montsalvatge's reputation has suffered from the immense popularity as an encore piece of his lazily tender, Caribbean-inflected 'Canción de cuna para dormir a un negrito', the penultimate of his five *Canciones negras*. The complete set is agreeably varied: a shrewd setting of one of Rafael Alberti's minglings of surrealist imagery with political comment, 'Cuba dentro de un piano', a high-spirited 'Canto negro' in an invented negro dialect, and so on. De los Angeles' recording of the set in its orchestral form (ASD 505) is greatly to be preferred to Caballé's of the piano version (EMI 16380). Charm and vulnerability are not among the latter soprano's most noticeable qualities, and she sounds positively embarrassed by the '¡Yambambó, Yambambé!' refrains of the 'Canto negro', while de los Angeles clearly loves everything about these songs, from the lovely hushed crooning of the 'Canción de cuna' even to the sudden anger of the closing line ('Now *Si* has turned to "Yes!"') of 'Cuba dentro de un piano'. Among recordings of isolated songs from the set, Merriman's of the 'Canción de cuna' (a real feeling of *négritude* to the grainily dark voice) and the 'Canto negro' (an edgy hint that it is not a jovial song at all) are well worth looking out for (EX 29 0654 3) and make one regret that she never recorded Ravel's *Chansons madécasses*, which in her hands they somewhat resemble. Montsalvatge's other songs, of which Caballé has recorded several (World Records CM 87), include an engaging but slighter collection of six Lorca settings, *Canciones para niños*.

Catalan composers

Two composers of distinctly greater substance are both, like Montsalvatge, from Catalonia, but the currency of their music has been restricted by their almost exclusive use of that once-suppressed minority language (a very substantial minority: Catalan is spoken by close on seven million people). Catalan culture has always been independent of the Castilian-speaking regions of Spain, looking rather towards France and to the Mediterranean, and referring back to a quite distinct political history (the closest relatives of Catalan are the *langue d'oc*, the language of the troubadours, and Provençal). The principal city of Catalonia, Barcelona, was until very recently (many Catalans would reject even that qualification) far more aware of artistic movements in the rest of Europe (often developing its own characteristic forms of them) than Madrid: the distinctively Catalan manifestation of *art nouveau* known as *modernisme* has left its mark on Barcelona, in the buildings of Gaudí, Domènech i Montaner, Puig i Cadafalch, Jujol and others, to a degree unparalleled in any other city. Painting of the *modernista* school was preoccupied above all with the portrayal of light (the links with French impressionism are obvious) and with urban life as a fit subject for the artist. The successor of *modernisme*, *noucentisme* ('nine-hundred-ism', i.e. the style of the 1900s) was neo-classical and lyrically Mediterranean, close to Cézanne and Maillol (and a seldom-acknowledged constituent of Picasso's monumental manner), and it is in this context, perhaps, that the songs of Eduard Toldrà (1895–1962) and Frederic Mompou (1893–1987) may best be appreciated: Toldrà as a *modernista* composer, Mompou as a *noucentista*.

Eduard Toldrà

The songs of Toldrà are mostly brief, simple and warmly lyrical, often with a touch of what Mompou has called 'urban popularism': 'light music', therefore, and genially urbane in the other sense of the word, but the best of them have a responsiveness to words, a refinement of melody, above all an innocent directness that raise them above the drawing-room trifles that they sometimes superficially resemble. Toldrà can sometimes take a simple verbal image, like the *bordoneig suau d'abelles* ('the gentle drone of bees') in his best-known song 'Maig', and with a musical phrase no less plain produce an effect that, in the mouth of a fine singer, is magically greater than the sum of its parts.

Michael Oliver

With very few exceptions his songs have been recorded only by Catalan singers, most extensively by Caballé and the baritone Manuel Ausensi. Of Caballé's two collections – one with orchestra, using the composer's own orchestrations (Vergara 110.002 LS), and one with piano (Edigsa 01L0481) – the former is the more important since it includes complete recordings of Toldrà's two best-known song-cycles, *L'ombra del lledoner* and *La rosa als llavis*. They are sung with real and evident affection, creamy beauty of tone and more expressive colouring than this artist sometimes employs; the record also includes 'Maig', and three other single songs. The other, shorter selection (one side of a disc otherwise devoted to Mompou) contains nothing that is not present on the Vergara record; made at a public recital, it is generally less well sung and marred by rather a lot of audience noise. Ausensi (Spanish Columbia C7111) has the advantage of an orchestra conducted by the composer himself (an advantage largely negated by the recording, which focuses on the singer quite excessively). His voice has a throaty, almost guttural vehemence and is not always perfectly steady, but his unaffected and unashamed sentiment and his enjoyment of the Catalan language are a good match for the almost (but not quite) naive directness of the music. Innocence is very close to sentimentality in his 'Cançó de l'amor que passa', he almost croons the ingratiating 'Canticel', but the expressive sincerity of his 'Maig', even the rueful laugh at the end of his 'Menta i farigola' remain obstinately in the memory.

De los Angeles has recorded Toldrà's songs much less generously than Caballé (and only in their orchestral settings) but often with an extra touch of fantasy and warmth. Her 'Canço de grumet' (from the *L'ombra del lledoner* cycle) is blithely light-footed, her 'Anacreóntica' charmingly points up a faint hint of Strauss in the vocal line, her 'Cançó incerta' (not recorded by Caballé) is hauntingly touching and her account of 'Maig' is exquisite: a raptly magical evocation of still summer warmth, the voice pure and poised (ASD 2517). Supervia's Toldrà recordings (some of them with piano) are also few but well worth seeking out for the depth of emotion she finds even in apparently slight songs: a poignant regret in 'Canticel' (Odéon 185006; Rubini GV 583), a ruefulness much closer to sorrow than Ausensi's in 'Menta i farigola' and 'Cançó de l'amor que passa' (respectively Odéon 184199 and 184186; both are included in Rubini GV 591 and OASI 533/4).

Frederic Mompou

Mompou's art is delicate, refined and reticent: it is wholly characteristic of him that he should have chosen the *Cantar del alma* of St John of the Cross as a song-text but should then have omitted all but six verses of the

142

poem and should have set them virtually unaccompanied, the piano providing only a simple prelude, interlude and postlude. At just over five minutes it is Mompou's longest song (almost his longest movement in any genre, indeed) and at the same time his most concentrated: it is curiously effective in its distilled, restrained earnestness.

His best-known set of songs, 'El combat del somni', is almost effusive by comparison, especially in its later orchestral version (indeed, the almost languishing beauty of its opening song, 'Damunt de tu només les flors', can easily mislead a singer into understating its intensity: it is an elegy over a flower-bedecked coffin). In its original form the cycle consisted of three songs; only Caballé's recording with the composer as accompanist (Vergara 701 STL) includes the fourth, 'Fes-me la vida transparent', which Mompou later added. Without its warm, still raptness other performances seem by comparison incomplete, and Caballé is heard here at her very best: the voice in immaculate condition, phrasing with great subtlety and finely responsive both to the text and to the supple *rubato* of her pianist. A later, 'live' recording, apart from omitting the final song, finds her in rougher voice (the lower notes are merely sketched) and her pianist, Rosa Sabater, cannot match Mompou himself in subtlety or accuracy (Edigsa 01L0481). The best of the other incomplete versions are those of Merriman (EX 29 0654 3) and (with orchestra) de los Angeles (ASD 2517). Merriman's voice darkens the music, not inappropriately, in 'Damunt de tu' and she succeeds better than most singers in giving a sense of finality to the third song, 'Jo et pressentia com la mar', by singing it with reflective gravity; Moore, her pianist, is outstandingly sensitive. Spurred on by the sparkling richness of Mompou's orchestration of 'Jo et pressentia', de los Angeles, by contrast, gives this song an eagerness that is no less attractive, but the combination elsewhere in the cycle of melting vocalism and rather over-rich orchestral colour gives the music an almost deliquescent aspect (there is more shadow and urgency to de los Angeles' earlier recording, with piano, of the opening slong alone SXLP 30147). Carreras' voice is rather too Italianate for these songs, but his love for them is evident in the generous *cantabile* of his 'Jo et pressentia' (concluding with a beautifully shaded *diminuendo*) and his expressive use of headvoice in the central song, 'Aquesta nit un mateix vent', and his accompanist, Martin Katz, is first-rate (Philips 411 478–1). Berganza's recording, with piano but in Castilian translation, of the first and third songs of the set only, has such eloquence and subtlety that one regrets all the more that she has not recorded the complete cycle in Catalan (Spanish Columbia CCL 32031).

Caballé's Vergara disc includes, apart from 'El combat del somni', a dozen of Mompou's other songs, the exquisitely simple and lyrical 'Pastoral' and the epigrammatic 'Comptines' (to French and Castilian as well as Catalan texts) seeming to confirm him as an elegant miniaturist, while the more urgent and openly eloquent 'Aureana do sil' and the soberly intense 'Cantar del alma' deny it (curiously but revealingly Mompou has said that his favourite painters are Vermeer . . . and El Greco).

Mompou is regarded as the most important Catalan composer of his generation and yet, at least outside Catalonia, he is inadequately represented in record catalogues. The quality of his best songs (and of his similarly subtle and concentrated piano music) makes one wonder whether other members of the Catalan school, such as Manuel Blancafort (b. 1897) might be no less worth discovering. While many of the younger generation of Castilian composers (still digesting their country's late exposure to modernism) have, like modernists elsewhere, abandoned the art song with piano accompaniment almost entirely, those of Catalonia (where modernism as well as *modernisme* has long been current) have not always done so. With the expatriate Schoenbergian Robert Gerhard (1896–1970) and his pupil Joaquim Homs (b. 1906) as father-figures (the latter is quite a prolific song-writer), such composers as Josep Casanovas (b. 1924), Josep Cercós (b. 1925), Josep Soler (b. 1935) and, in a more conservative idiom, Manuel Valls (b. 1920) have continued to contribute to the song repertoire, writing, like Mompou, what Pedrell might well have described in his native tongue as *musica català amb vistas a Europa*.

Mussorgsky

STEPHEN JOHNSON

Songs and Dances of Death (*Pesni i Plyaski Smerti*)

Arkhipova, Wustman	HMV ASD 3103
Borg, Prague Radio Symphony/Klima	Supraphon SUA ST 50390
Christoff, ORTF/Tzipine	1C 137–173 164–3
Diakov, Wyss	Accent ACC 140035
Kruysen, Lee	Telefunken 6.41998
London, Ulanowski	Am. Col. ML 4906
London, Taubman	Am. Col. MS 6734
Luxon, Willison	Argo ZRG 708
Nesterenko, Krainev	Melodiya S10 12935/6
Rebroff, Seidemann	Intercord INT 120 871
Rehfuss, Haeusslein	Decca LW 5037
Rosing, Foggin	Parlo. 78rpm SW 4/5; Artisco YD 3014
Saedén, Plasson	BIS LP 70
Sze, Smith	Iramac 6501
Talvela, Gothoni	Decca SXL 6974
Tavela, Aho	BIS–CD 325
Tourel, Bernstein	Odyssey Y 32882
Vishnevskaya, Rostropovich	Philips 6527 222
Vishnevskaya, LPO/Rostropovich	HMV ASD 3436

Sunless (*Bez Solntsa*)

Christoff, Labinsky	1C 137–173 164–3
Diakov, Wyss	Accent ACC 140035
Kurenko, Pastukhoff	Capitol CTL 7100
Nesterenko, Krainev	Melodiya S10 122935/5
Schenk, Starke	Colosseum 620
Slobodskaya, Newton	Saga 5357
Sze, Smith	Iramac 6517
Vishnevskaya, Rostropovich	HMV ASD 3221

Stephen Johnson

The Nursery (*Detskaya*)

Berganza, Requejo	Clavès CD 8204
Christoff, Labinsky	EMI 1C 137–173 164–3
Dorliak, Richter	Monitor MC 2020
Kurenko, Pastukhoff	Capitol CTL 7068
Price, Lockhart	RCA LSB 5001
Seefried, Werba	DG 410 847–1
Slobodskaya, Newton	Saga 5357
Söderström, Ashkenazy	Decca SXL 6900
Woolf, Bedford	Turnabout TV 34331
Zareska, Favaretto	French Columbia FCX 505

Songs and Dances of Death (*Pesni i Plyaski Smerti*); Sunless (*Bez Solntsa*)

During the summer of 1868, just a few months before getting down to work on the first version of *Boris Godunov*, Mussorgsky made several attempts to clarify his thoughts on musical realism. A letter from this period contains the following remark: 'My music must be an artistic reproduction of human speech in all its finest shades.' This is, in effect, the first article of Mussorgsky's artistic credo. He may have developed and enriched it in years to come, but the fundamental belief remained the same: the intonations and inflections of human speech were the composer's working material; what he had to do was work them into an artistically satisfying statement without decoration, exaggeration or romantic distortion.

A great deal has been written about Mussorgsky's ideas on realism, particularly in Soviet Russia. Indeed, a Mussorgsky-derived 'theory of intonation' has formed the basis of one of the classic treatises of Soviet musicology, Boris Asafiev's *Musical Form as Process*. Western commentators on the other hand have tended to be a little more sceptical: are Mussorgsky's ideas really that original? Isn't this just another variation on the notion of *stile recitativo* – the principles of the Florentine Camerata in nineteenth century Russian dress? Not entirely. Mussorgsky may have shared with composers like Jacopo Peri and Giulio Caccini a concern for clarity and directness of expression, but the kind of speech that he sought to recreate in music was very different from the exalted and rarified dialogues of classical antiquity. The everyday utterances of the ordinary people – this was to be the source of Mussorgsky's art. Like many members of the Russian *intelligentsiya* in the latter half of the nineteenth century, Mussorgsky believed passionately that the common people possessed enormous spiritual resources, despite their lamentable social

146

conditions. From them, from their everyday utterances, from their ancient stories and traditions, and especially from their music, the composer could forge an entirely new kind of art, powerful enough to challenge, and eventually supplant, the detested notion of 'art for art's sake'.

'Art representing beauty only, in the material sense, is crude childishness, art in an infantile stage. The subtlest features of the masses, the most searching investigation of those little-known regions and their conquest – such is the artist's true mission . . . To observe and study them by reading, observing, conjecturing, to probe it all to the core, and with it to feed humanity as with a health-giving food, never tasted before; there is a task for you, there is the joy of joys.'

But how does all this apply to works like *Sunless* and *Songs and Dances of Death*? After all *Sunless* was composed in a period of deep disillusionment after the apparent failure of the *Boris* experiment. If any work of Mussorgsky's deserves to be called 'subjective' or 'introspective' it is this cycle, with its central image of a solitary and alienated man, his moods fluctuating from boredom to anxiety to thoughts of self-extinction – a perfect counterpart, it is often said, for the Dostoyevskian 'underground man'. The once-revered masses have become the 'petty' and 'spiteful' crowd, from whom the hero turns in horror and disgust. And yet despite his depression and frustration at the incomprehension of critics and audiences, and despite the efforts of his friend and collaborator, the poet Arseny Golenishchev-Kutuzov, to dissuade him from continuing his experiments in musical realism, Mussorgsky never shifted from his basic position *vis-à-vis* the role of the artist. The music of *Songs and Dances of Death* and especially of *Sunless* contains some of the subtlest examples of Mussorgskian musical recitation, and the *Songs and Dances* in particular are rich in Russian popular elements. Communication is essential, no matter how small and intimate the audience, and the means to achieve it are the same as in *Boris* and *Khovanshchina*: the blending of the elements of recitative and melody – what Mussorgsky called 'the melody of life' – and the most characteristic features of the popular vocal and instrumental style, for Mussorgsky, and for many Russian composers after him, a truly vital musical vernacular.

And it is important to remember that Mussorgsky's concern for realism has its counterbalance. As he said, his music must be an *artistic* reproduction of human speech: the melody of life must also satisfy in purely musical terms. There has been a tendency, particularly amongst Russian singers, to emphasise the realistic at the expense of the artistic: to indulge in a kind of vocal acting that distorts Mussorgsky's melodic lines almost out of recognition. It was this kind of thing that aroused M. D. Calvocoressi's indignation in his 'Master Musicians' book on

Mussorgsky (published 1946):

> There exists no tradition for the interpretation of Mussorgsky's music. But one has long been forming which (abomination of abominations!) tends not to interpret it but regard it as raw material to be worked on and improved on . . . The song repertory stands in great danger. Of late years certain Russian singers have set a nefarious example by introducing gags, changes of tempo and tone, even grunts and hiccoughs, and gramophone recordings exist of these sins against the spirit. How one longs for an antidote.

Turning first of all to the *Songs and Dances of Death*, we encounter several examples of what Calvocoressi calls 'sins against the spirit'; indeed it is not difficult to identify at least one of the performers who so enraged him. Vladimir Rosing's recording, with accompanist Myers Foggin, first appeared in the mid-1930s. As an example of character acting, it is remarkable – intensely exaggerated but at the same time stylised in a way that reminds one occasionally of Eisenstein's *Ivan the Terrible*, but more often of the Wicked Witch of the West in the film version of *The Wizard of Oz*. Rosing's Death is a thoroughly insidious character, insinuating and wheedling rather than commanding, even in the grimly triumphant conclusion of the fourth and final song, 'The Field-Marshal'. Scene setting is often highly effective, and the closing pages of the 'Trepak' are poignant as well as ironic, but, as a whole, one would hardly call it an outstandingly musical interpretation. Rosing plainly does regard the text as 'material to be worked upon', and his *Sprechstimme*-like delivery frequently distorts both the shape and the rhythmic character of the vocal line. Heard once, it can be quite electrifying, but on repetition the effect quickly palls.

Artisco's LP transfer of Rosing's *Songs and Dances* puts the songs in Mussorgsky's order: 'Lullaby', 'Serenade', 'Trepak', 'The Field-Marshal', though the texts themselves are from Rimsky-Korsakov's revised version, published after Mussorgsky's death (Rimsky placed the 'Trepak' first, before the 'Lullaby'). Quite a number of recordings of *Songs and Dances of Death* use the Rimsky-Korsakov revision, in which Mussorgsky's often startlingly original harmonies are softened and 'functionalised', and the melodic lines are at times considerably re-shaped. Boris Christoff's complete cycle (recorded 1957) compounds the felony by making use of orchestrations by Labinsky, Lyapunov and Rimsky-Korsakov himself. It is known that Mussorgsky considered orchestrating these song, but if he had the results would almost certainly have been very different from these polished and rather tame efforts. Nevertheless, Christoff's performances are in an utterly different class from those of Rosing: strongly characterised, they are by no means unmusical. The anguish of the mother in

'Lullaby' is most affecting, and Death himself manages to be both malign and majestic, but the notes are there (despite the occasional 'swoon' or dramatically prolonged *portamento*) and phrases are finely and expressively shaped. 'The Field-Marshal' is thrilling, Christoff's rich, powerful tone sounding loud and clear above the tumult of the accompaniment. But Christoff made another, and to my mind still better recording of this song, this time with piano accompaniment (Rimsky's version again) played by Gerald Moore (RLS 735). Relieved of the need to establish a presence above the full orchestra, Christoff achieves far greater subtleties of characterisation, and there is a particularly strong sense of dramatic shape, with the final phrase truly climactic. The recording (dating from 1951) gives a recessed and emasculated piano sound, but the grandeur and immediacy of the performance is not seriously affected. Christoff has indeed 'probed it all to the core', and having done so addresses his audience with thrilling directness.

Five other singers use the Rimsky-Korsakov version of *Songs and Dances of Death*: Anton Diakov, Ivan Rebroff, Heinz Rehfuss, Jennie Tourel and Yi-Kwei Sze. Rehfuss – another recording from the early 1950s – sings in French, and the results are surprisingly effective. Rehfuss is a fairly light baritone (he certainly sounds so in the company of all these Russians), but his singing is so expressive and musical that one is soon prepared to put aside received impressions about how this music should sound. In the introduction to the 'Serenade' and the sad little lullaby at the end of the 'Trepak', Rehfuss' simplicity is most affecting, and although he does not share Christoff's feeling for the dance rhythms of the 'Trepak' (full-blooded Slavic energy and abandon would hardly be consistent with the tone of his interpretation), there is plenty of vitality. A civilised performance, it works because Rehfuss is able to involve the listener, to take him or her as it were into his confidence. His pianist, Hans Willi Haeusslein, is a discreet accompanist – perhaps just a little too much so at times.

If you consider the age of the Rehfuss recording, his use of the Rimsky text is not so surprising, and the same goes for Jennie Tourel. Quite why Diakov, Rebroff or Sze should have opted for it is another matter. None of these performances can be said to leave a particularly deep impression. Anton Diakov and the Chinese Yi-Kwei Sze both have strong firm voices with a great deal of chest resonance, but even the most dramatic moments in their interpretations tend to sound studied – applied to the music rather than drawn up from within it – and there's little in the way of poignancy. Also it sounds to me as if both Diakov and Sze are singing to the microphone rather than to an audience: not a very involving experience in either case. Ivan Rebroff's interpretation is better thought out and altogether more authoritative. A veiled, ghostly tone in the opening of the

'Trepak' gives way to rhythmic energy as the dance itself begins. The 'Serenade' is seductive in tone and acted with great aplomb. But although Rebroff is more musicianly than Rosing, it is his acting, rather than his singing, that catches the attention, and when he does show appropriate concern for the notes he can be disconcertingly flat. I find little to be enthusiastic about in Jennie Tourel's performance, in which the accompanist is the young Leonard Bernstein. At first Tourel's resigned sadness moves the hearer, but there is little variety overall, and although she succeeds more than many of the Russians in getting the notes, she seems to have made little effort to bring shape or expressive conviction to the music. A few genuinely perceptive moments in the quieter stretches of 'The Field-Marshal' hardly merit a recommendation.

There has been a number of recordings of excerpts from *Songs and Dances of Death*, of which the following are all, in their different ways, outstanding: Boris Christoff (discussed above) and Georgi Nelepp in 'The Field-Marshal', Feodor Chaliapin in the 'Trepak' (GEMM 170) and Mark Reizen in both these songs. All use Rimsky's text, and all but Chaliapin have piano accompaniments. The Russian tenor Georgi Nelepp recorded 'The Field-Marshal' not long before he died in 1957. It's a thrilling performance – urgent, strongly projected and finely characterised, with a powerful note of anguish in the culminating vision of Death triumphant. Chaliapin's 1929 recording comes perilously close to over-acting, and the coda (marked *poco a poco rallentando e diminuendo*) gets *very* slow. Nevertheless, it's a compelling performance, despite the ancient sound, and despite a rather drastic cut (bars 39–47). The Russian bass Mark Reizen was 85 when he recorded 'Trepak' and 'The Field-Marshal', and his voice is understandably unsteady in pitch and tone; even so it's an unusually eloquent and authoritative performance. To make the 'Trepak' dance convincingly at such an advanced age is no mean feat, but Reizen manages it with full honours, and his 'Field-Marshal' is no less impressive – commanding in fortes and full of insidious charm in pianos. More than any other singer, Reizen seems to me to vindicate Mussorgsky's theorisings about speech-melody: his singing is full of subtle inflections, yet the composer's pitch-relations and rhythmic patterns are obviously regarded as crucial. It retains the immediacy of speech without sacrificing its qualities as song (S10–13671).

Before passing on to those singers who favour the original undiluted Mussorgsky, there's one more version that we must consider: Kim Borg, with the Prague Radio Symphony Orchestra, conducted by Alois Klima. The orchestration used in this version is uncredited: it is apparently based on Mussorgsky rather than Rimsky, but the latter's order – 'Trepak' – 'Lullaby' – 'Serenade' – 'Field-Marshal' – is preserved. It is a subtle performance, not so gripping as Christoff's but undeniably moving. Death's lullaby over the dying child is achingly sad, and the 'Serenade' really does live up to the implications of its title – a seduction in song rather than a melodrama with musical accompaniment. Which only makes it all the more regrettable that the orchestration should be so fussy – so full of superfluous and distracting detail. The accompaniment to 'The Field-Marshal' is simply too noisy, and Borg often has to use all his vocal power to establish a suitable presence. It is still far from being a sustained bellow though: even here Borg's flexibility and musicality shine through.

Of the singers who perform *Songs and Dances of Death* as the composer wrote it, one, in my opinion, stands out: George London. There are two London recordings: the earlier, mono version features pianist Paul Ulanowski, and in the later one Leo Taubman accompanies. Both contain haunting performances of the opening 'Lullaby': the mother's pathetic remonstrations really touch the heart, and Death is a fascinatingly complex character, by turns alluring, consoling and grimly acquisitive. Dance rhythms in the 'Trepak' are well pointed, and in the *coda* one really feels the life ebbing away from the dying *muzhik*. London's earlier 'Serenade' has a beauty and poignancy which the second version captures only intermittently, but his later attempt at 'The Field-Marshal' achieves still greater richness of expressive nuance, and as with Christoff's earlier recording, there is a strong sense of purpose and dramatic shape. It should be added that London's Russian pronunciation is first-rate, and that every word seems to count – what a pity he never recorded *Sunless*.

Of the remaining performances, it is Irina Arkhipova who excites the strongest admiration. Like many Russian singers, she has a wide, intense vibrato, but she is capable of considerable tonal variation. There is a lovely ethereal quality about the opening of the 'Serenade', evocative of a clear, cold evening sky, and her sense of climax in the 'Trepak' is as strong as in any of the other recordings in this survey. The dialogue between Death and the mother in 'Lullaby' are quite gripping, as is the final climax of 'The Field-Marshal' – Death really struts in the final bars. Even so, her singing somehow is not quite as affecting as that of George London, for all the energy and intelligence – a charge one could level even more strongly at Benjamin Luxon. Luxon has obviously thought long and hard about his interpretation, and his vocal acting impresses at first, but after a while one begins to wonder if his style would not be more appropriate in one of those Victorian parlour songs that he has championed so enthusiastically. 'The Field-Marshal' works best, though even here Luxon's rather calculated melodramatics have an inauthentic ring. For an antidote one could do worse than turn to the Swedish baritone Erik Saedén – a comparatively light voice, but he acts well, without coarse theatricality, and his shaping of phrases, and indeed of the songs as a whole, is highly sensitive. Not a stirring performance, but often a gently

Stephen Johnson

moving one. 'The Field-Marshal' might have been more effective if Saedén had chosen a lower key: top notes sound strained in the final bars.

That leaves Bernard Kruysen, Martti Talvela, Galina Vishnevskaya and Evgeny Nesterenko. Vishnevskaya and Talvela have both recorded *Songs and Dances* twice: once with piano, and once in an orchestrated version. Vishnevskaya's orchestration is by Shostakovich, and it is easily the most impressive scoring available on record. Both of her performances have their impressive moments – the closing pages of the 'Trepak' have a strange kind of distant sadness, particularly impressive in the recording with piano, but elsewhere her acting makes Luxon sound restrained, in fact there are times when it borders on the hysterical. In the piano version, just before the 'Serenade's' final exultant *ti moya!* (you are mine!), there is a massive intake of breath that almost had me diving for cover.

Talvela commissioned his orchestration specially from the Finnish composer Kalevi Aho. As in the Borg version, this orchestration is full of extra detail: swirling harp *glissandi*, jingling sleigh-bells, and – inexplicably – chiming bells during the mother's outbursts in 'Lullaby'. Talvela has a fine voice, but in both recordings his involvement in the music seems to fluctuate. The version with piano is the more convincing – the 'Trepak' really dances, and the opening of the 'Serenade' is quite touching, despite slight insecurity of pitch – but generally speaking these are rather low-voltage performances. There is plenty of power in Nesterenko's version, but little subtlety. A very disappointing rendering altogether, not at all comparable with his fine *Sunless* (see below). His 'Field-Marshal' is delivered as an almost unrelieved bellow: *vse stikhlo* (all is quiet) says the text at bar 31 – it certainly isn't here! There's a good deal more poetry in the Kruysen version: a thoughtful performance, musically shaped with moments of insight, though lacking in power and conviction in 'The Field-Marshal', and his tight vibrato is not easy to take over long stretches.

And so to *Sunless*. Whatever one's opinion of the relative merits of the two cycles, there can be no denying the greater subtlety of Mussorgsky's realism in this group of songs. Scene setting and narrative are almost entirely absent (the nature of the text ensures that) and it is left to the piano to provide the illustrative elements – the steadily flowing waters in 'On the River' or the imagined death knell in 'Elegy'. The pace is often rapid, and the central character's thoughts – often strikingly contrasted – flow into one another in a manner that seems to anticipate the 'stream of consciousness' technique. On the face of it, *Sunless* seems to eschew the 'features of the masses': the hero of these songs renounces 'senseless day' and 'the busy streets', seeking solace in lonely nocturnal meditations and thoughts of death.

152

And yet, as in *Songs and Dances of Death*, the life of the vocal line often derives from the composer's involvement in the Russian musical vernacular. The building of paragraphs, even whole songs, on reiterated melodic cells – varied on repetition rather than developed in the classical sense – is an abiding characteristic of Slavic folk melody. Passages like the disturbed *allegros* in 'Elegy' are built up on repeated rhythmic patterns like those of certain Russian popular dance forms, and the lovely *andante cantabile* at the heart of 'At last an end to senseless day', in which the hero thinks nostalgically of a lost love, adds to this a melodic shape whose roots are also distinctly popular. And here, even more than in *Songs and Dances of Death*, it is vital that 'the reproduction of human speech in all its finest shades' does not result in unmusicality. *Sunless* contains some of Mussorgsky's most beautiful melodic writing. Anything approaching the pantomimic excess of a Vladimir Rosing would have disastrous consequences in music like this.

There have been far fewer recordings of *Sunless*. On the whole it has not attracted the more theatrically-inclined personalities – which given the nature of the music is probably just as well – but it has drawn fine performances from some of those singers whose *Songs and Dances of Death* were rather less enthusiastically reviewed above.

Take Vishnevskaya for instance. After her terrifyingly histrionic *Songs and Dances* one fears the worst, but her reading here is actually much more subdued and subtle, full of restrained intensity and imaginative tonal contrast. How effective is her sudden withdrawal into almost inexpressive coldness in the final bars of 'At last an end to senseless day' – one really feels the daydream evaporating. Occasionally I feel she misses the point, as in her heavy, plodding quavers in the agitated *allegro* episodes of the 'Elegy', but the concluding song, 'On the River', is hauntingly sad. Rostropovich's strong but by no means obtrusive accompaniment is an added bonus.

Nesterenko's *Sunless* comes as a welcome surprise. The recording catches a slight hardness in his voice, but Nesterenko uses his closeness to the microphone to great effect, creating a compelling intimacy, and never over-projecting. His rapid fluctuations in tone and expressive manner are balanced throughout by sensitive phrasing and pacing; moreover, Nesterenko has a strong feeling for the shape of the cycle as a whole, building steadily to a thrilling climax at the words *smerti zvon* (death knell) in the 'Elegy', without exaggerating Mussorgsky's notably restrained dynamics. Thoughts of self-destruction in 'On the river' now sound like a direct consequence of this chilling vision, rather than yet another passing mood.

Kruysen's thoughtful approach is altogether more fruitful in *Sunless*. There is more tonal variation too, and his confidential manner, amounting almost to a whisper in the opening of 'Elegy', draws the listener in most effectively; but again one is not exactly moved. Luxon, by contrast, seems to identify closely with the changing moods of *Sunless*. His performance lacks Nesterenko's sense of overall shape, but his characterisation is psychologically acute and not at all theatrical. Still, one wishes his blood would boil, or at least just simmer a little in the more passionate outbursts, particularly in the frenetic *allegros* of the 'Elegy'.

Once again, I was disappointed by Diakov and Yi-Kwei Sze. Diakov does very little to characterise or shape Mussorgsky's vocal lines, and there is a ponderous quality about some of the quicker passages. Sze's approach is slightly more humane, but his alternations of brooding darkness and quiet commiseration simply can't do justice to the many shades of meaning. He misses the irony completely in the concluding *i Bog stoboy* (and God rest your soul) of 'Ennui' – Mussorgsky has no intention of offering consolation here.

As for Manfred Schenk, who sings *Sunless* in a German translation, I hadn't realised just how repetitive the rhythmic structure of 'Within four walls' was until I heard his performance. For page after page the music takes on a relentless, plodding character, far more suggestive of the worst kind of Wagnerian narrative recitative than of the Mussorgskian 'melody of life'. Altogether more admirable are Maria Kurenko and Oda Slobodskaya. Kurenko's involvement is not entirely consistent, but there are some fine touches, like the sighing *skuchay* (boredom) of 'Ennui'. Perhaps Kurenko might have achieved more with the aid of a more responsive accompanist. Vsevolod Pastukhoff sails blithely through the opening of 'Ennui' and the 'death knell' in 'Elegy' is ludicrously underpowered. Slobodskaya is luckier in her accompanist, Ivor Newton, and although her voice was past its best when she made this recording, there is some highly expressive singing here. Slobodskaya really does make the vocal writing of 'Within four walls' and 'In the crowd' feel like speech, and yet there's actually very little bending of notes or phrases. Unfortunately 'On the river' is too insecure for comfortable listening.

Finally Christoff. Not a flawless performance: there is a feeling of strain in the *andante cantabile* lyricism at the heart of 'An end at last to senseless day', and Christoff's 'Ennui' has a quite inappropriate tonal splendour. But this is carping criticism: Christoff's singing is powerfully suggestive – one continually senses strong feelings smouldering beneath the surface – and extraordinarily intimate: one is somehow drawn into the singer's internalisings, raging with him at the 'rough, laughing crowds' and staring with him fixedly at the dark, swirling river. And here, as in *Songs and Dances of Death*, there is a truly uplifting vitality – 'the melody of life' – by no means at variance with the subject matter, and communicated directly to the heart of the listener.

154

The Nursery (*Detskaya*)

A really good performance of *Sunless* can be an uplifting experience; nevertheless it is something of a relief to turn to *The Nursery* after all that dark introspection. Amongst the songs, *The Nursery* marks the climax of Mussorgsky's realism: others may be equally lifelike, but few manage to combine the pictorialism, the recitative-like vocal style, and even the musical onomatopoeia, with such high artistry; the vocal line of 1, for instance, almost attains the quality of speech, yet at the same time one is aware of an apparently seamless process of motivic transformation. A performance must somehow keep these factors in balance. Interpretation must be musical, but it should also be vivid and naturalistic enough to make the listener 'suspend disbelief' – to compel one to accept that these are the spontaneous utterances of a child, and a very lively child at that.

Not surprisingly, most of the interpreters of *Nursery* on record have been women. The number of adult males who have been tempted to try it is very small, and only one appears in this survey: Boris Christoff. Even so there are problems for the female interpreter too – especially for those of riper years. A matronly tone destroys credibility, and exaggerated sweetness can be equally ruinous. Mussorgsky's little Misha[1] can be petulant, or just plain spiteful, and it's Mussorgsky's intention to portray his behaviour without adult sentimentality.

Nina Dorliak (accompanied by her husband, Sviatoslav Richter) is a fine example of how balance can be maintained. The first song is affectionately characterised, but the notes are all there and the phrasing is often very beautiful. She acts the other 'roles' (the Nurse in 2 and 5 and the consoling mother in 6) convincingly, without resorting to caricature to emphasise the contrast. At the same time she is always aware of the folk derivations in the vocal line – the lovely lullaby in 4 has a gentle and most unoperatic eloquence. Like Eugenia Zareska, Margaret Price and Simon Woolf she reverses the order of the last two songs and cuts the end of 7 in order to make a smoother transition – a pity, especially when the interpretation is generally of such high quality.

'It is particularly unfortunate' lamented *The Record Guide* in 1950 'that no record company should have decided to preserve the fascinating and authentic interpretations of Mme Oda Slobodskaya of the song cycle called *The Nursery*'. It wasn't until 1959 that a company rose to the challenge, and by that time Slobodskaya's voice was past its best: pitch is

---

[1] There seems to be a slight problem with names in *The Nursery* (assuming that it is the same child who is depicted in each song). In 2 the child refers to himself as 'Misha' and 'Mishenka' (diminutives of Mikhail), but in 5 he has acquired a 'brother Mishenka'. A momentary lapse of memory on Mussorgsky's part?

unsteady and the tone has an occasional quavery quality. Hers is obviously not the voice of a very young boy, and the acting, though highly characterful, has nothing of the disconcerting quickness of childish behaviour. Still there are lovely moments: strain may be evident in the higher regions of 4, but the singing has a smile, and the little encouragements to the doll ('Sleep, Tyapa, won't you!') are strangely touching.

Tonally, Maria Kurenko sounds much more convincing in these songs, even though the recording catches a certain hardness in her voice. Her manner is pleasingly relaxed, but to my mind somewhat under-characterised. In the folk-lullaby phrases that open 4 she is sweetly expressive, but the tiny recitative that follows ('Sleep, Tyapa . . . ') is lifelessly accurate. Likewise she sails through the climax of 6 without apparent concern for Misha's little accident. Ultimately, not a very memorable performance.

Zareska is altogether more convincing. She may not be quite able to match Dorliak's childlike purity of tone, but her characterisation is a good deal more vital than that of Kurenko. Song 4 is hauntingly beautiful – though one can't help wondering if she has momentarily forgotten that this is a child singing to a doll, not a real mother singing to a real baby. 6 is great fun, and the child–mother dialogues are touching and amusing.

I have now dealt with the Russians. Our next four ladies are west Europeans, and a fairly wide selection too: Margaret Price, Irmgard Seefried, Teresa Berganza and Elisabeth Söderström. Price achieves a beautifully pure tone, and her Russian pronunciation is exemplary. Her interpretation has some splendid moments – a sense of terrified fascination at the 'big black beetle' in 3, and a comical petulance at the end of 2 – but the first and last songs are a little too hurried for my liking, and I wish she could have been a little less rhythmically exact in 1. A minor complaint perhaps, but it does make me slightly uneasy, as does her reversal of the last two songs. True, Mussorgsky did write 7 before 6, but like Dorliak and Woolf, Price removes those last three bars of piano solo, presumably in the interests of smooth transition. It is a pity to lose that final flourish, a rather more convincing conclusion for this high-spirited cycle than the evanescent quavers at the end of 6.

At least Price and Dorliak *perform* 7. For some unaccountable reason Seefried omits it altogether. Does she consider 7 in some way inferior to the other songs? I can't think why she should. She also sings in German, and there's no doubt that her translation does affect the character of the cycle ('Grossmutter' for instance is a rather stiff substitute for the affectionate 'Babushka'), even of the child himself. His outbursts at Nurse sound positively vituperative when accompanied by a hail of German consonants. Despite occasional moments of insight, it is not a very attractive, nor a very comical performance. And even if she had included 7, I cannot imagine her doing justice to its agitated narrative style.

Berganza's performance is much more pleasing. On the whole she acts well, though her powerful and penetrating upper register (not helped by the recording) is a real drawback – again there is no way that this could be a child. A pity, for she is capable of real insight: passages like the encounter with the beetle in 3 and the list of names in 5 are handled with genuine comic flair. The other characters, the Nurse and the Mother, are perhaps a little too magisterial – could anyone really call the imposing personage in 5 'Nyanyushka'?

For a more consistently appealing performance one could turn to Söderström. Her acting is generally of such high quality that her matronly tone is easily overlooked. Both Söderström and her accompanist Vladimir Ashkenazy give the impression of having given every detail considerable thought, and yet there is nothing laboured or contrived in either singing or playing. But I have two reservations: firstly, the recording is highly spacious, suggesting that Söderström's nursery is an unusually large and sparsely furnished place; secondly, for all her eloquence, insight, and moments of real delight, Söderström's performance is perhaps a little short on comedy. Her 5 is affectionate, but not the funniest on record.

From time to time it has been suggested (once by no less a person than Boris Christoff) that a child would be the ideal interpreter for these songs, if only the music were not so technically demanding. Simon Woolf was 12 when he made his recording – rather older than one imagines Mussorgsky's Misha to be – but his performance has all the necessary purity of tone, with no hint of manly chest resonance. Woolf's interpretation has had distinguished admirers (Gerald Abraham for one) and it really is a creditable effort, despite the stilted English translation. Characterisation is on the whole convincing – even in the parts of nurse and mother. For me though, the combination of the ethereal Anglican choirboy tone with that less than comfortable translation is a barrier to complete enjoyment. And apart from singing 6 and 7 in reverse order (complete with the usual cut), Woolf substitutes a much shorter *coda* in 6, giving the song, and therefore the cycle, a curiously abrupt conclusion.

The final complete *Nursery* comes from Christoff. The notion of a grown man in the role of a very young child (not to mention mother and nurse) may strike one as faintly ludicrous, if not grotesque, especially when the singer possesses such a magnificently mature vocal instrument as Christoff. Nevertheless this is an unforgettable performance. Christoff acts with his usual aplomb (occasionally at the expense of melodic shape), and every detail seems to spring to life. His sense of pace is marvellous – quick on the whole, but with suitably generous pauses where necessary.

Stephen Johnson

Little Misha emerges as a strongly defined personality – more so than in any other interpretation – and it really is a delightfully funny performance. One's only regret is that one isn't able to *see* Christoff in these songs: the gestures and facial expressions that went with such spirited vocal acting must have been a treat to behold. One word of warning: the only modern transfer available at the time of writing comes in an EMI box set of the complete songs, arranged, unfortunately, in order of composition. Not only does this entail the reversal of 6 and 7, but it means that the songs are separated by others written at roughly the same time. So 'Yeremushka's Lullaby' and 'Peepshow' come between 1 and 2, and the 'Evening Song' of 1871 separates 5 and 7.

Before taking leave of *The Nursery*, I ought to mention two recordings of 5, both in English: one on a 7-inch 45rpm record (NBE 11092) by Nelson Eddy, and another from an LP entitled 'Songs of Enchantment', by Salli Terri. Terri's performance, accompanied by flute, oboe and string quartet, is the only version that really goes beyond the point of acceptable sentimentality, and the recording is dreadfully overblown. Nelson Eddy's version, however, is by no means reprehensible, despite its coarse recorded sound, and the intrusions of such Americanisms as 'say, Nursey' (Why do English translators persist in using the artificial-sounding 'Nursey' for 'Nyanya' – what's wrong with 'Nanny'?). Eddy's mock anxiety as the list of relations' names runs out is most effective, though his turning the last line into a joke at Nanny's expense is a bit of a liberty.

158

Tchaikovsky
Ten songs

DAVID M. JACKSON

Tchaikovsky wrote more than 100 songs, of which barely a handful are even moderately well-known – and one of which is too well-known for its own good. There are a number of reasons for this, some of which are better than others. In the West, language has been a barrier for performers and audience alike. With such a wealth of material available in the more 'readily accessible' languages, it is an adventurous and imaginative artist indeed who, not being a native speaker, will tackle Russian. That is not a good reason for neglect but it is an understandable one. A more serious reason is the character of Tchaikovsky's songs themselves. In the body of literature about the composer they are often referred to rather disparagingly, if at all. They seem mostly to have appeared in rather mechanically turned out groups of six (Ops. 6, 16, 25, 27, 28, 38, etc.) with suspicious regularity, as if the composer might have needed the money – and songs with piano had a considerably greater market value with publishers than a symphony, concerto, or, perish the thought, opera.

This seems an unfair inference to make about what is, after all, a reasonably substantial body of work spanning the composer's whole career. The songs are long overdue for re-examination and reappraisal. Certainly they largely fall into the category of 'Drawing-room Romance', and some of them are little more than that. Tchaikovsky was not Mussorgsky or Hugo Wolf. The majority of the songs take a text (not necessarily a distinguished one) with one mood or idea expressed, and depict that musically, with little in the way of finely etched reaction to verbal detail. In performance, however, these songs rarely fail to make their mark, and in the hands (and throats) of truly great interpreters they can seem masterpieces. That may be the crucial point about Tchaikovsky's songs: in a convincing, involving performance they can be great; because they are not all well-enough known to withstand a bad performance in the way that many Schubert or Schumann songs can, the listener may be tempted to dismiss the song with the bad performance.

159

David M. Jackson

The songs are explored on two Decca LPs by Elisabeth Söderström and Vladimir Ashkenazy, and between them they attain a remarkably high standard, making out a considerably better case for the songs than the anthology produced by Melodiya. Although this is sung by distinguished Russian artists – Arkhipova, Lemeshev, Mazurok and others – unfortunately the recording quality is variable and many of the interpretations are dull – as if the quest for completeness were more important than the individual songs. (This set omits the *Songs for Children* Op. 54.) Before going any further, I will list these recordings along with some of the others that are of importance. When discussing these records I will cite the number in brackets to the right of the record number:

Söderström, Ashkenazy	vol. 1 Decca SXL 6972 (1a)
	vol. 2 Decca SXL 7606 (1b)
Various singers and pianists	Melodiya D 026111/22 (2)
(86 songs on 6 discs)	
Christoff, Labinsky	HMV ALP 1793 (3)
Lemeshev, Kozel or N. Walter	Melodiya D 029713/4 (4)
Gmyrya, Ostrin	Melodiya D 011997/8 (5)
Obraztsova, Chachava	Melodiya S10 12265/6 (6)
Vishnevskaya, Rostropovich	HMV SLS 5055 (7)
Tear, Ledger	Argo ZRG 707 (8)
Fischer-Dieskau, Reimann	Philips 6514 166 (9)

'My genius, my angel, my friend' (Fet) pre-1860

The two pages of this, Tchaikovsky's earliest song, written when he was 17 or 18, look remarkably unimpressive. The accompaniment is particularly leaden in appearance. The vocal line, however, has a folk-like quality and the final *melisma* on 'moy drug' (my friend) is as effective and haunting as anything in the later songs. This little masterstroke is what makes the song tell in a number of recorded performances. Robert Tear (8) sings smoothly and persuasively – sometimes the self-conscious simplicity is dangerously near to being precious, but the overall effect is charming. Nina Isakova (2) is less successful at too slow a speed; the song loses shape. Her pianist Ye. Bruk sticks to her like glue, where a bit of positive leadership might have improved things considerably. Fischer-Dieskau (9) is better here than in many of the songs on this disc, singing simply and without the blustering quality that has marred some of his recent singing. The final phrase is quite haunting here, as it is with Söderström (1b), who makes the point best by singing straightforwardly and at a fairly flowing tempo. I was unable to find any earlier versions of this little song.

'Do not believe, my friend' (A. K. Tolstoy) Op 6 No. 1

The poet is saying 'When I tell you I no longer love you – don't believe a word of it!' and Tchaikovsky suggests that the singer is in love despite his better judgement. This could well have been a recognisable sensation for Tchaikovsky, who struggled all his life against his true nature. There are a number of fine performances on record. The singer needs a high, pure voice and sopranos with this type of production score the most success. The only man to have recorded it is Robert Tear, and, fine though he is, this is not really a man's song. He takes it faster than most and seems hard-pressed at the central climax, which may be caused by the difficulty encountered by a voice at the lower octave cutting through the heavy piano writing. The sopranos seem to have less trouble. Vishnevskaya has recorded it twice with Rostropovich, once in 1962 (Philips 6527 222) when the voice, less than ideally steady, is very beautiful though the slow tempo is enervating, and once in 1976 (7), where both performers make much more of the song, indeed too much: the waywardly fluctuating tempo, slightly whining vocal quality, and air of unrelieved tragedy over-power Tchaikovsky's music. This is not a tragic song, rather it has that brand of almost enjoyable melancholy which pervades so much of Russian art. Söderström understands this, and in her performance (1b) sings movingly, always involved but never self-indulgent. Margaret Price with James Lockhart (CFP 40078) goes slightly too far in the other direction: while the singing is ravishing in tone, she does not convey what the song is about. Tamara Milashkina (2) with V. Viktorov sings with beautiful tone, rather uninvolved in the outer sections and rather too wild in the middle one. The pianist indulges himself in too much expressive *rubato* for comfort. The novelty of an orchestra is all that recommends a version on 78 sung by Irra Petina (Am. Col. 72360–D), whose pleasantly bland singing tells us nothing new.

'A tear trembles' (A. K. Tolstoy) Op. 6 No. 4

The fourth song in the Op. 6 group is specifically for male voice (the vocal line is written in the bass clef). This is a simple strophic setting of two verses by Alexei Tolstoy (not to be confused with the novelist), with an extended piano postlude – a favourite device of the composer – and an unusual recitative-like introduction for the piano. This can sound effec-tive, boring or perfunctory according to the talent of the accompanist. One of the best is the composer Aribert Reimann playing for Fischer-Dieskau (9), who works wonders with the postlude too, making this final repetition of the vocal melody into an integral part of the song rather than

161

a tacked-on afterthought. Unfortunately Fischer-Dieskau is not on the same level of achievement here, and his effortful performance suffers from an uncharacteristic unsteadiness of pitch when the voice opens out for loud passages. While the singer's intelligence and musicianship ensure that this performance is not a failure, it is not one of his more successful efforts. Much more simple and effective is Ivan Rebroff with Herbert Seidemann (Intercord 185 814). Recorded in a reverberant acoustic, the voice sounds easy and natural, and the fairly swift tempo lets the song speak for itself. The postlude is well played, and if the final effect is no more than that of a superior Victorian parlour ballad then it works well on those terms. The best singing comes from Boris Christoff (3), whose powerful, gritty tone avoids the danger of being too lachrymose on the part of this 'trembling tear'! Unfortunately his pianist feels compelled to hurry the postlude in a dismissive way, robbing the song of the weight so successfully conveyed earlier. Ivan Kozlovsky in both his versions (on 78 Soviet 519, and LP Melodiya S 08555) is too much the histrionic tenor, although his commitment and idiomatic rightness are never in doubt. Andrei Ivanov (2) is pleasant of voice, but bland, and the pianism of G. Orentlikher is equally unmemorable.

'No, only he who has known' ('None but the lonely heart')
(Goethe, trans. Mey) Op. 6 No. 6

The masterstroke in this final song is the moment near the end, when after the climactic pause the voice sings a new counter-melody while the piano reiterates the opening theme. No matter how often the song is heard, this moment never fails to make its effect. The song has been done by so many singers of every type imaginable that it is hard to know where to begin. How to compare Schwarzkopf with Sinatra? As far as that goes, Sinatra (Fontana TFL 5082), even with soupy orchestra conducted by Axel Stordahl and an 'intro' filched from the 'Pathétique' Symphony, sings a very slow but rather marvellous version, and gets nearer to the meaning of the song than the mannered and self-conscious recording by Schwarzkopf with Gerald Moore (SAX 2265). Such is her obsession with tone production and beauty of sound that the emotional sense of the song is thrown out with the same bathwater as the sense of musical line or phrase. If one judges this great soprano by the standards she herself has set, this performance is most disappointing. Sadly, another great singer, Victoria de los Angeles, late in her career, suffers in much the same way, singing, as Schwarzkopf does, in German. Her version with Geoffrey Parsons (Polydor 2383 389) is scoopy and mannered singing, and becomes bathetic in the final section.

Fortunately, of the 30-odd recordings I have been able to hear, most have had something positive to say about this fine song. It is a danger-trap, as too much emotional over-indulgence can be fatal, while too detached a performance will make the song sound shallow. Performances in English and German abound, and there are one or two in French. Emmy Destinn translated it into Czech, presumably for her own use, but I have been unable to trace a disc of this. Of those in German, Schwarzkopf and de los Angeles have already been mentioned. Fritz Wunderlich with orchestra (Eurodisc 300 353) sings very beautifully but blandly, and the climax goes by almost unnoticed. Peter Anders with Hubert Giesen (Telefunken 648064/2) is a different thing altogether – swift-flowing tempo, and involved, committed singing combine to really moving effect. Ernestine Schumann-Heink aged 73 (Pelican LP 2008) is no more than a touching memento.

Gérard Souzay in French, on 78 (Decca M 633), is in superb voice and makes it sound like a *mélodie*. I have not heard Cesare Siepi on Parlophone RO 30003, also in French.

Versions in English suffer, as do all those not in Russian or German, from being a translation of a translation. When the words are sung as excruciatingly clearly as they are by John McCormack (DA 1112; GEMM 158) they become something of a trial. With a tortured and unyielding cello *obbligato* in tow, it is only the beautiful singing which makes this version worthwhile. Helen Traubel, with cellist Warwick Evans and Coenraad V. Bos, brings her heroic Wagnerian tones to bear in a slow but beautiful performance (Odyssey Y 31735). Her gorgeous sound almost overpowers the piano and cello. Where was the orchestra she needed? Playing for Tauber, it seems, and very nicely too, on a Parlophone 78 (RO 20518), with the voice velvety, and bang in the centre of every note. Joan Hammond with Gerald Moore and James Whitehead, piano and cello respectively (HMV B 9486), is rather too plummy. In the original Russian translation, as it were, one of the most authoritative versions and something of a touchstone by which to gauge others has to be Nina Koshetz (Veritas VM 113). Wayward in tempo to the point where one wonders at the tenacity of the pianist, Celius Dougherty, she nevertheless conveys the meaning of the song in a way rivalled only by Oda Slobodskaya (Saga XID 5050), whose voice was, by 1959, much less easy on the ear. These two communicate in a unique way, barely approached by other singers. Beside them, Jennie Tourel (American Decca DL 9981), with cello and piano, is beautiful but routine. Vishnevskaya and Rostropovich are certainly wayward in tempo, but to less effect, rendering the opening stanza shapeless, although Vishnevskaya's emotionally charged reading suits the song admirably. Margaret Price (CFP 40078) sounds marvellous but rather uninvolved, nor is she helped by the dull piano playing of James Lockhart. Beautiful singing and

David M. Jackson

much more is provided by Söderström (1a), whose restrained but deeply moving interpretation is ably matched by Ashkenazy's fine pianism.

Elena Obraztsova (6) is a bit over-emotional but the voice is strong and her darker vocal colour suits the song. Similar tone colour can be heard in a fine performance from Susan Kessler and Geoffrey Parsons on Meridian (E 77074), who convey a sense of the song's structure as well as its emotional content. The handling of the dramatic pause before the final reprise is particularly well done.

There are some fine performances on record from male voices too. One of the best is that of Pavel Lisitsian (2), whose heartfelt performance is marred only by an unwillingness to vary the dynamic level very much. Christoff's dark tones give a strength to his performance (3), making it tragic rather than melodramatic. Ghiaurov (Decca SXL 6530) is similar but has a more mellifluous quality. He seems less emotionally committed, however, as if concentrating too much on beauty of sound. Less successful than these two are Kim Borg (Supraphon SUAST 50499), whose vocal production is oddly masked, though there are some imaginative touches, and Boris Gmyrya (5) singing well, but self-indulgent, and hampered by a lumpy accompaniment. Robert Tear (8) gives a typically committed and imaginative performance, at a fairly swift tempo, but the singing and breathing are a bit too effortful for this to be completely enjoyable. Having listened to so many recordings for the purpose of comparison, I have been surprised at how the song itself has stood up to repetition. This is a fine song and deservedly celebrated.

'As they kept on saying "Fool" ' (Mey) Op. 25 No. 6

One of Tchaikovsky's most typically Russian songs, this is almost Mussorgsky-like in style and mood. It responds best to the kind of interpretation typified by Christoff (3), whose rough, folksy style suits the 'fool' who wishes to drown his sorrows in the pub rather than in the river. Although he interpolates a falsetto top G and has the accompaniment truncated at the end, this is forgivable after such a great performance. Fischer-Dieskau's version (9) has much to recommend it, notably the brisk tempo and sprightly rhythmic attack. If the voice shows a few signs of age that is a pity but not fatal to the success of the performance. Somehow, though, this fails to sound remotely like a Russian peasant singing, and we stay firmly in the drawing-room. Yuri Mazurok (2), though more idiomatic, is rather lifeless; the slow tempo is a real mistake here, robbing the song of much of its character. Of the two tenor versions I have heard, Peter Anders (in German – Telefunken 648064/2) is less successful than Robert Tear (8), lacking the latter's spring and character, although he has the more pleasant voice. In this song, however, beauty of tone matters less than character, rhythm, and the ability to put the words over. Leading in all these things is Christoff, although if you must have a version faithful to the letter of Tchaikovsky's score (if not so much the spirit) there is Fischer-Dieskau.

'Don Juan's Serenade' (A. K. Tolstoy) Op. 38 No. 1

The Op. 38 set contains two of the finest and most frequently sung songs – 'Don Juan's Serenade' and 'Amid the din of the ball', both of which have maintained a popularity unrivalled by most of the others.

As set by Tchaikovsky, this serenade is hardly a seductive piece; rather it is insistently importunate. This Don is unlikely to take 'No' for an answer from his 'Nisetta' (or 'Anita' as one particularly unhappy translation would have it). The tricky piano part poses problems for the accompanist: not so much negotiating the notes as endeavouring not to sound like one of the more boisterous nights in the Hall of the Mountain King! It needs to be fleet of foot, with as little resort to the sustaining pedal as possible. Vocally the song lends itself to a rather hectoring style which should be avoided, but isn't, by quite a few eminent singers who should have known better.

A couple of versions with orchestra can be dealt with fairly readily. Peter Dawson, though in fine voice (C 1327; HQM 1217), makes an effortful and unwinning Don, and as for the horrible English translation, the least said the better. Caruso (DA 114; several reissues) at a slow tempo is virile and effective; sung in French, this nevertheless reminds one more of Tosti than Tchaikovsky.

Edouard de Reszke, again in French, with piano (recorded 1903; Columbia 1223; Odyssey Y 35067), after a fast if approximate introduction, comes in at his own speed and produces a firm-toned, pleasant but unexciting performance. The only other translated version I have heard is Dennis Noble's in English (C 3637) – best left alone. Of the Russian versions, amongst the out-and-out shouters, and therefore unacceptable to me at least, have to be listed, sadly, Boris Christoff (3), Ghiaurov (SXL 6530), Fischer-Dieskau (9) and Gérard Souzay (RCA SB 6832). Others prove that the temptation to frighten Nisetta onto her balcony can be avoided. One of the best of these is Sergei Lemeshev (4), whose fleet and charming version shows just what can be done with this song. Nicolai Gedda (SAN 225) is also good, and his tone is more ingratiating than Lemeshev's. Another good tenor version is that of Robert Tear (8), with a particularly good accompaniment from Philip Ledger, who achieves an almost mandoline-like effect to underpin Tear's seductive performance.

The baritones and basses find it harder to strike the right note, but Pavel Lisitsian (2), Panteleimon Nortsov (Melodiya M10 46507 002), Boris

David M. Jackson

Gmyrya (5) and Kim Borg (SUAST 50499), all successfully lighten their voices. Ivan Rebroff (Intercord 185 814) is blandly disappointing.

'Amid the din of the ball' (A. K. Tolstoy) Op. 38 No. 3

One of Tchaikovsky's most successful fusions of poem and music, this seems popular with male and female singers alike. It lends itself to a wide variety of tempo, from the fast waltz to a more meditative pace, though the latter runs the risk of becoming maudlin, as with Sobinov (DB 892; Melodiya D 025209/12) and Kozlovsky (Soviet 519), both otherwise very fine. The other side of the interpretative coin is represented by Koshetz (Veritas VM 113), whose swift, vibrant performance, wayward in its rhythmic freedom, is a model of sung story-telling. Her tone may be rough, but this is easy to forgive for once. Disappointing is Slobodskaya (XID 5050) with Ivor Newton, she perfunctory and too scoopy, he matter-of-fact. Similarly uninteresting are Regina Resnik (Epic BC 1283), Mazurok (2), Irra Petina (Am. Col. 73360–D) with orchestra and Ivan Rebroff (Intercord 185 814).

Fortunately there are plenty of fine versions too, and those who opt for a swifter tempo seem to catch the essence of this song more readily. Among them are Margaret Price (CPF 40078), in ravishing voice; Vishnevskaya (7) – charming rather than serious about things; Anders in German with Hubert Giesen (648064/2) – passionate and involved. Finest singing of all comes from Souzay, in French, with Irène Aïtoff (Decca M 633), preferable to his later version in Russian with Dalton Baldwin (SB 6832). At a more moderate tempo but still very good are Tauber in English (RO 20549) with orchestra; Fischer-Dieskau (9) in fine voice and most atmospheric; Ghiaurov (SXL 6530) successfully lightening the voice.

Of the other versions, unmentioned here, many have something to recommend them, but the only outstanding recording yet to be cited is that of Söderström. Once again she strikes exactly the right mood and tone; reflective, yearning, while Ashkenazy works miracles with the deceptively simple piano part.

'Pimpinella' (words by the composer) Op. 38 No. 6

This popular Florentine song was transcribed by Tchaikovsky, while on holiday in Italy, after hearing a young street singer with whom he was extremely taken. There is little of the composer in it apart from some chromaticism and a couple of melodic alterations, where Tchaikovsky's

166

changes are actually less interesting than the original. A pleasant little song which tries perhaps too hard to be charming – especially as sung by Schwarzkopf, with Geoffrey Parsons (ASD 2404), who is too coy and winsome by far. Only in the final phrases does some real sunny charm break through, and we hear how the song should have sounded all along, as it does in Tauber's absolutely delightful version with orchestra – in English 'Fifinella'! – on Parlophone RO 20549. Charming too is Georgy Vinogradov (Supraphon B 23041) in Russian, but sounding as Italianate as Caruso in his 1913 recording (DA 119; RCA GL 84046). Singing, like Schwarzkopf, in the original Italian, he cuts the last verse but sings with real style and charm. Arkhipova (2) is a surprising choice for this song, and in truth she misses the mark by quite a bit. Her fine voice is too heavy for this bit of froth; her cries of 'No! No!' sound as if she meant them!

Undoubtedly the best here are Tauber in English and Vinogradov in Russian. No good modern version of the original Italian seems to exist.

'I bless you, forests' (A. K. Tolstoy) Op. 47 No. 5

John of Damascus apostrophises Nature, and in a final outburst states his wish to unite all of creation in his embrace. If not quite able to match the cosmic scale of the poem with music, Tchaikovsky nevertheless produces one of his best songs in response. It features a prelude and postlude for the piano, both of some length. In a number of recordings this postlude has been truncated, particularly where an orchestra replaces the piano. This is the case with Peter Dawson (C 2097), whose version is really only of interest as a souvenir of the artist. Preferable to this, although hampered with the same English translation, is Lawrence Tibbett (DB 1945): the voice is more magisterial and he makes more of the climax. Of a number of other recordings in English I have been able to hear only Dennis Noble (C 3637), who throws in the towel at the climax, just where he ought to be at his most powerful, but with Gerald Moore very fine in the prelude and postlude. I have not heard Roy Henderson (Vocalion X 9513) or Robert Radford (HMV 02367).

Of versions in Russian, the finest is that of Ghiaurov (SXL 6530), who has the warmth and breadth of tone to do justice to the sentiments expressed. The dynamics and the build-up to the climax are well handled. Also noteworthy are Ivan Petrov (Melodiya S 08555), similar in tone to Ghiaurov, and Boris Gmyrya (5) less than ideally steady of voice but powerful at the climax. Less interesting are Kim Borg (SUAST 50499) and Mazurok (2), both bland, Mazurok also hampered with a stodgy accompanist. A disappointment is Fischer-Dieskau (9): the voice sounds tired and the pitch is unsteady in places.

David M. Jackson

'Was I not a little blade of grass?' (Surikov) Op. 47 No. 7

This is a clever synthesis of folk and art song, with its memorable and affecting melody and subtlety of treatment. Each verse develops the vocal line, and more particularly the accompaniment, to reflect the structure of the poem (I was a blade of grass and they cut me down; I was a snowball bush and they made me into a whip; I was a young girl and they married me off to an old man). The stature of the song is brought out by Söderström (1b), whose moving voice is ideal at expressing this kind of sentiment, and Ashkenazy, who weaves the accompaniment skilfully round the voice. One can hear in this song the forerunner of Rachmaninov's early song 'The harvest of sorrow'.

There are overtly histrionic versions from Raina Kabaivanska (Cetra LPL 69005) and Vishnevskaya (7), both of whom sing well but tend to make too much of a meal of this basically simple song. A number of singers tinker about with Tchaikovsky's final melismatic flourish to verse 3, either to catch a breath or to avoid going up to the top B, or down to the bottom one! None of this matters so much as the cutting of the middle verse, which spoils Tchaikovsky's careful building up of the texture. Guilty of this are Natania Davrath (Vanguard VSL 11079), pleasant if unmemorable, and, unfortunately in an otherwise splendid version, Slobodskaya with Ivor Newton (Rimington RVW 104). Teresa Zylis-Gara recorded 'live' (Rodolphe RP 12392) is very beautiful, unfussy but atmospheric and vocally assured apart from a slight sense of strain at the very top. Irra Petina (Am. Col. 72361–D) is too lightweight by far and although the tone is charming, the orchestration is over-fussy and the mood is wrong. At the opposite end of the emotional scale is Obraztsova (6) transposed down a tone, whose dark voice conveys an air of tragedy from the start. Perhaps because of this she is driven to a wild conclusion, which though effective is a bit too squally to stand up to much repeated listening. Resnik (Epic BC 1384) and Tamara Milashkina (2) are both dull. It is Söderström and Ashkenazy who come closest to the heart of this song, as they do with so many others.

In this chapter I have been able to cover only a few of Tchaikovsky's songs. There are many more that repay attention and deserve to be championed by singers and pianists alike.

Rachmaninov
Ten songs

DAVID M. JACKSON

The songs of Rachmaninov contain some of the finest music he ever wrote. They appeared regularly throughout the active composing part of his life, but between leaving Russia in 1917 and his death in 1943, he included no original songs with piano in his rare compositional attempts.

Even the earliest set, Op. 4, contains at least two very fine songs which, while showing the influence of Tchaikovsky and others, have a strength and originality not to be found in Rachmaninov's contemporary piano and chamber pieces. He knew socially some of the greatest singers of the day – Chaliapin, Sobinov and Nezhdanova among them – and wrote specifically for their voices, often dedicating a song to the singer for whom it was intended. The accompaniments were written for the composer himself to play, and can appear tantamount to elaborate piano pieces – rather like an *étude–tableau* with vocal *obbligato* when seen on the printed page! In reality the balance between voice and piano is skilfully calculated; only occasionally will the pianist find it difficult to balance with the singer. Usually the voice is carefully positioned in relation to the piano textures, often well above it at climactic moments. The song 'Believe it or not' Op. 14 No. 7 is a good example, where the piano restlessly repeats chords beneath the voice, only allowed free reign in the postlude, which amounts to more than a third of the song's total 26 bars. On the singer's final note, the piano surges up eagerly to express its feelings – it would be unrealistic to expect anything else from one of the finest pianists of the century. These songs are full of similar opportunities for the pianist, and any accompanist who has not made their acquaintance should do so – and then begin the task of locating a singer with the requisite musicianship, range, and, rarest of all, linguistic ability to do justice to them.

On record they have not fared particularly well. The ten I have chosen to discuss here more or less chose themselves, because of the dearth of recordings with which to make comparisons. One song, 'The Dream' Op. 38 No. 5, I have included, even though I could find only four recordings of it, because it is possibly the finest song of all. It deserves to be better known for its deceptively simple opening, voice and piano gently inter-woven, and its masterful build-up, involving increasingly complex and beautiful piano figurations, until the ecstatic, soaring conclusion for the voice, followed by one of the finest pages of piano writing ever penned by Rachmaninov.

Any lover of these songs has cause to be eternally grateful to the team of Elisabeth Söderström, Vladimir Ashkenazy and Decca, for their recordings of the complete songs on four LPs. What wonderful singing and playing is preserved here (the number in brackets identifies them later in the chapter):

vol. 1 SXL 6718 (1a);   vol. 2 SXL 6772 (1b)
vol. 3 SXL 6832 (1c);   vol. 4 SXL 6869 (1d)

In addition to these there are various other LP collections of note:

Kurenko, Pastukhoff	Rachmaninoff Society RS 2 (2a)
Kurenko, Rosenthal	Rachmaninoff Society RS 5 (2b)
Koshetz, Dougherty	Veritas VM 113 (3)
Christoff, Labinsky	HMV ALP 1830 (4)
Gedda, Weissenberg	HMV ASD 2928 (5)
Tear, Ledger	Argo ZRG 730 (6)
Vishnevskaya, Rostropovich	DG 2530 725 (7)
Talvela, Gothoni	Decca SXL 6974 (8)
Various singers and pianists (82 songs on 5 discs)	Melodiya SM 04069/78 (9)

'Sing not to me, beautiful maiden' (Georgian Song) (Pushkin) Op. 4 No. 4

This is the best and most original of the Op. 4 set. Its sinuous, wailing theme immediately sets the nostalgic, rather exotic tone of the poem. It is particularly demanding for the singer in the closing bars, where a slow descent from a *pianissimo* top A has to be negotiated.

Jennie Tourel recorded it three times, transposing down so that the top A becomes F sharp, but the control in all three is admirable. Her first version (Am. Col. 71807–D) is the best vocally, rising easily to the big dramatic climax, and then beautifully poised in the final phrase. Her later versions (American Decca DL 9981; Am. Col. M. 32231) are less pure of tone, but more imaginative and committed, if a little self-indulgent in places; on the Decca recording she becomes so slow at the end that the shape of the phrase suffers. On her last version she is partnered by Leonard Bernstein, who gives an outstandingly imaginative account of the accompaniment.

Of Galina Vishnevskaya's two versions, that with Alexander Dedyukhin (SB 2141) is preferable to the later one with her husband Rostropovich (7). On the earlier version the song flows and the voice is well under control apart from a slightly wild moment at the climax; the final phrase is wonderfully evocative and nostalgic. The later recording is too slow and self-regarding, while the voice has become blustery. The slow tempo means Rostropovich has to speed up considerably for the two linking passages marked *meno mosso*! This miscalculation is also to be heard on both versions from Nicolai Gedda, and must therefore be a deliberate decision of the tenor; otherwise he is in fine form on both versions, passionate and expressive – the version with Gerald Moore (SAX 5278) being a whisker more beautiful than that with Alexis Weissenberg (5).

Christoff (4), Yevgeny Nesterenko (9) and Marti Talvela (8) all require rather excessive downward transpositions of a 4th or a 5th. All three are convincing, however; the generous voices of Nesterenko and Talvela sound particularly fine. In his moving and committed performance, Kipnis (VIC 1434) sings with superbly meaningful words and huge tone, rising easily to the song's climax.

A fascinating recording is that of John McCormack, in English, with Fritz Kreisler, no less, playing a violin *obbligato*, and Edwin Schneider at the piano (DA 457). The dialogue between voice and violin really works. McCormack's quirky, haunting pronunciation and the fine singing and playing all combine to make this a version to cherish. Of versions with orchestra, Edita Gruberova (Orfeo S 072831) sadly fails to convey any sense of meaning, seeing the song, inexplicably, as part of 'The Art of Coloratura' (LP title). Maria Cebotari in 1935 (Parlophone RO 20321), with shortened introduction and postlude, sings with an exciting, gipsy-like passion, a bit hectic at the climax, but very effective; Natania Davrath (Vanguard VSL 11085), with spicy touches of tambourine and harp, is clean and reasonably expressive if not outstanding. Lily Pons, slightly sour of tone, has cellist Bernard Greenhouse featured with André Kostelanetz (Am. Col. 7665–M). In a class of its own is the recording of Ivan Kozlovsky with the Bolshoi Theatre Orchestra and Israel Gusman (ASD 2539) – a marvellous over-the-top orchestration and consummate vocal style and expression, though the nasal tone will not please everyone. The finest versions with piano are: Christa Ludwig (SAX 5274), passionate and dark-toned; Irina Arkhipova (ASD 3103), immediately arresting, firm of voice and with superb diction; Robert Tear (6), impressive for the wonderfully imaginative playing of Philip Ledger, well and thoughtfully sung. Best of all, and I make no apology for the fact that I will turn to them again and again, are Söderström and Ashkenazy (1a), at a slowish tempo, but leaving room for an effective change to *meno mosso* where marked.

171

David M. Jackson

The final phrase is floated effortlessly; the whole performance is quite extraordinary.

'O thou my field' ('The Harvest of Sorrow') (A. K. Tolstoy) Op. 4 No. 5

This quintessentially Russian tragedy of ruined hopes and harvest with its folk-like melodic line, dramatic central 'storm' section, and closing vocal flourish, offers the singer much by way of both vocalisation and histrionics. It is marked *lento* by the composer; most performers opt for a flowing tempo, which works well. Though written for soprano or tenor, this song has proved attractive to lower voices too, and Christoff (4) and Talvela (8) both make much of the grim presence brought to the song by their dark voices. Talvela's downward transposition of a 5th (Christoff manages to keep it to a 4th) means that the piano is really growling in places, and the postlude is taken too fast by Ralf Gothoni, robbing the song of its full effect. Kipnis, with Celius Dougherty (VIC 1434), opts for a big declamatory tone and style, effective enough, but the difficult closing passage sounds effortful in the extreme: this is not as successful as his version of Op. 4, No. 4 on the same disc.

Nicolai Gedda (5), in the original key, goes all out for drama in his version, sacrificing beauty of tone in the process – Weissenberg's piano tone is also very harsh, and the speed is on the wayward and self-indulgent side.

Shirley Verrett (SB 6750) recorded 'live' at Carnegie Hall in 1965, gives a committed and well-considered performance at a swiftish tempo, but is let down by a recording which favours the voice far too much. Christa Ludwig (SAX 5274) is slower but beautifully controlled and her voice was at its peak when this recording with Geoffrey Parsons was made (c. 1966). She sings the closing *melisma* with every ounce of the drama required, while maintaining her beauty of tone.

Of three soprano versions, Natania Davrath (VSL 11079) proves to be more of a mezzo, transposing the song down into the same key as Ludwig and Verrett. She is rather hard-toned, but her sense of the words' meaning is strongly conveyed; Erik Werba makes too much of the left-hand tremolo during the 'storm', but judges the speed of the postlude just right. In the original key, Ninel Tkachenko (9) is on the slow side; she has a smooth voice which tends to harden under pressure; she becomes a bit of a shrieker towards the end. She also tries an ill-advised 'echo' effect at the very climax of the song, which doesn't come off; the repeated figure needs to be a full-voiced cry both times. Söderström and Ashkenazy (1a) take a fairly slow tempo. She declaims the opening in a plangent tone which she softens effectively for the quieter phrases. After a brief slackening of tempo for the 'storm', both artists open out for the climactic final page, and the difficult final 'cadenza' is memorably sung, while Ashkenazy predictably makes the most of his closing peroration.

'I have grown fond of sorrow' ('The Soldier's Wife') (Shevchenko, trans. Pleshcheyev) Op. 8 No. 4

The memorable opening phrase and its reappearance, repeated at the end, frame a concise little picture. The soldier's widow, left alone in a foreign country, has evoked a number of fine performances, one of them bizarrely enough from Christoff (4). Apart from the fact that he is the wrong sex, this is a very enjoyable version, slow and free in tempo and restrainedly dramatic. Tourel recorded two versions, both interesting in their own right. The earlier (Am. Col. 71807–D) has her in finer voice, but in both versions she uses the words to great effect, particularly in the central recitative-like section. On the later recording (American Decca DL 9981) she has the idea of doing the closing 'echo' phrase with closed lips, and this is very effective. Maria Kurenko (Capitol CTL 7068), rather thin of voice, gives a reasonable account at not too slow a speed, but remains unmoving. Ada Sari opts for an upward transposition of a 3rd, and then produces a slow and rather squeaky version (Muza L 0388), while Nadezhda Obukhova (9) goes down a 3rd from the original, and gives a slow, rather sour performance. Considerably more interesting is Slobodskaya (SXL 2299). Her feeling for words and phrasing make this a version to savour, only the sadly threadbare voice detracting from real enjoyment. Raina Kabaivanska (Cetra LPL 69005) and Söderström (1b) both give rather grandly tragic versions, but the voice that stays in the mind's ear is that of Tourel. Her gentle approach, blaming nobody, is exactly right for this song.

'Spring Waters' (Tyutchev) Op. 14 No. 11

With this uncharacteristic outburst of enthusiasm, for high voice and piano, Rachmaninov presents the performers with something of a problem: how to balance the voice against the full piano writing, without causing the singer undue strain, or the pianist to reign himself back unreasonably in this huge accompaniment. On record the problem is considerably less acute than in the concert hall, and on more than one occasion it seems that the engineer has done what nature cannot. A number of singers interpolate a penultimate high note (B flat if the song is being done in the original key) rather than the written one. This seems not unreasonable, although the melodic line really works better when left alone.

The earliest version I have heard is also the most disappointing.

David M. Jackson

Vladimir Rosing on a Parlophone 78 (R 20378) is effortful of voice, and choppy and careless of rhythm, while his pianist Hans Gellhorn is sorely taxed by the handfuls of notes required. Marjorie Lawrence (Decca M 602) has the right type of voice for this song, of a Flagstad-like amplitude and weight. Her (English) words are almost incomprehensible at first but become clearer, although she remains a bit too plummy for my taste. Both she and Rosing opt for the high note at the end. Nicolai Gedda's two versions share the fault of being shouted rather than sung. When he lapses into soft singing for the only moment of relaxation the song affords, one is immediately reminded of how lovely a tone he can produce. His earlier version (SAX 5278) is slower, with Gerald Moore striking a few wrong notes, but his later version has the steely and accurate Weissenberg (5), making things more exciting, at a faster tempo. Gedda also opts for the top B flat on the later version. In a recording with orchestra, odd in this song where the accompaniment is uncompromisingly pianistic, Kozlovsky (ASD 2539) gives a typically involved performance, wonderful at the soft passage to the words 'Spring is here!'. Lemeshev (Melodiya SM 29713/4) is disappointing – his wobbly tones at a plodding tempo are best left alone. Natania Davrath seems overwhelmed by Erik Werba's piano playing (VSL 11079), although she copes reasonably well and achieves a suitably ecstatic effect, while Verrett (SB 6750), in her 'live' recital, gives a fast well-shaped performance, eliciting rapturous applause from her audience. Tamara Milashkina (9) and Galina Vishnevskaya (7) have rather similar voices, tending to squall at the loud high moments, but whereas Milashkina has Berta Kozel making heavy weather of Spring's arrival, Vishnevskaya has Rostropovich, big in tone and very imaginative. Possibly the best singing of all comes from Elly Ameling on her 'Souvenirs' LP (CBS 76738). The balance may have been slightly adjusted in favour of the voice, but her pure tone rides easily over the piano of Dalton Baldwin, and she takes time to mould the music – taking an optional low B flat in the opening bars which most singers ignore. She also gives us, regrettably, the top B flat at the end; what a pity her usually flawless musical instincts should have lapsed here. Another soprano who sings the optional low note is Kabaivanska (Cetra LPL 69005), in a rather slower than average, but characteristically big-hearted performance. Probably the most musically satisfying version remains that of Söderström and Ashkenazy (1b) – the pianism in particular is unrivalled, while the singing perfectly expresses the anticipation and greeting of the new season.

'Lilacs' (Beketova) Op. 21 No. 5

One of the composer's most popular songs and one which he later transcribed for piano solo. Nothing happens during the course of the

174

song: it describes a pleasant garden and the poet's state of mind as she wanders there. The pure, smiling tone of Isobel Baillie, singing in English (Columbia DB 2303), suits this song admirably. A fairly fast tempo, as here, works well, but a slow tempo can be equally effective, as Jussi Björling proves on both his recordings (also in English, but a less satisfactory translation). The first (DA 1890; RLS 715), with orchestra reminiscent of Mahler's 'Ich atmet einen linden Duft', is very slow and superbly sung. His version with piano (ALP 1187) is similar in effect. The voice is perfectly poised and rises to the song's sustained climax very tastefully indeed.

The light voice of Kurenko (CTL 7063) is nicely used here, at a flowing tempo and with well-pointed words. Nina Koshetz (3) is too wilful and wayward, robbing the song of shape. Preferable is either of Slobodskaya's versions on 78, although the 1931 (HMV EK 113) with Percy Kahn finds her in better voice than in 1938 (Rimington RVW 106) with Ivor Newton. She moulds the song carefully, warm of voice and expression, and the gentle twinge of chromaticism at the climax is perfectly judged. Neither of Gedda's versions is an unqualified success – though in 5 the tempo moves well and his tone is an appropriately intimate *mezza voce*. He opens out rather too much in the middle section, however, and then inexplicably sings some different (wrong?) notes towards the end. His later version (Melodiya S10 13977/8) has all the right notes, but seems too mannered and has extremes of dynamic unsuitable for this little piece. An interesting recording is that of Dmitri Smirnov with Gerald Moore (DA 752; GV 75), nasal-toned but a marvellous way with the text. The falsetto high A flat interpolated at the end seems unnecessary. One of the best performances comes from Arkhipova (9), with controlled dynamic range and pin-point accuracy of pitch, yet capturing all the expression to be found in the song. Söderström (1c) is nicely relaxed and the song floats along with just a touch more warmth in the central, more expressive section. The only bass to have attempted this delicate piece is Kim Borg (Supraphon SUAST 50499), who transposes it down a 3rd, and sings a sensitive performance with mellow, solid tone; if it seems a shade restrained, that is an error in the right direction.

'How fair this spot' (Galina) Op. 21 No. 7

Considered by many to be the finest of all Rachmaninov's songs, with its skilful interweaving of the vocal and piano textures and responsive word setting, this song is ruled out for many singers on purely technical grounds. The climax of the song consists of a cruelly difficult *pianissimo* top B natural, which has to appear as from nowhere, and if the singer cannot bring this off, then the whole effect of the song is spoiled. Those who have committed a version to disc are, on the whole, those who can manage this fiendishly taxing moment. Only Kurenko does less than well here (2b), getting the top note, but not *pianissimo*, and suffering from pitch problems elsewhere.

Such is the lure of the 'fair spot's' beauty, that two basses have recorded it. Christoff transposes down a 4th and at the crucial moment sings not the top note as written, but a lower option (presumably of his own devising). After the initial shock has worn off, this works quite well, and his solid tone and careful shaping of the phrases make this a worthwhile version. Talvela (8) follows Christoff's example (down a 5th this time) and with his great voice and the fine playing of Gothoni in support also makes this a memorable version.

The famous recording by McCormack with Edwin Schneider (DA 680; EX 29 00563) deserves its reputation, though the quirky pronunciation of the English translation is not to my taste.

Of two versions with orchestra, that of Lily Pons with André Kostelanetz is little more than a showpiece, particularly the top note, but Kozlovsky (ASD 2539) is another matter entirely. Love it or hate it, and I could never hate it, this version is really *hors concours* with its thick, almost syrupy orchestration and nasal singing. However, the superb atmosphere of hushed, ecstatic reverence, and Kozlovsky's seemingly interminable but perfectly placed top note can never seem too much of a good thing. Recorded within a year of one another, in 1938 and 1939 respectively, Slobodskaya (Rimington RVW 106) and Koshetz (3) are rather similar. Both voices sound rather worn and both surprise us pleasantly when it comes to the climax. Slobodskaya particularly fine here; unfortunately, Ivor Newton accompanies her unresponsively and plays the wonderful closing bars in a matter-of-fact way. Not so Moore for Gedda on the earlier of the tenor's two versions (SAX 5278). Moore's command of tone excels in this great accompaniment, and Gedda sings a beautiful, poised performance, better even than his later version with Weissenberg, good though that is (5).

Pianism of the first order is also to be heard from Sviatoslav Richter, superb in support of soprano Nina Dorliak, who turns in a good if unmemorable performance (9), and of course Ashkenazy with the inimitable Söderström (1a), whose silvery quality of voice enables her to turn in the best performance of all.

One remaining version should be mentioned: that of the Russian soprano Elena Katulskaya, recorded in 1913 when she was about 25. Her controlled gleaming voice is a marvel, and can be enjoyed in admittedly wretched sound (2–23761; GV 528).

'Christ is risen' (Merezhkovsky) Op. 26 No. 6

The Op. 26 set produced a number of declamatory songs such as this one, which is not a celebration as the title might suggest, but rather a reflection by the poet on what kind of world the resurrected Christ would see today. This dramatic and gloomy song suits the gritty tones of Christoff (4) ideally; his Boris-like reading is grimly impressive. Unsubtle but very exciting is the impression left by the massive voice of Talvela with Gothoni similarly electrifying in the accompaniment (8).

Söderström (1d) really has the wrong voice for this song but she darkens her tone effectively and produces an interesting reading at the original pitch. Other high voices have tended to transpose up. Kozlovsky (9), sounding like the Simpleton from Boris Godunov this time, gives an enthralling and wide-ranging performance, but Gedda (5) is too lachrymose, though he uses the words to dramatic effect.

Peter Dawson singing in English with orchestra (HMV B 8196) is dramatic and incisive, though he sings a glaringly wrong note at one point, and the orchestra under Lawrance Collingwood is lacklustre to say the least. The Russian baritone G. M. Yurenev (HMV EK 136) gives a well-shaped performance, but the voice is tight in tone and becomes strangulated at the big moments. One final version, and a most interesting one, is that of Koshetz (3), who transposes up a tone, and whose slightly sour tones suit the mood well. She is effortful and dramatic, and very bitter in this most pessimistic of songs. If a choice were to be made, I would opt for Talvela or Christoff, but would not want to do without Kozlovsky.

'To the Children' (Khomyakov) Op. 26 No. 7

With the possible exception of 'Lilacs' this is probably the most widely popular of the songs. Rachmaninov, always the fond father, responded warmly to the text of the poem. The deceptively simple construction hides a careful development of mood and key until the final page with its feeling of calm resignation.

Of the recordings in English, there are two by John McCormack, one with piano alone (DA 1112; GEMM 158) and one with Kreisler performing a wholly unnecessary violin *obbligato* (DA 680; EX 29 0056 3). Edwin Schneider is the pianist in both, and the version without violin is much the better of the two. McCormack sings with warmth and sincerity, and even his odd pronunciation seems to add to the charm of this version. Richard Crooks (Club 99 CL 502) is too self-regarding in his enervated performance. David Lloyd (Col. DB 2124) is more straightforward.

David M. Jackson

Eileen Farrell's glorious voice does full justice to the sentiments expressed in the song (33CX 1553), although she is dangerously slow. The Russian baritone Andrei Ivanov (9) is also slow, and his weepy style is completely wrong, though the voice itself is pleasant enough. Gedda (5) and Tear (6) both give suitably restrained performances, both are accompanied most imaginatively and both use their best honeyed tones, Gedda only beginning to push a little too much at the very end.

Schwarzkopf, in English, with Gerald Moore (SAX 5268), sings with beautifully controlled tone, although her pronunciation is rather odd in places. Slobodskaya (SXL 2299) and Koshetz (3) both sound past their prime but use their voices to moving effect. Söderström (1c) produces a flow of lovely tone, responsive as always to the text, and Ashkenazy brings out previously unheard details in the accompaniment.

'Vocalise' Op. 34 No. 14

This wordless song was written for the high, pure voice of the soprano Antonina Nezhdanova and is unusual in that it has become better known as an instrumental piece than as a song. There are far more non-vocal recordings of it than the eight vocal versions discussed here. This is a supremely taxing piece for the singer, and the amount of listening pleasure to be gained from some of these recordings is minimal. In the original key, the final phrase climbs to a climactic top C sharp, although a lower option is given. Unfortunately Kozlovsky (9) goes for the top, and the sound is unbearably stressful; this is not a pleasant experience. Similarly, Gedda is too forced and effortful.

Easiest on the ear are Anna Moffo with Stokowski's American Symphony Orchestra (LSB 4114), although her blandly sexy approach becomes monotonous, and Suzanne Murphy with the Scottish National Orchestra conducted by Neeme Järvi (Chandos ABRD 8476), using Rachmaninov's own orchestration. The distant placing of Murphy coupled with her smooth tone and fine musicianship makes this the best version with orchestra, and possibly the best all round. Pons with Kostelanetz (LX 1209; D3M 34294) sings with too many intrusive aspirates, and suffers pitch problems.

Kurenko (2a), transposed down a tone, sings nicely but ignores most of the dynamic markings. Söderström (1a) is glorious and even boasts a good trill, but Vishnevskaya (7) is disappointingly effortful, although she takes the low options where available.

178

'The Dream' (Sologub) Op. 38 No. 5

There can be only one possible recommendation for this wonderful song, and that has to be Söderström and Ashkenazy (1a) – superb singing and playing both technically and emotionally. The other versions with piano are Kurenko (2a), who has to strain for the notes and conveys no sense of repose in the final phrases where it is crucial, and Natalya Shpiller (9), whose sour, rather wobbly singing puts her out of the running immediately, although Lev Oborin plays the final page very well.

One more version needs to be heard: Kozlovsky with the Bolshoi Theatre Orchestra and Israel Gusman (ASD 2539) in an almost unbearably lush arrangement, slow and ecstatic throughout.

Scandinavian song

ROBERT LAYTON

No records exist of Jenny Lind or Christina Nilsson, though the first interpreters of Sibelius' songs, Ida Ekman (1875–1942) and Aino Ackté (1876–1944) did make fleeting appearances on the gramophone. Ackté, for whom Sibelius composed 'Luonnotar', possessed an exceptionally wide *tessitura*. She recorded Grieg's 'Jeg elsker dig' in Paris in 1905 (Od. 36868), while Ida Ekman, who sang some Sibelius songs to Brahms, recorded 'Svarta rosor' ('Black roses') (G & T.83546) in Helsinki the following year. Even through the generous surface noise, it is evident that Ackté had a thrilling voice of real power, and one can only regret that nothing survives of her Salome. Although the Finnish singers of the period (Eino Rautavaara, Irma Tervani (Ackté's sister), and Maikki Järnefelt and Abraham Ojanperä were all recorded and have been transferred to microgroove (Scandia SLP 541), it wasn't until the 1930s that any serious attempts were made to explore the songs of Sibelius and Kilpinen, two highly-contrasted figures. Sibelius composed almost a hundred songs, most of them to Swedish texts: Kilpinen, on the other hand, composed some seven hundred, mainly to German and Finnish poets.

Although his contribution to song does not rank alongside that of Mussorgsky or Wolf, Sibelius certainly deserves a more honoured place in the firmament than many commentators have been inclined to accord him. Composers who have poured their inspiration solely in this medium, like Kilpinen or to a much lesser extent the Swiss master, Othmar Schoeck, are a case apart. However, among those for whom song is not a primary or exclusive preoccupation, Sibelius can more than hold his own. As with the Grieg songs, some of the most popular have served to hinder the music-lover from exploring the less familiar, and it is such songs as 'Svarta rosor' and 'Flickan kom ifrån sin älsklings möte' ('The Tryst') that one encounters more often on record rather than such strange and haunting masterpieces as 'Jubal', 'Teodora' and 'Höstkväll' ('Autumn evening'). Another factor is the relative inaccessibility of the Swedish language as far

180

as non-native singers are concerned, for like the Grieg songs, those of Sibelius do not sound at all well in translation. Only five are in Finnish, though these are among the most simple and direct in utterance. Nine are in German, in which Sibelius was reasonably fluent, and one is in English, in which he was not, but the vast majority are in the language with which he grew up as a child, Swedish. Sibelius' inspiration was fired by the nature poets writing in Swedish, be they Finnish, such as Runeberg, Wecksell and Tavaststjerna or mainland Swedish, like Karlfeldt, Fröding and Rydberg. Sibelius' setting of Rydberg's 'Höstkväll' is among his very greatest and most self-revealing songs, and in the hands of a Flagstad encompasses an enormous range of feeling. Not all of Sibelius' poets are of Rydberg's stature but most of them are of quality, and all are linked by their highly developed feeling for the northern landscape and its desolate melancholy and grandeur. Runeberg was undoubtedly the poet he loved most deeply, an enthusiasm shared by Brahms, no less, and roughly a quarter of his output in the genre is of Runeberg settings. Even so, the great Lieder singers of the LP era, Schwarzkopf, Fischer-Dieskau, Souzay, and Prey have fought shy of this body of song, though Schwarzkopf did record some Grieg as well as Sibelius' 'Säv, säv, susa' ('Sigh, sedges, sigh'). To the best of my knowledge, no non-Nordic singer has recorded 'Höstkväll' and Flagstad's, the first on record (SXL 2030), remains unsurpassed. The voice was still glorious and she enters the heart of this extraordinary miniature tone-poem with its wide compass and almost Wagnerian grandeur and breadth. Nilsson's has a cool magnificence that is entirely appropriate but it is marred by one or two moments of insecure intonation (SXL 6185). Krause's in the complete set is one of his less successful. It is always intelligent and atmospheric – but much is lost when we hear it in the monochrome of the piano, and it does not match the widely spanned seemingly effortless line of Flagstad.

The challenge posed by language did not deter Astra Desmond from recording Grieg for Decca and championing Sibelius in the concert hall (and in a perceptive essay in Gerald Abraham's 1947 Symposium). Nor did it inhibit Marian Anderson from recording another of his greatest songs to words of Tavaststjerna, 'Långsamt som kvällskyn' ('Slowly as the setting sun') with Kosti Vehanen (DA 1580). Indeed she recorded five altogether in 1936–7. This is a song that haunts the listener with its concentration of mood and atmosphere but the success of her record rests rather more on the thrilling sound she produced than the interpretative insights that a native singer, such as Aulikki Rautavaara, who recorded for Parlophone, could bring. Although twenty-eight songs were recorded on coarse-groove records, some like 'Säv, säv susa' in numerous duplications, the advent of LP drastically increased his representation. The poem by Gustav Fröding is so rich in verbal music that setting it must have

Robert Layton

been a daunting task, and Flagstad's poignant account still reigns supreme. It was recorded by Björling on 78s (DA 1797) and then later at a concert in Gothenburg conducted by the legendary Nils Grevillius only a few weeks before Björling's death (RB 6620), a glorious but operatic account that misses much of the intimacy and melancholy of the poem. Nicolai Gedda's 1969 recording (ASD 2574) is less histrionic but conveys the character and poignancy of its closing bars to excellent effect. Even so in terms of vocal beauty, it is no match for Tom Krause in 1963 (SXL 6046) as far as poetic insight is concerned. I am tempted to say that Hynninen's 1975 account (Harmonia Mundi HMC 5142) is perhaps the most affecting of all. (That issue translated 'Sigh, sedges, sigh; beat, waves beat' as 'Roseau, roseau, chuchotez, vagues, vagues agitez-vous', which may be why French singers have fought shy of it!)

Kim Borg's mid-1950s anthology of sixteen songs with Erik Werba for Deutsche Grammophon (DGM 19113) is one of the pinnacles of the Sibelius song discography. It was somewhat overshadowed by Kirsten Flagstad's classic set, which was a pity as no one has given a more affecting account of the simple Finnish settings 'Souda, souda, sinisorsa' ('Swim, duck, swim') and 'Illalle' ('To evening'), which Flagstad sings in Swedish. Made at the very height of his powers, Borg gives all the songs on this record with rich sonority and a marvellously variegated tonal palette, and above all with the artistry that conceals art: it all sounds so completely natural and effortless, and the sense of line in the Finnish settings is quite masterly. Kim Borg's performances are the epitome of style in that one never questions whether it is even possible to sing these songs in any other way! Although the two anthologies from Tom Krause (SXL 6046 and SXL 6314) brought a number of marvellous songs such as the setting of Bertel Gripenberg's 'Narcissen' ('Narcissus') into circulation, it was the appearance of the Complete Songs from Decca that must be accounted the great event of the 1980s in this field (Argo 411 739–1ZH5). In its different way this was as important for Sibelians as were the pre-war volumes of the Hugo Wolf Society. Many of the songs, including two of the very greatest, 'Jubal' and 'Teodora', had, amazingly enough, never been recorded on LP before. 'Teodora' must have come as a revelation to many collectors, for in its over-heated expressionism it comes close to the Strauss of 'Salome' and 'Elektra'. Tom Krause is superb here: just listen to the subtlety with which he prepares her entrance, 'hon kommer, kejsarinnan, hon nalkas, Teodora' ('she comes the Empress, she is drawing near, Theodora'). The vast majority of the songs falls to his lot, the remaining dozen or so coming from Elisabeth Söderström and Vladimir Ashkenazy. Krause's voice has lost some of its youthful freshness and bloom but none of its black intensity. If you put his earlier accounts of, say, 'Vilse' ('Astray') or 'Narcissen' ('Narcissus'), both

182

delightful songs, alongside the later ones, you will notice the firmer focus and fresher timbre of the voice in the earlier but the keener interpretative insight and feeling for character in the latter. His performances are authoritative and majestic. 'Jubal' is to a poem of the Swedish poet and painter, Josephson, who inspired the Op. 58 settings. The piano part is, as often in Sibelius, fairly simple and the burden of the musical argument rests with the voice – the reverse of Wolf. But what a vocal part it is! It ranges with great freedom over a compass of almost two octaves; indeed, so intense is this writing and that in its companion, 'Teodora', and so full of dramatic fire that, in spite of 'The Maiden in the Tower', one wonders whether he could not have become an operatic composer. (He still toyed with operatic plans right up to 1913.) Söderström floats this line to wonderful effect. (I have been unable to track down a copy of the only previous recording by Aune Antti on Polydor 57175.) Of the German settings the real masterpiece is 'Die stille Stadt' which has the concentration and atmosphere of a miniature tone-poem: indeed, its serenity, beauty of line and sense of repose mark it out from the others. Here is a song of great distinction and refinement of feeling, but again it has been grievously neglected for apart from the Argo set, Taru Valjakka (Finnlevy SFX 11) and Hynninen (Finlandia CD FA 202) would seem to be the only other artists to have recorded it.

Another great song, 'På verandan vid havet' ('On a balcony by the sea') is more familiar from Flagstad's and indeed Krause's earlier record with Pentti Koskimies. Its intense questing chromaticism points to the Wagnerian shadows that crossed Sibelius' horizon in the 1890s. Like so many of his great songs, this comes into its own in the orchestra, for Sibelius was never wholly at ease with the piano. I find Irwin Gage in the Complete Edition excessively vehement in these opening bars. Pentti Koskimies gave more sensitive support in the earlier record, but again this is a song that needs the orchestra. Hynninen has recorded it with piano in 1975 and a decade later with orchestra and both vocally and interpretatively is peerless. He seems totally attuned to the melancholy and mysticism Rydberg evokes. Another Fröding setting, new to the gramophone, 'Bollspelet vid Trianon' ('Ballgame at Trianon'), is among the most delightful, and its charm and subtlety quickly win one over. Söderström points the contrast between recitative and the pastiche pastoral style with great artistry, and in this instance the piano writing has great finesse – and so, too, it goes without saying, has the playing of Vladimir Ashkenazy! But there are so many riches here that take one by surprise: songs like 'Soluppgång' ('Sunrise') and 'Lasse Liten' ('Little Lasse') are finely characterised with something of the concentration and atmosphere you find in his finest miniatures.

'Luonnotar' is a special case: it is half-song, half tone-poem, which

Robert Layton

Ackté first sang at the Gloucester Festival in 1913 and the vocal part is very demanding indeed. It is also one of his most strangely mysterious and imaginative creations. Luonnotar is the mistress of the air in Finnish mythology. From the emptiness of space, she descends to the oceans and the waves carry her; she roams the oceans for 700 years. It has an extraordinary sense of mystery and an intensity unusual even in Sibelius. It wasn't until the late 1960s–early 1970s that it was recorded by Phyllis Curtin (Bernstein), Gwyneth Jones (Dorati) and Taru Valjakka (Berglund). An earlier recording from 1934 by Helmi Luikkonen (World Records SH 237) was rejected at the time as the result of record wear tests. Valjakka on HMV and Häggander on BIS come closest to the spirit of this work. Söderström in her recording with Ashkenazy (SXDL 7517; CD 400 056–2DH) suffers from a wider vibrato and shriller timbre than is usual from this artist. Of the songs on Flagstad's celebrated LP only half were scored by the composer himself. The soprano Mari Anne Häggander and Jorma Hynninen have recorded all of Sibelius' original orchestrations with the Gothenburg Symphony Orchestra under Jorma Panula for BIS (LP/CD 270). Apart from such rarities as 'Koskenlaskian morsiammet' ('The Rapids-Rider's Brides') there is a song of haunting beauty, 'Serenade', newly discovered among Sibelius' papers by Erik Tawaststjerna. It dates from 1895, the period of the *Lemminkäinen Legends*, and is a setting of Stagnelius, a Shelley-like figure in Swedish poetry, to whom Sibelius was much attached. It has the greatest delicacy and atmosphere, and its whispering *pizzicato* strings are wonderfully suggestive.

Kilpinen

Hynninen is also a masterly interpreter of Yrjö Kilpinen (1892–1959), whose hold on the catalogue whether on shellac or LP has always been tenuous. His stature far outstrips his meagre representation on record, and the finest of his songs withstand comparison with Wolf, whose successor he was at one time proclaimed. Kilpinen was trilingual, speaking Finnish with his father, Swedish with his mother and immersing himself in German as a student. He remained aloof from contemporary trends: his idiom is unexploratory and his harmonic vocabulary does not go much beyond Wolf, and yet at his finest he creates a strangely distinctive world. He is a master of the vignette and distils a powerful atmosphere and a keen psychological intensity with the greatest economy of means. The classic pre-war Kilpinen Song Society set by Gerhard Hüsch and Margaret Kilpinen (HMV DB 2594–98; LV 80) included the two of the Morgenstern cycles, 'Lieder um den Tod' and 'Lieder der Lieder' and 'Mondschein' to words of Jalkanen, a haunting song, as concentrated in feeling and mood as Wolf or Schoeck. These were among Hüsch's most intense performances for he gets inside these masterly cycles as few others since. Kim Borg, too, gave an unforgettable reading of two of Kilpinen's Swedish-language songs, both Lagerqvist settings, in a 1960 recital record (DG SLPM 138 060). 'Som ett blommande mandelträd' ('Like blossoming almonds') and 'Om tiotusen år' ('In ten thousand years') capture the luminous otherworldly quality of this poet and the performances have an eloquence and a lyrical poise that elude so many interpreters. Grateful though one is to have other anthologies, such as that Tuula Nienstedt (soprano) and Matti Tuloisela (bass-baritone) give us on Da Camera Magna SM 90013, it offers *vin ordinaire* by the side of the heady vintages of Borg and Hynninen. Moreover, to use the tedious euphemism, not all of Kilpinen's songs are of equal interest, and there are a fair number of these on this disc. However, among modern recordings, Hynninen's anthology comprising the early songs, the Leino settings, the Koskenniemi songs, and the Tunturilauluja, Op. 52–5 (some of which Talvela recorded for Decca – SXL 6522). These are virile, thrilling performances that form an excellent introduction to the composer.

Grieg and Norway

There is a long and flourishing tradition of folk song in Norway, but it was not until the 1840s that the publication of Lindeman's *Norske Fjeldmelodier* drew the attention of Norwegian composers to its riches. It was the impact of this and subsequent volumes, as well as the rising fortunes of Norwegian letters during the Romantic period, that did much to stimulate the growth of the Norwegian art song during the second half of the century. Not long after the famous encounter between Nordraak and Grieg in the early 1860s we find Grieg responding to the growing fascination for Norwegian folk music. His debt to it emerges in the melodic contours and rhythmic inflections, the habits of musical speech, as it were, and in the preponderantly strophic design. Even *Haugtussa* (The Troll Maiden), composed in 1896–8 and Grieg's finest song cycle, makes little use of the elaborate devices of integration that we encounter, say, in the great Schumann song cycles, and all but one of its eight numbers rest on predominantly strophic foundations. In this predilection for the simple strophic design, Grieg is not alone, for other Scandinavian composers regarded it with favour, including Nielsen and Rangström. Yet compare, say, the settings of Bjørnson's 'Princessan sat højd i sitt jomfrubur' by Kjerulf and Grieg, and it is obvious that Grieg created in a few brushstrokes a mood picture that is stronger in atmosphere. Fine though the Kjerulf song is, it is the Grieg that resonates in the memory and which completely proclaims its strong artistic identity, and it is equally

Robert Layton

evident that he has completely absorbed the folk song into his blood-stream. Hardangar music and folk song are not the only sources of inspiration but they do play a much greater part than is the case in Denmark and Sweden, perhaps because Norwegian folk music is such a rich resource.

According to Grieg, his wife Nina was the finest interpreter of his songs, but she was never recorded. Flagstad recorded songs by Grieg's precursors, two by Halfdan Kjerulf on an acoustic Odeon, one by Rikaard Nordraak on Columbia DN 51. As for Grieg himself Flagstad recorded *Haugtussa* three times with the same pianist, Edwin McArthur: first in 1940 (DB 5833–36), then again ten years later (RCA LM 1094) but it is their 1956 recording when the voice was perhaps too matronly (LXT 5237) that has effectively displaced them. A setting of poems by Arne Garborg, written in the Norwegian *landsmål*, the dialect of rural Norway as opposed to *riksmål* the language of the educated urban Norwegian, they have never gained more than a peripheral place in the repertoire outside Scandinavia. The story tells of a young maid who through her supernatural insights and the suffering she undergoes, including unrequited love, wins through to greater self-understanding and tranquillity. In terms of characterisation Flagstad, for all her weamth and richness of vocal colour, was never quite the equal of Aase Nordmo-Løvberg on HMV (7EBN1/2), never released outside the Scandinavian territories, and made before the voice began to develop the hard timbre that affected her in the upper register in the 1960s. Nor did her 1957 recital of Grieg and Strauss (33CX 1409) receive the wide currency it deserved. Whatever their merits, subsequent versions of this great cycle by Edith Thallaug with Kjell Bækkelund (Philips 854006 AY) and Ellen Westberg Andersen and Jens Harald Bratlie (Simax PS 1011) offer no definitive answer to the challenges offered by this cycle. Nor, to be frank, did the Swedish soprano, Siv Wennberg, who recorded it in 1973 with Geoffrey Parsons (HQS 1345). The voice has remarkable tonal beauty and power, but the absence of vibrato in the upper part of the register inevitably weakens her colour. It also serves to expose her occasional habit of attacking a note from below, very slightly below but discernibly so. There are certain mannerisms (she lingers over the 'l' in *lengtande* (longing) and 'Li' in the first line of 'Möte' to unpleasing effect) and vowels tend to swamp consonants. A Grieg recital, which must be numbered among the classics, however, is Flagstad's 1957 anthology that includes 'Fra Monte Pincio', 'Med en Primula veris' ('With a Primrose') and 'Millom rosor' ('Among the roses') (LXT 5264). Her masterly pacing, sense of vocal colour and command of atmosphere are not to be faulted. Mention must also be made of Knut Skram's fine collection entitled *Norske Romanser* with Robert Levin of some of the Vinje settings

186

that appeared in 1970 (Philips 6507 001), which fills a gap and offers singing of fine intelligence and style.

Even if we still need a great modern performance of *Haugtussa* the song repertoire before and after Grieg is reaching the gramophone. Two LPs of Kjerulf's songs in the Norwegian Cultural Council's series (NKF 30 003 and 005) give a glimpse of the foundations on which Grieg built. With the generation following Grieg, few of Sinding's songs maintained more than a peripheral hold on the catalogue (rightly so, one would be tempted to say, on hearing such conventional pieces as 'Leit etter Livet og liv det' ('Take hold of life and live it') that Flagstad recorded (LXT 5237), yet a song such as 'Sylvelin' tells a different story, and possesses a touching simplicity. Perhaps the finest examples of Norwegian *romans*[1] after Grieg are to be found in the work of Ludvig Irgens Jensen and Sparre Olsen but the former's *romanser* are more praised than played nowadays. His settings of Hans Bethge's *Japanischer Frühling* have a distinctive quality and a delicacy of feeling that is well captured by Karin Langebo in her 1971 recording (Philips 6597 005). Arne Dørumsgaard (b. 1921) enjoyed a brief vogue in the early days of LP and twenty-two of his songs were recorded by Flagstad and Gerald Moore (ALP 1140) (the authors of *The Record Guide* called them 'uneventful'), and his *Canzone scordate*, transcriptions of early music, enjoyed the advocacy of Gérard Souzay (LXT 2835) but in the 1960s his talent turned to literary rather than musical expression.

Fartein Valen (1887–1952) ploughed a lonely path in Norwegian musical life and reacted against the post-nationalist folk-inspired musical language of the 1920s in Norway. Like Skalkottas in Greece, he evolved an idiom that has some of the qualities of the second Viennese school, yet is spiritually quite independent of it. If his often poignant harmonic language seems to make little contact with that of any other Norwegian composer of his day, his music evokes the atmosphere of isolated northern latitudes. His orchestral songs include a setting of Hans Bethge, and the *Zwei Chinesische Gedichte* together with his Whitman setting 'Darest Thou now O soul' are eloquently presented by Dorothy Dorow (Philips 6754 001). These songs have some of the sensuousness of Delius and the emotional complexity of Alban Berg. Another composer, just a little younger than Fartein Valen, is Sparre Olsen (1902–85), whose musical language is highly diatonic, even though he studied in the 1930s with Valen, and was a keen admirer of both Schoenberg and Hindemith at a time when these masters were not fashionable in Norway. He has steeped himself in Hardangar music and his music has an authenticity of feeling to which I find it impossible not to respond. The *Edda songs* were

[1] The *romans* is the equivalent of *Lied* in German or *mélodie* in French.

recorded in the 1950s by Eva Prytz with consummate artistry (Mercury MG 900002), which Toril Carlsen does not quite match (Philips 410 445–1). These songs have a folklike dignity and great beauty and if his is not a major personality, it is a sympathetic and distinctive one.

Denmark and Nielsen

Norway was not the only Scandinavian country to witness an upsurge of interest in song. In Denmark at the beginning of the century we have Christoph Ernst Friedrich Weyse: in Sweden we have Geijer, Almqvist and Adolf Fredrik Lindblad, whose songs were so much admired by Mendelssohn, but these have not enjoyed the same exposure as either Weyse or his successor, Peter Heise (1830–79), who wrote no fewer than 200 songs in his relatively short life. Weyse was born in 1774 and migrated from Germany and made his home in Denmark: he is generally thought of as 'the father of Danish song', Denmark's Schubert and so on. They are artless in their simplicity and of surpassing beauty. The delightful songs that Nielsen wrote throughout his life owe much to this much neglected composer and if you juxtapose, say, Weyse's 'Natten er saa stille' to words by a Golden Age poet, Johan Ludvig Heiberg, and 'Underlige Aftenlufte', one of Nielsen's greatest songs, to a poem by Oehlenschläger, the debt even within the limited canvas and conventions of the strophic miniature is striking. Both were recorded in the 1940s by Aksel Schiøtz and have been transferred to LP. This artist's incomparable legacy, embracing Weyse, Gade, J. P. E. Hartmann, Henrik Rung, has been collected on five LPs (HMV E051 37021/5). His accounts of the Nielsen songs have been surpassed neither in artistry nor beauty and subtlety of vocal colour. Nielsen's songs have none of the psychological subtlety of Kilpinen or the nature mysticism of Sibelius, but stem from the artless simplicity of Weyse. The gramophone has done nothing like justice to their genius, and apart from Schiøtz, only one record made in the 1960s has offered twelve of them, including such masterpieces as 'Æbleblomst', 'Irmelin Rose' and 'Underlige Aftenlufte', sung by various Danish singers (Philips AY 836 750). Ib Hansen's account of 'Irmelin Rose', for example, is beautifully shaped and imaginative in its colouring. But the shadow of Aksel Schiøtz looms large in this tradition, so large indeed that Danish singers have been reluctant to record them at all. No doubt until a Danish singer of world standing like Schiøtz emerges, Nielsen songs will be slow to claim their rightful place either on record or in the recital room. But similarly, one must add, until a great Norwegian artist appears to fill the gap left by Flagstad and Nordmo-Løvberg, Grieg will also suffer neglect. Astonishingly, there is still no complete set of Grieg.

Sweden

Last, but not least, Sweden, which has produced more than its fair share of singers. Indeed, thanks to artists such as Elisabeth Söderström, Kerstin Meyer and Håkan Hagegård, the songs of Stenhammar, Peterson-Berger, Rangström and so on are heard in the concert hall outside Scandinavia more often than Danish and Norwegian repertoire. Although singers as distinguished as John Forsell and Aulikki Rautavaara recorded Sjögren, Stenhammar and Rangström in the days of 78s, only a handful of songs was listed in WERM and Adolf Fredrik Lindblad, a key figure in Swedish song, remained unrepresented. Swedish opera singers were well represented on shellac, but the *romans* repertory was not. As far as LP collectors are concerned, the ground was broken by a 1957 anthology by Elisabeth Söderström and Erik Saedén with Stig Westerberg at the piano (Swedish Society Discofil LT 33127–28) which ranged from Erik Gustaf Geijer to Ture Rangström. (Bellman falls into a special category: a poet who set his original verses to existing music and not the other way round.) Erik Gustaf Geijer (1783–1847) was also a poet, and an important one as well as a philosopher, but he was musically gifted and is now represented by an LP devoted to his songs and a rather Mendelssohnian Piano Quartet (Caprice CAP 1274), and Carl Jonas Love Almqvist (1793–1866) has also had a whole record to himself, a 1974 BIS issue (LP 13). However, it is Lindblad who possessed the most natural melodic talent and though few of his two hundred songs are recorded, Söderström made a strong case for the four songs she included on her recital record with Jan Eyron, devoted to repertoire favoured by Jenny Lind (SXL 6195).

Given the poor representation of Grieg, Kilpinen and Nielsen, it is small wonder, perhaps, that the even less familiar Swedish song repertoire should languish unattended. The first side of a valuable 2 LP set (CAP 2019) issued in 1986 to mark the bicentenary of the Swedish Academy is devoted to settings of poets of the Gustavian age (Bellman and Johan Henrik Kellgren through to Tegnér, by composers such as Joseph Martin Kraus and Bernhard Crusell). The second includes a Berwald setting, compositions by Carl Jonas Love Almqvist and Erik Gustaf Geijer, who were active as composers as well as poets. The second LP brings settings of Strindberg by Rangström, two fine Stenhammar songs, one of which, 'Prins Aladin (sic) av lampan', to a poem of Fröding, is highly original and quite unlike the Stenhammar we know from the symphonies, and the same applies to its companion, 'Moonlight'. There is also a charming account of Peterson-Berger's setting of Karlfeldt's 'Längtan heter min arvedel' ('Longing is my heritage'), very different from Sibelius' celebrated song from the Op. 86 group (1916) but nonetheless quite magical, particularly when it is as gloriously sung as it is by Sylvia Linden-

189

Robert Layton

strand. These LPs are well planned with intelligent changes of voice and mood.

Only a handful of Rangström's songs has received attention: his settings of Runeberg's 'Den enda stunden' ('The only moment') and Bo Bergman's moving, dignified 'Bön i natten' ('Prayer in the night') must be among the most recorded of his songs. Söderström captures the simple eloquence of the Bergman setting perfectly in her 1957 recital. Birgit Nilsson included it in her 1965 anthology, 'Songs from the Lands of the Midnight Sun', though it strikes me as less moving in its orchestral form (SXL 6185). (I must admit that I have not been able to track down a copy of Rautavaara's version with the composer conducting on Telefunken.) Söderström's 1969 recording of the *Idyll*, fifteen Runeberg settings taken from a Swedish Radio broadcast (EMI 7C 053–35162), is an indispensable part of any collection, and is coupled with Kerstin Meyer's performance of Gösta Nystroem's finest songs *Sånger vid havet* (*Songs by the sea*). The songs of Stenhammar are perhaps best served by Erik Saedén, an artist who has never achieved (perhaps because he has not sought) international exposure. His vocal splendours are second to none and his imagination and artistry such that one regrets his reluctance to travel. He has recorded Stenhammar's *Visor och stämningar* (*Songs and moods*), ten songs dating from 1909–10, and some of the most captivating of his *romans* compositions (EMI 4E 053–35116).

One can only regret that Nicolai Gedda had not been able to break a lance for Stenhammar earlier in his career. He has recorded twenty of the songs, including such fine examples of his art as 'I skogen' and the 'Adagio', a setting of Bo Bergman, accompanied by Jan Eyron on the small Bluebell label (BELL 147), but it would be idle to pretend that Gedda's voice has the timbre or bloom of his prime. And much the same must be reported of his survey of Peterson-Berger's songs on the same label. The Swedish *romans* repertoire from Geijer through to Rangström and Gunnar de Frumerie is enormously rich, and there is much that still awaits the attention of the gramophone.

Bartók and Janáček

DAVID MURRAY

Bartók: Five Songs, Op. 16 (after Endre Ady)

Kovács, Fellegi	Hungaroton SLPX 11603
Laszlo, Holetschek	Nixa WLP 5283
Leanderson, Leanderson	BIS LP 43
Sass, Schiff	Decca SXL 6964
Seiner, Salter	Apollo Sound AS 1007

Janáček: Zápisník Zmizelého (The Diary of One who Disappeared; poet anonymous)

Blachut, Štěpánová, Páleníček	Supraphon LPV 319
Frydlewicz, Soukupová, Kvapil	Panton 11 0216
Gedda, Soukupová, Páleníček	Supraphon C37 7541
Häfliger, Canne-Meijer, de Nobel (in German)	Philips ABR 4041
Häfliger, Griffel, Kubelik (in German)	DG 138 904
Keller, Wirz, Venzago	Accord ACC 140007
Přibyl, Márová, Páleníček	Supraphon 2414
Schreier, Lahusen-Oertel, Lapšanský (in German)	Eurodisc 200 045
Tear, Bainbridge, Ledger (in English)	Argo ZRG 692
Válka, Hošáková, Páleníček	Esta M.5158–61 (78 rpm)

Just north and east of Austria, you might think, song was all but blighted from the turn of the century. Neither Western concert programmes nor record catalogues suggest otherwise: a little Szymanowski surfaces from time to time, and a little Kodály and one Enescu cycle, but beyond them there are only the song cycles listed above. It is quite possible nonetheless that there are further discoveries awaiting, for Czech and Hungarian composers like Janáček and Bartók faced a peculiar difficulty in their time – the practical necessity of German translation. Publication on anything more than a local scale required it. Unfortunately Czech, a Slavic language, has syllabic patterns that are hard to match in Western tongues; and Hungarian (which is hopelessly Finno Ugric: no articles, no prepositions, no gender) doesn't work at all.

Bartók and Janáček had to accept many musical compromises so as to secure German publication. (Even in the Boosey & Hawkes edition of Bartók's Op. 16 songs that I have in hand, there are only German and English words; worse still, the translators are identified but not the original Hungarian poet!) Each of these composers could at least wield the influence he had earned in other musical forms, whereas – who knows? – other composers in the former provinces of the Austro-Hungarian Empire who were chiefly devoted to solo song may have disappeared unpublished. Imagine, for example, a Hungarian equivalent of Hugo Wolf . . . Nowadays singers hasten to learn Czech for Janáček's operas, and Hungarian for *Duke Bluebeard's Castle*; perhaps there will be a spin-off in the form of new middle-European discoveries.

Meanwhile the Bartók and Janáček cycles keep a marginal foothold in the Western repertoire, each with its own difficulties. In the case of the Janáček *Diary*, the obvious ones are the inclusion of small but essential parts for solo mezzo and a trio of female voices, and the unbrookable demand for top Cs from the tenor protagonist at the very end of the cycle. There are subtler difficulties in Bartók's Op. 16: the piano part requires a concert soloist, and the Symbolist poems of Endre Ady – Magyar-laconic and suggestive in the original – suggest too much in too few syllables for any Western translation.

All the recorded versions of the Bartók are sung in Hungarian, and all but Rolf Leanderson's by sopranos or mezzos. In fact the vocal line never goes above the stave (F-sharp is the highest note), and Ady's first-person stance is perceptibly masculine despite the linguistically undetermined sex. Since most of the poems are erotically fraught, it is odd that the cycle has had so little attention from male singers.

These were Bartók's last solo songs, composed in spring 1916. His one opera, *Duke Bluebeard's Castle*, was already five years old, but most of his mature music was still to come. Op. 16 belongs with Op. 15, a similar song set with inferior texts, and came immediately after the Op. 14 Suite for piano. There are a few echoes of the *Bluebeard* idiom, especially in the fourth song 'Alone with the sea'; but the level of dissonance is much higher, and the voice is often in tonal conflict with the piano (Bartók had perfect pitch, and his singers need it too). The lyrical address is always intimate, even when exacerbated; the piano carries an expressive burden of greater complexity and breadth, and the even-numbered pieces need something like virtuosity as well as astringent passion. I have not discovered whether Bartók was familiar with Schoenberg's 1908 George cycle, *Das Buch der hängenden Gärten*, but he certainly knew Schoen-berg's seminally atonal Op. 11 piano pieces, and the Ady songs share that musical climate. In detail there are no closer resemblances: in fact these songs are like no others except the sibling Op. 15 set. Their dramatic effect can be formidable.

It is less than that in the recordings by Magda Laszlo and by Katinka Seiner. Laszlo is careful, earnest, too mild by far, though sensitive and effective in the third song (mournful reflections on a lonely bed). She doesn't rise to the intensity of the fourth, and her pianist Franz Holetschek – much blotted in the recorded sound – is never imaginative enough nor brilliant enough. For Seiner, Timothy Salter's accompani-ment remains just a scrupulous accompaniment (not really fluid in the Debussy-ish pianism), and Seiner herself – properly committed and con-cerned – sacrifices the cutting edge of many a phrase to her frail, tremu-lous manner. The expressive range of the cycle is reduced, and her habit of taking slow unaccompanied phrases far slower than Bartók's markings reduces it further. (There is a common misapprehension that the Ady songs make an awkwardly slow sequence: soulful lingering over what looks like 'recitative' ensures that impression, and obscures the taut construction of each song.)

The other two female performances are steadier and stronger, with the advantage of piano-partners who are independent soloists. Eszter Kovács and Ádám Fellegi are faithful to the composer's tempi, as one would expect in Hungaroton's comprehensive Bartók collection. Though Kovács is described as a soprano, her dark mezzo timbre suits the songs well, and Fellegi is not only assured but eloquent. Somehow the *forte* climax of 2 misfires. Sylvia Sass, a genuine soprano, offers still more cool authority and subtler colouring of individual words and phrases, with a fine vehemence in the right places. She also gives the sharpest point to the contrast between short interjections and long lines, which is essential to Ady's prosody and exactly rendered by Bartók. With the benefit of András Schiff as partner – occasionally a touch too restrained, but always lucid, refined and searching – this performance exercises the bleak dramatic grip that belongs to the cycle.

It is a great pity nevertheless that the performance by Rolf and Helene Leanderson (sister? wife? – the sleeve doesn't say) appears only on an obscure BIS record called 'Songs of Love and Death', for in important musical respects it is the best model available. The male Leanderson does not have a fascinating personality like Sass, nor her acute identification with the material; but his more objective, 'public' delivery has its own attractions, which include very clean line and tone, and excellent pitch (I cannot judge how idiomatic his Hungarian may be, but he uses the words articulately). Above all the Leandersons respect Bartók's pacing: the cycle does *not* seem predominantly slow, and the significant pauses never exceed the just musical measure. The result is that each piece sounds an entirely convincing *song*, and not only a dramatic soliloquy. Ms Leanderson is good, a bit careful, without the flair of Fellegi or Schiff, and too loud in the middle of 2. In 3, however, the baritone's gentle intensity is beautifully found. I feel sure that the composer would have thought his musical intentions were realised here with distinguished loyalty and insight.

Where the young Bartók's Ady songs retain a private, prickly air, old Janáček's musical transformation of the anonymous 'Diary' is all candour and undisguised warmth, a mature composer's recreation of excitable innocence. The 'naive' poems are like that, too: they appeared in Janáček's local newspaper billed as private effusions by a farm lad (the 'one who disappeared'), unearthed after he had absconded with his gypsy sweetheart – but it is incredible that anybody ever believed the story! Only recently has it been generally admitted that for the alleged situation, the poems are too good to be true – too knowing, too dense with hindsight, too artful with telling details: in short, too like Wilhelm Müller's *Schöne Müllerin*. (The current conjecture is that the poet was a literary friend of the newspaper editor.) Whether Janáček himself really believed the authorship tale or not makes no difference. What he made from the verses, filled out with his own vast sympathetic resource, is radiantly persuasive.

I mentioned earlier the awkward demands the cycle makes. Among them is the sort of tenor required: one with the mature artistry to do justice to Janáček's subtleties *and* to shape the dramatic profile of the whole cycle, but one who also captures the accents of a lusty young voice – for youthful fervours and stammers are so much written into the protagonist's music that greyer voices must sound a little false, at best second best. It is easier for a veteran singer to represent *Schöne Müllerin* or *Frauenliebe und -leben* than the *Diary*, because the more operatic Janáček trades directly upon the material freshness of a young man's timbre (and those daunting top Cs).

The age of the pianist is of course immaterial; and Josef Páleníček, who was four years old when the *Diary* was composed in 1918, has played it on record from the days of 78rpm (with Válka) to 1984 (with Gedda, himself in his sixtieth year). In the old Válka performance he was lively and impatient, with Blachut in 1953 at once more imaginative and more authoritative. By 1978, with Přibyl, he was testier and more aggressive, inclined to hammer; discretion returned in the collaboration with Gedda (he sounds dampened in the 'Oxen' song at Gedda's disappointing tempo). In all those accounts, his idiomatic sympathy is remarkable. A seasoned Janáček pianist is a treasure in the *Diary*, for he has a grand, independent role in the foreground – and of course the crux of the drama, when the hero loses his virginity *al fresco* (the apposite 'poem' consists of nothing but asterisks), is richly enacted by the piano alone.

Czech has an inalienable claim upon the *Diary*, though for live performance the language of the audience may beckon. Adjusting German or English to the music is frankly a compromise, unnecessary for records accompanied by bilingual texts; Janáček's notorious concern with the expressive speech-patterns of his own language resists effective translation. That said, the recordings in non-Czech are rather impressive. Robert Tear sings in English as if he were determined to show how much communicative sense *can* be wrought from the (unavoidably stilted) translation, and he is thoroughly musical, though his timbre is a special taste. His Zefka is Elizabeth Bainbridge, smooth, clear-toned and alert, if always a concert-singer – how much impersonation her role invites is an arguable matter – and the female trio is good. At the piano Philip Ledger is expert and full of good sense, sometimes prosaic.

Peter Schreier's *Diary* voice is uncomfortably close to his Mime voice, laced with some near-falsetto and some chalky tone. Much self-conscious art is expended on the German declamation, and the high level of nervy anxiety has a disheartening sameness despite all the refined intelligence. One misses any sturdy simplicity. The women are unexceptionable, the pianist merely unexceptional – solid, competent, blandly metronomic.

Ernst Häfliger's two recordings in German are separated by a decade. In 1954, with Felix de Nobel as a graceful, reticent partner (inclined to smooth the corners of dotted notes), he sounds fresh and sensitive, but never remotely like a farm lad, and the folk-dance song (no. 20) has salon manners. Cora Canne-Meijer is well attuned, but too grandly sonorous for wild little Zefka. The lesser ladies are excellent, nicely distant (they must serve as a sympathetically detached Chorus). The strenuous ending goes badly. It has far more exciting thrust in Häfliger's later recording, where the tenor doesn't seem older but simply more resourceful, and direct instead of dreamy. Kubelik proves a superlative accompanist, straight and tough where de Nobel was fluently suggestive. There is a forward, specifically personal Zefka from Kay Griffel; this time the women are a *Frauenchor* (as too obviously on several other recordings – Janáček was right to prescribe just an intimate trio). This admirable performance enlists the *Diary* into the mainstream *Lieder* tradition, with some confident gains as well as some sacrifices.

The renditions in Czech are richly various. I bitterly regret having been able to find only half of the Válka cycle on 78s, and no information about J. Válka himself, for his superbly cultivated performance with Páleníček stands apart from modern ones. His fine period operatic tenor is crisply forthright, objective rather than intimate; it belongs to a past era of sing-

David Murray

ing, and it is quite possible that Janáček would have intended nothing more subjectively histrionic than Válka's polished style admits. Certainly one feels no expressive lack: a scale of degrees of evident 'involvement', in the modern manner, would be simply inapplicable.

Beno Blachut's 1953 account concludes with impressive high Cs, despite earlier evidence of some wear (thrown cruelly into relief by the light, seductive Zefka of Štěpánová, though she was in fact seven years his senior). His gentle intensity commands unstinting respect. Not only is the central dialogue vitally delicate, beyond anyone else's range, but he is uniquely successful in capturing the shy young hero's irrevocable growing-up, the 'before' and 'after' of his crisis. Lustier tenors sound imperceptive by comparison: only Blachut fully captures the depth of the diarist's overnight transformation, his newly charged state of rapturous independence combined with manful shouldering of responsibility. Since that is what the *Diary* is about, Blachut sets a standard despite his passing frailties.

Vilém Přibyl has the advantage of a more virile timbre, but for all his forceful drama and apt, pungent simplicity he sounds the same hearty chap throughout. (The devout distress in 19 goes for very little.) There are plenty of heartfelt details, represented in uniform close focus by the recording, like Páleníček's overbearing contribution. Together with Libuše Márová's *hors concours* Zefka, they make a creditably gripping performance – for Márová eschews conventional gypsy-vampery in favour of shy, simple passion, vulnerable and unpractised: that rings touchingly true. It is a pity that the 'Oxen' song, which crystallises the hero's 'before' state (Přibyl's natural vein), should be technically so clumsy.

Matched with Věra Soukupová's strong, decidedly mature Zefka, Miroslav Frydlewicz's fervent young tenor – betraying some Eastern European bleat in high passages – suggests a Manrico/Azucena pair, which cannot be right. The terms of his unconditional surrender in 18 are hefty, and the final Cs come with desperate effort. The special distinction here is earned by the pianist, Radoslav Kvapil: in the first songs he seems excessively literal about note-values, but as the drama intensifies he shows his true mettle. He wields big rhetoric in 12, barely suppressed electricity in 13 (the wordless solo *exposé*), and brilliant delicacy in the tremulous 16. Every *Diary* pianist should measure himself against Kvapil's example.

The newest versions have their own attractions. Gedda is scrupulously impassioned, and manages to sound miraculously young (with brave Cs at the end) even though the bloom has gone from the voice. The duologues are limp, however, with Gedda registering only a kind of generalised distress, and thereafter there is too much earnestly applied Acting.

Soukupová is again mature to excess, with a dull penchant for making a *crescendo–diminuendo* on each and every main note. Gedda's idea of making the folk-dance song a drunken effusion has grisly results; the female trio is again too opulently a chorus. The rewards of intelligent experience are still substantial.

I know nothing about Peter Keller, who is perhaps Swiss but certainly cultivates an elevated French style of delivery. Some may find that precious in the *Diary*; I was reminded – disarmingly – of Jacques Jansen, and of Bernard Kruysen's bated-breath sensitivity in Fauré. In the 'Oxen' song Keller finds beautifully exact contrasts, irresistibly affecting. Clara Wirz's gypsy girl is appealing but simpler, edging toward shameless operatic vamp; Mario Venzago's keen commitment at the piano is sometimes hard-fingered. I should still count this eagerly loyal performance among the best on record. Among it, the Blachut and Přibyl versions and maybe the period Válka and later Häfliger, Janáček's inexhaustible cycle gets delved into very thoroughly, leaving a sum impression greater than the individual essays in interpretation. It is surely a mark of a great work that it leaves room for so many realisations, with a guaranteed character that will survive many another fresh reading – especially in the original, inalienable Czech.

Britten

MICHAEL KENNEDY

For a composer who enriched the vocal repertory so prolifically, Benjamin Britten wrote comparatively few solo songs, if we except his many delightful folk song arrangements (which are not considered here). He preferred to group the songs into cycles or sets to which he imparted such unity and cohesion that it is rare in a recital to encounter a single item extracted from a cycle. He is unique among British composers in having written a masterpiece in each of five languages, English, French, German, Italian and Russian. He also favoured the song-cycle with orchestral accompaniment in the manner of Mahler and Berlioz (and of Elgar's *Sea Pictures*), but with the difference that there are no alternative versions with piano accompaniment. His model, therefore, may be assumed to have been Mahler's *Das Lied von der Erde*, which would be unimaginable in anything but its full orchestral dress, rather than the same composer's *Lieder eines fahrenden Gesellen*, which is effective with piano. Nevertheless of the many compositions now to be surveyed, only five are for voice and orchestra. Equally, with the exception of folk songs, none of the songs with piano was later provided with an orchestral accompaniment, as was Richard Strauss's occasional practice. This is scarcely surprising in view of Britten's genius as a pianist. His piano accompaniments are so complete in themselves that any further embellishment might be regarded not merely as superfluous but as impertinent.

Three Early Songs

Mackie, Vignoles	CDC 7 49257–2
Luxon, Willison	CHAN 8514 (CD)

1. Beware
2. O that I had ne'er been married
3. Epitaph: The Clerk

These three early songs were slightly revised in 1968 and published in

1985. 1 was composed in 1923 when Britten was 9, 2 a year earlier and 3 in 1926. Already Britten's responsiveness to a text and his innate sense of drama are evident. Neil Mackie's approach is in the Pears tradition, Benjamin Luxon's slightly more dramatic. Both performances are excellently recorded.

Quatre chansons françaises

Gomez, Rattle, CBSO   HMV ASD 4177

1. Nuits de Juin
2. Sagesse
3. L'enfance
4. Chanson d'automne

Britten's first orchestral song cycle – we ought, perhaps, to re-name it in English the *Four First Songs* – was composed in the summer of 1928 when he was fourteen years old, between leaving preparatory school at Lowestoft and entering Gresham's School, Holt, Norfolk, yet it was not performed until March 1980, three and a quarter years after his death. These four French songs were written as a present for his parents' wedding anniversary and demonstrated to them, if they got the message, that their youngest child was already a composer and could follow no other occupation. That he was already formidably equipped for such a vocation is evident from every bar of this astonishing work. The assurance with which Britten had absorbed the styles of Chausson, Ravel and Debussy, with hints of Wagner at the end of 4, is a less remarkable feature of this music than the evidence it provides of the already nearly mature composer – mature not only in the ability to manipulate a musical language but in his approach to an overall philosophical and thematic conception. For the two poems by Verlaine and two by Hugo were obviously carefully chosen to illustrate the boy-composer's dawning preoccupation with the themes of lost innocence and the poignancy of the past. Already, too, the themes of night and dreams creep into the text – all Britten's orchestral song-cycles deal in some way with them. Yet the most startling single pre-echo is 3, in which a child plays games and laughs while his mother is dying. Here the embryonic opera composer may be perceived. A solo flute depicts the child's laughter, his song and his games, prescient of Britten's ability to epitomise a dramatic situation in orchestral terms in his operas.

It is this dramatic element that is most strongly characterised in Jill Gomez's performance, with Simon Rattle conducting, and 3 therefore emerges as the strongest composition. Her brilliant rather than lustrous tone is less well suited to bring out the sensuousness of 1, though Rattle

Michael Kennedy

loses no opportunity to emphasise the bewitching nocturnal qualities of its scoring – the orchestra includes harp and piano. (One recalls with particular pleasure Heather Harper's singing of this song in the first broadcast performance.) Gomez's diction is somewhat indistinct in 2, possibly the finest of the songs by reason of its lucid orchestral textures and its easy command of the variety of moods in Verlaine's poem (set by Vaughan Williams in 1908 as 'The Sky above the Roof'), but she gives an appropriately ecstatic lift to the *Liebestod* conclusion of 4. The orchestra's flute and oboe soloists are particularly distinguished and are also recorded with a musicianly sense of balance and proportion.

Tit for Tat

Shirley-Quirk, Britten   Decca SXL 6608
Luxon, Willison   Chandos CHAN 8514 (CD)

1. A Song of Enchantment
2. Autumn
3. Silver
4. Vigil
5. Tit for Tat

In the preface to the published score of *Quatre chansons françaises*, Britten's erstwhile amanuensis Colin Matthews writes that the orchestral parts required virtually no editing. The songs in *Tit for Tat*, written roughly contemporaneously with the French cycle and some after it, up to 1930, were published in 1969 in Britten's lifetime. In a note written at the time, Britten said he had composed 'well over 50 songs' between 1922 and 1930, many being settings of poems by Walter de la Mare. He chose five for publication which he considered to be 'as complete an expression as is possible from a composer in his early teens'; and he admitted that he had decided to 'titivate them a little . . . Once or twice when the fumblings were too obvious, the experienced middle-aged composer has come to the aid of the beginner . . . I do feel that the boy's vision has a simplicity and clarity which might have given a little pleasure to the great poet . . . ' Again it is not the obvious influences on Britten which are significant here, but the glimpses of what he was to become. The best song is 5, because it is the most characteristic of Britten the man, who hated blood sports and cruelty. In this he was no doubt encouraged by his teacher Frank Bridge, but these attitudes went deeper and further back, as his childhood fondness for de la Mare itself proves. 5 is a trenchant indictment of Tom Noddy, the poacher of fish and fowl and of hares and rabbits, 'the murderer through the green woods', and the music is spontaneous, deeply felt and knows exactly where it is going and how. The previous four songs

200

– and it was surely the 'experienced middle-aged composer' who knew to place 5 last – are exercises in wistful nostalgia, with 3 a night-piece that was to have many successors. It is really extraordinary that a child should have composed 2, with its economy of gesture, and the born dramatic composer is no less obvious – and perhaps more subtly obvious – in 4 than in 5. John Shirley-Quirk sings the cycle with the authority that the composer's chosen interpreters automatically absorbed from him, and Britten's accompaniment in no way condescends to the young composer's illustrative shafts.

Benjamin Luxon's recording, with David Willison as his pianist, finds the singer in excellent voice, relatively free from the vibrato that sometimes mars his performances. Whereas Shirley-Quirk's performance seems weighted throughout towards the climax of 5, Luxon makes more of 3. The Chandos recording is not ideally balanced, with the voice placed in the background.

Our Hunting Fathers

Pears, Britten, LSO	BBC REGL 417
Söderström, Armstrong,	HMV ASD 4397
Orchestra of Welsh National Opera	

1. Prologue
2. Rats Away!
3. Messalina
4. Dance of Death
5. Epilogue and Funeral March

Britten described his Op. 8 as 'my real Opus 1', in other words the work in which he knew Britten had become Britten. He designated it a 'symphonic cycle' and the term is amply justified. Although for voice and orchestra, the voice is treated instrumentally and the cycle is in every respect a forerunner and companion piece of the *Sinfonia da Requiem* of a few years later. *Our Hunting Fathers* is the most radical and pioneering work Britten wrote. Written in 1936 when he was 22, it has no parallel in the English music of its day. No British composer had written for the orchestra with such virtuoso savagery and, in the context of 1936, it is not surprising that the players behaved badly at the first rehearsal and that the critics were baffled after its first performance at a Norwich Festival. The tragic outcome was that this explosive work was virtually neglected during the rest of the composer's lifetime and has achieved recognition at its proper valuation only since he died. It is the ripest fruit of the collaboration between Britten and W. H. Auden. The texts of 1 and 5 are by Auden, who modernised the anonymous text of 2 and chose 3, also

Michael Kennedy

Anon., and 4, which is Thomas Ravenscroft's poem about a partridge-hunt. The ostensible theme of the cycle, as its title implies, is condemnation of man's cruelty to animals in blood sports, the theme of de la Mare's 'Tom Noddy', but Britten used this as an analogy for the blood-sports that were occurring in Europe in 1936, hence the deliberate juxtaposition of 'German' and 'Jew', names of hounds or hawks (it is not clear which) in the Ravenscroft poem. The music is a series of elaborate *cadenzas*, for the singer, for the woodwind and brass, and for the strings. Perhaps only a young composer would have dared to pile on the emotional agony as Britten did here, first with the shrieks of 'Rats Away', then with Messalina's florid wailings of 'Fie' as she mourns her dead monkey, and then the 'whurrets' and hunting cries as the predators chase their prey, the orchestral sound dominated by *glissandi* on horns and yelps from trumpets and woodwind.

Our Hunting Fathers was written for the voice of Sophie Wyss, the Swiss soprano who was one of Britten's first champions and also gave the first performance of *On This Island* and *Les Illuminations*. Unfortunately no recording of her in Britten's music (except folk song arrangements) has survived, if indeed any existed, but she heads the list of distinguished interpreters who were fully committed to his works. Not until 1982, when the BBC issued on its commercial label a studio broadcast given in 1961, was a recording available. The soloist was Peter Pears, with Britten conducting the London Symphony Orchestra. It is in many ways an indispensable document, not merely because the composer conducts the music with extraordinary intensity and whiplash energy, but because Pears was at the very peak of his mature form and delivers the text with exemplary clarity and intelligence. The precision of his singing is ground as sharp as a knife; and there are memorable individual flashes of interpretative insight, such as the final 'Amen' in 'Rats Away!', where the irony is delicately suggested rather than stressed. The acrobatic feats required in 'Rats Away!' pose no problems for Pears, and he is equally agile in the roll-call of names. It is a measure of his artistry, too, that he sings the extravagantly elegiac *melismata* of Messalina's song so convincingly that he makes the listener temporarily forget that this is essentially a woman's music. Trust him, too, to sing the text of the Prologue and Epilogue with a fluency that disguises the difficulties Britten encountered in setting its complexities (the Epilogue and Prologue, in that order, were composed last). Possibly the work might have languished for a shorter time on the fringe of Britten's popularity if the top and tail had been omitted – the coda of the Epilogue today seems almost embarrassingly a pastiche of Shostakovich, though it is no less astonishing that it should have been composed by a young English musician in 1936. Astonishing, too, is the orchestral virtuosity displayed in the 'Dance of Death' (forerunner of its equivalent in the *Sinfonia da Requiem* of 1940), in which the rhythms and cries of the hunting-field are metamorphosed into a savage commentary on events in Abyssinia and Spain. Some English musical opinion in 1935 had found it hard to assimilate the furies unleashed in Walton's First and Vaughan Williams' Fourth Symphonies; it did not want to know Britten's even fiercer apophthegms. The 'Dance of Death' has its own prologue and epilogue, the words taken from Ravenscroft's 'Hawking for the Partridge'. The incredible *glissando* cadenza of 'Whurret', followed by the catalogue of hawks' names, is sung by Pears like some kind of mystical incantation. At the end, just the two names 'German' and 'Jew' are chosen for repetition, sung *sotto voce* and interpolated into the sinister recapitulation of 'Whurret'.

Elisabeth Söderström recorded *Our Hunting Fathers* in 1983 with the Orchestra of Welsh National Opera conducted by Richard Armstrong. It is right that a Swedish soprano should take over a role created by a Swiss soprano and neglected by most British sopranos with the honourable exception of Heather Harper, whose performance at a Prom with Haitink ought to have led to a commercial recording. There is a touching link with the composer, too, for Söderström sang *Our Hunting Fathers* at the 1976 Aldeburgh Festival, which was to be Britten's last, and the record sleeve has a moving picture of them together at this time. Söderström's performance is characterised strongly and has the incisiveness the music requires. Her recital of the hawks' names is more effective than Pears', not because of better singing but just because it sounds better, as does the whole work, with a soprano – the 'Fie fie' of Messalina is an obvious case with which to prove this point. Thanks to the advantages of digital recording, the orchestral detail comes through more clearly than in the BBC disc; and the harmonium-like woodwind accompaniment in the 'Mark, Matthew, Luke and John' episode of 'Rats Away!' is beautifully played by the Welsh opera orchestra.

Cabaret Songs

Walker, Vignoles   Meridian E77056

1. Calypso
2. Johnny
3. Tell me the Truth about Love
4. Funeral Blues

These four songs were written in collaboration with Auden in the period 1936–9. Composer and poet had in mind the artistry of Hedli Anderson, who specialised in singing 'light' revue songs of high quality somewhat in the style of the Brecht–Weill cabaret songs which became famous in the

Michael Kennedy

Berlin of the inter-war years. They are an early example of Britten's brilliant and innate capacity for absorbing a musical style and, transcending pastiche, making it part of his own. Astonishingly, they were not published until 1980, when one of the first singers to seize eagerly upon their wit and melody was Sarah Walker. Her recording, with Roger Vignoles as accompanist, is part of a recital given at Dartington Hall, Devon, in 1982, to an appreciative and (where it matters) mainly silent audience. 'Calypso' (1) was the last to be composed, dating from 1939 when Britten and Auden had left England for America. It is a railway song of a kind in which Britten was later to excel in setting Hardy's 'Midnight on the Great Western' in *Winter Words*, with an identical *ostinato*. It is a reminiscence of the Auden–Britten success in the documentary *Night Mail* of 1935–6, and it signals their swift assimilation of an American idiom which was to result in 1941 in the flawed but genius-touched 'operetta' *Paul Bunyan* (to the ill-concealed chagrin of certain American composers). 'Johnny' was composed on the afternoon of 5 May 1937, Britten in the morning having composed the 'Nocturne' of *On This Island*. It sounds like a folk song; then in the third verse the mention of going to the opera invites a parody so affectionately true that one need no longer wonder where the rustics' 'Pyramus and Thisbe' in *A Midsummer Night's Dream* came from; and the last wistful verse is a Britten 'dream' song, another Nocturne. 'Tell me the Truth about Love' is the most 'obvious' cabaret song of all, composed in 1938, and a homage, both in the text and the music, to the art of Cole Porter. It is a delicious song, not least because of its subcutaneous poignancy and vulnerability. 'Funeral Blues' was the only song of this quartet which was at all widely known at the time of its composition. It was part of the music for the Auden–Isherwood play *The Ascent of F6*, first performed on 26 February 1937 at the Group Theatre in London, and became known as 'Funeral Blues'. Its original accompaniment, in the theatre, was for two pianos and percussion, and the text differed from the published version.

If Britten ever felt that these songs were too closely tied to the political and social mood of 1937–8, time has proved him wrong. They are good songs, evocative songs. Sarah Walker sings them with stylish humour and deep insight, though the high notes put her under strain and her voice becomes shrill and metallic. Vignoles' accompaniments are impeccable.

On This Island, Op. 11

Pears, Britten	BBC REGL 417
Troxell, Kozma	McIntosh MC 1003
Johnston, Ibbott	Pearl LIL 300
Tear, Ledger	HMV HQS 1310

204

1. Let the florid music praise!
2. Now the leaves are falling fast
3. Seascape
4. Nocturne
5. As it is, plenty

(Two extra settings)

Mackie, Vignoles   HMV CDC 7 49257–2

6. To lie flat on the back
7. Night covers up the rigid land

This is not a song cycle, but a song collection, all but one of the poems being taken from Auden's 1936 volume *Look, Stranger!* (published in the United States as *On This Island*, which Auden preferred). Britten added 'vol. I' to the title, implying that another set was planned. (Other Auden settings dating from 1937 have now been unearthed and recorded.) He wrote the first of this set, 4, on 5 May 1937 – a setting of a lyric in the Auden–Isherwood play *The Dog Beneath the Skin*, first performed at the Westminster Theatre on 12 January 1936 – and the last in October five months later. The first performance was given in a BBC broadcast on 19 November 1937 by Sophie Wyss, with Britten accompanying – 'her English is obscure at times', the composer commented. But a private performance had been given on 15 October at Britten's London flat by a friend he had first met earlier in the year, Peter Pears, to an audience of Christopher Isherwood and Lennox Berkeley. (In his diary Britten wrote: 'Peter sings them well – if he studies he could be a very good singer. He's certainly one of the nicest people I know, but frightfully reticent.') The first song gave Britten most trouble: by late September 1937 he had revised the opening about six times. It is a liberating song, both Handelian and neo-classical, its florid opening in D major giving way to a funereal G minor section. The words refer to a failed love affair, but in such ornate and privately allusive language that Britten's task in reconciling the text's ceremonious and intimate contrasts was clearly great. He succeeded superbly.

Curiously, of this collection Pears and Britten recorded commercially only the first song, in October 1955 (ECS 545). Their performance of the complete set was issued by the BBC in 1982, the tape of an Aldeburgh Festival relay from Blythburgh Church on 18 June 1969. If it seems trite to say that the performance represents the fruit of 32 years' knowledge of the songs, it remains the truth. We are conscious as we hear this interpretation of all that followed *On This Island*; the pre-echoes of the *Winter Words* cycle are prominent. 2 and 4 are also innovative songs of their day, the first with a pattern of semiquaver duplets which was to become a fingerprint, the second one of the earliest of several great 'sleep' songs, *bel canto* in its vocal style, its arches of melody representing the sleeper's breathing. 3 captures the 'leaping light' of the poem; 5 is another cabaret song, false accents underlining the false sentiments. Pears seems a trifle self-conscious in 5, as if its brittle satire was difficult for him to recapture in 1969. His singing of 4 is unsurpassed.

Robert Tear, recorded in 1973 with Philip Ledger as a sensitive accompanist, is uncomfortable in the low register of 1 and his diction is unclear in 2. A lulling, hypnotic performance of 4, though. David Johnston (1972) has an even better pianist in Daphne Ibbott and it is a pity the recording is so 'boxy' in sound quality. Like Tear, he is taxed by the range of 1, especially in the lower notes. Women frequently sing *On This Island*, though there is no clear preference as in the case of *Our Hunting Fathers*. The American soprano Barbara Troxell, a pupil of Elisabeth Schumann and a Pamina and Elvira for Beecham and a Marschallin for Bernstein, is more successful than anyone else on record in capturing the mood and style of 5 – her performance refutes suggestions often made (and implied by me above in my comments on Pears) that this song has 'dated'. She is fine, too, in 4 and the whole interpretation is strongly dramatic. Tibor Kozma is an excellent accompanist, favoured by the recording engineer at the expense of the singer. Made in 1953, this was an enterprising disc. It also includes performances of a beautiful Auden setting probably intended for vol. II of *On This Island* – 'Fish in the Unruffled Lakes' (November 1937) and of two rarities, the vocal duets 'Mother Comfort' (words by Montagu Slater) and 'Underneath the Abject Willow' (Auden). No doubt following Schumann's celebrated example, Miss Troxell sings these duets with herself. The Auden is particularly interesting: the poem was an invitation to Britten to embark on a warmer relationship and the composer parodied it by setting it jauntily (not taking the words seriously) and for two voices (impersonally). 'Fish in the Unruffled Lakes' is also included on Johnston's disc, with a song from Britten's boyhood, the charming Belloc setting 'The Birds' (1929).

Since Britten's death his executors have unearthed and released several hitherto unperformed songs which were intended as part of the set and were discarded, usually because they did not 'fit' rather than because he judged them inferior. Two Auden settings, intended for a successor to *On This Island*, and composed in October 1937, have been recorded by the tenor Neil Mackie, accompanied by Roger Vignoles. Both poems, 'To lie flat on the back' and 'Night covers up the rigid land', were aimed directly at Britten, for whom Auden had an unreciprocated passion. The first, 6, is set wittily and lightly, as if Britten was rejecting the hints, while 7 recaptures the mood and the gentle lilt of 4. Also from 1937 is a song, 'Not even summer yet', which Britten composed to words by Peter Burra, a writer and critic who was at school with Pears and was killed in a plane crash in 1937. Britten set the poem for Burra's sister, a singer. It is in his most successful melancholy vein, wistful and affecting, but with a strong middle section. Mackie sings it beautifully.

Les Illuminations

Pears, Goossens, New Symphony Orchestra	Decca LXT 2941
Pears, Britten, ECO	Decca 417 153–2
Harper, Marriner, Northern Sinfonia	HMV SXLP 30194
Schreier, Kegel, Leipzig Radio Symphony Orchestra	Decca SXL 21179
Mock, Sokoloff, La Jolla Musical Arts Society, San Diego, Orchestra	Alco ALP 1211
Hallin, Comissiona, Stockholm Philharmonic Orchestra	RIKS LP 4
Rendall, Wallberg, Bavarian Radio Symphony Orchestra	Da Camera SM 691513
Tear, Giulini, Philharmonia Orchestra	DG 2531 199
Teyte, Ranck (piano)	GHP 4003

1. Fanfare
2. Villes
3. (a) Phrase
3. (b) Antique
4. Royauté
5. Marine
6. Interlude
7. Being beauteous
8. Parade
9. Départ

This was the first of the vocal works in which Britten deliberately set foreign texts in order, as Peter Pears has written, 'to mediterraneanise' his music. The strange Rimbaud prose-poems, with their vivid imagery, their fantasy, their invocation of a world of lost innocence and their undertones of homosexuality, appealed to Britten, who was probably introduced to them by Auden. Rimbaud himself, Pears said, appealed to Britten as one of the world's 'lost sheep'. To recapture the intensity of his childhood impressions, Rimbaud sometimes resorted to hashish, and his writing, almost untranslatable, has a parallel in English in Coleridge's 'Kubla Khan'. Britten recognised the musical possibilities and it is a measure of his genius that he did not use the full orchestra to illustrate the kaleidoscopic tone-colours suggested by the text but limited himself to strings.

Michael Kennedy

He had already, in 1937, written a masterpiece for strings, the *Variations on a Theme of Frank Bridge*, in which his inventive parody had full play. *Les Illuminations* (1938–9) is its vocal equivalent, with the strings imitating the rest of the orchestra – the 'trumpet' fanfare at the start, for an obvious example – and the soprano voice an essential feature of its colouristic plan. Even Pears does not make the use of a tenor convincing, though it is sanctioned by the composer's use of the term 'high voice'. It is another Sophie Wyss work: she sang two of the numbers – 'Being beauteous' and 'Marine' – in Birmingham and London before the first performance of the complete cycle in London on 30 January 1940, conducted by Boyd Neel.

So, I would place at the head of the several recordings of this marvellous work, prodigal in its tunefulness, that made in 1970 by Heather Harper with the Northern Sinfonia, conducted by Neville Marriner. Her clear diction is a basic asset but one that is treasurable. The cadenzas in 'Marine' are dazzlingly well sung, and at the end of 'Phrase' she floats the triple piano high B flat on 'danse' with exquisite tone, its slide down an octave so gracefully done, making the transition into the slow B flat dance of 'Antique' even more magical. In 'Royauté', where a couple dementedly believe they are king and queen, she is profoundly poignant. Marriner begins the Interlude too loudly (compare Britten's own recording) but otherwise obtains a very truthful account of this fascinating score. The excellence of the playing in 'Being beauteous' points up a more than vague similarity to the introduction to Act 3 of Puccini's *La bohème* in the illustration of falling snow. It is known that the march theme in 'Parade' originated as part of the discarded string quartet *Go play, boy, play!* (1933–6), and one wonders if this movement was the first to be composed since the recital of names – 'Chinese, Hottentots, gipsies, simpletons, hyenas, Molochs . . . ' – is much nearer than the rest of the work to the harsher style of *Our Hunting Fathers*.

Another soprano recording of particular interest is that by Maggie Teyte, made (with piano accompaniment only, alas) at a concert in the Town Hall, New York, on 15 January 1948 during what, amazing to account, were her first New York appearances (she sang her last Mélisande during this visit). She was 59 and it is a tribute to her taste that she should have selected this work for this occasion. The voice betrays signs of frailty at the top of its range and is deficient in tone-colour. But her singing is always sensitive, her diction exemplary and her performance of 'Antique' something to savour for its lyrical line. Margareta Hallin's performance with the Stockholm Philharmonic is not in the Harper league, good though it is, and Sergiu Comissiona's slow and deliberate tempi rob the work of some brilliance. Alice Mock's voice is small and weak when extended, but she sings the text expressively in excellent French, particularly 'Royauté'. The La Jolla strings have knotty problems with Britten's decorative writing and are not helped by the primitive LP recording, but Sokoloff had a marked affinity with the music and his slower march in 'Parade' is effective.

Pears recorded *Les Illuminations* twice. His first recording was made in 1954 with Eugene Goossens conducting the strings of the New Symphony Orchestra. He is in good and incisive voice, his soft singing of wondrous beauty, 'Ce sont les villes' a clarion call. The recording is of its time, the opening strings fanfare fuzzy rather than sharply defined. In 1966 he re-recorded it, with Britten as conductor – and what a joy it is to hear the strings of the English Chamber Orchestra play for the composer. What vivacity, colour and (in the 'Interlude') desolation he conjures from them, what subtlety of rhythm and phrasing in 'Antique'. Pears sounds under strain in some of the more testing passages, though the artistry and insight are unimpaired, as is his sustained high *legato*. The performance as a whole recaptures youthful zest and *joie de vivre*.

Three other tenors have recorded *Les Illuminations*. Robert Tear's (1979) is with Giulini, who uses a large body of strings and gives the music the full treatment, with precise and clear virtuoso playing by the Philharmonia. This is less 'aesthetic' a performance than Pears'; the music sounds tougher and less impressionistic but no less original. Giulini's *allegro energico* in 2 is heavier than the composer's, he obtains a majestic start to 4 and in 6 he achieves a gorgeous range of colour, making it sound like a study for a *Peter Grimes* interlude. In 5 Tear's cadenzas are less fluent than Pears's and his lower register is strained in 8. But this is a large-scale approach to the piece, risking and not entirely escaping inflation. The operatic tenor David Rendall's recording is of a studio performance in Munich in 1977 with the Bavarian Radio Symphony Orchestra, whose playing under Heinz Wallberg is meticulously accurate but a little stiff. Rendall has a richer voice than Pears or Tear, though his French is less good than theirs. He brings a feeling of urgency to the music and the shading of tone in 3b is admirable.

I like the invigorating opening tempo set by Herbert Kegel for Peter Schreier's recording with the Leipzig Radio Symphony Orchestra. The playing is notable for many subtle nuances which show how carefully the performance was prepared. Schreier sings beautifully, of course, but his is generally a characterless interpretation, much less in sympathy with the essentials of Britten's score than Kegel.

Seven Sonnets of Michelangelo, Op. 22

Pears, Britten	HMV RLS 748
Pears, Britten	Decca 417 183–1

Michael Kennedy

Rolfe Johnson, Johnson   Hyperion A 66209
Tear, Ledger   HMV HQS 1310
Young, Watson   Argo RG 25

1. Sì come nella penna (XVI)
2. A che più debb' io mai (XXXI)
3. Veggio co' bei vostri occhi (XXX)
4. Tu sa' ch' io so (LV)
5. Rendete a gl' occhi miei (XXXVIII)
6. S'un casto amor (XXXII)
7. Spirto ben nato (XXIV)

The *Michelangelo Sonnets* are a watershed in Britten's work. They were his first song cycle written especially for the voice of Peter Pears; and at the same time they celebrate that in Pears Britten had found not only a musical partner but a life partner. They are also another stage in his deliberate distancing of himself from a too obviously English tradition. Yet it should be noted, when we consider Britten's four foreign language song cycles, that only that in Russian, written specifically for a Russian singer who was a friend, has attracted performances by singers of the nationality concerned. Schreier, it is true, recorded *Les Illuminations*, but not the *Hölderlin-Fragmente*. How many Italian singers sing the *Sonnets*? Which French singers the Rimbaud? Incidentally, it is sometimes forgotten that Delius composed songs in German, French, Norwegian and Danish, in addition to English.

The *Sonnets* were composed between March and October 1940 and were completed in Amityville, Long Island, where they were privately performed at the home of Dr and Mrs William Mayer, hospitable hosts to Britten and Pears. The first public performance was not given until nearly two years later, in London in September 1942, five months after Britten's return from America. The songs were recorded two months later. This first recording is unsurpassed, and one would even say unsurpassable, in its passion, urgency, sensuousness and its youthful audacity. Pears' voice is ringing and firm, Italianate in a Schipa-like way, his diction perfect even in the fastest passages. The double-dotted rhythms of 2, the proud declamation of 1, the chaste classical lines of 3, the amorousness of 4 and 6, the serenade of 5 and the grandly noble eloquence of 7 – all shine as brightly as new-minted coins in the utter conviction of this performance, to which Britten's contribution at the piano is no less wonderful, with touches such as the dove-like cooing in 4 which anticipates *Noyes Fludde*. And if, over 40 years on, the music's 'novelty' can be seen as an extremely skilful manipulation – as in *Les Illuminations* – of familiar and unrevolutionary devices such as *ostinati* and arpeggios and a refraction of well-established tonal procedures, this knowledge seems of little importance:

the music itself still sounds to be opening magic casements. The same artists' 1954 recording is also a memorable performance, with the bonus of maturity. If Pears' voice has lost some of its youthful brilliance and gained some mannerisms, it has also gained in artistic insight and percipience. Voice and piano are intertwined in a total re-creation of the moments of the music's creation. 2 is even more mercurial, 7 still more moving.

The first tenor besides Pears to record the *Sonnets* was Alexander Young in 1953 in what was almost certainly his own first recording, a brave choice. It was made for the enterprising small company Argo, and the sound is no longer acceptable, especially that of Gordon Watson's excellent piano accompaniment. The performance, though, is certainly acceptable, with vocal trumpet-tone in 1, an impressive *legato* line in 3 – how beautifully 'Il sole' is sung at the end – and an intimate teasing style for 4 until its solemn close. Only in 7 is one conscious of the gap between this and Pears; the last line is uncomfortably fragile. The Tear–Ledger performance has no weakness where 7 is concerned and 3 is again especially beguiling. The virtuosity of the music seems nearer to the surface than with Pears and Britten. Anthony Rolfe Johnson's singing of the *Sonnets* is very much in the Pears tradition where tonal restraint is concerned, although he is not afraid to broaden the emotional expression in 3 and to bring an extra resonance to the beginning of 1. His rapid enunciation of 2 is done with skill and clarity. He is partnered by Graham Johnson, whose personal knowledge of Britten's methods is at all times evident in his playing of the piano part. Aided by an excellent modern recording, he almost rivals the composer in the expressiveness of the postlude to 7.

Serenade for Tenor, Horn and Strings, Op. 31

Pears, Brain, Boyd Neel Orchestra/ Britten	Decca 417 183–1
Pears, Brain, New Symphony Orchestra/ Goossens	ECS 507
Pears, Tuckwell, London Symphony Orchestra/Britten	Decca 417 153–2
Schreier, Opitz, Leipzig Radio Symphony Orchestra/Kegel	Decca SXL 21179
Schreier, Damm, Slovak Chamber Orchestra/Warchal	OPUS 9112 1577
Bressler, Froelich, Musica Aeterna Orchestra/Waldman	VC 81507
Kozlovsky, Polekh/Rozhdestvensky	Melodiya D 9045

Michael Kennedy

Tear, Civil, Northern Sinfonia/Marriner	HMV SXLP 30194
Tear, Clavenger, Chicago Symphony Orchestra/Giulini	DG 2531 199
Partridge, Busch, London Philharmonic Orchestra/Pritchard	Classics for Pleasure CFP 40250

Prologue
1. Pastoral (Cotton)
2. Nocturne (Tennyson)
3. Elegy (Blake)
4. Dirge (Anon.)
5. Hymn (Jonson)
6. Sonnet (Keats)
Epilogue

The *Serenade* is a masterpiece of English song to rank with *On Wenlock Edge*, *Dies Natalis*, and the best of Purcell. To those who were musically responsive in the mid-1940s, it was a case of 'bliss was it in that dawn to be alive', as, one after another, we made awed acquaintance with Britten's *Michelangelo Sonnets*, the *Hymn to St Cecilia*, *Rejoice in the Lamb* and this *Serenade*, all written within a few months, Vaughan Williams' Fifth Symphony, Walton's *Henry V* music, Tippett's *Child of Our Time* and, to crown it all, *Peter Grimes*. Yet in some respects it was perhaps the first impact of this *Serenade* that still vibrates strongest in the memory, possibly because of the unusual combination of voice and horn, certainly because English poetry had rarely been set to music like this. Then, the plan of the work itself is so effective and affecting, a succession of nocturnes of varying and contrasted kinds. There may have been a few dissenting voices and pens, but for hundreds upon hundreds of music lovers it seemed that the *Serenade* was one of music's treasures, and so it still seems. It was recorded in May 1944, seven months after its first performance, the only difference in the recording studio from the Wigmore Hall being that Britten conducted instead of Walter Goehr. The youthful Pears is superb, characterising each song ideally, producing a firm *legato* in the glorious picture of sunset that opens the cycle after the horn's Prologue, singing out strongly in the Tennyson setting, chilling the blood in the 'Lyke-Wake Dirge', performing impeccable coloratura acrobatics in the 'Hymn to Diana' and, in the final Keats setting, achieving an almost hypnotically beautiful grace of line and phrase to match the text and Britten's inspired setting. And what can one write of Brain's horn-playing except to assert that it justifies use yet again of the overworked epithet 'legendary'? The individual timbre, the glints and gleams of brass tone which were his secret, the perfect control of swelling and fading, the contrast between light and shade – these have never been excelled in this music and have been equalled only in his second (LP) recording of the work with Pears in 1954 when Eugene Goossens conducted (listen, for example, to the muted playing at fig. 6 in the second verse of the Tennyson Nocturne). Pears is in his prime in this later recording. In his third (1963) recording Britten again conducted and the horn is played by Barry Tuckwell, Brain having been dead for nearly six years. The incisive string-playing is the best feature of this version. Pears' sensitivity to the text is as finely tuned as ever but his singing lacks the richness of the earlier record-ings and there is some unsteadiness. Tuckwell plays too loudly and fails to supply the magic and poetry.

Robert Tear's 1979 recording with Giulini and the Chicago Symphony Orchestra presents this singer at his best, and Dale Clavenger is a dis-tinguished partner on the horn, the Epilogue being played and recorded most evocatively. Together they make the Blake 'Elegy' the high point of the work. In 5 the singing of the opening is too *staccato*; the effect is like an elocution lesson. *Leggiero* it is not! As in *Les Illuminations*, Giulini uses a full symphonic body of strings which gives the music an almost too sophisticated richness. Yet the magnificence of 2 is undeniable; rarely can it have sounded so romantic. Tear adopts a more traditional 'Aldeburgh' style in his earlier (1970) recording with Alan Civil (horn) and the Northern Sinfonia under Marriner, but in no respect does it rival the Pears–Britten recordings, for all its virtues.

What does an international star like Peter Schreier make of this work? Where the English words are concerned, the answer must be 'heavy weather'. Gallant as the effort is, the result is sometimes unintentionally funny. Nevertheless, the singing is beautiful, Herbert Kegel is an attentive accompanist and Opitz a good horn-player. The last verse of 1 is drawn out too long and the slow 2, though romantic enough, endangers the setting's momentum. Schreier recorded the *Serenade* again in 1983 in Bratislava with Peter Damm as the horn player and the Slovak Chamber Orchestra conducted by Bohdan Warchal. The English pronunciation has improved slightly, though the result is still like a performance featuring Erich von Stroheim. Yet Schreier clearly loves and understands the work, and one result of his unidiomatic vowel sounds and pronunciation is to show how exactly Britten matched his music to the English language. The colour of the music is altered, even violated, by Schreier. I hope this does not sound chauvinistic, for it is still a pleasure to hear such a fine tenor in this work. For sheer beauty of timbre and for attention to every nuance of dynamics he is in the highest league. In 2, the *da lontano* effect is magical and the drama of 3 is tensely conveyed, while the elaborate 5 is virtuoso singing. Once one has reconciled oneself to the East European sound of the horn (an instrument made in 1972, the sleeve tells us), Damm's play-ing is superb. The string playing is among the finest on record in this work, with accurate and expressive *pizzicato* in 5 and a really rich sound in 6.

The American tenor Charles Bressler has in Ralph Froelich the best player of the horn part after Brain. In 3 he almost rivals Brain in the range and expressiveness of his performance. Charles Bressler has a light, pleasant voice which tightens under pressure. His diction is first-rate. The strings of the Musica Aeterna Orchestra had been taught the work thoroughly by Frederic Waldman, it would appear, and the engineers were notably successful in capturing the basses' *pizzicato* in 3.

My preference for a recorded interpretation of the *Serenade* after Pears–Britten is that by Ian Partridge and Nicholas Busch, with the LPO under Pritchard. This is elegant singing, in no way etiolated, the texts delivered with a Pears-like intelligence and sensitivity. Partridge's is not a big voice, but on record it is big enough, especially as Pritchard's accompaniment is so good, with superlative playing by the LPO and Busch a highly accomplished partner.

The Russian performance – sung in Russian – is a severe disappointment in view of the Soviet Union's interest in Britten's music and to those who, knowing how well Gennady Rozhdestvensky conducted British music when he was in charge of the BBC Symphony Orchestra (1978–81), expect something special from him here. His contribution is much the best, as it happens, but tempi are almost all too slow and there is no impression that anybody understands much about the work. Polekh, first horn of the Bolshoi Opera Orchestra, is something of an artist, but he has to play a nasty instrument. He takes the Prologue very slowly and plays it well. The almost legendary Ivan Kozlovsky, with whom he gave the first Russian performance of the *Serenade* in the autumn of 1961, is misparted here. His first entry in 1 is neither *piano* nor *dolcissimo* and the performance of 2 is nothing short of a travesty, with the 'dying, dying' phrases converted into exaggerated echo effects at a ridiculously slow tempo merely in order to display vocal virtuosity. Show him a passage marked *piano* and he will give you a *forte* nearly every time. Much of this performance is grotesque: the use of falsetto in 4, for instance. But the Keats setting, 6, is rather beautifully performed and gives a glimpse, though too late, of what this recording could have been.

The Holy Sonnets of John Donne, Op. 35

Pears, Britten	HMV RLS 748
Pears, Britten	Decca SXL 6391
Young, Watson	Argo RG 25
Gilvan, Capon	Oryx 1925

1. Oh my blacke soule
2. Batter my heart
3. Oh might those sighes
4. Oh to vex me
5. What if this present
6. Since she whom I lov'd
7. At the round earth's imagin'd corners
8. Thou hast made me
9. Death, be not proud

The Donne Sonnets have the severity and power of sculpture compared with the romantic oil-painting of the *Serenade*. The Michelangelo Sonnets may seem almost frivolous set beside these chiselled sermons. Nor is this contrast surprising, since the Donne settings were composed in one week while Britten was feverishly ill after returning from Germany in 1945 where he and Menuhin had played to concentration-camp survivors. Only one of the nine songs, 6, is lyrical, the remainder are craggy, and the tension of the cycle, rarely relaxed, is maintained by use of a particular harmonic groundplan or rhythmic pattern. It is a great song cycle but an exhausting one, for performer and listener.

Again I have no hesitation in preferring the first Pears–Britten recording made in 1947. Pears' voice has its youthful vigour and brilliance, and it has now matured and become Brittenised, after the experience of singing Peter Grimes at Sadler's Wells and elsewhere. His dramatic attack on the opening of 1 sets a standard for the whole performance, with the composer's playing a nonpareil – the virtuosity in 2, for example, and the quicksilver semiquavers of 4. And what a song is 3, its hesitant rhythm and its unusual word-stresses a throwback to Elizabethan usage. That the 1945 Purcell anniversary (the 250th of his death) was a factor in Britten's inspiration is evident in 7, where the clangour of trumpets sounds in the piano, vying with the voice until the singer has the field to himself at the end. Purcellian ornamentation is an influence in 9, too, one of Britten's favourite *passacaglia* movements. Pears sings this magnificently, as he does the turbulent 5. It is only in 6, on the word 'loved' in the first line, that he sounds insecure, and it is in this lovely song in his second recording, made again with Britten 22 years later in 1969, that he is under strain when the opening phrase returns an octave higher. But the sense of growing panic in the middle of 8, the scherzo quality of 4, the energy of 1 and the emotional power of 3 are as strongly projected as of yore.

Alexander Young's 1953 performance with Gordon Watson is no carbon-copy of Pears' but an individually thought-out interpretation, nobly sung and poetically accompanied, and a refutation early on that Britten's vocal music, though so closely tailored to Pears' style and timbre, is strong and good enough as music to transfer to a different sort of performance and lose nothing in the process. Raimund Gilvan's performance, with Frederic Capon a reliable accompanist, suffers from a lack of variety in tone-colour and from such affectations of diction as 'steel' for 'still' and 'peelgreem' for 'pilgrim'. His singing of 3 is of some distinction.

A Charm of Lullabies, Op. 41

Watts, Britten	BBC REGL 417
Greevy, Hamburger	Decca SXL 6413
Hodgson, Swallow	Pearl SHE 559
Watkinson, Crone	Etcetera KTC 1046 (CD)

1. A Cradle Song (Blake)
2. The Highland Balou (Burns)
3. Sephestia's Lullaby (Greene)
4. A Charm (Randolph)
5. The Nurse's Song (Phillip)

This song cycle, composed in 1947 for Nancy Evans, who was co-creator with Kathleen Ferrier of Lucretia in Britten's *The Rape of Lucretia* at Glyndebourne in 1946, has tended to be rated rather far down the scale among its composer's vocal works. It is certainly less ambitious than the Donne or Rimbaud cycles, less scarifying than the Auden and less cobweb-blowing than the Michelangelo, but it is another facet of Britten's penchant for disciplining himself by setting himself a narrowly defined task, in this case to build a work from five lullabies. By definition, a lullaby offers little scope for variety, yet Britten succeeds (rather more, I now think, than when I wrote my book on him six years ago) in making an engaging song-cycle, with more contrasts than could be imagined. It shows him, too, re-entering the more traditional realm of English song, a move that would not have been welcome to his profoundest admirers at the time. A technical feature is a move towards a more direct simplicity of utterance. It is almost as if he had put the neo-baroque behind him. The piano parts, as well as the vocal writing, are less demanding.

The Third Programme broadcast by Helen Watts and the composer on 3 December 1962 was issued as a commercial recording in 1982 and is part of the disc which includes *Our Hunting Fathers* and *On This Island*. It is good to have the composer's playing of the accompaniments and Helen Watts' singing is always accurate and cultured, with excellent diction, but it is all rather bland. She is best in 1, a song which might have strayed from *The Rape of Lucretia*. Bernadette Greevy's performance is not very subtle, nor is her diction as clear as it ought to be; Hamburger's accompaniment is the better half of this duo. Alfreda Hodgson takes more

216

risks, characterises each song more strongly, and makes much more of 4, a *furioso* lullaby, with her peremptory opening 'Quiet', a good joke in itself with its clash of D and C sharp. 5 is the finest of the set and both she and Watts enjoy its quiet intensity. Keith Swallow's playing throughout is more flamboyant than Britten's and more forwardly recorded, emerging as more effective. Carolyn Watkinson perhaps underplays the ironies, notably in 3, and is reticent about projecting the mood of each song. Tempi are too relaxed – the interpretation is a shade too respectful, whereas to be convincing the music needs taut savagery. Tan Crone's accompaniment is sensitive.

Winter Words, Op. 52

Pears, Britten	Decca 417 183–1
Tear, Ledger	HMV HQS 1310
Gilvan, Capon	Oryx 1925
Irving, Werba	BIS LP 61
I. Partridge, J. Partridge	Enigma VAR 1027
Rolfe Johnson, G. Johnson	Hyperion A 66209

1. At day-close in November
2. Midnight on the Great Western (The journeying boy)
3. Wagtail and Baby (a satire)
4. The little old table
5. The Choirmaster's burial (the tenor man's story)
6. Proud songsters
7. At the Railway Station, Upway (The convict and the boy with the violin)
8. Before Life and After

Unpublished 'discards'

Mackie, Vignoles   HMV CDC 7 49252 2 (CD)

9. The Children and Sir Nameless
10. If it's ever spring again

Six years passed between composition of *A Charm of Lullabies* and the Hardy settings *Winter Words*, years during which Britten wrote *Billy Budd*, *Spring Symphony*, and *Gloriana* among other things. Although not a cycle, *Winter Words* – 'lyrics and ballads' – is almost closely organised enough to rank as one. The tonal progression is from D minor in 1 to a final D major. The selection of contrast is careful. Each song is Britten at his most colourfully inventive (only the last is philosophical or intellectual); and in each song his musical identification with the ironic nature of

Hardy's poetry is extraordinary. With these settings, Britten reclaimed the kingdom of English song as his natural habitat.

Pears and Britten gave the first performance in Harewood House in October 1953 during the Leeds Festival and recorded it five months later. No other partnership approaches theirs in execution and interpretation: so exactly *right* is the performance of each song that it is as if we were present at the actual moment of creation. Britten's piano-playing captures every nuance and subtlety of the text, and such imitative passages as the bird-song of 3, the creaking of wood in 4, the railway sounds in 2 and the violin in 7 have a magic that only genius of a special kind can create. Pears, too, is at his zenith. Even that unsteadiness which often afflicted him in the recording studio is little in evidence. In 5, one of the best narrative songs by an English composer, he conveys the authoritarian priggishness of the vicar without recourse to caricature: just a change of tone-colour, an inflection, and the wretched man stands before us. As for 8, a claimant for the title of Britten's greatest song, it is sung with a moving visionary quality which goes to the heart of Hardy's poetry – 'A time there was . . . when all went well', words which returned to Britten at the end of his life when he wrote his *Suite on English Folk Songs* in which a Hardyesque mood prevails.

Against this competition Ian and Jennifer Partridge offer a comparable impression of variety within unity and outstandingly good performances of 1, 3, 5, 7 and 8 and very good ones of the rest. The recording quality is superior to Decca's for Pears and Britten. I like Robert Tear's *Winter Words* the best of his recordings of Britten songs with piano, but the brilliance of certain individual songs rather than the consistent excellence of the whole is the impression left by this recording, in which Philip Ledger, for all his skill, cannot match the composer. In 3 one is forcefully reminded of 'Now the leaves are falling fast' from *On This Island*. Raimund Gilvan is very good in 2 but overdoes the vicar in 5, while his pianist in 3 reminds us that this would be an acceptable standard if we did not know what extra a Britten can draw from the wagtail's prinkings in 6/16.

Even if Anthony Rolfe Johnson kept to what one may call 'the Pears line' in his recording, accompanied by the ever-sensitive Graham Johnson, there are passages where choice of a slower tempo enables him to point up both the irony and the intensity of the poems. In 2, for instance, the line 'What past can be yours?' is invested with a profound sense of mystery, while the performance of 5 is in every respect masterly and a reminder that Rolfe Johnson has sung some of Britten's operatic roles with distinction. He imparts a richer sonority than Pears achieves to the climax of 8, but is less at ease in the near-whimsicalities of 3 and 6. This is altogether a memorable performance of songs that seem to grow in stature as each year passes. Whereas in the Britten–Pears recording one can sense that *Winter Words* was still a new work, Rolfe Johnson's approach to it acknowledges its classic status and goes on from there.

Although one can understand that a woman would want to sing these songs, the fact is they do not transpose well for the female voice, as has been shown even in the case of Janet Baker. Dorothy Irving's 1974 broadcast of them, with Erik Werba a splendid pianist, has some good moments, but the narrative songs succeed less than the 'philosophical' ones and it would need a better singer than Irving to convince me that 5 should ever be sung by a woman.

Britten discarded two songs, both of high quality, and it is good that they have been released as individual items and recorded by Neil Mackie and Roger Vignoles. 9 is a typical Hardy poem – Sir Nameless disliked children, who have their revenge on his effigy – and Britten has set it jauntily. 10 is one of his long, unfolding, intensely serious melodies, its line being expressively drawn by Mackie. It would be a tragedy if these two fine songs were not to achieve wide currency.

Songs from the Chinese, Op. 58

Pears, Bream	RCA SB 6621
Brown, Williams	CBS 61126
Schéle, Holeček	BIS LP 31

1. The big chariot
2. The old lute
3. The autumn wind
4. The Herd-boy
5. Depression
6. Dance song

Why are these wonderful settings of Arthur Waley's translations from the Chinese not better known? In their epigrammatic austerity, imaginative flair, and bitter-sweetness of mood and in the use of guitar instead of piano, they are among Britten's highest achievements. The songs are all short, but they are all heaven in a grain of sand – and they are not even discussed in *The Britten Companion* of 1984! The guitar is not used as any king of pseudo-Chinese onomatopoeia but because it occurred to Britten that it was the perfect instrument to accompany these tender, fragile, dreamlike texts and songs. It can suggest desolation, too, in the use of *glissando* in 5, with its anguished last line 'Though my limbs are old, my heart is older yet'. They inhabit an atmosphere unlike any other Britten songs. They chill the heart and warm it simultaneously.

The songs were written for Pears and Julian Bream in 1957 and their

219

subsequent recording was made in 1969 (it includes a memorable performance of 'Happy were he', Essex's second lute song from *Gloriana*).
The gap of 11 years between the Aldeburgh Festival first performance and
recording is sadly indicative of a pattern in the attitude to some of
Britten's music after its *War Requiem* high-noon. But the result enshrined
a great interpretation, with each song polished and honed until every last
subtle turn of phrase, textual or musical, makes its full impact. Yet that
poetic singer Wilfred Brown is almost equally convincing in a performance of even closer intimacy between voice and guitar, the amazing
mixture of triumph and tragedy in 6 being particularly poignant, with
John Williams a perfect partner. Unlike the Hardy set, these songs do suit
a soprano. The Swedish Märta Schéle, whose English is very good,
recorded them in 1975 with a Czech guitarist, Josef Holeček. Her pure,
clear and strong voice and excellent diction are heard to ravishing advantage in 2; and the soprano register emphasises a consanguinity between 5
and the Governess' lament in *The Turn of the Screw*. Balance between
voice and guitar is exceptionally fine in this sought-after recording of a
work that grows in importance at each repetition.

Nocturne, Op. 60

Pears, London Symphony Orchestra/Britten   Decca 417 183–1
   (*obbligato* instrumentalists: flute, A. Murray; cor anglais, R. Lord;
   clarinet, G. de Peyer; bassoon, W. Waterhouse; horn, B. Tuckwell;
   timpani, D. Blyth; harp, O. Ellis)
Tear, Academy of St Martin-in-the-Fields/Marriner   Argo ZRG 737
   (*obbligato* instrumentalists: flute, W. Bennett; cor anglais, N. Black;
   clarinet, T. King; bassoon, C. James; horn, I. James; timpani, T. Fry;
   harp, D. Watson)

1. On a poet's lips (Shelley)
2. The Kraken (Tennyson)
3. The Lovely Boy (Coleridge)
4. Midnight's Bell (Middleton)
5. The September Massacres from *The Prelude* (Wordsworth)
6. The Kind Ghosts (Owen)
7. Sleep and Poetry (Keats)
8. Sonnet 43 (Shakespeare)

The *Nocturne*, composed in 1958, was Britten's first song-cycle with
orchestra for 15 years, since the *Serenade*. Like its predecessor it is an
anthology piece, and this time evening has passed into night and the
poems are presented as dreams. The scoring is for tenor, seven *obbligato*

(or *obligato*, as Britten preferred) instruments and strings, and the work is in C major, here used as a key for darkness rather than light. Song 1 is accompanied by strings only but in the subsequent settings an *obbligato* instrument is added, and all the instruments are used in the last song, 8. A rocking figure for strings suggests the sleeper's regular breathing and acts as a *ritornello*, so that the music is continuous. The scoring is marvellous: poetic, evocative, imitative, seductive. Only in some of the vocal writing is it possible to find an increased reliance on formulae that have become mannerisms – and word-painting (distinctive, of course) predominates over musical substance. Yet the work is a success, and it is important because the Owen setting must have been a starting-point for the *War Requiem* of 1961. As always, Britten's choice of solo instruments is apt and inspired: bassoon for Tennyson's sea-monster; harp for Coleridge's moonlit 'lovely boy'; horn for Middleton's repertoire of night-sounds (owl, cat, dog and bell); drums for Wordsworth's meditation on the French Revolution; cor anglais lamenting Owen's doomed youth; flute and clarinet for Keats' invocation to sleep, the strings silent until the word 'Sleep' is first uttered. Then the strings lend their full glory to the Shakespeare setting which crowns the work, as Keats had crowned the *Serenade*, with an aureole of Britten melody at its most impassioned (and an explicit avowal of why the work is dedicated to the widow of Mahler, for Mahler's spirit is here invoked).

Britten's own recording (1959) with Pears and seven instrumentalists several of whom were specialists in his music has an authority that can never be superseded. At the risk of monotony, I can only repeat that Pears' insight into music and text is incomparable. He is in superb voice here, capturing the atmosphere of each song, and the LSO players match him in sensitivity. The contrast between the fancifulness of the Middleton setting and the insomniac fever of Wordsworth's terrifying vision, and among Tennyson's submarine horrors, Owen's chilling elegies, and Coleridge's silvery sensualities, is conveyed by this singer in a way that Tear perhaps knows he cannot approach and tries too hard to present in a different way, emphasising where no emphasis is needed. Nor are Marriner and his soloists rivals to Britten and the LSO in musicianship and virtuosity.

Sechs Hölderlin-Fragmente, Op. 61

Pears, Britten   Decca 417 313–1

1. Menschenbeifall
2. Der Heimat
3. Sokrates und Alcibiades

4. Die Jugend
5. Hälfte des Lebens
6. Die Linien des Leben

Songs and Proverbs of William Blake, Op. 74

Fischer-Dieskau, Britten   Decca 417 313–1
Luxon, Willison   Chandos CHAN 8514 (CD)

1. The pride of the peacock . . . London
2. Prisons are built . . . The Chimney Sweeper
3. The Bird a nest . . . A Poison Tree
4. Think in the morning . . . The Tyger
5. The Tygers of Wrath . . . The Fly
6. The Hours of Folly . . . Ah, Sunflower!
7. To see a world . . . Every night and every morn

The Poet's Echo, Op. 76

Vishnevskaya, Rostropovich   Decca 417 313–1

1. Echo
2. My Heart
3. Angel
4. The Nightingale and the Rose
5. Epigram
6. Lines written during a sleepless night

Who are these children?, Op. 84

Pears, Britten   Decca SXL 6608

1. A Riddle
2. A Laddie's Sang
3. Nightmare
4. Black Day
5. Bed Time
6. Slaughter
7. A Riddle
8. The Larky Lad
9. Who are these children?
10. Supper
11. The Children
12. The Auld Aik

(Discards)
Mackie, Vignoles   HMV CDC 7 49252 2

13. Dawtie's devotion
14. Tradition
15. The Gully

A Birthday Hansel, Op. 92

Pears, Ellis   Decca SXL 6788

1. Birthday Song
2. My Early Walk
3. Wee Willie Gray
4. My Hoggie
5. Afton Water
6. The Winter
7. Leezie Lindsay

Four Burns Songs, Op. 92a (from above)

Kenny, Crone   Etcetera KTC 1046 (CD)

5. Afton Water
3. Wee Willie Gray
6. The Winter
4. My Hoggie

The Hölderlin settings were composed in 1958, after the *Nocturne*. In them Britten returned to a foreign language for the first time since 1940. They are short and spare, but there is no austerity of emotion. Indeed 2 and 3 are among the most touching songs he ever wrote, while 1 has the vigour of a Michelangelo setting and 4 suggests to this listener links with *A Midsummer Night's Dream*. With the hindsight afforded by *Death in Venice*, a listener today might feel that Britten's Aschenbach is the 'author' of 3. In all the songs, notably 5, the piano part is of amazing subtlety and difficulty. The composer's playing is a text-book of instruction in itself. Pears, in this 1961 recording, is again Britten's ideal interpreter. This is nowhere more evident than in 6, a stylistic and emotional link with the sombre mood of the Blake *Songs*, composed in 1964 for the German baritone Fischer-Dieskau and recorded with him a year later. As the *War Requiem* showed, Britten realised this artist's capacity for compassionate melancholy. Blake was a memorable choice for him. The result was a song cycle more sombre than any since the

Michael Kennedy

Donne, and its terseness, economy and suppressed anger find unchallengeable expression in Fischer-Dieskau's performance. Each song is prefaced by a proverb so that the cycle is continuous. The proverbs act as a *ritornello* which has all twelve notes arranged into three four-note shapes; until Proverb 7 these occur only in the piano part while the singer's declamation is in the style of the church parable *Curlew River*. But at 7 the voice has a 12-note phrase. Decca's recording, although made in the Kingsway Hall like most other Britten records, has a boxy quality not found in the Hölderlin songs, for example, but it captures the many-shaded emotional and tonal range of Fischer-Dieskau's singing and the majesty of Britten's playing, though better piano tone is heard elsewhere.

Luxon's performance, with David Willison as sturdy accompanist, is more lyrical and reflective, although there is plenty of dramatic force when required. The fact that he is singing his native language, unlike Fischer-Dieskau, allows him to give an exciting and swift-moving account of 4, and in general the words emerge not only with more clarity but also with a more natural flow and emphasis.

Uncanny penetration into the strengths and capabilities of a singer is again demonstrated in Britten's Russian song cycle of poems by Pushkin, *The Poet's Echo*, composed for Galina Vishnevskaya, for whom the soprano part in *War Requiem* was written. They prolong the sombre mood of the Blake songs in a shorter work wherein there is no unifying *ritornello*. The cycle's unity lies in the 'echo' (a major seventh), symbol of isolation. There is no reply to the echo. Deeply as Britten entered into the Italian, French and German national personalities for his earlier cycles, he became almost more Russian than the Russians in *The Poet's Echo*. The Shostakovich affinity which began in the 1930s here found its apotheosis thirty years later, spurred by the admiration and friendship of the composer himself and of his two great compatriots, the cellist Rostropovich and his wife. With Rostropovich as pianist, Vishnevskaya gave the first complete performance of *The Poet's Echo* in Moscow in December 1965. Their recording has a discreet extra resonance which intensifies the drama of the pauses (as the reply to the echo is vainly awaited). Vishnevskaya's powerful, emotion-laden voice, not 'beautiful' but immensely full of character and excitement (the kind of voice Britten preferred), is magnificently exploited by each song. 4 is among the composer's finest, and 1 and 6 convey the essence of Pushkin in a way that obviously deeply moved these Russian interpreters of English music. This is a large-scale performance in every sense.

The 12 Soutar 'lyrics, rhymes and riddles' which make up *Who are these children?*, composed in 1969, show Britten reverting to the 'protest' songs of his youth, perhaps impelled by Vietnam, Northern Ireland and student riots. Soutar (1898–1943) was a Scottish socialist and his 1941

224

poem from which this song cycle takes its name was written after he had seen a photograph of a hunt going through a bomb-damaged village and watched by children – cannon-fodder, as it were, for the composer of *Our Hunting Fathers*. There are four protest songs – 3, 6, 9 and 11 – and they are in English, interspersed among the shorter dialect songs of which Britten originally set eleven. Hunting-calls in 9, the wailing of air-raid sirens in 11 – Britten's imitative ability never deserted him, and his playing of the piano part on the recording has all his old magical brilliance. It was recorded in November 1972, six months before his stroke put an end to his pianistic career. *Who are these children?* is two cycles in one, the innocent children's songs and the songs of the world of war and pain. The one encroaches upon the other and the final song is devastating – 'The Auld Aik's down' ('The old oak's down'). And as Britten told Graham Johnson[1] in 1971, 'It really is down, you see; it's the end of everything.' For him, too, shortly afterwards. Pears' voice is occasionally tested by these songs, but the artistry is as great as ever, the understanding as acute. It is surprising that this cycle has not had many performances, for it is direct and appealing in the manner of the earlier songs. If some listeners felt that Britten had moved into remoter climes in his German and Russian and Blake cycles, in the Soutar songs he had come back to them. Three settings which did not fit into the final scheme of *Who are these children?* have been recorded by Neil Mackie, accompanied by Roger Vignoles. They are simple in outline and, while perhaps adding nothing to our knowledge of Britten, they repay the unaffected directness of Mackie's approach.

After his heart operation, when composing was an immense physical effort to him, Britten wrote one more song cycle, again largely in Scottish dialect, for it comprised seven Burns settings in honour of Queen Elizabeth the Queen Mother's 75th birthday in 1975. *A Birthday Hansel* is for voice and harp, originally Pears and Osian Ellis, who recorded it. The harp links the songs, which are free from the anguish and questionings of Soutar, though 'The Winter' is a serious and splendid song.

Four of the songs were arranged for voice and piano in 1975 by Colin Matthews, with the composer's approval. The original songs are continuous, so in changing the order Matthews had to provide endings to each song and he chose the sombre 'My Hoggie' as an ending rather than the exciting 7. Yvonne Kenny, accompanied by Tan Crone, sings with warmth and charm, but also with a slight deficiency in tone-colour. The well-recorded performance is rather stiff in its method of presentation.

It adds no lustre to Britten's songs to imply, as some of his disciples have seemed to do, that before he came on the scene all was fuddy-duddy in

---

[1] G. Johnson, 'Voice and Piano' in *The Britten Companion* (London, 1984), p. 306

English song-writing and that he alone trod an enlightened path. The songs of Parry, Delius, Vaughan Williams, Gurney, Finzi, Ireland and many others (q.v.) are part of the glory of English music. If it seems to some that Britten's are its crowning glory in this field, they may also be its final glory, for since his death no successor has arisen. In one respect they are unique. Although particular singers have been closely associated with particular composers – Gervase Elwes and Mark Raphael with Quilter, for example – the voice and mind of Peter Pears are not only the interpretative source of Britten's songs, they are an essential ingredient of the music. Whatever replaces the Pears element in Britten must be different. His recordings are a documentation of authenticity that removes any need for musicological speculation. Pears, too, summed up once and for all Britten's place in English music when he wrote as long ago as 1952,[2] 'if Britten is no innovator, he is most certainly a renovator'. It is that work of renovation that Pears himself has fixed in the musical conscience.

[2] P. Pears: 'The Vocal Music', in *Benjamin Britten, a Commentary on his works from a group of specialists*, ed. Mitchell & Keller (London, 1952), p. 73

English song[1]

JOHN STEANE

For most listeners, as indeed for most singers, English song begins with Dowland. The mediaeval and early Tudor periods are represented in the current record catalogues, but the proportion of solo to part-song is small and, in what must be a selective survey of a wide field, Dowland and the other Elizabethans provide the appropriate starting-point.

In the early years of the gramophone, and even up to the time of the Second World War, Dowland's name was of small interest to the record companies. In the pioneering first volume of the *Columbia History of Music*, edited by Percy Scholes and issued in 1930, Cecile Dolmetsch accompanied by lute and viol contributed 'Awake, sweet love' (5715) from Dowland's *First Book of Songs* published in 1597. She sang it with a tiny, white, piping voice of exceptional purity, a world distant from the standard tone of the professionally trained singer in the twentieth century. In one sense this had the effect of removing Dowland from his own age, the relatively familiar past of Shakespeare's time, to an era more remote. Yet the artless freshness and (despite a most expert and exquisite trill) the absence of anything that suggested operatic or 'classical' training had its attractiveness. It could well be that the line of English sopranos specialising in early music, and extending to the present day in singers such as Emma Kirkby, had its origin in those two or three minutes of shy singing audible beneath the sizzling surface of an Old Columbia black-label which, as far as I know, has not been thought worthy of reissue on LP.

It was another voice, however, equally far from the recognised norm, that showed to the record-buying public for the first time something of Dowland's true greatness as a song-writer. Alfred Deller, styled counter-tenor, came from the ranks of what church choristers then knew as the altos. There seem to be plenty of them about at present, but they were pearls of great price to any choirmaster in those days. Even so, it was taken for granted that the alto would not be called upon, in the general

---

[1] The songs of Benjamin Britten are discussed separately, in the previous chapter.

way of things, to sing a song or aria in church or concert. Deller changed that. He was also part of a movement which altered the taste of the musical public, directing its interests backwards in time from Handel to Purcell and then further, to the Elizabethans and beyond.

Deller's records of 'In darkness let me dwell' and 'Sorrow, stay' (C 3951 and C 4178; HLM 7234) showed clearly that Dowland was indeed the great song-writer that the text-books proclaimed him to be. Their melancholy found fine expression in that voice which had such unusual resources of coloration and depth. Deller could also increase or diminish the vibrancy of his notes so that his voice would ring out strongly in phrases such as 'my music, hellish, jarring sounds' and then would hollow itself out to an almost unearthly spirit-tone at points like the long-held 'arise' in 'Down and arise I never shall'. He re-recorded these songs as late as 1977 in a three-record album devoted to Dowland (Harmonia Mundi HM 244/6). By then the resonance had diminished but not his individuality and imaginative absorption, the mark of a distinguished artist to whom English song owes much.

British singers such as Deller were not the only ones to show appreciation of Dowland. Aksel Schiøtz, a Danish tenor of wide culture and fine sensitivity, recorded several songs with his customary good taste and clear diction (DB 5270). The American, Roland Hayes, whose programmes ranged so widely over the whole field of song, included in one of his late albums (1953 A 440 Blue Label 12–3) 'Come again, sweet love doth now invite', which was also recorded, though not issued till many years later, by Elisabeth Schwarzkopf (ALP 1435501). The approach here is typical of many singers in that period who saw such songs as rather solemnly hymn-like. More recently Frederica von Stade (CBS 76728) has recorded 'Come again', beautiful in tone but still solemn in mood and slow in tempo. Comparison with Janet Baker (HQS 1091) introduces a more lively rhythmic sense and a quite different, outward-going style in what is after all an 'addressed song'. In Baker's record, the first words, 'Come again', issue so imperative an invitation that her listener's hand reaches out almost by reflex for the engagements book.

Still, Dowland and his contemporaries do not really call for the 'great' voices. A light, flexible, firm and pure sound is wanted, and this is what the group of singers in Anthony Rooley's Consort of Musicke has sought to provide. Their recordings of Dowland's three songbooks (Oiseau-Lyre DSLO 508–9, 528–9, 531–2) form the most valuable contribution to the gramophone library in this field. They strike a balance between treatment of the pieces as part-song and solo lute-song, and, when a solo version is offered, the singers most frequently used are Emma Kirkby and the tenor Martyn Hill. Both of these voices, particularly at the time when the first volume was recorded, are heard as slender and light in body; they are also (and this seems to conform to the doctrine of their school) as nearly free from any kind of vibrato as the human voice can be. The effects of the doctrine can also be heard in the voice of the bass soloist, David Thomas, who sings 'His golden locks' in Book One with non-vibrant, softened tone from which his true bass quality has all but disappeared. With this goes the habit of swelling on individual notes in a way that is perhaps suggested by the sound often produced by viols. There will be listeners to whom these characteristics of the group will be at best a mild irritant. The charm and skill of Emma Kirkby (in 'Wilt thou unkind' or 'Weep you no more', for example) and Hill (as in 'Love stood amazed' in the Third Book) are potent nevertheless, and the whole enterprise earns deep gratitude for its sensitive performances, scholarly presentation and fine recording.

Martyn Hill is also one of several singers who have recorded more widely in the Elizabethan repertoire. Lute songs by Thomas Campion, Robert Jones and Robert Johnson ('Away, delights' especially striking in form, with admirably sustained phrasing by the singer) appear in a recital called *Music with her Silver Sound* (Turnabout TV 34443 S). Ian Partridge (Hyperion 166095) brings a rounder, sweeter tone to a Dowland/Campion recital; and, with more animation if less sheer vocal beauty, Frank Patterson with lute accompaniment by Robert Spencer (Philips 6500 282) has just the right open-air, spontaneous feeling for Dowland's 'Fine knacks for ladies' and a communicative way with words in Rosseter's 'What then is love but mourning'. A delightful account of that song ranks among the pleasures of a comparable recital by Peter Pears and Julian Bream (made in 1956, reissued on ECS 549), supremely distinguished by the responsiveness of both artists to 'In darkness let me dwell' and, incidentally, by Pears' demonstration of breath-control in 'It was a lover and his lass'.

At a more advanced age, his predecessor in that, as witness his 1928 recording with the young Gerald Moore (4985; OPAL 806), was the famous operatic and Lieder singer John Coates. Deller was another who delved into the wider school of Elizabethans: *Byrd and his age* (Vanguard PVL 7035) is a particularly good collection, including Byrd's 'Elegy on the Death of Thomas Tallis' ('Tallis is dead and music dies'). Another of Byrd's elegies but here on the tricky subject of Mary, Queen of Scots ('the noble famous Queen, who lost her head of late') is heard in a recital by James Bowman (EMX 2101), divided usefully into sections, 'At Court', 'In the theatre' (with some original Shakespeare settings) and an Italian group, affording an opportunity for comparisons. The Early English Music Group has a similar anthology (RCA RL 25110), which the tenor (often sounding like what I understand by the term counter-tenor) Paul Elliott brings to an engaging conclusion with Morley's 'See mine own sweet jewel'. Emma Kirkby also has a graceful programme called *Time*

John Steane

stands still (Hyperion A 66186), songs of mutability and metamorphosis, recorded 'live' at Forde Abbey in Dorset. Among recitals devoted to a single composer are fine ones by the Consort of Musicke: Morley (*Aires and Madrigals* Oiseau–Lyre DSDL 708, with a lovely performance by Kirkby of 'Sleep, slumb'ring eyes'), Byrd (*Psalms, Sonnets, Songs, Sadnes and Pietie* DSLO 596, with John York Skinner fine in the sombre 'O that most rare beast') and Coprario (*Funeral Teares*, music for the death of Mountjoy, Earl of Devonshire in 1606, DSLO 576).

Although more than a century lies between the birth of Byrd (1543) and that of Purcell (1659), the same singers predominate in recordings of his songs, and on the whole they sing in similar style. Deller's famous original recording of 'Music for a while' in 1949 (C 3890; HLM 7234), with its characteristic 'lifts' of the voice and its pure tone inseparable in the memory from such phrases as 'how your pains were eased', was a landmark in the whole renaissance of interest in early music – which at that time meant anything before Bach. Of course a great deal *had* happened to English song in the interim. The florid baroque manner of the opening phrases of 'Sweeter than roses' (C 4044; HLM 7234), or the *fioritura* on the word 'tormenting' in the *Epithalamium* (C 4044; HLM 7234) is foreign to the Elizabethans but very much home-ground to Deller, who produces some of his most full-voiced tone as well as a strong feeling for the mood of these songs.

Purcell's time was probably the golden age of the English counter-tenor, but the new lease of life which the voice has had since Deller first restored it (or the 'alto' – arguments about nomenclature are endless) to favour has been international. Most recently at the time of writing, the Australian Andrew Dalton has recorded a Purcell recital clearly in the tradition (Etcetera ETC 1013). He makes a strong emotional appeal and includes some of the finest solos, such as *The Queen's Epicedium*, 'Lord, what is man' and 'Sleep, Adam, sleep and take thy rest'. The 'Evening Hymn' is taken a shade too briskly, and for that lovely song with its masterly ground and gently swinging Alleluias one might prefer to return to Deller (C 4144), Ian Partridge (ASV ALH 963) or Emma Kirkby (Oiseau–Lyre DSDL 713), whose Purcell recital brings out a possibly unsuspected gift in the singer for strong characterisation with the dramatic monologue 'Mad Bess'. Partridge's includes the subtle *Morning Hymn*, a responsive performance though less strongly projected than by Pears on Decca 411 919–1.

Purcell was not, of course, a discovery of the post-war generation, though the depth and extent of his work probably were. In the early 1920s Elsie Suddaby recorded 'Hark, the echoing air' (E 354) with much the same airy tone and nimble fluency as Kirkby in the recital mentioned above. In 1941 Isobel Baillie made a more substantial contribution with

230

'The Blessed Virgin's Expostulation' (Columbia DX 1031; RLS 7703): it has lovely touches, such as the softening of 'Was it a waking dream', yet there remains something too literal, and the last line in particular ('But oh I fear the child' – such an imaginative stroke in the writing) needs more insight and feeling. Among the men, the baritone Keith Falkner recorded three songs ('The Aspiration', 'I love and I must' and 'If music be the food of love') with clear diction and smooth runs (ROX 134; HQM 1238); also, most unusually for 1935, with a proper 'continuo' accompaniment of harpsichord and cello. The heavy brigade of basses concentrated on 'Arise, ye subterranean winds' taken from incidental music to the Dryden version of *The Tempest*. Norman Allin (Col. 9929 and L 1414; EX 29 0169) and Robert Radford (D 530; HLM 7054) are both dated in style and in the genuineness of their bass quality, which seems nowadays to have gone the way of the real contralto. Best of all in the pre-war catalogues remains very probably the voices of the Manchester School Children (Col. 9909; SEG 7705) in their famous, ever-fresh record of 'Nymphs and Shepherds', the catalogues being as blissfully ignorant as the children themselves that the song came from a show called *The Libertine*.

With the post-war Purcell boom, Pears recorded an impassioned account of 'The Queen's Epicedium (DB 6763; RLS 748), Maggie Teyte's version of 'Nymphs and Shepherds' appeared, coupled with 'Fairest Isle' (DA 1790; RLS 716), then Kathleen Ferrier's excellent 'Hark, the echoing air' (Decca LXT 5324) and, further from the beaten track, Astra Desmond's fluent if somewhat subdued 'From rosy bowers' (Decca M 509). A more dramatic account of that solo is included in a Purcell recital by Helen Watts (Oiseau Lyre OL 50173), by which time we are well into the age of LP, as the catalogues have begun to place what had been known as single songs into the context of their role as theatre music; hence, perhaps, strictly outside the scope of this chapter. Again the soloists of the Consort of Musicke have been prominent, this time with the Academy of Ancient Music under Christopher Hogwood, who have produced eight volumes of Purcell's theatre music to date, in the invaluable Florilegium series on L'Oiseau Lyre (DSLO 504, 514, 550, 561, 590, 414 173–1, 414 174–1). Excellent alternatives to some of them are provided by John Eliot Gardiner's Monteverdi Choir and Orchestra (*The Fairy Queen* Archiv 2742 001, *The Tempest* Erato STU 71274, *The Indian Queen* Erato STU 71275). Many of the songs now have to be looked for in such collections or in context. Meanwhile, solos occasionally appear on their own, exceptionally fine examples being Janet Baker's 'Sleep, Adam, sleep' and 'Lord, what is man' (HQS 1091). Kathleen Battle, with James Levine at Salzburg (DG 415 361–2), sings 'Come, ye songsters' from *The Fairy Queen*, 'Music for a while' and 'Sweeter than roses' with

delicate tone and winning tenderness. 'The Blessed Virgin's Expostulation', now with richer tonal colouring and a more imaginative realisation of the last line (a lovely effect is the soft, long-drawn 'oh') takes a step
nearer perfection in a performance by Frederica von Stade (CBS 76728).

No major English song-writer occurs within half a century of Purcell,
either before or after. Earlier is William Lawes (1602–45), and the
Consort of Musicke have come up with an admirable collection of his
Dialogues, Psalms and Elegies (DSLO 574). His brother Henry, who
wrote the incidental music for Milton's *Comus*, also has some 'dialogues'
recorded by Kirkby and Hill on DSLO 587. Later come William Boyce
and Thomas Arne, born and dying within a year of each other and spanning the eighteenth century with representative grace. Boyce's 'Tell me,
lovely shepherd' is lightly, charmingly sung by Baker in the record
mentioned above, and was a pleasant item in the late catalogues of the
'78' era, sung by the small but characterful soprano voice of Margaret
Ritchie (C 3983). Thomas Arne's Shakespeare settings are given in recital
by Alexander Young (CSD 1572), and the Canadian mezzo, Maureen
Forrester, also took part in this record singing the famous *Ode to
Shakespeare* ('Thou soft-flowing Avon') with warm tone and due
decorum. April Cantelo (Oiseau–Lyre SOL 50036) is clear and fresh in a
similar repertoire. A particularly lovely example of Arne's expressive and
melodic gifts is 'O ravishing delight': recordings are by Isobel Baillie (Col.
DB 2121; RLS 7703), Valerie Masterson (Pearl SHE 590), and, with more
imaginative absorption, by Yvonne Kenny recorded 'live' at the Wigmore
Hall on Etcetera ETC 1029.

There follows a long period without a great deal to recommend it. The
English songs of Haydn and Beethoven hardly belong here and have been
discussed in *Song on Record* vol. 1. The latter part of the eighteenth century and the first half of the nineteenth offer little otherwise. 1823 is
perhaps a year to remember as in it Sir Henry Bishop supplied what almost
became a second national anthem – 'Home, sweet home', which began
life as an air in his opera *Clari*. Its independent existence dates back to the
age of Adelina Patti, whose record, made when she was over sixty, is short
of breath but still uniquely touching (03053; RLS 711). Melba (03049,
DB 351; RLS 719), Tetrazzini (DB 527; GEMM 220/7) and Galli-Curci
(DB 602, DA 1011; CDN 1004) followed in multiple versions. 'Lo, here
the gentle lark', a setting by the same composer of four lines from Shakespeare's *Venus and Adonis*, also enjoyed a prolonged and glamorous
existence in several recordings by Melba (03047, 03090, DB 348; RLS
719), two best-selling ones by Galli-Curci (DB 258, DB 1278; CDN
1004), and a less famous but equally charming version by Maria Ivogün
(Bruns. 10174; Preiser LV 68). Lily Pons (DB 2502), Gwen Catley (C
3214) and Joan Sutherland (Decca 410 147–1), with their respective

flautists, have been among their most conspicuous successors. 'Home, sweet home' also features in a recital by Ann Mackay (Meridian E45 77076), comprising 'Romantic songs and ballads' from the period; they are pleasantly sung, but one would only wish the artist better material.

In the second half of the century a number of composers, Sullivan among them, wrote songs – quite apart from 'The Lost Chord' – that survive as graceful melodies with some generous feeling. Right from the heart of Victorian England we have Sir Charles Santley's recording, made in 1903 but embodying the taste and practice of the earlier age, of 'Thou'rt passing hence, my brother' (02015). In recent years Felicity Palmer's inclusion of 'My dearest heart' in a song recital (Argo ZK 45) provides an example of the 'Victorian ballad', while Roy Henderson (Decca M 583) and Janet Baker (ASD 2929) in the Schubertian 'Orpheus with his lute' have something better.

It fell to Parry and Stanford, only a few years younger than Sullivan, to lead the revival of English song. Happily, the prejudice against them, strong in the post-Victorian age, has lifted so that they are now reasonably well represented in the record catalogues. How slow the companies were to show interest in what might be called the English 'art-song' can be gauged from the vehemence of a review by Herman Klein, veteran critic of *The Gramophone* magazine, in October 1931. John McCormack had two songs by Parry on the Special List at that time (DA 1172), and Klein wrote: 'It is the very type of song record we want and need so badly, and possibly the finest English song record yet issued . . . Once for all, if we do not support it at least as well as the far more luxurious symphonies, we shall deserve no more.' The songs were 'Three aspects' and 'There', and, truth to tell, neither the songs nor the performances are quite as exceptional as all that. But, as Klein pointed out, there are nearly a hundred of Parry's English lyrics in print, and his view was that 'for what they say and their eloquence in saying it' they will 'stand up pretty well to any of the German Lieder'. His advocacy, if it was heeded at all, would probably have been seen as an amiable eccentricity on the part of an old man with no interest in 'the music of the future'. But as it happens, the future (being our present) has shown more appreciation of such things than ever seemed likely in the 1930s.

A whole recital devoted to Parry is given by Robert Tear and Philip Ledger on Argo ZK 44, introducing some delightful songs such as 'A Welsh Lullaby', 'From a city window' and a lively setting of Meredith's poem 'Marian'. 'Love is a bable' stands out as among the most characterful, though Tear's voice and manner hardly satisfy as Kathleen Ferrier's did: the song was a favourite in her recitals, and to anyone who does not have memories of her as she was in those concerts, life and liveliness personified, her record (BBC REGL 368) will seem an excellent example of her art. Tear's recital also includes many of the Shakespeare settings such as a fine version of 'When icicles hang by the walls', particularly well sung too. 'O mistress mine' is done with great verve by Baker and Moore (and a delightful accompaniment he has to play) on ESD 100642, and for this song and the whole resourcefully compiled programme, not to be missed is Sarah Walker's recital with Graham Johnson called *Shakespeare's Kingdom* (Hyperion A 66136). HMV's *Treasury of English Song*, compiled from recordings made on 78s (EX 29 0911), is another invaluable set, with Parry most charmingly represented by 'To Lucasta' and 'To Althea' attractively sung by Robert Irwin (C 3821).

On appropriate occasions, Stanford had a popular touch and a melodic facility that made his songs more readily appealing to most of the earlier generation of singers. Sir Charles Santley would sing 'Father O'Flynn' and Plunket Greene 'Trottin' to the fair' (E 82 and Col. DB 1377 respectively), neither of them with much voice left in their old age but with a great charge of good humour and with impeccable diction. Norman Allin, with the broadest of brogues and varied 'acts' worthy of a Chaliapin, was ordained Father O'Flynn in 1929 (Col. 5856; GEMM 173), and Peter Dawson (B 3838) proposed his health too, though less expansively. Equally popular, and rightly so, were the *Songs of the Sea*. Dawson (B 4482/3) was ideal in the quieter numbers, while in the patter of 'The Old Superb' his tone wanted a little more body and his vowels told of Melbourne rather than Plymouth Hoe. Benjamin Luxon (ASD 4401) has coupled them with the later *Songs of the Fleet* (from which Dawson made a superb record of the Farewell, C 2694): full-blooded and sensitive, the performances show just how good they are. Individual songs have been well recorded by Norman Bailey (DSLO 20) and John Shirley-Quirk (Saga 5473) among others, and the tenor James Griffett has a Stanford recital on Hyperion A 66049, best when he can work idiomatically on the 'character pieces' such as 'Colonel Carter' or when the mood is quiet and simple as in the haunting folk song, 'The Willow Tree'.

The great English composer of the period, of course, is Elgar, remembered as a song-writer principally through *Sea Pictures*. His single songs are heard most conveniently on record in a recital by the baritone Brian Rayner Cook, with Roger Vignoles accompanying (Pearl SHE 526). Early recordings are included in *Elgar's Interpreters on Record*, a valuable collection issued by the Elgar Society (ELG 001): John Coates, in resonant voice and with strong temperament, sings 'In the dawn' (rec. 1915 on 02584), Tudor Davies gives an imaginatively dramatic performance of 'The River' (D 1908), and Rosina Buckman, full-hearted in the phrase 'the memory smouldered to a dull regret' in 'Pleading' (03718): these are among the best. 'Pleading', one of Elgar's first songs, was also beautifully recorded by Walter Hyde (4–2119; GV 5) and with some

234

characteristic *portamenti* by Maggie Teyte (DA 1807). 'Shakespeare's Kingdom', one of the last, set to words by Alfred Noyes, gives its title to the excellent recital by Sarah Walker mentioned earlier. The *Treasury of English Song* (also mentioned above) selects 'In the dawn' by Coates, 'Speak, music' in an impressive version by the characterful Eric Marshall (E 428), and the light, well-poised voice of David Lloyd is heard in 'Is she not passing fair' (Col. DB 2117). Recently Hildegard Behrens, of all people, revived the haunting 'Queen Mary's Lute Song' (HMV CD 747–5512).

For the *Sea Pictures*, Janet Baker's classic version with Barbirolli (CDC7 47329–2) remains unmatched. Yvonne Minton with Barenboim (CBS 76579) has fine moments, such as the quietly reflective 'skies impassive o'er me'; so does the strong, imaginative Felicity Palmer (CDC7 47329–2). Two well-loved contraltos of an earlier era recorded the cycle on 78s: Muriel Brunskill (Col. 9170/2) in the 1920s and the affecting Gladys Ripley, twice (C 3498/500, 1946, and XLP 30009, 1854). But one returns to the Baker recording for the full depth of spirit and vividness of communication. The most popular of these songs, 'Where corals lie', surprisingly and attractively exists in a recording from around 1928 by the once famous Dutch contralto Maartje Offers (DB 1761). It is also the only one of the songs recorded (in 1912) by the great original, Dame Clara Butt: sensitively shaded, intensely individual and memorable (03299; HLM 7025). Elgar himself conducted the Welsh contralto Meila Megane in 1922, and 'Sabbath Morning at Sea' (D 576), more impressive in tone than in style, is included in an anthology of British mezzos and contraltos on HLM 7145.

Comparable to Elgar in the relatively incidental place of the song in his total work is Delius. The pre-war issues include some solos sung by Dora Labbette, light of voice and well-focused, with Beecham as her piano accompanist. Many years later when Beecham's Delius recordings were collected on LP, some previously unpublished matrices by Labbette were added (World Records SH 324). Lovely examples are 'Twilight Fancies' and 'The Nightingale', though in general her virginal whiteness of tone hardly allows the songs full scope. Heddle Nash, delicate in style, strong in personality, recorded 'Shall we roam, my love' and, with superb playing by Gerald Moore, 'Love's Philosophy'. Both are included in this boxed-set and the latter, exciting in its passion and vigour, occurs again in the *Treasury of English Song*. Later, Peter Pears sang 'To Daffodils' with finesse and fitting simplicity (Argo ZK 28/9). Partridge includes six Delius songs in his English song album (Oxford University Press OUP 155/6), best for the atmospheric performance of 'Twilight Fancies'. Graham Trew (Hyperion A66085) may be too decorous in the surprisingly vigorous setting of 'Spring, the sweet spring', while in Elizabeth

John Steane

Harwood's recital (Conifer CFRA 120), its Delius group ending with 'It was a lover and his lass', it is the setting itself, angular and over-sophisticated, that checked enthusiasm.

More substantial, both in output and catalogue-representation, are the songs of Vaughan Williams. The *Songs of Travel* have now several complete recordings, and individual items have had a place since the 1910s. Gervase Elwes, his gently-edged voice at some disadvantage with the top-cut of old recording methods, sings gracefully and opens out well in the last verse of 'The Roadside Fire' (rec. 1916 Col. L 1074; HQM 1114). Peter Dawson (B 1698; RLS 10 7705 3), with more sharply etched tone, gives a sturdy account of 'The Vagabond', and his fine *legato* sustains beautifully the ending of 'Bright is the ring of words' (B 1355; RLS 10 7705 3): intermittent irritants are certain features of pronunciation such as the insistence on full value for secondary syllables such as the 'en' in 'even'. Very likeable in these three songs is Robert Irwin, whose versions (B 9504/5) are selected and splendidly transferred to LP in the *Treasury* (EX 29 0911 3).

Good as the songs are individually, they are still better in sequence. Shirley-Quirk's recital of 1963 (Saga 5473) was one of the most popular of song recordings, and rightly so, for it brought to notice not only the best young English baritone of his time but also the cohesion of the *Songs of Travel* as a cycle. Published versions of the music in two 'sets' had not included the *Epilogue* ('I have trod the upward and the downward slope'), posthumously discovered among Vaughan Williams' papers; with its reminiscences it does much to 'bind' the songs as a whole. Benjamin Luxon sings them with less well-focused tone (Chandos CD 8475) but with broad phrasing, some passion at the climaxes and excellent piano accompaniments by David Willison. The orchestral version, completed by Roy Douglas, is magnificently played by the City of Birmingham Orchestra under Simon Rattle (CDC7 47220–2), with Thomas Allen as soloist. A genuine enrichment of sound marks all of these, with, for instance, a spangled, almost Ravellian descriptiveness in the magical 'Thick as stars at night' passage. Thomas Allen's resonant, evenly produced voice gives great pleasure throughout, though some extra individuality and personal involvement is needed to bring the performance to full imaginative life.

On the reverse side of that record is *On Wenlock Edge*, sung by Robert Tear, again with full orchestral accompaniment. Here the voice production is less even and the habit of aspirating groups of notes on the same syllable irritates. The first verse of 'In summertime on Bredon' provides an example of that, and, more happily, of the evocative orchestration. The opening of the cycle has never sounded so exciting in recordings, where hitherto the original scoring for piano quintet has been preferred. Gervase

Elwes, tenor of the first performance, recorded the songs in 1919 (Col. 7363/5): musical taste and sound vocal method combine with the flavour of the period to help the old recording still to weave a spell. Not so with its successor by Steuart Wilson (Decca F 1649/51; ACL 303). Far better is Martyn Hill with the Coull String Quartet and Graham Johnson (Hyperion A66017), also giving a lovely account of 'In summertime on Bredon'. On HQS 1236, Ian Partridge's greater warmth and beauty of voice support an equally sensitive reading.

Partridge is the singer in several other important Vaughan Williams recordings. The *Four Hymns* of 1914 and *Merciless Beauty* (1921) are coupled on HQS 1325, both of them having a wide range of mood and calling for just that kind of gentle grace which one associates with this singer. In this recording there is also an incisiveness and power of *crescendo* and *marcato* that are less characteristic. The later and more austere *Blake Songs* he recorded finely with Janet Craxton (HQS 1236); a version by Robert Tear is on Argo ZRG 732. Then, in the two-record album of English songs mentioned already (OUP 155/6) Partridge introduces one of Vaughan Williams' earliest songs, 'How can the tree but wither' (1896), unmistakably himself even then. Of the four songs set to poems by the delightfully named Fredegond Shove (also included here), 'The new ghost' is a small masterpiece previously known on record in the strangely anxious, haunted voice of Jennifer Vyvyan (Eclipse ECS 589).

Luxon also has the Fredegond Shove songs in his recital (Chandos CD 8574). *House of Life*, to poems by Rossetti, proves less characteristic though it contains the exquisite 'Silent Noon'. But the real satisfaction of Luxon's record lies in two short songs from the composer's last years: 'Tired' (1956), an affectionate, modest setting of a poem by his wife, and 'In the Spring' (1951), a delicate and subtle gift to the William Barnes Society. The famous Barnes poem, 'Linden Lea', is also in the recital and has been recorded many times before. Rather too slowly but with a smiling manner and beautiful tone, Heddle Nash sings it on B 9719 (EX 29 0911 3). McCormack (DA 1791; EX 29 0007 3) draws a less beautiful line of sound but is more free and spontaneous with the words. Nash's 'Silent Noon' (C 4210; HQM 1089) catches to perfection, with Moore, the serenity and stillness of Dante Gabriel Rossetti's poem and the composer's setting. Shirley-Quirk (Saga 5473) sings both 'Linden Lea' and 'Silent Noon' with fine quality and masterly phrasing. He is also the excellent soloist in the *Five Mystical Songs* recorded by the Choir of King's College, Cambridge, under Willcocks (SLS 5082). Stephen Roberts, with the Northern Sinfonia under Hickox, provides a clean and well-recorded alternative (EL 27 0305 1). The fourth of those settings of poems by George Herbert, 'The Call', opens Janet Baker's *Anthology of English Song* (Saga XID 5213): it was her first recital record, and by the second verse of that song, with its shining facial expression and pointed, outgoing tone, she has impressed as a great singer in the making. Her unaccompanied recording of 'Bushes and briars' (ASD 2828) reminds us that folk song was as fundamental to Vaughan Williams' art as the chorale was to Bach's. A good recital of his folk song arrangements, performed by Tear with Philip Ledger and Hugh Bean (HQS 1412), represents this passionate involvement: 'As I walked out' is the title-song.

Folk song exercised less influence on the song output of Holst, who was the composer closest in most matters to Vaughan Williams. *The Dream City*, a cycle of poems by Humbert Wolfe, is heard with orchestration by Colin Matthews in a first recording, coupled with *Savitri*, on Hyperion A 66099. Patrizia Kwella's voice production, with its habitual swelling of individual notes, may not attract, but some of the songs are lovely in sound and deep in feeling: 'Envoi' and 'Journey's End' (with a magical opening) are examples. Three other Wolfe settings are sung by Ian Partridge (Enigma VAR 1027), the last of the set, 'The Floral Bandit', being a brisk, rather amusing little piece with a reference to 'Who is Sylvia' and a way of suiting action to words at the end ('breaks off her music in the middle' it says – and it does). 'Persephone' is still curiouser: accent, rhythm, nuance, accompaniment, intervals, all (one would suppose) present special difficulties, though not to Pears and Britten, who give a spirited account on Decca ECS 545. A more traditional style of writing and of singing is found in 'Lovely kind' as sung by Peter Dawson (B 1750; EX 29 0911 3), a model of sound method and tasteful sincerity.

The writer to whom folk song mattered possibly most of all was Percy Grainger. Apart from his being a great collector, he pioneered the use of recording to preserve traditional songs in the actual voices of country people. Of his own arrangements the best-known, 'Six dukes went a-fishing', was coupled by Pears and Britten on DA 2032 with 'Waly, Waly', one of Britten's own arrangements. Ears, more surprisable in those days, listened with interest to the fate of 'the royal duke of Grantham'. 'They took out his bowels' we gathered, but Pears' tone conferred a certain spirituality on the operation. The attractively swaggering 'Jolly Sailor's Song' was recorded at the same time but not issued till the publication of the Pears–Britten HMV recordings collected on RLS 748. Two excellent miscellanies called *Salute to Percy Grainger* (SXL 6410 and SXL 6872) highlight the originality of this fertile mind; and in *Shakespeare's Kingdom* by Sarah Walker (Hyperion A66136) one of the most haunting items is Grainger's final arrangement of the original version of Desdemona's Willow Song.

Distinct from the folk-orientated song-writers and midway in a line of composers who looked outwards from their English centre is the increasingly interesting figure of Frank Bridge. He wrote a bolder, broader type of song than was current in his time. Early compositions, from 1901 to 1908, well sung by Patricia Wright and Stephen Varcoe, appear on Pearl SHE 577. Among the four later songs recorded by David Johnston (SHE 551), 'Where she lies sleeping' brushes the mind lightly forward to the Lullaby in *The Rape of Lucretia*. One wonders whether Bridge's most famous pupil heard the song and remembered it, perhaps subconsciously, years later. The group included in this record ends with 'Love went a-riding', best-known of Bridge's songs and associated particularly with Kirsten Flagstad, who would send her concert audiences home with the final note ringing in their ears. Her recording (DA 1588; EX 29 0911 3) may not quite match the memory but it still takes flight and rides high. The other 'Pop' is 'Go not, happy day', and that, correspondingly, was Kathleen Ferrier's song. Here the recording is up to reality: smilingly done on PA 172. Many others have recorded it, most recently a Ferrier Award winner, Anne Dawson (Hyperion A66103). She groups it with other songs by Bridge, among them 'Come to me in my dreams', which deserves the popularity it once looked like achieving when adopted in late years by the silky-toned Tauber (RO 20554; EX 29 0911 3). Pears, delicate (some might say prissy) in 'Go not, happy day', has Britten accompanying with miraculous lightness and clarity (ECS 545). In another recital (ZK 28/9) he sings a number of less familiar pieces, each of them strong in ideas, with the setting of Yeats' 'When you are old' finding Pears at his best and most characteristic. Bridge is still recalled principally for his instrumental music, but it is good to see the considerable song output finding a place.

For several others in this period, the writing of songs was at the very centre of creative life. Roger Quilter, in particular, wrote little else. The disparagement of his songs represents them as superficial and soft-centred, and indeed they rarely elicit any very disturbed kind of response. Yet the time of writing these notes has just seen the arrival of a recital by Elly Ameling (Philips 412 216), where Quilter's 'Weep you no more, sad fountains', juxtaposed with Dowland's setting, makes a most lovely impression, the soprano phrasing with the special touch that has an audience holding its breath. This was so, too, when Ferrier sang 'Now sleeps the crimson petal' (M 680; ACL 309); the shading, poise and beauty of tone are exquisite. McCormack (DA 1111; EX 29 0056), Teyte (DA 1807; RLS 716) and Derek Oldham (B 2870; EX 29 0911 3) also bring their unmistakable personal qualities to it. A late Heddle Nash record (B 10265) has a delightfully buoyant 'It was a lover and his lass', also recorded, with a distinct family resemblance, by his baritone son, John Heddle Nash on C 4255. First among the original Quilter singers, Gervase Elwes (L 1055, 1074, 1119) graces the well-behaved melodies with his gentlemanly style and mellow voice. With a fastidiously light touch Quilter himself accompanies Mark Raphael, dry-toned though

John Steane

good with words: there were six records in the old Columbia catalogue (DB 1583, 1598, 1602, 1629, 1643, 1648), three of the sides included in the *Treasury* album. Slightly richer in tone, though hardly as much as one would like, Graham Trew sings a Quilter group on A66026; among them, less than a minute long, is his setting of 'Hark, hark, the lark', a charming miniature. Elizabeth Harwood (CFRA 120) also finds an unusual song, 'The Fuchsia Tree', an old Manx ballad but still very Quilteresque. She ends with the more familiar 'Love's Philosophy', for which we would probably turn to Janet Baker and Gerald Moore (HQS 1091). That song opens the first thoroughly recommendable Quilter recital record (Hyperion A66208). David Wilson-Johnson and David Owen Norris perform with sensitivity and conviction, and several lesser-known pieces come to light. Even so, as with Reynaldo Hahn among French song-writers, the final impression is of a distinctive gift not quite robust enough to sustain a whole programme.

Defence of Quilter, should one be needed, comes from a possibly unexpected quarter. Peter Warlock wrote that 'If it were not for the songs of Roger Quilter there would have been no Peter Warlock'. This may not necessarily constitute a self-evident recommendation, and in any case the influence is not all that readily apparent. A world away from Quilter, for example, is Warlock's exploration of bleak landscapes in *The Curlew*, with its desolate emotions rendered in the cry of the cor anglais and the indeterminate motions of the string quartet forming a disconsolate background to the solo voice. First to record the work in pre-war days was John Armstrong (NGS 163/5), then came René Soames (C 7934/6), pleasant, indeed too pleasant. A fine version by Partridge with Janet Craxton and the Music Group of London (HQS 1325) strikes an appropriate chill, with a little gratuitous warming by the resonant acoustic. Alexander Young's record (Argo RG 26) is worth noting, and the absence of one by Pears is worth regretting. He does include several of Warlock's songs in recitals: 'Yarmouth Fair', its vigour compensating for the lack of a more full-blooded tone, is on ECS 545, with 'Piggesnie' and – a touch of *The Curlew* in its strange, otherworldly idiom – 'Along the stream' on ZK 28/9. Partridge devotes a complete side to Warlock in his *English Songs* album (OUP 155/6), the half-pained, half-easeful setting of Fletcher's 'Sleep' suiting him admirable. Robert Tear interpolates two groups of songs (including a less enjoyable performance of 'Sleep') among choral works sung by the Louis Halsey Singers (DSLO 27). A recital by Norman Bailey, with twenty-six songs (DSLO 19), presents as comprehensive a view as we have at present. Songs such as 'As ever I saw' need more charm, and others such as 'The Fox' want more subtle expressiveness. Bailey is best in the catchy 'Elere lo'; his accompanist, Geoffrey Parsons, excels throughout. Among earlier British artists who recorded

240

songs by Warlock are Roy Henderson (M 514, 519, 563), Nancy Evans (B 9332; EX 29 0911 3) and Parry Jones. Two of his records (DB 1443 and 1489) have a side each represented in the *Treasury* Anthology; but the best is 'The Fox' (DB 1521), no great delight to the ear maybe, but a sharp piece of characterisation that stays vividly in the mind once heard.

Warlock, who died in 1930, takes us into the interwar years, but we should pause briefly to look at two composers who but for the tragedy of the war would surely have been important throughout the period. Among the fallen was George Butterworth, remembered most as a song writer for his settings of Housman's *Shropshire Lad* poems. 'Is my team ploughing?' offers opportunities for an imaginative colorist whose resonant 'man alive' will contrast with the pallid ghost-voice. Keith Falkner (B 9064; HQM 1238) makes nothing of this, and his 'lads', dead or alive, clearly attended a Very Good School Indeed. Shirley-Quirk (Saga 5473) is more imaginative and performs the whole set well; Luxon too (ZRG 838). Pears (ECS 545), without exaggerating his effects, achieves the most eerie ghostliness in the last song, and a tenor to record the cycle complete is Anthony Rolfe Johnson (Polydor 2460 258), who does it with clear diction and intelligent phrasing. Other songs of Butterworth are rare. Graham Trew has some on Hyperion A 66037 (and a complete 'A Shropshire Lad' on Meridian E 77031/2;, and Luxon adds 'Bredon Hill' to his *Shropshire Lad*, an attractively bold and individual setting, with 'On the idle hill of summer' as the most haunting of all.

Another victim of the war, though he lived on in mental institutions till 1937, was Ivor Gurney. *Ludlow and Teme*, another Housman cycle, has been well recorded by Martyn Hill; with its accompaniment of piano and string quartet it makes a natural coupling for *On Wenlock Edge* (A 66013). Gurney sets many of the same poems as Butterworth, and though his ideas are less instantly memorable there is probably a more sensitive imagination at work; certainly the performance itself is finely attuned to the moods of both words and music. Partridge has a dozen songs by Gurney in his album mentioned earlier (OUP 155/6). These include 'Severn Meadows', the only important setting of one of his own poems: affectionate music of a sweetness that becomes doubly moving as one thinks of its origin in the trenches. These delicate, gentle vocal lines suit Partridge ideally, and particularly beautiful are the hushed setting of Edward Thomas' 'Snow' and the soft ending of 'All night under the moon'. On VAR 1027 Partridge sings Gurney's 'Under the greenwood tree', unusual in that a minor tonality prevails, facing with the pluckiness of its jaunty rhythm the realities of 'winter and rough weather'.

The age into which these men should have survived was rich in talent, and most English composers of those years wrote songs. Moeran, Rubbra, Bax, Michael Head, Howard Ferguson, as well as the more 'popular' writers like Graham Peel, Armstrong Gibbs, Frederick Keel, Eric Coates and Haydn Wood. Two others emerge as most distinguished and prolific: John Ireland and Gerald Finzi. Ireland has indeed been nominated by William Mann as perhaps the most important English songwriter between Purcell and Britten.

The large corpus of his work has been well served by Lyrita records in association with the Ireland Trust. Benjamin Luxon is the principal singer in three volumes (SRCS 65, 66, 118) which, among them, were intended 'to include all that it is thought the composer would want'. Hardy and Housman are favoured poets, as with so many song-writers of this period; others less expected include Aldous Huxley, whose fine poem 'The Trellis' inspires one of the loveliest songs, and Sylvia Townsend Warner: her 'Hymn for a child' injects a little irony into the story of the boy Jesus at the Temple and brings out a relatively unfamiliar quality of sharpness in the composer. Luxon is a good choice of singer: he has the sensitivity and intelligence not to thicken the lines and coarsen the colours, but there is also a good manly straightforwardness and vigour, to provide as far as a singer can a corrective to the frequent impression of a wandering, uncommitted vocal line. Much of the strength of these songs lies in the piano part, and Alan Rowlands plays throughout with skill and understanding. In some the accompaniment is subordinated, as in the attractively simple 'Mother and Child' songs, sung by Alfreda Hodgson, or 'Hawthorn Time' among the tenor settings assigned to John Mitchinson. In that last song, Ireland is on the verge of commitment to melody, and, after many in these volumes that retreat just as that verge comes into view, one may well find uncommunicative this 'private' musical voice (as William Mann puts it), 'unconcerned with the great popularity that accrued to his jolly songs'. If 'I have twelve oxen' and Benjamin Luxon's clear enjoyment of it are representative of the 'jolly songs' in performance, one can only wish for more of them (that 'jolly songs' are inherently less valuable than 'private' melancholy ones is a common assumption; indifference towards the public's pleasure being a feather in the artistic cap seems often to be another).

The most popular of Ireland's songs, of course, is 'Sea Fever'. In his recording, Luxon pays attention to precise details of notation, where the general tendency has been to make free. Roy Henderson is urgent and scrupulous (Decca M 526), Robert Irwin (B 9073; EX 29 0911 3) a bit lightweight. Paul Robeson's deep resonant simplicity (B 3976) earns gratitude, probably more so than Robert Lloyd's rougher treatment (ASD 3345); Norman Bailey (DSLO 20) helps make vivid 'the flung spray and the blown spume', and Shirley-Quirk (Saga 5473) provides in addition exemplary firmness and beauty of tone. In the Hyperion collection *The Sea* (A66165) Thomas Allen brings both strength and refinement. A forthright early record of 'I have twelve oxen' by Peter Dawson deservedly survives (B 1137; RLS 10 7715 3). Several versions of 'Land of lost content' have come and gone, Anthony Rolfe Johnson's (Polydor 2460 258) being one of the more transitory, and Peter Pears' (ZK 28/9) probably the most permanent. Even so, there are times when his curious 'ee' vowels combine with other vocal idiosyncrasies and with the seemingly directionless drift of the music to suggest something dangerously close to self-parody.

A feeling of 'lost content' pervades much of the song-writing of this period. The malaise of *L'entre deux guerres* played its part, yet if these composers could but have known it they were writing in what now seem enviable conditions. By this time English song had developed well beyond the limitations of the 'drawing-room ballad', and yet music had not yet entered the phase when atonality and serialism were to drive a wedge between 'serious' composers and the general music-buying public. Finzi, whose talent once seemed to be the diluted last drippings of a dying tradition, now begins to look more like a culmination. He certainly has most to show in the record catalogues.

Three recitals on the Lyrita label cover a major part of his output. He had a great love for Hardy's poems, and three sets of ten songs each show him to have been a reader after Hardy's own heart, one of those 'finely-touched spirits' whom he could trust for 'right note-catching'. *A Young Man's Exhortation* (1933) sung by Neil Jenkins and *Earth and Air and Rain* (1936) by John Carol Case are coupled on SRCS 51: Jenkins good when not too loud or too high, Carol Case good when not too low (in this respect Benjamin Luxon manages better in his recording on ZRG 838). *Before and after Summer* (1949), also sung by Carol Case, impresses deeply, and the seven-song set called *Till Earth Outwears* (1958) suits Robert Tear well, especially in the solemn, imaginative setting of 'At a lunar eclipse' (SRCS 38). Anne Dawson, commanding attention in her first solo record (A 66103), also sings *Till Earth Outwears*, 'I look into my glass' registering firmly as a small masterpiece. The lovely Shakespeare settings, *Let us Garlands Bring*, beautifully orchestrated and assembled as a collection for Vaughan Williams' birthday in 1942, are perhaps most beguiling of all: John Carol Case again, not quite in best voice though always singing with taste and exemplary diction. Coupled with this on SRCS 93 Ian Partridge sings *Two Sonnets of John Milton* and *Farewell to Arms*, both of them compositions of rare grace and unostentatious strength. The Hardy settings are also collected in an invaluable two-record album issued in 1985 (Hyperion A66161/2). Stephen Varcoe continues in the tradition of Carol Case but with a youthful freshness of voice. Martyn Hill, a touch too genteel in 'Budmouth Dears', is ideal in 'At a lunar eclipse' and 'The Sigh'. The piano writing, usually delicate,

243

sometimes vigorous, has an able exponent in Clifford Benson, and the songs themselves give steadily growing pleasure.

The larger-scale work *Dies Natalis* (1940) was recorded first by Joan Cross (Decca K 1645/7; ECM 834) when just a little past her best, then by Wilfred Brown (World Records CM 50) and recently by Philip Langridge (ZRG 896). Some later songs, *Oh fair to see* Op. 136 and the very last of all, 'Since we loved', written in August 1956, are included by Partridge in a recital called *Finzi and his Friends* (A 66015), with seven miscellaneous songs well sung by the baritone Stephen Roberts. Among the separate recordings, not to be missed is Janet Baker's singing of two of the Shakespeare songs, 'Come away, death' and 'It was a lover and his lass' in her memorable *Anthology of English Song* on Saga XID 5213; marvellous control and ability to communicate evident in the young singer, as she was then, almost at the start of her career.

After Finzi it is tempting to write 'Finis'. Of course English song does not end there; the rest is not silence. But in several senses the line traced in this chapter stops, for the time being at least. From Dowland to Finzi song has been melodic, and melody, however subtle, has been understood to exist within the limits of key and time indicated by their signatures on the stave. Accompaniments, however complex, have still been accompaniments to the voice. With few exceptions, performance has been within the scope of amateurs, and the music could and would be performed in the home. Now comes the great divide. The dominant figure is Britten, whose songs, with the possible exceptions of his folk arrangements, can hardly be performed by any but professional musicians. Tippett goes still further beyond the amateur. Meanwhile the guitar succeeds the piano as the popular instrument, and the microphoned 'pop' vocalist provides the average man and woman (or more importantly boy and girl) with their concept of 'the singer'. The main line of melodic writing is deflected into the kind of composition practised by Lennon and McCartney or Elton John. Somewhere or other there must be people who still sing and play for pleasure and who buy new songs in the way people once bought Quilter's Shakespeare songs or Frederick Keel's *Salt Water Ballads*. For the most part 'sheet music' now means those musically, and often verbally, illiterate outlines of top-twenty numbers, while the work of 'serious' composers produces songs which there are few to sing and almost as few to love.

The record catalogues reflect this. Britten's songs, the subject of a separate chapter, have been recorded less frequently than might have been expected. *Boyhood's End* and *The Heart's Assurance*, works of comparable importance, form the major part of a Tippett recital record (DSLO 14) by Philip Langridge and John Constable. Langridge, less distinctive than Pears, who recorded them previously (DA 34), sings with well-placed tone and is unfailingly clear and intelligent in his dealing with words. Constable masters the difficult piano writing superbly, for instance, in 'The Dancer', the fourth song of *The Heart's Assurance*. Pears, like Langridge, has also recorded the *Songs for Ariel* in a recital of modern British song including Alan Bush's *Voices for the Prophets*, accompanied by the composer, and as ever shows himself the most understanding of singers (ZK 28–9). He too sings Walton's *Anon in Love* and Fricker's musing, slightly awkward setting of 'O mistress mine', both with guitar by Julian Bream on RCA SB 6621. Richard Rodney Bennett's *Tom o' Bedlam's Song* (cello accompaniment) is not merely well but greatly performed, with the slow smile, the beating maddened indignation wonderfully caught; and in the same album (ZK 28/9) Priaulx Rainier's *Cycle for Declamation* again has Pears at his finest, singing with intense imagination and command of vocal colour. The apparently unattainable extremes of the human voice are exploited in Peter Maxwell Davies' *Songs for a Mad King*, which find their astonishingly able exponent in Julius Eastman (Unicorn RHS 308). He follows, apparently without turning a hair, the score's injunctions to move from treble high C to bass low G sharp on one syllable and to produce a chord of F minor on another.

At such a point, song, further from home than ever, can hardly avoid making another change of direction. Just possibly (but does this ever happen?) it may rejoin the long and pleasant road it once followed, and on which the gramophone record has pretty faithfully followed its tracks.

This is the best hope, for the alternatives are not pleasant to contemplate. In one direction: the restrictive practices of modern composers, among whom once or twice in a century there may or may not arise a Benjamin Britten. In the other: adolescent gravel-voices, synthesizers, and rubbish amplified to facilitate premature but merciful deafness.

American song

WILL CRUTCHFIELD

Ned Rorem has probably written more American art songs than any other composer and probably, also, more about them than any other critic. One could do worse, therefore, than turn to him for a description. 'The genre may be defined', he wrote in a lively note for a New World Records anthology, 'as the musical setting of a lyric poem for one voice with piano accompaniment. The setting is by a specific American composer as opposed to anonymous or collective authorship; is self-contained as opposed, say, to an aria, which is part of a whole; and is strictly as opposed to approximately notated like so-called popular songs, which can be rendered by any voice in any arrangement at any speed. "Art song" is our answer to the German Lied or the French *mélodie*, which implies a through-written recital song as distinct from a *chanson*.'

A definition is required, and especially so for American song, because when all is said and done America's greatest contributions to song probably lie in the 'approximately notated' masterpieces of Gershwin, Kern, Porter and the rest, and in the spirituals and frontier songs of 'anonymous or collective authorship'. But to venture on that territory would be to veer off from the concerns of this book, and to face a body of recordings impossibly vast for the space of a chapter.

Even when, following the definition, we reluctantly omit from consideration folk-song arrangements, spirituals, works with multiple voices or instruments, pop-songs of all kinds (and that can be a tricky line to draw), the field is still large, for though the art song has grown an offshoot rather than a main branch in America it has flourished notably in this century. So, since this is to be a survey not of American song but of American song on records, let us further limit it to those songs that have attracted significant artists in sufficient numbers for critical comparison to be in question.

Interpreted by that 'objective' standard, the evidence suggests that America has produced one great song composer, Charles Edward Ives, and two strong secondary figures, Samuel Barber and Charles Tomlinson Griffes. After that, there are composers who have attracted a modest following with many songs, and others who have attracted a long list of singers with one or two. I would not proceed on this basis if I felt it did frequent injustice to the material or artists involved – and where occasionally it does, at least parenthetical mention of some 'excluded' recordings can offer redress.

My main reservation concerns Stephen Foster, who may well have thought his songs 'strictly notated' – and no doubt their simple notation was deemed complete by the amateur performers who made up their original audience ('market', we would say today). But I should like to dodge Foster, first because the vast majority of performances are in arrangements – they assume, in other words, that the originals were 'approximate' – and second simply because his evergreen melodies have been recorded so often that there would hardly be room to discuss anything else.

I must deal first and foremost with Ives. He was, we know, almost debilitatingly ambivalent about his very relationship to music, and also about the impulse to contact anyone else through it. Working by day in the business world of Manhattan, he composed for about 20 years in near-total artistic isolation. But towards the end of that period, just before he stopped composing, he sent out privately published editions of his Concord Sonata for piano and a bewildering collection of 114 songs. These set in motion the slow process of recognition that ran through the remaining thirty-odd years of the composer's strange life: contact with the American avant-garde, publication, John Kirkpatrick's landmark performance of the Concord Sonata in 1939, the Pulitzer Prize in 1947. It has gone on since his death in 1954, and the songs have been at the centre of it. The initial collection – pieces dating from 1888 to 1920 – contained sentimental trifles, elegant and serious art songs on European models (it was a habit formed by Horatio Parker's practice of having his students reset the texts of great songs, so Ives has an 'Ich grolle nicht', a 'Songs My Mother Taught Me', a 'Lotosblume' and so on), raucous popular songs and war songs, visionary reachings in music after Transcendentalist thought, knotty and dissonant struggles with tough texts, witty miniatures, undisciplined outbursts . . .

These were supplemented in the 1930s and afterward by separate publications combining excerpts from the original 114 (sometimes significantly revised) with others that brought the eventual published total to some 150, not counting multiple versions. So bizarre, uneven, sometimes forbidding and often puzzling an output had to be sorted through and figured out before the masterpieces in it could become the common property of American singers. The leading artists of the 1940s and 1950s did not know quite what to make of Ives, but their successors gradually studied him, and the activity since the composer's centennial in 1974 has been specially remarkable. Instead of being left alone for a while, as often happens to over-exposed composers, Ives has clearly been accepted into the active song repertory. Well over a hundred of his songs have now been commercially recorded, most in multiple versions. Thirty-eight have been done four times or more, while some of the most popular have attracted as many as a dozen interpreters. And the most satisfying recordings, by and large, are the more recent ones.

That is not to say that nothing memorable arose from the first grapplings. The very first of all, Radiana Pazmor's 'General William Booth Enters Into Heaven' (NMQR 2–4; NW 247) is a stunner. She leads as boldly as Booth himself 'with his big bass drum', with a firm stride and wonderfully pure, strong tone. The declamation is telling, and she switches beautifully into a 'singing' style for the refrain ('Are you washed in the blood of the lamb?'). For the bugle calls she has the flexibility of a well-schooled vocalist; for the quick shifts ('Yet – in an instant . . . '), the responsiveness of a theatre singer. Hard to beat! Donald Gramm's version (Desto DST 6411–2) is very good, with a special beauty and warmth for 'Jesus came from the court-house door', and Marni Nixon makes this the highlight of her lively collection – but her raw timbre sends one back to Pazmor, whose version though abbreviated for 78s still gives fullest measure in this remarkable song. She recorded no other Ives commercially, but did make some broadcasts which survive; issue of them would be most welcome.

The first recorded collection of the songs, a half-dozen issued on Musicraft 78s in 1939 (now on CRI SRD 390) with Mordecai Bauman, is a lovely success. Bauman, a warm-voiced, slightly (but not unappealingly) nasal baritone whom I take to be of foreign origin, chose straightforward songs and approached them much as Peter Dawson might have done, with firm, well-managed manly tone, forthright expression, general musicality. But even in these pieces there are twists, problems and undertones that little of the Peter Dawson repertory represented. 'Ann Street', over as it is in less than a minute, is a little tricky just to get right, and Bauman's rhythm is tentative. 'Charlie Rutlage' raises a problem that recurs in Ives, that of going back and forth between song and speech. The action-packed middle section of this ballad (about the death of a cowboy) is recited over a busy accompaniment; Bauman does it in a kind of chant that is not especially dramatic – but later interpreters who have been more specific in their declamation have sometimes run aground on the singsong quality of the verse, which becomes rather wretched when the context of rhymed song is taken away. (In the sung sections, Bauman gives a likeable hint – not too much – of the style that came to be known as 'country-Western').

'Evening' (the best Milton art song I know) goes well, and the charming 'Two Little Flowers' elicits a delightful grandfatherly chuckle. And surely Bauman's 'The Greatest Man' has not been equalled since. This is one of Ives' most popular songs, but a fragile one, just one step away from maudlin, because of the sappy poem (it is about a boy's naive admiration for his father). The music is fresh and lively: it has plenty of songful consonance, but warmed with constant unobtrusive chromaticism that is functional, not just decorative. Right from the opening 7th chord, bouncing on its toes to a resolution on which it will light only fitfully, the piece has a springy harmonic rhythm which culminates in one of the best final cadences ever penned. Bauman finds precisely the simple, true tone for it, feeling the childish pride ('we ketched *five* newlights'), with just the right unselfconscious softening for the sentimental lines, and a great manly slap on the back for 'that's the stuff!'. The opposite is embodied in Roberta Alexander's recording, on her generally disappointing all-Ives disc: she begins with a set face, a caricature of childishness, which almost guarantees that nothing to follow will be heard as springing from sincere impulse. (A curiosity is that both Bauman – who may not have been a native English-speaker – and Alexander tell of Dad going to find not 'minners' (minnows) but 'minors' down by the creek! Better not to think about that one.)

But when as likeable a singer as the New York City Opera tenor Ernest McChesney cast his net a bit wider for a collection of seventeen songs (Concert Hall C–7) a decade later, it was to gather mostly problems. McChesney has just the right sweet tenor, clear and forward, for the sentimental 'A Night Song', and the flexibility of his tempo is appealing. When those virtues will suffice, as in 'Mists' or 'Night of Frost in May', he is good. But in 'Two Little Flowers', where they should go a long way, he is confused by the *ostinato* accompaniment (the pattern is one quaver short of the length of a bar, and so goes in and out of phase with the voice). Confusion mounts in the 'Cradle Song', where Ives alternates two-four and six-eight with the untraditional specification that the quavers (rather than the beats and bars) be equal. The singer does not seem to have decided whether or not 'Harpalus' is a joke; he hasn't got the one-two punch for the end of '1, 2, 3', and so on it goes. There is also the problem of keys: Ives wrote determinedly for baritone; McChesney transposes liberally, usually to good effect, but with bizarre result when in 'The Circus Band' he raises one 16-bar section by a fourth with the surrounding matter in its original key!

A great step forward was taken in 1954 when Overtone Records issued

24 songs on an LP (Overtone 7) with Helen Boatwright accompanied by Kirkpatrick himself. At the time of compiling his admirable 1968 Ives discography, Richard Warren called this 'my favourite Ives record', and hearing her true, delicate, firm tone in 'Abide With Me' one instantly understands why. There is also a good Protestant strength of spirit about the final lines, but in general a reticence of characterisation hampers one's appreciation of this disc today (now that it does not bring, as it must have in 1954 and even in 1968, the joy of discovering the songs themselves). And if the earlier collections were weighted towards the charming and slight in Ives, and fought shy of the stronger songs, this one plunges in ('General Booth' again, 'The Swimmers', 'Tom Sails Away' and others) without finding their measure. Still, the singing is unfailingly lovely and the playing extremely clear and vital. By the time of her second Ives collection (Am. Col. M4–32504, recorded in 1969 but not published until the composer's centennial in 1974), Boatwright had gained somewhat in character but lost in ease of production. It is still valuable, though, for the inclusion of some beautiful songs that are otherwise unrecorded (and some, in the versions used here, unpublished). Especially good are three items from the small cluster of strange, spare, fascinatingly exploratory songs that Ives wrote after effectively giving up composition in 1921: 'Peaks', 'Yellow Leaves', and a telling dirge on Ariel's 'Full Fathom Five'. Both these collections benefit from Kirkpatrick's special knowledge of the multiple source materials that lie behind the published Ives editions, and both do honour to a pioneering singer.

But nearly three decades after Bauman's set the catalogues still did less than justice to the range of Ives' songs. A collection by Corinne Curry appeared in 1963, but the singing is not vivid and the piano playing misses a number of important points (Cambridge 1804); the tenor Ted Puffer introduced many important songs in two 1965 discs (Folkways FM 3344–5), but his style and voice were not on a level with his enterprise, and he makes bland listening. Marni Nixon's half-LP in 1967 (Pye GSGC 14105) helped a good deal (clear and relaxed in 'Ann Street', enthusiastic and effective in 'The Swimmers' until the vampish whisper at the end). She is always accurate, and always alive, even if the interpretations are rarely evocative and the voice (almost a Broadway sound at times) somewhat threadbare.

The contribution of Evelyn Lear and Thomas Stewart (CBS M 30229) helped more. First of all, in Stewart the ideal singer of the hearty vernacular songs was found. In 'The Circus Band', 'They Are There' and 'Charlie Rutlage', his big grainy baritone and strong masculine style embody to the letter the side of Ives that was a rambunctious Yankee boy who never grew up. Nor is a deeper responsiveness lacking: Stewart's vocal means will not fully encompass the possibilities of 'Autumn' and 'The Things our

Fathers Loved', but in both, his firm, natural soft singing conveys a gentleness born of strength. A drawback is that when the strength is displayed the voice takes on a gruff, insistent, cross sound. Still, the combination of elements is just right for the stern injunction of 'In Flanders' Fields': a burden of honour laid by the dead on the shoulders of the living. And Stewart's 'At the River' addresses and solves convincingly the problem of the displaced beats and pitches in the hymn tune arrangement: he is a rough-hewn revivalist (perhaps the 'Old John Bull' of Ives' recollections, the 'best stonemason in town', in whose off-key bellowing could be heard 'the music of the ages') whose vigorous rendition carries him with conviction and unconcern out of tune and time.

That simple song, incidentally, is one of the most variously interpreted in the Ives canon. With Boatwright or William Parker it is a simple hymn sung with feeling and lovely tone, the pensive polytonal accompaniment speaking for itself; for Marni Nixon, going very slowly, it is a private, contemplative recollection; Cleo Laine is an old blues mama croaking out a half-remembered tune from long ago; Jan DeGaetani is as always effortlessly accurate and observant of the tiniest instructions; Fischer-Dieskau tries rather unfortunately to sound American on 'gathurr' and seems to have no point of reference for the song (somewhat as though Cleo Laine had tried to sing 'Du, du liegst mir im Herzen'), but Stewart's version satisfies markedly more than the rest.

Evelyn Lear's portion is less rewarding – she was not in the best of vocal health at the time, and two songs re-done on a later live recital (Pelican LP 2012) come off better there. But in one piece she is memorable for creating a strong mood: 'Grantchester', where one has almost a physical sensation of lying 'day-long . . . flower-lulled in sleepy grass'. And in the last line of 'Maple Leaves' she is one of the few singers to find any response to the rather startling image ('like coins between a dying miser's fingers').

It was Jan DeGaetani whose splendid 1976 collection on Nonesuch (H 71325) set a high watermark for Ives recordings. It stands as the best all-Ives collection and general introduction to the composer's songs. The opening sounds could not be more promising: rich, deep, relaxed sonorities from Gilbert Kalish for the 'contented river', the Housatonic at Stockbridge. Kalish's contributions are magnificent throughout: he is even better than Kirkpatrick as a clarifier of Ives' potentially murky textures, but his clarity never becomes clinical or precludes a rich cushion of piano sound. At 'thou beautiful', the singer's tone is a tiny thread, almost inert in its calm observation, and as beautiful as the image itself (though Stockbridge is no longer the best place to watch the Housatonic: it is now bordered with a golf course). At the pickup to the climax, ('Ah, there's a restive ripple') Kalish's command makes all the difference, and the ending is superbly realised.

Will Crutchfield

Next comes the pair of 'Memories', brilliantly contrasted and beautifully sung; then 'From *Paracelsus*', a noble utterance of a noble song (Ives could rise in music to Browning's impassioned, lofty thought here); then a neat and bright 'Ann Street', later a full-hearted 'In the Mornin'' (a moving Negro spiritual arrangement made well after Ives had abandoned composing); a stunning realization of 'Like a Sick Eagle', an eerie 'Farewell to Land' (superbly accurate, and with the very sound of the 'night winds' sighing in the voice) and so on and on. The songs that want an expansiveness of tone and phrasing leave one wishing for more even while admiring, and there are times when the relaxed style can seem to verge on passivity, but there is an underlying strength and certainty that compel and reward attention.

Of the half-LP of Ives the same pair produced in 1983 for Bridge Records (BDG 2002) it need only be said that it was eagerly awaited, that it did not disappoint, and that it contains several of Ives' very finest ('West London', 'Down East', 'Tom Sails Away', 'Afterglow' and a smart, sparkling 'Side Show' that makes the unsteady waltz sound like a record with skips in it, or like a machine on the blink).

A fascinating thing has been to watch how Ives has fared as he has penetrated into the international repertory. Almost 40 Ives titles have now been recorded by non-Americans, and several of the songs have found their best realisations in these recordings. Neither the notion that Ives is parochial in appeal nor that only Americans can find the right vantage point for him (true enough, perhaps, in the relatively few works that depend entirely on what to us are patriotic tunes) can survive these artists' explorations.

The biggest name among them, though, presents a fascinating problem case. Fischer-Dieskau's collection (DG 2530 696), appearing shortly after DeGaetani's in 1976, gave his admirers and the composer's a rough time of it. The baritone was not in his best voice, and there is no getting around the embarrassing fact that his is one of the least accurate recordings of the more difficult dissonant songs. He gets half-a-tone off partway through 'A Farewell to Land', and stays that way to the end. 'The Swimmers' has almost as many wrong notes as right (and it matters, not because there is any real tonality until near the final lines, but because the voice is often supposed to be in octaves with the right hand of the accompaniment). A great deal of 'Ann Street' is off too, and it seems that when Fischer-Dieskau knows he's 'swimming' in this sense, he turns to a sort of ranting straight tone, half-spoken in an unattractive way. Embarrassing, too, are a few of his attempts at an American accent though that is less problematic than some of his critics would have it, since only four or five of the songs are American in reference.

But when all is said and done, the vitality of this collection puts it

252

among the best few. First of all, there are several unmitigated successes: the lovely group of German songs, the powerful Matthew Arnold setting, 'West London', the delicate and beautifully realised art song 'Autumn'. Even in the others, Fischer-Dieskau is in there grappling with the music and the thoughts, sweaty and rough, excited and involved. In 'The Swimmers' he may shout and approximate; no one else seems to feel as he does the exultant swing ('out of the foam I lurched, and rode the wave'). Erik Saedén's recording may capture better the steadiness of motion, the sense of time slowed, that is there in the physical act of swimming – but not the 'feverish intensity of life' that is its metaphor here. In 'West London', it is Fischer-Dieskau who understands the structure as Ives has: first part observation – and neither Boatwright (1976), DeGaetani (1983), Puffer nor even the vivid Marni Nixon paints the scene as he does – and second part impassioned comment. 'Above her state this spirit towers', says the poet, as the transcendentalist strain in Ives bears the music toward a conclusion in which the 'vernacular' and visionary idioms are eloquently combined; Fischer-Dieskau follows.

But that is the sort of contrast that one finds repeatedly. As one turns from someone else's version to his, the pulse quickens as a new order of vitality fills the room; turn to someone else's again and it is at first hard to concentrate because the singer's own concentration seems less intense. Not that Fischer-Dieskau's version is always the best: far from it, in some cases. But one cannot fail to be aware of *presence*, and then of the way the songs seem to need and reward an interpretative presence of such dimensions. Above the occasional roughness of voice and less than thorough preparation, his spirit towers.

Two Ives sides have come from Sweden. Erik Saedén (C 053–35162) jumps right in with a hearty 'Circus Band', and is at his best in 'The Greatest Man' (he especially seems to enjoy seeing Miss Molly Cottontail on the run when Dad goes hunting). But Saedén was a veteran vocally by the time the recording was made (1966, though it was not published until a decade later), and sometimes finds the tessitura uncomfortably high, as in 'Requiem', a Robert Louis Stevenson song that still awaits a satisfying recording (though Kirkpatrick plays the big piano part splendidly on Boatwright 1974). Nor does the Swedish baritone capture any real feeling of sickness, of mortality's heavy weight, in 'Like a Sick Eagle'. That one is tricky, partly in the sense that it is a 'trick' song, with the voice invited (in the second published edition) to slide through quarter tones on the way to each pitch. Saedén doesn't attempt this; Roberta Alexander, in addition to the parodied-sounding expression, substitutes a monotonous half-step *Portamento* for the quarter tones. DeGaetani (1976) is superb: her near limpness of tone and rhythm capture the feeling perfectly, and she and Kalish make memorable the slow, effortful progress to the cadence (a rich and agonizing promise of C major that cannot be reached).

The other Swedish disc is a rare treasure, though. The Ives half of Kerstin Stahl's recital on Caprice (CAP 1187) just may be (startling as the thought is) the most consistent in its satisfactions of any Ives collection on record. Stahl, of whom I had never heard until this record appeared, is more vibrant and outgoing than DeGaetani, more accurate and tonally beautiful than Fischer-Dieskau, more varied than Thomas Stewart. Though a delicate lyric soprano, she can put pressure on the middle voice without losing its beauty and poise. Her English is splendid, and she has a way of finding things in the songs that others have missed. 'Old Home Day' is a good example: Ives dodges in and out of quoted and quote-like material in his most wistful and well-integrated way; what Stahl catches is the sensuousness of the out-dodges, savouring the music's beauty and mystery side by side with the rugged street songs in a way that Ives rarely did in words, but often in tones. (The optional printed *obbligato* isn't included; no great loss, as Boatwright II, where it is incorporated into the piano part, shows. Raymond Beegle's vocal ensemble does 'Old Home Day' as a series of solos on Vox); Douglas Perry's clear tenor, heard also in a sentimental 'Karen', makes it worth having, and the set also contains a satisfying version of 'Canon' by Rosalind Rees.)

To 'The Things Our Fathers Loved' Stahl brings a beautiful vibrancy and generosity of phrase. More: the song is *reflective* from its first line – one realises instantly what state of mind is involved. Then feeling floods in at 'summer evenings': all the associations that are to come in the song have struck the singer just then, and are implicit in her sound. 'The Housatonic at Stockbridge', generally successful (despite a rather clinical separation of the left-hand notes by the pianist Kerstin Aberg), asks for one thing she apparently cannot do, to hold the final F at a strong *forte* while the piano shifts beneath. But such disappointments are rare. In 'Grantchester' the mood is not as immediate as with Lear, but the phrase 'and felt the Classics were not dead' brings a smile and a light touch: happy thought. 'The Cage' has just the right biting understatement; 'Down East' lilts longingly and, at the end, movingly (as it does also in De Gaetani's second collection).

Such characterful touches are elusive in the Ives group recorded by Carolyn Watkinson in Wigmore Hall (Etcetera ETC 1007), though the tone is clear, the diction splendid and the accuracy impressive. 'Walking' has a firm stride ('A big October morning') that irresistibly calls Janet Baker to mind (she has sung some Ives, but not recorded it as yet). In 'Tom Sails Away' she catches an opportunity that no one else seems to have noticed, unostentatiously and delightfully imitating a train whistle where the text mentions one. But I have run out of examples; 'Grantchester', and indeed most of the group, is forthright and uninterestingly interpreted.

A problem posed by 'Grantchester' and 'Walking' in common with several other Ives songs is that of speaking over accompaniment. In 'Grantchester', where the song turns a corner from thought to feeling, the line 'but these are things I do not know' is given a rhythm (an unconvincing dotted one) but no pitches. It just doesn't work; in every single recording it is an almost embarrassing moment. The end of 'The Swimmers' runs 'knowing I was its master (sung), not its slave! (spoken)', and frankly the most persuasive solution to this has been Boatwright's: instead of dropping the octave on 'master', she keeps both syllables on upper D, then sings the last three words on the lower.

The problems of the recitation in 'Charlie Rutlage' have already been mentioned. In 'Walking' the matter is different: the piano interlude describes, we are told by the composer's marginalia, first a funeral going on at a church, then a roadhouse dance. Ever since Boatwright did it in 1954, singers have read the marginalia aloud – again, rarely to convincing effect. Jan DeGaetani takes this further, announcing the two streets that intersect little Ann Street in the interludes, and crying out 'Hear the trombones!' when Ives prints that injunction under the piano part of 'Circus Band'. I can only assume that some listeners find this more effective than I do; it almost always rings false to me.

On the other hand, the cry of 'Curtain!' when the overture is done at the opera house in 'Memories' always brings a smile, and Elly Ameling's smile for it in her mixed recital on CBS 76738 is as winning as her tender tone for the second 'memory'. Ameling, one gathers, would like to record more Ives: happy prospect. I hope we have more, too, from William Parker, the wonderfully cultured American baritone who joins Ameling in EMI's Poulenc set (q.v.) and who included nine Ives songs (four in French) in the first of his two splendid American song recitals on New World (NW 300 and 305). His deep, warm tone is effective in the four hymn-based songs; it is ideal when coupled with his loving pronunciation and persuasive style in the rarely heard French settings. One might wish that the extraordinary Rumanian soprano Yolanda Marculescu, now resident in Milwaukee, had chosen those (her affinity for French being what it is) instead of five German songs for inclusion in her interesting anthology of 'American Composers – Foreign Poets' (Orion ORS 685); the tone is lovely and the style responsive, but the response is inhibited by a general feeling of less than full comfort with the language.

There remains the most recent Ives disc, ETC 1020, with Roberta Alexander, a soprano who has recently scored a Metropolitan Opera success as Gershwin's Bess. This is the kind of record one tends to call 'commendable' without really meaning to commend it. Commendable is the fact that an artist with plenty of operatic work should find the curiosity and take the time to deal with important but difficult songs from her country. Less so is the impression that more time was needed: there are occasional slight inaccuracies, and (far worse) a prevailing blandness, yielding at times to a caricature ('Charlie Rutlage', 'Greatest Man' and others) that makes one wish for the blandness back. Still, her voice is often a fine one, and the piano parts are beautifully played by Tan Crone.

There are still other isolated Ives items in various anthologies, but though few of his important songs still await first recordings, a fair number await first distinguished ones. A complete set, with full annotation and accounting for variant versions, would be a project of manageable proportions, one would think; of course, it wouldn't be worth it if artists who could make the songs meaningful and memorable weren't on hand – but my impression is that the moment is ripe.

A footnote: in addition to what is discussed above, there are several Ives collections on 'fringe' labels – budding companies that never quite bloomed, or vanity-press operations – that find their way into libraries but not into channels of sale. Few of these are rewarding, and some are excruciating, but one I should mention if only because I participated. While an undergraduate at Northwestern University, I accompanied Walter Carringer in a collection of then-unrecorded early songs on Brewster BR-1299. At this distance in time I find I have no great admiration for the piano playing, but there is a fond spot in my heart for Carringer's warm tenor, and I flatter myself that we caught the verve of some of the love-songs better than subsequent attempts have done.

No other American composer has found anything like such a following as Ives among performers for a wide body of songs, but several have found an even greater one for a few beloved items. Charles Wakefield Cadman, for instance, though he was a 'serious' enough composer to have written in a variety of chamber and symphonic forms, was identified to the near-exclusion of all else with a small handful of songs, above all 'From the Land of the Sky-Blue Water' and 'At Dawning'. The former comes from a group of American Indian melodies, harmonised and 'idealised' by Cadman. A lovely pentatonic melody, sugary (but not quite syrupy) accompaniment, sentimental words about a captive maid: it is as unsurprising that singers of the 78 era found it irresistible as that their successors have quietly let it drop. The list goes on and on – from starry names like Nordica (30486; SYO 11 and various other reissues) and Gluck (Victor 659) to forgotten ones like Florence Hinkle (60079) and Mary Lewis (1140), with Alice Nielsen (A–1732) and Evan Williams (871) in between, all singing with the purity and resonance of tone that were so regularly cultivated in those days, and all with a general warmth of feeling, though not with particular imagination. Edith Mason

(Brunswick 10177) had at least the imagination to see the possibility of repeating the second half (orchestra first, voice rejoining at end, like a pop song), and the second time round she adds a stunner of poised *pianissimo* B flat – this after singing the song with voice and phrasing so lovely as to stand out even after the pure-toned ladies mentioned above. Hers is surely the best; others include Jeanette MacDonald (2055; tender and unpretentious), Maggie Teyte (a late broadcast, rather determined-sounding: REGL 369) and the single modern recording, William Parker's (on NW 213, devoted to the Indianist movement); his fine manly tone would have earned rather more admiration 75 years ago, I imagine, than would that of many of his present-day colleagues.

Even more ubiquitous than this was 'At Dawning', a song whose sentimental strains became so much a part of the national consciousness that Ives could write a parody ('On the Counter') without a single direct quote, but unmistakable in reference. Charles Kullman (4592M), Alfred Piccaver (M 419) and Richard Tauber (RO 20524) sang it; likewise Nelson Eddy (DA 1585 and ML 4343), John Charles Thomas (B–60055, 10167), Joseph Hislop (DA 819), Risë Stevens (M 654). One can hear many a nice *piano* note and graceful *portamento* without finding anything to lodge in the memory or recommend the piece; just as one is about to endorse its fall into oblivion, there comes Mary Garden (4369; NW 247 and other reissues), singing very slowly with the most fragile, deliciously shaded tone and with spacious, unhurried phrasing, as though the hackneyed words were brand new and thrilling. It makes an extraordinary effect (and it is nice to hear from the recording accompanied by the composer on a late Nordskog acoustic, of all things, that Cadman paced the song with similar breadth). Others that stand out are McCormack's (DA 303), with a ring of passion in the voice at 'love anew to me is born', and Schumann-Heink's, boomed out with all-embracing motherly warmth on a broadcast made in the singer's seventy-third year. It was not Isobel Baillie's kind of song: her 1926 HMV test sounds not so much chaste as dutiful – though there is an uncharacteristic interpolated high note at the end; nice to know she had it in her (RLS 7703). One would be curious to hear Paul Robeson's version (B 8731); there is also a modern one by Stuart Burrows (SOL 324) that has not come my way.

Rogers' 'At Parting' and Rasbach's 'Trees' are similar songs ('art songs' but sentimental in a way that doesn't make one long for a return to the age of sentiment) that achieved comparable attention, but sorting through them would add little of interest here; better to take leave of this genre of American song with another sally into Indianism, Lieurance's 'By The Waters of the Minnetonka'. All sorts of exotic people show up for this one – not just Madame Melba (DA 334; RLS 719), pure-toned and steady at 59, though typically perfunctory with the melody, but Princess Watawaso

(Victor 18431), Os-ke-non-ton (American Col. A–3173), and Lieurance himself playing it on Indian flute (21972). Playing the tune in all its primitive plainness, that is, and a very different thing it is without the sweet sevenths and ninths we then hear as Clement Barone, Galli-Curci's flautist, plays Lieurance's usual arrangement. The 'conventional' versions include Frances Alda (the gorgeous tone floating over what would come to be thought of as a Hollywood-style oohing and aahing chorus on the acoustic (Victor 527)), Culp (DA 149), Schumann-Heink (Victor 1198 and a broadcast (Pelican 2008), lavishing affection and imaginative care on the repetitive phrases), Nielsen (American Columbia A 1732, catching a foxtrot feeling to the rhythm) and several others that I haven't heard.

Not just America's Indians but India's fascinated our composers for a time, with Rabindranath Tagore's poems a favourite source. John Alden Carpenter (1876–1951), a serious and (but not here) experimentally inclined composer, made a cycle from the 'Gitanjali' collection that won the Nobel Prize in 1912, and one of its songs became especially popular: 'When I Bring You Coloured Toys'. It is a little unfair to the several fine singers who have recorded it that Conchita Supervia should have made an unforgettable version (HMA 1), exquisite from the first line, savouring the child to whom the song is sung as though she could hardly hold herself back from covering it with kisses. What a chuckle, tease, scolding and gleeful appreciation (all at once) in the line about 'your greedy hands!'.

There is nothing like this in the other records, but Rose Bampton (Victor 1628; NW 247) sings with a smile, delicate top notes, and affectionate shaping of lines. Donald Stenberg (Educo 4006) is engaged and expressive, but there's no sense of a *child* being addressed. That is there in John Kennedy Hanks' version (DWR 6417), and Glenn Darwin's (Victor36224) is warm, gentle and fatherly. Flagstad (LM 2825, unpublished until 1965) sings with surprising lightness and character, with some verve in the line about 'song and dance', she's helped by Edwin McArthur's quick, elegantly buoyant accompaniment. Alexandra Hunt's performance (in a recording of the complete cycle on Orion ORS 77272) gives the impression of being modelled on Flagstad's, but the voice is clouded and effortful by comparison.

Another well-known Tagore setting was Richard Hageman's 'Do Not Go, My Love', whose perfumed atmosphere is not as likely to appeal today as once it did. Bampton's version (DA 1855; NW 247) is the best in that it captures basic elements most uninhibitedly: the lush languor, the possessiveness, the starting up from sleep and subsiding. In the ripe-toned, scooping attacks one feels immediately the 'eyes heavy with sleep', and the contrasting middle section is vivid. Marguerite D'Alvarez (Victor 1116; Club 99–73), by contrast, sings with general *legato* and expression but no particular sense of atmosphere ('I start up' is as languid as any other line). Hanks starts with a good 'Eastern' sounding touch: an effective performance. Others have their moments: an old-fashioned upward *portamento* from Tudor Davies (E 504); a delicate utterance at 'to touch you' from Dino Borgioli, as though the beloved were a butterfly (LB 24; EX 29 1169 3); impressive soft notes from Zinka Milanov (LM 1915), whose emphatic grandeur makes an otherwise rather lugubrious effect; a fine *messa di voce* on the last F sharp from Jeanette MacDonald (2047). This song has escaped us, though, I think; Dale Moore revives it on his 1973 American LP anthology (Cambridge CRS 2715), but the mood just isn't there.

Of slightly earlier vintage, but belonging with these European-style recital songs, is a red-blooded setting of Kipling's 'Danny Deever' by Walter Damrosch (1862–1950), a through-composed gripper on a strophic base. The classic recording here is David Bispham's savage, chilling account (the piano-accompanied version (30016, from around 1906) is on NW 247, along with Bispham's amusing account of his adventures with the song; there is a better-recorded orchestral). Richard Bonelli (Brunswick 5166) and Reinhold Werrenrath (Victor 74827 and 6638) imitate Bispham with lesser intensity, but Brownlee (E 553) thinks for himself, with fast, clipped questions, a haunted *mezza voce*, horror in the sergeant's explanation of the crime, and broad phrasing at the climax. It is Leonard Warren, though, who successfully challenges Bispham with a contrasting conception of equal power. He makes it something broad, rolling, Mahlerian ('Tambourg'sell' and 'Revelge' both come to mind, and the chilling drum rolls in this orchestration help). He maintains the contrast between the two voices with splendid success even in the most agitated passages, and the magnificent power of the voice makes the climax unforgettable. (I have not heard Owen Brannigan's version or Malcolm McEachern's.) This song should have been perfect for Lawrence Tibbett, but his 'off-the-air' version (Voce 107) fails to catch fire.

The Warren is on LM 147, a rare 10-inch LP of Kipling songs that also includes Frank Tours' 'Mother O' Mine', of which Emilio de Gogorza (V 1107), John McCormack (DA 314), Richard Crooks (DA 1528) and more recently the McCormack revivalist Robert White (ARL1–1968) have also made endearing records. But here again, as so often in these early records, we are on the fine line between 'art' and 'popular' songs in those days; indeed most of these singers probably never drew it. One other composer who was distinctly 'art', and not terribly popular on records until after his premature death, was Charles Tomlinson Griffes (1884–1920). His European style was an easy target when reformers began to call for a truly American music, but an individual voice of refinement and distinction has been increasingly heard in him in recent years.

Griffes wrote over 60 songs, about half of them in English. There are

Will Crutchfield

two worthwhile anthologies on record: New World NW 273 with Sherrill Milnes, Olivia Stapp and Phyllis Bryn-Julson, and Musical Heritage Society 824678M (43 songs done by the four winners of the 1980 Naumburg competition: Faith Esham, Irene Gubrud, Jan Opalach and Lucy Shelton). Griffes' apprenticeship was in Berlin, and many of the best songs are German. One of these, a Brahmsian setting of 'Auf geheimes Waldespfade', turns up fairly early on records in a version by Elizabeth Rethberg that ought to be ideal but has not come my way. Young Eleanor Steber (Victor 10–1071, NW 247, in English) sings it with a Rethberg-like purity of tone and cleanness of attack, and a most delicate kind of lingering. Rather than swelling out in the obvious way at the peak of the first verse ('Dearest, there to dream of thee!'), she sustains the quiet mood, and the voice has a specific tone of sadness for the end of the second. A few notes are less than perfectly poised, but that is because a high standard has been set; Irene Gubrud (MHS), Sherrill Milnes (NW) and Yolanda Marculescu (Orion), all in German, do not match it, and, though each has merit, all three make something a little less special out of the piece. When Milnes lets his voice out we remember the magnificent quality it had at its best, and Marculescu is expressive, but they walk rather briskly down the 'lonely forest pathway'. (I cannot help mentioning the utterly delicious 'Berceau de Gertrude Stein', by Virgil Thomson, that precedes this song on Marculescu's record.) Darwin and Hanks (in English) offer, respectively, a reliable *legato* rendition and an energetic, frankly operatic but somewhat strained one. 'An old song resung', meanwhile, is good fodder for the Manly American Baritone. Leonard Warren took it with him to Russia (LM 2266), singing with a balladeer's relish for the sapphires and the gold and a very well balanced *pianissimo* – not easy here! – for the second verse. The sinking of the ship loses something from Warren's inability to attack sharply, and the big standard Mephisto laugh as she goes down is disappointing (though it must have provided a point of contact for Chaliapin's compatriots in the audience), but the face changes abruptly to seriousness for the chilly observation at the end ('the broken glass was clinking as she sank among the wrecks'). Opalach (MHS) seems laboured in his attempt on the hearty style; William Parker's version (NW 305) is more strongly sung, and Stenberg (Educo) makes the song work with a relish that seems to elude the (perhaps) more self-conscious young singers. Hanks throws himself into it even more luridly, with some shouting and a tone of black humour at the end.

Another oft-recorded Griffes song is 'The Lament of Ian the Proud', in whose harmonies and excitability one senses the kinship to Debussy that is so notable in Griffes' orchestral works. Indeed he orchestrated the 'Lament', but that is not the version Ezio Pinza used when he sang it on the radio with orchestra in 1944. Voce 108, a collection of Pinza broadcasts, shows a voice still wonderfully firm and beautiful, and a general expressivity rather than a specific enquiry into the sometimes obscure text of William Sharp/Fiona MacLeod. The composer's orchestration is heard with Bryn-Julson (NW) and it has a sweep to it, but Seiji Ozawa luxuriates; the song rambles and the vocal part seems shapeless (the big *accelerando* is completely ignored). Hanks, with piano, has a sense of how to portray a soul 'weary and blind' yet keep energy in the line, but his voice will not take the stress of the high-lying climaxes. Esham (MHS) sounds unfortunately tremulous and stressful in this; not the right thing for her vocal character. Elizabeth and Robert Suderburg, in their 'American Sampler' (University of Washington Press), immediately bring out sharper rhythms, stabbing accents and a more flexible pulse, but the vocalism is insecure. Dale Moore's record – like Pinza's somewhat general in its merit, but naturally more idiomatic – is probably the best realisation of the piece.

There are a few other figures it would be wrong to pass over before moving on to the post-war composers. Mrs Beach, all sentimental effusion but considerable in the musical wherewithal that backs it up; Ethelbert Nevin, whose oft-recorded 'Mighty Lak' a Rose' draws from the dim wax a rare glimpse of Nordica's personality (it recalls, but faintly, the Patti of 'Comin' thro' the rye' and the like); Ives' teacher Horatio Parker (a beautiful pair by Gogorza and Mrs de Gogorza (Emma Eames) is on NW 247); Edward MacDowell, and still more. We might close, as singers did their recitals, with 'When I have sung my songs' by Ernest Charles; its rolling lines, sentimental tone, obvious (but satisfying) climax just don't fit the current American understanding of the song recital. But it was a favourite for good reason. Bidu Sayão, John McCormack and Jeannette MacDonald recorded it expressively, Ponselle and Flagstad with great richness (comparison of Flagstad's 78 with her LP version shows how comfortable she eventually grew in English, and how smooth her phrasing became in consequence), but the best of all, probably, is Eileen Farrell on a little-remembered recital (33CX 1553) of songs and ballads with George Trovillo accompanying. In both beauty and amplitude of tone she bears comparison with either Ponselle or Flagstad, and she has a naturalness of expression all her own.

On the whole, though, it is not entirely with regret that one leaves this era of American song recordings. One sometimes reflects that Ives could have benefited from some of these singers – but more often that they could have benefited from some of his music. But even as Ives was laying down his still-unnoticed pen, a more promising school of American songwriters was finding its bearings – largely in Paris, where from the 1920s to the

1950s composers like Aaron Copland, Virgil Thomson, Samuel Barber, Ned Rorem and others went, either to study with Nadia Boulanger or simply to evade the weight of German influence at home.

Copland has not been a prolific songwriter, though his folksong arrangements have become a recital staple (Peter Pears, William Warfield, Marilyn Horne, William Parker, Shirley Verrett and others have recorded them enjoyably). There are two versions of the 1950 *Twelve Poems of Emily Dickinson* with the composer at the piano, Adele Addison brighter and more youthful-sounding on CBS 61993 than Martha Lipton on Amer. Col. ML 5106, but neither capturing any more than Copland himself did the anxious, complicated side of Dickinson. (Frederica von Stade included 'Why do they shut me out of heaven' in her live recital on CBS 37231); there are two excerpts each on Hanks' first LP and on Nancy Tatum's American collection with Geoffrey Parsons on Decca SXL 6336, which finds the soprano's big voice insufficiently flexible or secure to give much pleasure in the repertory chosen. A fairly extensive search has failed to turn up any copy of Robert Tear's or Sandra Browne's British recordings of the Dickinson songs on this side of the Atlantic.

In some of Samuel Barber's songs one hardly seems to have left the world of Ernest Charles after all, for Barber grew up on that kind of music and remained faithful to Romantic harmony. But if his stance was always conservative, his perceptions were subtler and more complicated, his compositional craft more refined, than the earlier American songwriters. Ned Rorem is different: American in poetic affinities and outlook but almost wholly French in musical descent. His best songs have a lucid immediacy that makes them stick, and there is a bittersweet strain of Poulenc in some of them that evokes the model without seeming merely imitative. The two are paired in most American singers' minds as our best song composers of recent memory, and also on a New World release (NW 229) where Philip Ramey, in clever and illuminating sleeve-note interviews, elicits from each composer words of condescension about the other's songs.

This is a most recommendable sampler drawn from three sources: Victor 78s on which Barber sings his own *Dover Beach* with the Curtis String Quartet rather better than Fischer-Dieskau sang it later with the Juilliard; an unpublished Columbia tape of Pierre Bernac and Francis Poulenc in Barber's 'Mélodies passagères' (Barber might have sung those better too, but it is good to have them as they are); and a Columbia LP of Rorem's songs accompanied by himself, disappointing only in that this reissue of half of it means likely consignment of the rest (last seen on Odyssey 32 16 0274) to oblivion. Donald Gramm, Regina Sarfaty, Phyllis Curtin, Charles Bressler and Gianna d'Angelo are the singers. I would have chosen the songs differently, but the most popular one ('Early In the

Morning', an example of the Poulenc flavour) is there in a warm, round voicing by Gramm. Some strong pieces left behind on the Odyssey disc are 'O you to whom I often and silently come', an elusive, succinct Whitman *frisson* of a few seconds' length; 'The Lordly Hudson', Rorem's first published song, the only one Barber admitted liking, a fine flowing apostrophe; and 'Visits to St. Elizabeth's', a harsh, mechanical *moto perpetuo* whose text is Elizabeth Bishop's response after visiting Ezra Pound in his psychiatric confinement.

This last is one of the surprisingly few Rorem songs to have been recorded thrice. Sarfaty sings it with biting accents. Neither she nor Rorem the pianist seems responsive to the passages that turn lyrical (without ever breaking the motion); one imagines Rorem the composer to have written them as a kind of salve, an access of compassion amidst the harsh repetitive sing-song of observation). Mildred Miller on the valuable Desto American anthology (the one with Gramm's 'General William Booth') gives a softer interpretation but still does not particularly reflect the shift of musical feeling. Rosalind Rees, in a recent Rorem recital (GSS 104, again with the composer accompanying) gives a performance still harder, faster and more relentless; 'Bedlam' is practically yelled each time.

The other two songs I know in multiple versions are the 'Christmas Carol', a fluent strophic song with varied accompaniment and coda, done best by Rees but pleasantly and fleetly by Bressler (Hanks is vocally unkempt in this though musically attractive), and 'What sparks and wiry cries', a poem by Paul Goodman, best in the uncompromising strength of Phyllis Curtin's recording on CRI 238. The words are wonderfully American in utterance, and she makes her voice hard and wiry to match the text. Rorem played the song much slower and more deliberately than for Rees, who catches a folk-like lyricism; Hanks is overtaxed by the high notes.

Barber has also been recorded less often than one would expect from the prominence he has or used to have, on American song recitals. Leontyne Price has performed many of his songs expressively and with incomparable tone, but has not recorded any since the fresh, vibrant set of the Hermit Songs with the composer in 1954. Even though she has retired from opera, it is not unreasonable to hope that she might put the cycle, *Despite and Still*, which he wrote for her and still awaits any recording, on disc. Three early groups of song have proved attractive to a number of artists. From Opus 2, 'The Daisies' is a sweet little lyric that wants recording by a fresh-voiced lyric soprano; Moore has to work for lightness. Ludmila Ivanova, on a rare ten-inch Melodiya (D 12261/2), offers the intriguing opportunity of hearing it in Russian, expressed (not ineffectively) as though it were by Rachmaninov.

She also does the whole trio of Opus 10 songs ('Rain has fallen', 'Sleep now', 'I hear an Army'), which have been recorded often but not yet persuasively, and one is gradually aware of the limitations of her rather hard tone. Moore sings all three with reasonable conviction; Joan Patenaude (who debatably includes Barber in 'Songs of the Great Opera Composers', MHS 3770) is vocally not quite up to their demands; Glenda Maurice is in good control but brings little character to two of the songs on her Etcetera recital (ETC 1002), and Fischer-Dieskau, though commanding and vigorous, was tempted into shouting in 'I hear an Army', from a live concert with the Chamber Music Society of Lincoln Center, issued by Musicmasters. Marilyn Cotlow, the first singer of Menotti's *The Telephone*, recorded 'Sleep now' on 78s (Victor 10–1467), not very lyrically; one starts to criticise her accompanist for inattention to some expressive markings in the postlude, and then notices that they were not in the song's first edition. Stenberg and Hanks, on records already mentioned, also sample this group of songs, and the same interpreters line up in a number of recordings from Opus 13, but the character of the performances does not insist on staying in the memory in most cases. One of the exceptions is Fischer-Dieskau's vital 'Nocturne', another Maurice chattering vividly in 'Secrets of the Old'. Maurice and Fischer-Dieskau should also be mentioned for three songs on (translated) foreign texts, Opus 45; they were written for the baritone, who gives hammy Deutsch humour to 'A green lowland of pianos' but is eloquent in parts of 'O boundless, boundless evening'.

But these songs still await the recordings they should have, as do all but a few of the better songs of Theodor Chanler, Richard Hundley (some nice work by von Stade on CBS 37231), Paul Bowles, John Duke and the others a music critic hears making the sounds of vocal recitals in New York.

The American avant-garde, meanwhile, has been little interested in the piano-accompanied song (Elliott Carter's mature vocal works have ensemble accompaniment, as do all but one – a memorable Whitman cycle recorded by DeGaetani on Bridge BDG 2002 – of George Crumb's haunting death meditations for voice; Berio has written excitingly for the voice of the late Cathy Berberian, but not art songs). John Cage does have a thrice-recorded piece that just qualifies for inclusion, 'Wonderful Widow of Eighteen Springs', in which the singer intones the text (adapted from 'Finnegan's Wake') on three notes (B, E, A in the score, but any transposition is allowed for the sake of production 'without vibrato, as in folk-singing' in a 'low and comfortable range') while the outside of the closed piano is tapped, rubbed and beat upon. In the live 1958 performance by Arline Carmen with the composer accompanying (Koby 1499–1504), voice and piano lines are only very approximately coordinated. Berberian and Bruno Canino (Wergo WER 60054) are much more precise; the vocal part is done in an affected croon, straight pop rather than folk style. A *bit* of feeling intrudes on the drone at 'win me woo me wed me', but the most effective of the three is Rosalind Rees (TV 34727) with the guitarist David Starobin at the piano, hushed and intent. The singing is purer, the accompaniment softer, the slide at the end more agonizing. (More Joyce settings are collected on Lyrichord LL 83 by Patricia Neway, the Alceste of the old Giulini recording and first Magda in *The Consul*.)

But 'Wonderful Widow' is not 'song' in the sense that the traditional recitalist understands it; nor, from the opposite end of the spectrum, are the massive soprano and orchestra pieces of David del Tredici and Joseph Schwantner. And if the 'New Romantic' movement is leading American composers and traditional recitalists once more in each other's direction, the gramophone has not yet begun to reflect it.

Encore

JOHN STEANE

Asked to list 'the best things in life', one would probably not come up immediately with 'encore-time at a concert by a great singer' as part of the answer, yet there cannot be many occasions when happiness is so keenly felt and widely shared. Sometimes it is almost a tangible presence: for a moment a stranger arriving in the midst might feel that it would be possible to put out a hand and touch it.

It also shares with the more commonly acknowledged 'best things' the advantage of being free, a kind of bonus, that little bit extra, the bargain brought home from market that makes all the difference. Encore-time has another quality too, a delicious sense of freedom both for the artist and the audience. The singer is free to make a personal choice more or less on the spur of the moment; the audience is free to hope for its favourites, and even (especially if there is an Italian contingent) to call for them. There is a release from the serious musical and literary responsibilities that infused the earlier pleasures of the evening with just a suggestion of hard work. The artists have also earned another kind of freedom; having successfully braved the trial which to some extent every recital is, the singer has won the freedom of the hall, been taken to the audience's heart not so much as a visiting celebrity but now as a personal friend. The audience has become a family, the concert a party.

This is at best. At worst, of course, encore-time can turn civilised audiences into greedy children. Cultivated artists become buskers and occasionally something much less honourable than that. Gramophone records at least spare us these ultimate degenerations, and, even if a special magic of the live occasion may prove elusive, the encore-song still deserves a place in any liberal record collection. I daresay a good many evenings with the great composers have ended most contentedly with the works of a writer of no great name, or perhaps with something by Anon. himself.

Simplest is often best. When Janet Baker sings 'Bushes and briars' unaccompanied (ASD 2828) nothing more is wanted: verses, melody, singing, all are simple and perfect without a word, a note, an inflection too many or out of place. When Kathleen Ferrier sings 'Blow the wind southerly' (Decca F 9300; SPA 172) the singer is so identified with the song that it is difficult to separate the one from the other. Unaccompanied song can also be remarkably international in the immediacy of its appeal. Teresa Berganza opens and closes her recital of old Spanish songs (DG 2530 504) with simple unaccompanied melodies, the first of them, 'Rosa das rosas', from the thirteenth century, particularly haunting in the quiet strength of sincerity and the singer's pure, boylike tone. Hugues Cuénod's recitals of mediaeval and renaissance song include some splendid examples in all three volumes, Italian, French and German. The German album for instance (CLP 1847) has a song called 'Kettenton' depicting Death as a decent fellow who does an honest job of work and enjoys his food and drink. The French troubadour songs (Westminster XWN 18683) end with the anonymous 'Lai des amants' charmingly done with graceful use of the head voice which Cuénod carried so wonderfully into his old age (his unaccompanied singing of a song by Machaut at the Wigmore Hall when he was well over eighty remains among the memories of a lifetime).

Accompanied, a folk song often loses something of its true nature and yet can still have a magical effect. In his recording of 'The Siberian Prisoner's Song' (DB 21383; RLS 735) Boris Christoff sings with a simple piano accompaniment, giving a deeply impressive performance with an involvement and technical command very akin to Chaliapin's in 'Night' on DB 2145. At the other end of the vocal spectrum, the clear pure soprano tone of Alma Gluck floats gently and bewitchingly in two folk songs of Little Russia (DA 240; Club 99–30). Many singers have made a special place in their repertoire for the folk songs of their own country. The Czech soprano Jarmila Novotna's *Songfs of Lidice* for example are affectionately sung to strong piano accompaniment by Jan Masaryk, the President (DB 6157; GEMM 261/2). They include 'Dobru noc' ('Good-night'), one of the national songs which the great Emmy Destinn taught her Algerian lover Dinh Gilly and recorded with him (Victor 88498), fascinating voices both of them. For Elisabeth Schwarzkopf the Swiss song ''s Schätzli' made an irresistible end-of-recital piece, recorded originally as one of a group inherited no doubt from her famous teacher Maria Ivogün. We can hear Ivogün's more delicate voice in a recording from 1932, some short time after the great days of her career but still most appealing in its artless style and girlish tone (DA 4402; 7ER 5116). Schwarzkopf's later version (SAX 2265) shows a complete mastery of resources: variety, communication, inner happiness and laughter, the

John Steane

voice itself in radiant condition. Throughout the middle years of her career, that song was Schwarzkopf's just as the song of the smiling carnation seller ('Clavelitos') belonged to Victoria de los Angeles.

Whenever a classically trained singer turns to folk song, inevitably the smooth, cultivated purity of line, richness of tone and stylistic polish remove it from the cottages and the cornfields. It is so to some extent with de los Angeles herself, who has done as much as any other great concert artist for her native Spanish music. Many folk song recordings by her are still of the utmost beauty even so. The Sephardic 'Una hija tiene el rey' (ASD 452), the gentle melancholy of 'Ay luna que reluces' (SLS 5233) or the hauntingly simple, guitar-accompanied 'El rossignol' (DA 1970; ASD 3085) are all enchanting examples. For French song there is that splendid artist, highly individual in tone and style, Vanni-Marcoux (examples are Breton and Bearnaise songs, DA 4812 and K 6991 on Club 99–101). For Dutch, one cannot do better than with Elly Ameling, whose saucy variant of the 'Vergebliches Ständchen' is included in a recital record, CBS 76738 (called 'Mother', it tells of the wooer applying to be let in and actually admitted by mother herself on guarantee of so many thousand guilders in the bank). Scotland, its glens and lochs brought indoors to the accompaniment of a grand piano, is pleasantly evoked by Joseph Hislop in the 'Herding Song' (DA 444 or DA 789; RS 308) or by Isobel Baillie in 'Ca' the yowes to the knawes' (Col. DB 2076). For the livelier type of Scottish song there is 'Whistle and I'll come to you', with a choice between Baillie again (Col. DB 2111; RLS 7703) and the equally accomplished Evelyn Scotney (E 450). The great madames of old tended to favour Scottish airs in their programmes, and 'Twas within a mile of Edinburgh Town' has the sexagenarian Adelina Patti telling the tale with all the animation and much of the freshness of a young girl (03064; RLS 711). English folk songs interested them less, though the story of 'Pretty Polly Oliver' has rarely been told with more vividness and variety than by the great Polish soprano Marcella Sembrich in a late recording of 1919, for many years unissued (matrix Vic B 22800–1; IRCC L 7037). Certainly the man and maid in 'Oh no, John' have never exchanged question and answer more eloquently than they did in 1932 through Conchita Supervía (RO 20193; Rococo 5230).

As to Italy, the folk song proper seems to have merged with or perhaps been submerged by those broad-phrased, open-throated songs about Naples and Sorrento. Voices other than the tenor tend to feel themselves as intruders here, and in the old days the record catalogues were full to the brim with Italian tenors 'in Neapolitan' and evidently in their element too. Some are open and simple as the day is sunny. 'Santa Lucia' as sung by Caruso (DB 142; ORL 314) has a fine, manly dignity, the last verse broadening out with almost the majesty of a national anthem. 'O sole mio' as sung by Fernando De Lucia (2–62701; RS 305, and Fono. 92701) is a song of almost aristocratic elegance. When 'Torna a Surriento' is sung by Giovanni Martinelli (DA 740; LV 230) it has the tragic concentration of an operatic aria; then as led slowly and sadly, phrase by phrase, to its full-voiced climax by the mighty Ruffo, it assumes a character that is almost epic (DA 353; CO 323). There are also the jolly ones. An absurd piece of rumtitum called 'Tarantella sincera', marked on some of the old labels 'tenor/humorous', has Caruso at his most genially expansive (DB 141; EC 70001/8). Beniamino Gigli radiates *bonhomie* in the raucous 'Quanno a femmena vo' (DA 763; GEMM 151), and the lyrical grace of Tito Schipa takes to the streets and crowded cafés in 'Marechiare' (DA 1114; SC 847) and 'Chi se nne scorda occhiù' (DA 1054; GEMM 219). Sometimes the tunes are so broad, with so much of the old-time music hall in them, that they can scarcely be taken seriously at all – but then, they never asked to be. 'Stretti, stretti, nel'estasi d'amour', the words of the banal refrain used to plague the sensibilities of Aldous Huxley, who would quote them when he wished to typify Italian crudity in musical taste. It is difficult to be severe, however, when 'La Spagnola' (for so the song is called) is performed with the polished manner of Renato Zanelli (7–52145) or for that matter with the incorrigible chirpiness of Gigli (DA 1711; BLP 1099).

These things do have composers. If, as well as exhibiting the normal melodic flair, a song also carries a suggestion of developed musical form, then it is quite likely to be by Tosti. 'A vucchella', 'Luna d'estate' and 'L'ultima canzone', three of his best-known songs, can boast a distinctly graceful coda: Rosa Ponselle in the first two (DA 1035; CDN 1006–7), Ezio Pinza in the third (DA 908; LV 146) are rich and rare in quality. The once celebrated 'Goodbye' has a somewhat dowdy, droopy melody until it lets fly in the final phrases: magnificently dark baritonal Caruso is best here (DB 131; ORL 307). For the finer qualities of a Tosti song there is one called 'Non t'amo più', sung by Luciano Pavarotti with restrained passion and flawlessly sustained lyricism (Decca SXL 6650), or by Aureliano Pertile with overwhelming commitment (DA 1008). Not to be missed either (how hard it is to let these things go by as one starts to recall them) are Tito Gobbi's saddened tones and Gerald Moore's *cantabile* in the accompaniment of 'Malia' (RLS 738), an unusually tender Luisa Tetrazzini (DB 538; GEMM 220–7) and a characteristically subtle De Lucia (Phonotype C 2435) in 'Aprile'. Mattia Battistini is at his unmatchable best in a group of these, including 'Ancora' and 'Ideale', all collected in the great EMI Battistini edition (EX 29 0790 3). Broader and more impetuous, 'L'alba separa' might have been written to celebrate the glories of the tenor voice and bring the house down at the end of a recital. Jussi Björling at the Carnegie Hall in 1955 ('live' on SER 5706) or in an earlier studio recording (DA 1931; HLM 7038) sings superbly, as with considerable refinement in the quieter phrases does Pavarotti (SXL 7013). Carreras in a recital of Tosti's song (Philips 9500 743) takes it slowly, opens out at the phrase 'il sole eterno' and produces quite a thrilling climax. Caruso's old record (DA 121; GV 504), less expansive in tempo, broadens from illimitable resources of sheer voice, and is still supreme.

With the greater composers we are not now concerned. We will admit Leoncavallo though, composer of the famous 'Mattinata'. Well sung by Pavarotti (SXL 7013), it gives its name to the whole recital, complete with symphony orchestra, in an expensive-sounding arrangement with all the technical sophistications of stereophony and so forth at its service. Somehow, all too much. Sentimentally, perhaps, there is an extra charm and authentic period flavour in Pertile (DA 1008) coming through a crackle of 1928 shellac, barnstorming the climax but working towards it from a *pianissimo* at which one holds the breath, a real piece of encore magic. Further back still, Caruso, for whom the song was written, lyrical and free-throated in 1904, shows his infallible instinct for *rubato*, and is fortified by an almighty thump from the enthusiastic composer, who accompanies on the piano (DA 546; GV 504). Mascagni too was responsible for a few of these songs: 'Stornelli marini', thrillingly sung by Gigli (DA 1052; GEMM 205), fills a couple of joyful minutes, and the 'Serenata' as sung by Gobbi (HLM 7018), Martinelli (DB 337; LV 271), or Bergonzi (CBS 73747) remains in the mind long after more musically interesting songs have gone.

With few such exceptions, the high masters of the genre have names not to be found in the average dictionary of music and musicians: names such as De Curtis, Barthèlemy, Bixio and Buzzi-Peccia. Bixio wrote the music for Schipa's film of the late thirties, *Vivere*, the callow theme-song of which (recorded on DA 1558; QLP 8125) will never sound quite the same again to anyone who remembers its bitterly ironical role in another film, *The Garden of the Finzi-Contini*. More likeable is De Curtis' theme-song 'Non ti scordar di me' written for Gigli and sung by him with honeyed voice and ingenuous pathos on DA 1458; GVC 500; more recently it has become Bergonzi's favourite final encore, when many a *furtiva lagrima* moistens the eye (recorded on CBS 73747). Then there is Luigi Denza: 'Occhi di fata' we remember him by, a song for baritones like Battistini, Riccardo Stracciari (a joyous collection of such songs on his early electrics transferred to LP on Club 99–29) and Gobbi (DA 1887; HLM 7018). Occasionally one comes upon something that sounds genuinely like a folk song: 'Canta a timuni' as sung by the young Giuseppe Di Stefano (DA 1877; RLS 756) is an example. Occasionally, too, a new one appears in a recording by a modern singer, as, for instance, Nicolai Gedda sounding sunnily Italianate in a delightful piece called 'Stornelli capricciosi' (SLS

5250). Such songs are the best consolation for a missed Italian holiday; though the consolation may not be without sadness either, for the Italy which these songs were part of is so largely a thing of the past.

This is probably almost as true of Spain. Certainly the proud waxed-moustache and hats-off-to-a-lady style of Emilio de Gogorza has no modern counterpart. Of his several records of 'La paloma' the last (DA 782) is probably the best and remains a model of suave strength and virile grace. His duets with Schipa (DA 976) are charmers too, relics of the old musical evening at home when duettists would sing in thirds, the process being known as 'singing seconds'. Gone also, like the grand style of film stars of old, is the flashing charm and rattlesnake voluptuousness of Conchita Supervía – though of course there was much more to her art than anything of that sort. 'Hay en mi jardín' (HLM 7039) is a multi-coloured enchantment, and a song called 'Lo frare' (Odéon 185005; SHB 72) presents a marvellously vivid picturebook encounter of great big robber–friar and timid little peasant, overshadowed by the still more formidable personage of the victim's wife. Vivid also are 'Cançó de l'amor que passa' and 'Pajarico triguero' (Odéon 185012 and 185018, both on GV 591); but what a difference it makes to the enjoyment when the words or at least summaries of them are available, as in such LP collections they really should be. The zarzuelas provide a rich store of encore songs, such as those on LP by Plácido Domingo (SXL 6988), José Carreras (Philips 9500 649) and Montserrat Caballé (SXL 6792). The tenor idol of the 1920s, Miguel Fleta, recorded some excerpts that show well what a spellbinder he could be; for a single song, with the spinning out of half-voice, the fascinating reserves of power and dark richness of tone backed by a variety of quaint orchestral devices, 'Nostalgia andaluza' might be recommended (DB 1025). With so many of these singers one song will lead to another, at it seems was habitual in encore-time at concerts by the adored Lucrezia Bori. Her unmistakable tone should be sampled first in pre-electric recordings, such as the 'Malagueña' (DA 131); then, if under the spell of this strangely childlike yet patrician singer, it is worth risking a silly catchy tune with spinning *moto perpetuo* accompaniment called 'Seguedille' (DA 1039; Rococo R 32), though hardly sounding like one.

The French and Germans probably do well to take their encores from composers represented in the main body of the programme. Wolf's 'Elfenlied' or 'Er ist's' are miniatures apt for the purpose; or something big and bosomy like Strauss' 'Zueignung' is often welcomed. Otherwise there is what might be called the Tauberlied: 'Wien, du Stadt meiner Träume' is the archetype (Tauber sings it in German on Odéon O 8341; RLS 7700, and in his special kind of English on RO 20467; SLS 5065). There are also songs about the Prater, Grinzing and so forth, sung with verve and enthusiasm by Lotte Lehmann (Odyssey 32 16 0179). Erich

271

John Steane

Kunz's rather creepy Viennese songs with Schrammel orchestra, such as 'Mei Mutter war a Wienerin' (LB 90) will suit some tastes; his student songs, such as 'Doktor Eisenbart' (USD 731) probably have a more wholesale appeal. Julius Patzak's disc of Heurigen songs recently reissued (Decca 414 178–1) is full of that Viennese tenor's plaintive charm.

Ernestine Schumann-Heink's benign yodelling in 'I und mei Bua' banishes inhibitions of certain kinds (Victor 88139; Rococo R 11), and she also recorded one of the most charming of French encore songs, Delibes' 'Bonjour, Suzon', but sings it in English (Victor 87168; Rococo R 27). The tragic Claudia Muzio produces the most winning of smiles in that song (Pathé 67347 in English, or Columbia BQ 6000 on EX 29 0163 3 in French), as did Supervia, delicious as ever, adding Delibes' 'Eglogue' as a companion piece (RO 20180; GV 580). Sentimental French songs of the pink-postcard type figured in the repertoire of Vanni-Marcoux, who was particularly fond of those by Paul Delmet (Club 99–104). Other examples, and not without grace and humanity, would be old Lucien Fugère singing 'Les vieilles de chez nous' (D 13043; Club 99–2) or the admirable Robert Couzinou in 'Le temps des cerises' (Club 99–76), or Paul Reimers, light of touch, right of tone, in 'Le coeur de ma vie' (45063). Edmond Clément sings 'Chanson lorraine' and others with immaculate French elegance (64223; TQD 3049), and Emma Calvé uses her so-called 'quatrième voix' to astonishing effect in 'Ma Lisette' (033054; RLS 7705). 'Au clair de la lune' always recalls to the collector's mind Yvonne Printemps with harpsichord, unusual in those days (DB 1625; 2C 051–12092). She is also to be heard in some of the songs written for her, such as Poulenc's 'Les chemins de l'amour' (DA 4927; FDLP 1088), in which the more recent version by Jessye Norman (Philips 9500 356) is like whipped cream to Printemps' white wine. For all such songs it is worth looking out Yolanda Marculescu, idiomatic and stylish in Satie's 'Je te veux' and 'La Diva de l'Empire' (Orion ORS 76240).

The English 'ballad' as it was commonly called has partly returned to favour with joint recitals by Robert Tear and Benjamin Luxon (EMD 5528) or solos by Robert White, who specialises in the McCormack repertoire and sings beautifully on, for instance, RCA RL 13442. Here he opens with 'The Old House', which McCormack sang at the end of his London Farewell in 1938, recording it with restrained but infectious emotion a few years later (EX 29 00073). The swelling heart that just withstands the stress of farewells beats in McCormack's 'Terence's Farewell to Kathleen' (DA 1396; EX 29 00073) and in the later version of 'Kathleen Mavourneen' (DB 1200). Melba tried her hand at the Irish song, and to exquisite effect, in 'Come back to Erin' (3616; RLS 719). Maggie Teyte brought a similarly clean vocal method and a more communicative style to 'Oft in the stilly night' (DA 1804; RLS 716), a heart-felt piece of singing and one of the best of her records. From the inter-war years songs like Eric Coates' 'I heard you singing' become newly attract-ive with the lapse of time (Hislop, DA 818; RS 308); and his 'Bird Songs at Eventide' has been known to impress persons of superior taste and unsuspecting gullibility when introduced as 'Les oiseaux dans le soir' and sung with much skill by Thill (LF 110; 2C 061–12079). We can then go back to the old days of ballad concerts by robust baritones such as Peter Dawson ('The Bandolero', C 1659) or 'real' basses such as Norman Allin and the now almost forgotten Harry Dearth (dramatic as a Chaliapin in 'The Lowlands Low', D 213). Clara Butt, not a full-time exponent of 'Land of Hope and Glory', trills and treads the gossamer in Herbert Brewer's 'Fairy Pipers' (X 300; GEMM 168); and from way back in the Victorian age itself Charles Santley survives to tell with unsurpassed vividness the tales of Simon the Cellarer and the Vicar of Bray (E 82; RLS 7705).

There are American counterparts. Stephen Foster was a favourite with the tenor Richard Crooks, and 'Old Folks at Home' was a speciality not only of Melba (3619; RLS 719) but also of Calvé, who would use it to make the cowboys weep (03092; Rococo 10). She enjoyed 'Dixie' too (Pathé 3196; GV 57), as did the unsmiling, matriarchal and magnificent Emma Eames (85061; Rococo 29). In recent times Frederica von Stade has caught the right flavour, if with just a pinch too much of icing sugar, in 'Jenny Rebecca' (CBS 76728), while Shirley Verrett's 'He's going away' has strong feeling without sentimentality (RCA SB 6750). In the same programme (part of a concert recorded 'live' at the Carnegie Hall) she also goes boldly into Copland's 'At the River', as with sumptuous richness did Marilyn Horne in her recital at La Scala, Milan (CBS 74105), adding ('per dire arrivederci') 'Jeannie with the Light Brown Hair'. Spirituals, when sung by the great, tend to be sophisticated in one way or another. Paul Robeson, still phenomenal in quality of voice, was heavily committed to Lawrence Brown's arrangements, which was perhaps a pity, but Marian Anderson comes close to the real thing in the deep, free-throated tone of 'Tramping' (DA 1669), as does Roland Hayes with the syncopations of 'Plenty good room' (DX 1132). A different treatment of spirituals, musically much more sophisticated, and perhaps too ready for the night-club, comes from Barbara Hendricks with the brilliant Russian pianist Dmitri Alexeev (ASD 173 1681). She also sings a collection of songs by Gershwin, again with musically sophisticated accompaniment this time by the Labeque sisters and so inventive that it constitutes a takeover bid as far as the composer's work is concerned (Philips 9500 987). Gershwin, Cole Porter and Irving Berlin being now 'classics', their songs appear ever more naturally at encore time. Sarah Walker, 'live' at Dartington Hall

(Meridian E 77056), clearly enjoys such things; but it is Elly Ameling, in a record called *After Hours* (Philips 6514 284), who accomplishes the most remarkable transformation, both on the songs and on herself. Gershwin's 'Someone to watch over me' and Vernon Duke's 'Autumn in New York' are comfortable, civilised and refreshing as an early evening cocktail at the Algonquin.

Other voices, other encores. To the Russian (or Bulgarian) bass belong songs with balalaikas, such as accompany Nicolai Ghiaurov recorded in his prime (SXL 6659) and Boris Christoff a little beyond his (DG 2536 115). Chaliapin had a chorus of Russian emigrés in Paris to make merry with in some of his last recording sessions, and again happiness is almost tangible (DA 1371). Then there are the coloratura sopranos with their songs about birds, preferably with flute *obbligato*. In our time it was Joan Sutherland who revived these, such as 'The Gypsy and the Bird' and 'Parla' (SET 247–8), songs which in the 1920s were beguilingly if less dazzlingly recorded by Amelita Galli-Curci (DA 928). Airs and variations used to abound; 'Ah, vous dirai-je, maman' is a famous example, eliciting astounding scales and *altissimi* from Frieda Hempel (DB 352; COLH 135) and further wonders from Gabrielle Ritter-Ciampi (Pathé 0382; RLS 743). Benedict's 'Carnival of Venice' seems a little less brainless when the exquisite art of Lotte Schoene is bestowed upon it (Kristall 06502; GV 16), yet on returning to Tetrazzini (DB 689; GEMM 220–7) or Toti dal Monte (DB 821 or DB 1001) one finds sparkle, energy and virtuosity compensating delightfully enough.

Then there is the art of doing what might be termed 'your own thing', either in the form of self-accompaniment or in some instances actual composition. Giuseppe Anselmi, tenor beloved of the ladies, was one who had a little repertoire of his own pieces, collected on records from rare originals on GV 64. Several of the grand ladies took over at the piano: Melba in 'Home, sweet home' and others (03049; RLS 719), Sembrich, a highly proficient pianist, very neatly in Chopin's 'The Maiden's Wish' (Victor 88100; IRCC L 7087). Then, within the memory of most of us, there is Victoria de los Angeles, whose return to the platform with guitar in hand always released the great depths of affection, though a pang of sadness was felt too because everyone knew that when the song she always sang on these occasions, 'Adiós, Granada', was over, it would be time to go home. There are several records of her singing this to her own accompaniment, the one which best captures the essence of encore time coming 'live' from the Festival Hall in London, preceded as on most of those lovely occasions by the song of the carnation seller, 'Clavelitos' (ASD 3656).

Several such recordings exist, taken 'live' from the concert hall and conveying in a miraculous way the feeling of occasion. Some have been mentioned in this chapter, such as Verrett at Carnegie Hall and Horne at La Scala. Others take us back further: to, say, the farewell in New York of the seventy-year old Giuseppe De Luca, enchanting his audience with an absurdity called 'Marietta' sung in his Italian English and with an endearing and quite personal kind of humour. In another late New York concert he was joined by his contemporary, Martinelli, making them laugh and love the occasion with their duet 'I mulattieri' (Celebrity CEL 500). In recordings like these the feeling of the audience rising to meet a loved artist is almost palpable, and as listeners we are momentarily enabled to join in the party, to become members of the family and share the general happiness.

It is strange, perhaps, that at the end of such a journey as is chronicled in two books through the vast realm of recorded song, with all the masterpieces of the great composers behind us, we should find a special place in the affections for such small things as these. But so it is, on records as in the concert hall. Song and singer, after all, are interdependent, and it is often through such songs as these that we best come to appreciate the individuality of the singer. That in turn helps us to catch the special flavour of a singer's art and enriches our understanding of it when we hear it again in the masterpieces of the repertoire. But there is also an intrinsic pleasure which needs no outward references for its justification. It is a pleasure that is better having been worked for. Encore time is right for it, and it is a time, I would say, that has been responsible for much concentrated delight, a delight without which musical life would be distinctly the poorer.

Index of singers' names

Ackté, Aino, 180, 184
Addison, Adele, 262
Alavedra Montserrat, 133
Alda, Frances, 258
Alexander, Roberta, 249, 253, 255
Allen, Thomas, 87, 90, 236, 242
Allin, Norman, 231, 234, 273
Ameling, Elly, 3, 9, 18, 22, 40, 42, 46, 55, 58,
   60–1, 65, 68–9, 72, 78, 82, 84–6, 91, 93,
   95, 98–9, 102–4, 110, 118, 124–5, 174,
   239, 255, 268, 273
Anders, Peter, 164, 166
Anderson, Marian, 181, 273
Angelici, Martha, 63
Anselmi, Giuseppe, 274
Antti, Aune, 183
Arkhipova, Irina, 145, 151, 160, 167, 171,
   175
Armstrong, Sheila, 3, 11
Armstrong, John, 240
Ausensi, Manuel, 142

Bacquier, Gabriel, 13, 40, 48, 65–6, 74, 104,
   109, 126
Badía, Conchita, 134–7
Bailey, Norman, 234, 240, 242
Baillie, Isobel, 175, 230, 232, 257, 268
Bainbridge, Elizabeth, 191, 195
Baker, Dame Janet, 3–4, 6, 10–11, 21–2, 29,
   32, 37, 41, 49–50, 61, 66–7, 69, 71, 73,
   99–100, 104, 106, 110, 115, 219, 228,
   231–5, 237, 240, 244, 266
Baldin, Aldo, 138
Balguerie, Suzanne, 125
Baltsa, Agnes, 3–4, 9, 11
Bampton, Rose, 258
Barber, Samuel, 262
Bardac, Emma, 82
Barrientos, María, 130, 133
Bastin, Jules, 87, 90
Bathori, Jane, 39, 50, 52, 80, 96, 98, 100,

104, 108
Battistini, Mattia, 269, 270
Battle, Kathleen, 68, 231
Bauman, Mordecai, 248–9
Beegle, Raymond, 254
Behrens, Hildegard, 3, 9–10, 235
Benoit, Jean-Christophe, 48, 50–1, 104–8,
   112–13, 115, 117, 126
Berberian, Cathy, 264
Berganza, Teresa, 104, 131, 134–5, 137–8,
   140, 143, 146, 156–7, 267
Bergonzi, Carlo, 270
Bernac, Pierre, 16–17, 20–1, 24, 26–7, 31,
   37, 39, 41–5, 54, 57, 63–4, 69–72, 74, 78,
   82, 89, 100–1, 104–5, 107–9, 112, 117–19,
   120–3, 126, 262
Berton, Liliane, 125
Billot, Étienne, 63
Bispham, David, 259
Björling, Jussi, 175, 182, 269
Blachut, Beno, 191, 194, 196–7
Boatwright, Helen, 250–1, 253, 255
Bogard, Carole, 78
Bonelli, Richard, 259
Borg, Kim, 145, 150–1, 167, 175, 182, 185
Borgioli, Dino, 259
Bori, Lucrezia, 271
Boué, Géori, 18, 33, 47, 50–1, 53–4, 60, 67,
   93, 96
Bourdin, Roger, 41, 51–2, 63, 93, 101
Bouvier, Hélène, 16, 18, 20, 22–3, 25–7, 29,
   31–2, 35–7
Bowles, Paul, 264
Bowman, James, 229
Brannigan, Owen, 259
Bressler, Charles, 211, 214, 262–3
Brohly, Suzanne, 62
Brown, Wilfred, 219–20, 244
Browne, Sandra, 131, 135, 262
Brownlee, John, 259
Bruyère, Jules, 19, 29

277

Index of singers' names

Bryn-Julson, Phyllis, 260–1
Buckman, Rosina, 234
Burrows, Stuart, 3, 11, 70, 78, 257
Butt, Dama Clara, 235, 273

Caballé, Montserrat, 93, 96, 131, 134–8,
    140, 142–3, 271
Calvé, Emma, 40, 49–50, 272–3
Canino, Bruno, 264
Canne-Meijer, Cora, 131, 195
Cantelo, April, 15, 232
Carey, Michael, 86–7
Carlsen, Toril, 188
Carmen, Arline, 264
Carol Case, John, 243
Carreras, José, 138, 143, 270–1
Carringer, Walter, 256
Caruso, Enrico, 165, 268–70
Catley, Gwen, 232
Cebotari, Maria, 171
Cernay, Germaine, 13
Chaliapin, Feodor, 150, 169, 267, 274
Christoff, Boris, 145–6, 148–51, 154–5,
    157–8, 160, 162, 164–5, 170, 172–3,
    176–7, 267, 274
Clement, Willy,. 19, 67, 74, 78, 272
Coates, John, 229, 234–5
Command, Michèle, 91, 96–7, 99
Consort of Musicke, 230–3
Cotlow, Marilyn, 264
Couzinou, Robert, 272
Crabbé, Armand, 58–9
Credi, Nadine, 99
Crespin, Régine, 3–4,. 7, 18, 23, 26, 29, 32,
    36, 57, 59, 65, 67, 72, 74, 99, 104, 108,
    111, 126
Croiza, Claire, 16–17, 24, 35, 55–6, 58,
    71–4, 86, 96–7, 119
Crooks, Richard, 177, 259, 273
Cross, Joan, 244
Cuénod, Hugues, 42, 68–9, 78, 80–1, 91, 93,
    96, 102, 267
Culp, Julia, 258
Curry, Corinne, 250
Curtin, Phyllis, 84–5, 93, 95–6, 184, 262–3

dal Monte, Toti, 274
Dalton, Andrew, 230
D'Alvarez, Marguerite, 258
Danco, Suzanne, 3–4, 7, 11, 41, 56, 78, 82,
    91, 94–5, 99–101, 104–6, 112–13
d'Angelo, Gianna, 262
Daniel, Susan, 131, 135
Daniels, Lise, 87–8
Darwin, Glenn, 258, 260
Davies, Tudor, 234, 259
Davrath, Natania, 172, 174

Dawson, Anne, 239, 243
Dawson, Peter, 165, 167, 177, 234, 236, 238,
    243, 248, 273
Dearth, Harry, 273
DeGaetani, Jan, 106, 115, 251–5, 264
de Gogorza, Emilio, 259, 271
Deller, Alfred, 227–30
Delman, Jacqueline, 60
de los Angeles, Victoria, 3–4, 8–9, 11, 23–4,
    33, 54, 60, 66, 78, 94, 99, 104–5, 110–12,
    129–34, 136–7, 139–40, 142–3, 162–3,
    268, 274
De Luca, Giuseppe, 275
De Lucia, Fernando, 269
Dens, Michel, 19, 25–6, 34, 38, 40–1, 48
Denza, Luigi, 270
Dercourt, Rose, 125
Derenne, Paul, 55, 78, 81, 87–8
de Reszke, Edouard, 165
Desmond, Astra, 181, 231
Destinn, Emmy, 163, 267
Devries, David, 24
Diakov, Anton, 145, 149, 154
Di Stefano, Giuseppe, 270
Dobbs, Mattiwilda, 44, 65
Dolmetsch, Cecile, 227
Dolukhanova, Zara, 131
Domingo, Placido, 271
Doria, Renée, 55–6, 60, 69, 73, 84–5
Dorliak, Nina, 146, 155–6, 176
Dorow, Dorothy, 98, 187
Dubuis, Madeleine, 94, 98
Duke, John, 264
Dutey, Jacques, 55
Duval, Denise, 125

Eames, Emma, 261, 273
Eastman, Julius, 245
Eddy, Nelson, 66, 158, 257
Ekman, Ida, 180
Elliott, Paul, 229
Elwes, Gervase, 236–7, 239
Endrèze, Arthur, 50, 54, 61, 63
Esham, Faith, 260–1
Evans, Nancy, 216, 241

Falkner, Keith, 231, 241
Farrar, Geraldine, 41
Farrell, Eileen, 66, 96, 99–100, 177, 261
Fellegi, Ádám, 193
Ferrier, Kathleen, 216, 231, 233, 239, 267
Fischer-Dieskau, Dietrich, 16, 41, 78–9, 81,
    83–4, 93, 101, 104–8, 111, 115–16, 121,
    160–2, 165–6, 181, 222–4, 251–4, 262,
    264
Flagstad, Kirsten, 181–4, 186–8, 239, 258,
    261

278

Index of singers' names

Fleta, Miguel, 271
Forrester, Maureen, 232
Forsell, Jan, 189
Friant, Charles, 18–19, 28, 51
Friedmann, Gérard, 75, 77
Frijsh, Povla, 61
Frydlewicz, Miroslav, 191, 196
Fugère, Lucien, 272

Gall, Yvonne, 50
Galland, Danièle, 21
Galli-Curci, Amelita, 232, 274
Garden, Mary, 95–6, 257
Gaudin, André, 61, 78
Gauthier, Eva, 17
Gedda, Nicolai, 58, 75, 77, 93, 118, 124, 138, 165, 170–2, 174–8, 182, 190–1, 194, 196–7, 270
Gehrman, Shura, 87, 89
Ghiaurov, Nicolai, 164–7, 274
Gigli, Beniamino, 269–70
Gilly, Dinh, 267
Gilvan, Raimund, 214, 216–18
Gluck, Alma, 49, 256, 267
Gmyrya, Boris, 160, 164–5, 167
Gobbi, Tito, 269–70
Gomez, Jill, 98, 106, 114, 132, 135, 138, 199–200
Graf, Kathrin, 106, 115
Gramm, Donald, 248, 262–3
Greevy, Bernadette, 3–4, 10, 216
Gregory, Jane, 59
Grey, Madeleine, 105–6, 112, 114, 125
Grieg, Nina, 186
Griffel, Kay, 191, 195
Griffett, James, 234
Gruberova, Edita, 92, 171
Gubrud, Irene, 260
Guillamat, Ginette, 69

Hadour, Yvon le Marc', 89
Häfliger, Ernst, 191, 195, 197
Hagegård, Håkan, 189
Häggander, Mari Anne, 184
Hahn, Reynaldo, 43, 52–4
Haley, Olga, 58
Hallin, Margareta, 207–8
Hamair, Julia, 99
Hammond, Joan, 47, 163
Hanks, John Kennedy, 258, 260–4
Harper, Heather, 104, 110, 200, 203, 207–8
Harrell, Mack, 30, 34
Harsanyi, Janice, 78
Harwood, Elizabeth, 235, 240
Haskin, Howard, 19, 21
Hayes, Roland, 228, 273
Heddle Nash, John, 235, 237, 239

Hempel, Frieda, 274
Henderson, Roy, 167, 233, 241–2
Hendricks, Barbara, 94–5, 97, 273
Herbillon, Jacques, 16, 19–20, 23, 25–7, 29, 31, 33, 35–8, 55, 57, 60, 66, 68–709, 72, 75, 77–8, 81, 85–8, 90
Herzog, Colette, 97, 125
Hill, Martyn, 40, 42, 44, 48, 50–2, 54, 58, 60, 66, 228–9, 232, 237, 241, 243
Hinkle, Florence, 256
Hislop, Joseph, 257, 268
Hodgson, Alfreda, 216, 242
Horne, Marilyn, 99, 131, 262, 273–4
Hunt, Alexandra, 258
Hüsch, Gerhard, 184–5
Huttenlocher, Philippe, 107, 116
Hyde, Walter, 234
Hynninen, Jorms, 182–5

Iriarte, Ana Maria, 131
Irwin, Robert, 234, 236, 242
Isakova, Nina, 160
Ivanov, Andrei, 162, 178
Ivanova, Ludmila, 263
Ivogün, Maria, 232, 267

Jackson, Richard, 104, 109, 127
Jansen, Jacques, 43, 94, 101, 116, 197
Järnefelt, Maikki, 180
Jenkins, Neil, 243
Joachim, Irène, 93, 96, 98
Johnston, David, 204, 206, 239
Jones, Gwyneth, 184
Jones, Parry, 241

Kabaivanska, Raina, 168, 173, 174
Kahn, Percy, 175
Katulskaya, Elena, 176
Keller, Peter, 191, 197
Kenny, Yvonne, 223, 225, 232
Kessler, Susan, 164
Kilpinen, Margaret, 184
Kipnis, Alexander, 172
Kirkby, Emma, 227–30, 232
Kolassi, Irma, 61, 68, 72, 84–5, 87–8, 91, 99–100, 105–6, 111, 115
Koshetz, Nina, 163, 166, 170, 175–8
Kovács, Eszter, 191, 193
Kozlovsky, Ivan, 162, 166, 171, 174, 176–7, 179, 211, 214
Krause, Tom, 181–3
Kruysen, Bernard, 16, 19–21, 23, 25–7, 29–31, 33–8, 60, 66–8, 70–2, 78, 81, 87–8, 90–1, 93, 100–8, 112, 115, 117, 126, 145, 152–3, 197
Kullman, Charles, 257
Kunz, Erich, 271

279

Index of singers' names

Index of singers' names

Palmer, Felicity, 63, 65, 68–9, 78, 82, 104–6, 108, 112, 114–15, 125, 233
Panzéra, Charles, 16, 19–20, 23–8, 30–6, 38–9, 46, 51, 54, 56, 59, 61–3, 67, 70, 72, 75–6, 78–81, 87, 90–90, 100, 102, 132
Parker, William, 118, 124, 251, 255, 257, 260, 262
Partridge, Ian, 18, 28, 34, 36, 58, 84, 66, 75, 77–8, 212, 214, 217–18, 229–30, 235, 237–8, 240–1, 243–4
Pastukhoff, Vsevolod, 154
Patenaude, Joan, 264
Patterson, Frank, 3, 12, 229
Patti, Adelina, 232, 268
Patzak, Julius, 272
Pavarotti, Luciano, 269–70
Pazmor, Radiana, 248
Pears, Peter, 78, 83, 118, 121–2, 199, 201–3, 205–9, 211–15, 217–23, 225–6, 229–31, 235, 238–41, 243–5, 262
Peignot, Suzanne, 119
Perry, Douglas, 254
Pertile, Aureliano, 269–70
Pérugia, Noémie, 86–7, 89
Petina, Irra, 161, 166, 168
Petrov, Ivan, 167
Piccaver, Alfred, 257
Pinza, Ezio, 260–1, 269
Planel, Jean, 35, 51, 53
Plantey, Bernard, 102
Pons, Lily, 59, 91, 93, 95–6, 171, 176, 178, 232
Ponselle, Rosa, 58, 99, 261, 269
Prey, Herman, 181
Přibyl, Vilém, 191, 194, 186–7
Price, Leontyne, 3, 10, 60, 66, 68, 263
Price, Margaret, 18, 20, 32, 102, 135–7, 146, 155–6, 161, 163, 166
Printemps, Yvonne, 272
Prytz, Eva, 188
Puffer, Ted, 250, 253

Radford, Robert, 231
Raphael, Mark, 239
Rautavaara, Aulikki, 181, 189–90
Rautavaara, Eino, 180–1, 189–90
Raveau, Alice, 63–4
Raynet Cook, Brian, 234
Rebroff, Ivan, 145, 149–50, 166
Rees, Rosalind, 254, 263, 265
Rehfuss, Heinz, 145, 149
Reimers, Paul, 272
Reinhart, Gregory, 61, 71, 87–8, 90
Reizen, Mark, 150
Rendall, David, 207, 209
Resnik, Regina, 137, 166, 168
Rethberg, Elizabeth, 260

Rhodes, Jane, 16, 18, 20, 22–3, 25–7, 29–30, 32, 35, 37
Ricciarelli, Katia, 57
Richardson, Marilyn, 136
Ritchie, Margaret, 232
Ritter-Ciampi, Gabrielle, 274
Roberts, Stephen, 237, 244
Robeson, Paul, 242, 257, 273
Rodde, Anne-Marie, 55, 84–6, 92, 94
Rodriguez de Aragón, Lola, 133–4
Rogatchewsky, Joseph, 41–2
Rolfe Johnson, Anthony, 53, 127, 210–11, 217–19, 241, 243
Rosing, Vladimir, 145, 148, 150, 153, 174
Ruffo, Titta, 269
Russell, Anna, 92

Saedén, Erik, 145, 151, 152, 189–90, 253
Santley, Sir Charles, 233–4, 273
Sarfaty, Regina, 262–3
Sari, Ada, 173
Sass, Sylvia, 191, 193
Sauvageot, Maurice, 62, 65
Sayão, Bidu, 18, 47, 98, 261
Schéle, Märta, 219–20
Schenk, Manfred, 154
Schenneberg, Eliette, 49, 53
Schiøtz, Aksel, 188, 228
Schipa, Tito, 269–71
Schoene, Lotte, 274
Schorr, Friedrich, 25
Schreier, Peter, 191, 195, 207, 209–11, 213
Schumann, Elisabeth, 134, 257
Schumann-Heink, Ernestine, 163, 258, 272
Schwarzkopf, Elisabeth, 47, 63, 93, 121, 162–3, 167, 178, 228, 267–8
Sciutti, Graziella, 75, 77
Scotney, Evelyn, 268
Seefried, Irmgard, 146, 156
Seiner, Katinka, 191, 193
Sembrich, Marcella, 47, 268, 274
Sénéchal, Michel, 27, 94, 118, 123–4
Shelton, Lucy, 84, 260
Shirley-Quirk, John, 3, 12, 200–1, 234, 236–7, 241–2
Shpiller, Natalya, 179
Sibille, Madeleine, 78
Simoneau, Leopold, 16, 18, 21, 24–5, 27–8, 30–1, 34–6, 38
Sinatra, Frank, 162
Singher, Martial, 75, 77, 79, 83–4, 87, 90, 102, 107, 116
Skinner, John York, 230
Slobodskaya, Oda, 145–6, 154–5, 163, 166, 168, 173, 176, 178
Smirnov, Dmitri, 175
Soames, René, 240

281

Index of singers' names

Sobinov, Leonid, 166, 169
Söderström, Elisabeth, 146, 156–7, 160–1, 164, 166, 168, 170–4, 176–9, 182–4, 189–90, 201, 203
Soukupová, Věra, 191, 196–7
Souzay, Gérard, 3, 12, 16, 19–20, 23–6, 28–9, 31, 33, 35–6, 38, 41, 44, 46, 49–50, 54–6, 60, 63, 65, 68–72, 74–5, 77–8, 80–2, 85–98, 100–2, 104–9, 111–12, 115–18, 121–3, 132, 163, 165–6, 181, 187
Stahl, Kerstin, 254
Stapp, Olivia, 260
Stappen, Suzanne, 79, 84
St Cricq, Henri, 35
Steber, Eleanor, 3, 6, 10–11, 14, 260
Stenberg, Donald, 258, 260, 264
Štěpánová, 191, 196
Stevens, Risë, 257
Stewart, Thomas, 250–1, 254
Stracciari, Riccardo, 270
Streisand, Barbra, 59
Suddaby, Elsie, 230
Suderburg, Elizabeth, 261
Supervia, Conchita, 130–1, 134, 138, 142, 258, 268, 271–2
Sutherland, Joan, 232, 274
Swarthout, Gladys, 18, 48, 93
Sze, Yi-Kwei, 145, 149, 154

Talvela, Martti, 145, 152, 170–2, 176–7, 185
Tatum, Nancy, 262
Tauber, Richard, 166–7, 239, 257, 271
Tawaststjerna, Erik, 184
Tear, Robert, 15, 160–1, 164–5, 170–1, 178, 191, 195, 204, 206–7, 209–13, 217–18, 220–1, 233–4, 236–8, 240, 243, 262, 272
Te Kanawa, Dame Kiri, 3, 8–9, 18, 21–2, 32, 36–7, 57, 105, 110
Terri, Salli, 158
Tervani, Irma, 180
Tetrazzini, Luisa, 232, 269, 274
Teyte, Dame Maggie, 13, 17–18, 21, 23–4, 27–8, 32–4, 44–9, 52–3, 57, 64, 66, 69, 72, 83, 91, 94, 96–8, 100–1, 105, 207–8, 231, 235, 239, 257, 272
Thallaug, Edith, 186
Thill, Georges, 34, 38, 53, 57, 67, 74–6, 78, 273
Thomas, David, 229, 257
Thursfield, Anne, 66
Tibbett, Lawrence, 167, 259
Tkachenko, Ninel, 172
Touraine, Geneviève, 96, 125
Tourel, Jennie, 13, 18, 37, 48, 63, 75–6, 96, 99, 105, 109, 145, 149–50, 163, 170, 173
Tragin, Lucienne, 95

Traubel, Helen, 163
Trew, Graham, 235, 240–1
Troxell, Barbara, 204, 206
Tuloisela, Matti, 185
Turp, André, 75

Vaguet, Albert, 62
Valjakka, Taru, 183–4
Válka, J., 191, 194–7
Valletti, Cesare, 13, 18, 24, 28, 34, 48, 51, 58, 62, 65, 67, 93, 95–6
Vallin, Ninon, 13–14, 16–19, 21–4, 33–4, 39, 42–4, 47–51, 53–4, 56, 60–2, 67, 70, 72, 74–6, 78, 132
van Dam, José, 105–7, 112, 117
Van Dyck, Ernest, 62
Vanni-Marcoux, 30, 52–3, 64, 268, 272
Varcoe, Stephen, 239, 243
Veasey, Josephine, 3, 12
Verhoeven, Jacques, 60, 63, 66, 69, 75, 77
Verlet, Alice, 40, 42
Verrett, Shirley, 131, 137, 172, 262, 273–4
Vieuille, Jean, 63
Villabella, Miguel, 41, 54, 78
Vinogradov, Georgy, 167
Vishnevskaya, Galina, 59, 145, 152–3, 160–1, 163, 166, 168, 170–1, 174, 178, 222, 224
Vivers, Huguette, 61
von Stade, Frederica, 3–4, 9, 58, 60, 63, 67–9, 71, 91, 95, 99, 105–6, 110–12, 115, 228, 232, 262, 264, 273
Vyvyan, Jennifer, 237

Walker, Sarah, 12, 63, 79, 83–4, 93, 98–101, 203–4, 234–5, 238, 273
Warfield, William, 262
Warren, Leonard, 64, 259–60
Watawaso, Princess, 257
Watkinson, Carolyn, 216–17, 254
Watts, Helen, 216, 231
Weikl, Bernd, 13–14
Wend, Flore, 91, 94–5, 98, 101
Wennberg, Siv, 186
Werrenrath, Reinhold, 259
Westberg Andersen, Ellen, 186
White, Robert, 259, 272
Williams, Evan, 256
Wilson, Steuart, 237
Wilson-Johnson, David, 240
Wirz, Clara, 191, 197
Woolf, Simon, 146, 155–7
Wright, Patricia, 239
Wunderlich, Fritz, 163
Wyss, Sophie, 63, 78, 82, 202, 208

Index of singers' names

Index of accompanists' names

Index of accompanists' names

Giesen, Hubert, 163, 166
Gilbert, Goeffrey (flute), 115
Gothoni, Ralf, 145, 170, 172, 177
Gouat, Simone, 75, 78, 84–7
Greenhouse, Bernard (cello), 171

Haeusslein, Hans Willi, 145, 149
Hahn, Reynaldo, 50, 53–4
Hamburger, Paul, 52, 216
Harty, Hamilton, 40
Holeček, Josef (guitar), 219–20
Holetschek, Franz, 78, 191, 193
Höll, Helmut, 104–5, 107–8, 112, 116

Ibbott, Daphne, 204
Isepp, Martin, 91, 96, 103
Ivaldi, Christian, 16, 25

Jansen, Rudolf, 42
Johnson, Graham, 12, 14, 41–2, 44, 48, 104, 109, 127, 135, 138, 210–11, 217–18, 225, 234, 237

Kalish, Gilbert, 251, 253
Katz, Martin, 132, 143
Kegel, Herbert, 213
Kilpinen, Margaret, 184
Kirkpatrick, John, 250, 253
Kosimies, Pentti, 183
Kozel, Berta, 160, 174
Kozma, Tibor, 204, 206
Kreisler, Fritz (violin), 171, 177
Kubelik, Rafael, 191, 195
Kvapil, Radoslav, 191, 196

Labeque sisters, 273
Labinsky, Alexander, 145–6, 160, 170
Laforge, Jean, 13, 91
Lapšanský, 191
Larrocha, Alicia de, 131, 134–6
Lavilla, Félix, 134
Leanderson, Helene, 191, 193
Ledger, Philip, 160, 165, 170–1, 191, 195, 204, 206, 210–11, 217–18, 233, 238
Lee, Noël, 16, 20, 25, 27, 35–7, 78, 87, 91, 94–5, 98, 100–5, 107–8, 112, 145
Levine, James, 13, 99
Lieurance (Indian flute), 257, 258
Lockhart, James, 102, 146, 161, 163
Long, Kathleen, 78

McArthur, Edwin, 186, 258
Marshall, Frank, 130
Masaryk, Jan, 267
Meedintiano, Ivana, 97
Melba, Nelly, 274
Moore, Gerald, 21, 28, 32, 41, 46–7, 49, 53, 58, 61, 65–6, 78, 83, 91, 94, 97, 99, 131, 143, 149, 163, 167, 171, 174–6, 178, 187, 229, 235, 237, 240, 269

Newton, Ivor, 67, 145–6, 154, 166, 168, 175–6
Norris, David Owen, 240

Oborin, Lev, 179
Opitz, 211, 213
Orentlikher, G., 162

Páleníčik, Jan, 191, 194–5
Panzéra-Baillot, Madeleine, 23, 28, 35, 61, 75, 78, 87
Paraskivesco, Théodore, 55, 75, 77–8, 84–5, 87
Parsons, Geoffrey, 162, 164, 167, 172, 186, 240, 262
Partridge, Jennifer, 36, 75, 217–18
Pastukhoff, Vsevolod, 145–6, 154, 170
Pleeth, William (cello), 115
Polekh (horn), 211, 214
Poulenc, Francis, 24, 45, 57, 71–2, 78, 82, 95–6, 101, 104–5, 107–8, 117–21, 123, 125, 127
Puig-Roget, Henriette, 25

Quilter, Roger, 239

Raveau, Alice, 63
Ravel, Maurice, 105, 108, 112
Reeves, George, 35, 75
Reimann, Aribert, 160–1
Richard, Jean-Charles, 91, 100–1, 104, 107–8, 112, 126
Richter, Sviatoslav, 146, 155, 176
Rostropovich, Mistislav, 145, 153, 160–1, 163, 170–1, 174, 222, 224
Rowlands, Alan, 242

Sabater, Rosa, 143
Salter, Timothy, 193
Sembrich, Marcella, 274
Schiff, András, 191, 193
Schneider, Edwin, 171, 176–7
Seidemann, Herbert, 145, 162
Soriano, Gonzalo, 60, 133, 135
Spencer, Robert (lute), 229
Starobin, David, 265
Suderburg, Robert, 261
Swallow, Keith, 216–17

Taubman, Leo, 62, 145, 151
Tordesillas, José, 130
Trovillo, George, 261
Tuckwell, Barry (horn), 211, 213

285

Index of accompanists' names

Tunnard, Viola, 15

Ulanowski, Paul, 13, 145, 151

Vehanen, Kosti, 181
Venzago, Mario, 191, 197
Vignoles, Roger, 87, 98, 100, 198, 203–6, 217, 219, 225, 234
Viktorov, V., 161

Walker, Nina, 87

Walter, N., 160
Watson, Gordon, 210–11, 214–15
Weissenberg, Alexis, 137, 170–2, 174, 176
Werba, Erik, 146, 174, 182, 217, 219
Westerberg, Stig, 189
Whitehead, James (cello), 163
Williams, John (guitar), 219–20
Willison, David, 145, 198, 200–1, 222, 236
Wustman, John, 57, 145

Zubal, Franz, 75, 77